At the Elizabeth Park Rose Gardens,
West Hartford, Connecticut

Following pages: Old Westbury Gardens, New York

America's
Public Gardens

300 of the Best Gardens to Visit
in the U.S. and Canada

by Mary Zuazua Jenkins

Contents

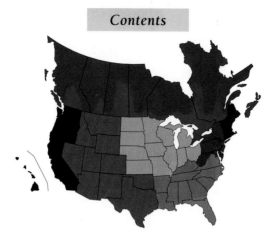

Contents

CHAPTER 2
Mid-Atlantic ———— 64

Ladew Topiary Gardens, Maryland

Contents

Hibiscus 'Tequila Sunrise'

CHAPTER 3
The South ————— 142

Contents

Powell Gardens, Missouri

Contents

Torch ginger

Contents

CHAPTER 7
Canada————354

Butchart Gardens, British Columbia, Canada

Our Garden Heritage

AT THE DAWN OF THE NEW millennium, Americans in increasing numbers are discovering the joys of visiting gardens. Traditionally, we have been more disposed to spend leisure time enjoying unembellished nature, a consequence of our history and the size and diversity of our landscapes. Clearly this is changing as more and more of us try our hands at creating our own versions of paradise outside our homes. As the English did generations ago, we are learning that spending time in a garden can be an experience of peace and beauty, a way of looking inward for contentment rather than outward for diversion.

The *National Geographic Guide to America's Public Gardens* is a fresh and informative compendium of North American gardens open to the public. The gardens represented here include both the well-established and well-supported traditional gardens and the exceptional, newer gardens that reflect the passions, talents, sensibilities, and sometimes quirkiness of their creators—gardens that are quintessentially American in outlook.

These latter gardens are the focus of The Garden Conservancy, an organization founded in 1989 to help preserve outstanding gardens for posterity. We know that the great majority of important private gardens created in the first part of the 20th century have vanished or been abandoned. We are working to ensure that this not happen to significant gardens in existence today. By contributing to an awareness of America's garden heritage, this book supports our efforts.

While mindful of the gardening traditions of other nations, Americans have discovered ways to garden that are inspired by their landscapes. With this guidebook, readers can visit these gardens for their horticultural enrichment and pure delight. As an earlier garden lover wrote:

"A Garden is the only complete delight the world affords, ever complying with our variable and mutable Minds."

Francis H. Cabot
Founder and Chairman, The Garden Conservancy

Crystal Springs Rhododendron Garden, Portland, Oregon

How to Use This Guide

The NATIONAL GEOGRAPHIC GUIDE TO AMERICA'S PUBLIC GARDENS presents the best gardens to visit in the United States and Canada. We have defined "public" as any outdoor or indoor garden open to visitors, either on a definite calendar schedule or by appointment. The gardens were selected on the basis of several years of research, recommendations from a wide range of knowledgeable sources, and garden visits. The criteria for selection were varied: historic importance, grandeur, renowned landscape design, notable botanical institutions, creator's vision or quixotic interpretation, rare and unusual plant collections, extravagant exhibitions, and interesting ideas for the home gardener. The selections reflect the influence of tradition, the ingenuity of American gardeners, and the splendor and diversity of our natural resources.

Huntington Botanical Garden, San Marino, California

The guide is divided into regions and the regions into states, each beginning with an important or elaborate garden; other gardens follow in geographical sequence. If the garden is not located in a major city, its distance from a city, town, or nearby garden is given in the information block at the end of the garden description. You can find the locations of these towns or cities on the map on pages 14-15.

To the best of our knowledge, information about every garden is correct as of press time. Note that small and private gardens may not have set hours, so it would be wise to call before you go. Though many gardens are wonderful year-round, it's also best to phone ahead for up-to-date information on floral displays; they do not always bloom according to calendar date. An information block with the following data follows each garden entry:

- Miles from the closest garden, major city, or town.
- Street address and telephone number.
- Hours, days, and months open. Most gardens close Thanksgiving and Christmas. For other holidays, it may be advisable to call ahead. (Note: Opening times apply to gardens and grounds only. Houses, gift shops, restaurants, libraries, and conservatories often have different hours.)
- Total acres for the garden (and grounds when relevant).
- Quick reference to each garden's special collections.

I hope this book inspires many pleasurable garden experiences.

Mary Zuazua Jenkins

Data Key

■ **GARDEN** (12 miles northeast of City) 123 Main Street, Town, State 01234 **TEL:** (000) 123-9876 **OPEN:** Daily dawn-dusk, June through Oct. **TOTAL ACRES:** 2.3 **SPECIAL COLLECTIONS:** Azaleas, perennial borders, fruit trees, fountains, wildflowers   **ZONE 3** A C F G H HO L P PA R T V WS

The | ZONE # | for each garden is referenced to a map on pages 14-15, drawn according to studies conducted by the U.S. Department of Agriculture. A helpful guide for the gardener, this map shows the climate zones or growing zones used in many gardening books and nursery catalogs. The map divides North America into 11 hardiness zones with Zone 1 the coldest, and Zone 11, a tropical area found only in Hawaii and southern Florida, the warmest.

A Pets Allowed
Dogs must be leashed.

C Conservatory or Greenhouse
Conservatories often charge a fee when there is no fee for the garden. Most conservatory hours differ from garden hours, opening later and closing earlier. Exhibitions vary in seasons and themes, so call ahead.

F Fee
Indicated when there is a fee for the garden, conservatory, or parking.

G Gift Shop

H Handicap Access
This often means some degree of wheelchair accessibility. Important to call ahead.

HO House Open
Historic house or museum on the premises.

L Library
Horticultural reference library open to the public.

P Parking
Lots or street parking.

PA Picnic Area

R Restaurant
Full menu, café, snack bar, or afternoon tea.

T Tours
Any kind of tour—varying from guides at the site to formal tours with reservations required. Gardens will often make special arrangements for groups.

V Visitor Center
A formal information center— usually found at large gardens. Many other gardens have information at a kiosk or gift shop.

WS Web Site
Many gardens have their own Web site with reliable, updated information. Some sites are maintained by universities or state and city tourist offices and require more patience to access. Search for the specific garden name or through:
http://cissus.mobot.org/ AABGA/member-list.html

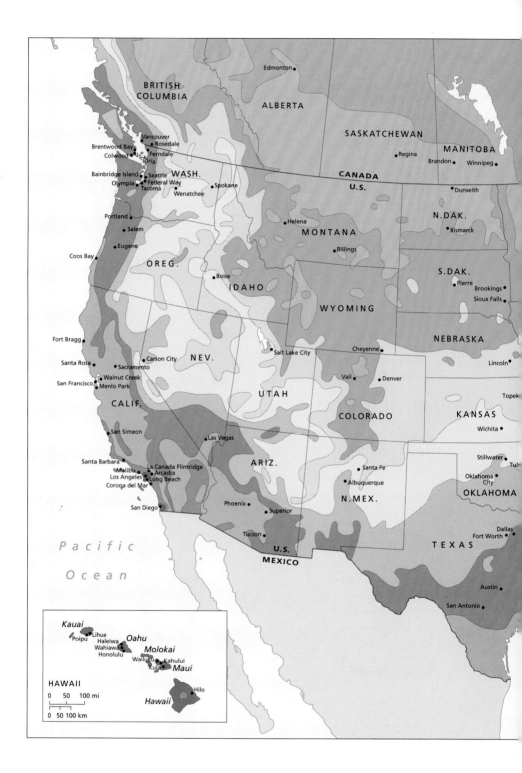

BRITISH COLUMBIA
Vancouver
Brentwood Bay • Rosedale
Colwood • Ferndale
Victoria
Bainbridge Island • Seattle
Olympia • Federal Way
Tacoma
Wenatchee
Spokane

WASH.

Portland •
Salem •
Coos Bay •
Eugene •

OREG.

Boise •

IDAHO

Fort Bragg •
Santa Rosa •
Carson City •
Sacramento •
San Francisco • Walnut Creek
Menlo Park

NEV.

CALIF.

San Simeon •

Santa Barbara •
Malibu • La Cañada Flintridge
Los Angeles • Arcadia
Corona del Mar Long Beach

San Diego •

Las Vegas •

ARIZ.

Phoenix •
Superior •
Tucson •

U.S.
MEXICO

Edmonton •

ALBERTA

SASKATCHEWAN

MANITOBA
Regina •
Brandon • Winnipeg •

CANADA
U.S.

Dunseith •

N. DAK.
Bismarck •

Helena •

MONTANA

Billings •

S. DAK.
Pierre •
Brookings •
Sioux Falls •

WYOMING

NEBRASKA

Salt Lake City •
Cheyenne •

Lincoln •

Vail •
Denver •

UTAH

Topek

COLORADO

KANSAS

Wichita •

Santa Fe •

Albuquerque •

N. MEX.

Stillwater • Tul
Oklahoma •
City

OKLAHOMA

Dallas •
Fort Worth •

TEXAS

Austin •

San Antonio •

Pacific

Ocean

HAWAII

Kauai
Lihue •
Poipu • Haleiwa
Wahiawa •
Honolulu

Oahu

Molokai

Wailuku • Kahului
Kula • Maui

Hilo •
Hawaii

0   50   100 mi

0 50 100 km

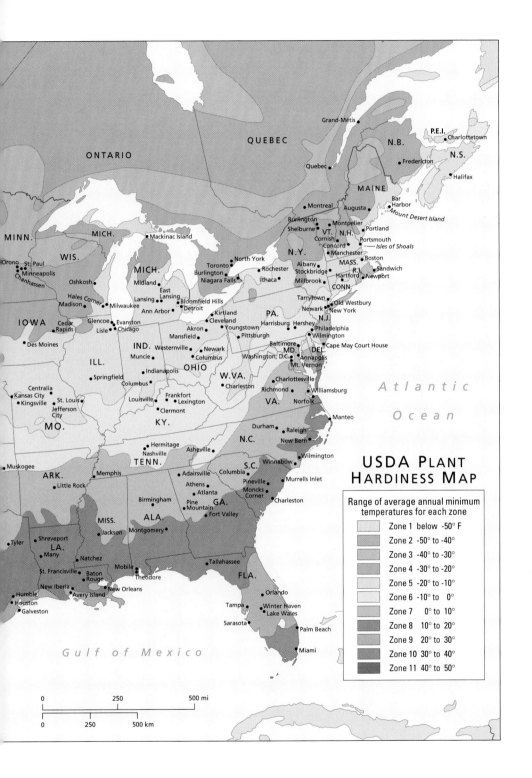

USDA PLANT HARDINESS MAP

Range of average annual minimum temperatures for each zone

	Zone 1 below -50° F
	Zone 2 -50° to -40°
	Zone 3 -40° to -30°
	Zone 4 -30° to -20°
	Zone 5 -20° to -10°
	Zone 6 -10° to 0°
	Zone 7 0° to 10°
	Zone 8 10° to 20°
	Zone 9 20° to 30°
	Zone 10 30° to 40°
	Zone 11 40° to 50°

0   250   500 mi

0   250   500 km

CHAPTER 1

NEW ENGLAND

■

Maine

New Hampshire

Vermont

Massachusetts

Rhode Island

Connecticut

*In Asticou Azalea Garden
(Maine), crabapple trees
sheathed in white blossoms
frame brilliant azaleas.
A Japanese-style stone bridge
spans a tranquil pond.*

Asticou Azalea Garden
Northeast Harbor, Mount Desert Island

Mention Mount Desert Island and, for many people, the windswept headlands and towering evergreen forests of Acadia National Park come to mind. But Mount Desert also holds many smaller gems, gardens that thrive in the shadow of the island's genteel summer "cottages." Despite its high northerly latitude, the island's microclimate is almost as gentle as that of England or coastal Japan, thanks to the tempering action of the sea.

While most gardens here remain in private hands, two—Asticou and Thuya (see separate entry) in the village of Northeast Harbor—welcome the public in season. These gardens exist in large part due to the efforts of two lifelong residents of Mount Desert Island: the plant collecting of Beatrix Farrand, one of America's most famous landscape architects and horticulturists, and the extraordinary preservation work of Charles Kenneth Savage.

Although Asticou calls itself an azalea garden, it manages to be much more despite its mere 2.3 acres. Created on this site in 1957, Asticou is actually the botanical heir of a much older and larger garden cultivated across the island in Bar Harbor in 1914. That was the year Beatrix Farrand inherited Reef Point, her family's summer retreat; over the next quarter century she made her waterside home the site of extensive test gardens for native flora, traditional annuals, and perennials.

At their peak, Farrand's private gardens held perhaps a thousand specimens, including 250 azaleas, 175 rhododendrons and laurels, and scores of choice evergreens. However, in her later years, Farrand realized that Reef Point would not become the self-sustaining horticultural study center she had envisioned and announced plans to sell her best specimens.

Fellow Mount Desert resident Charles Savage, a self-taught landscape designer, as well as an artist, musician, conservationist, innkeeper, and public-spirited citizen, decided that something had to be done to keep Farrand's outstanding botanical collection on the island. With financial help from longtime neighbor and Farrand client John D. Rockefeller, Jr., Savage set about finding new homes for Reef Point's plants.

Savage first chose a swampy area of alders and cattails opposite the fine old Asticou Inn operated by his family (and named after a chief of the local Abenaki Indians). With the deadline for moving Farrand's plants looming, Savage had to transform this uninspiring site into a viable garden in the shortest possible time. Beginning in 1956, he oversaw the clearing and dredging of the swamp, laid out ponds and a meandering stream bed, brought in truckloads of fill to raise and sculpt the surrounding terrain, and arranged specimens from Farrand's plant collection according to his new design. Somehow, Savage completed the herculean task in less than two years.

Still, there was much to be done. In subtle ways, the garden that visitors see today is still a work in progress, with new materials added yearly. Although Savage will always be credited as the designer, Asticou has since benefited from the contributions of Japanese horticulturist Osamu Shimizu, American landscape architect Patrick Chasse, azalea specialist Fred Galle, and others. The resulting serene landscape offers many of the traditional

Banks of intense magenta azaleas are among the 50 varieties that thrive in Asticou Azalea Garden. A parallel serpentine stream connects man-made pools in this Zen-influenced garden.

hallmarks of a classic Japanese stroll garden. Here are stepping-stone paths, natural stone bridges, cascading waterfalls, stone-lined "river" courses, and pagoda-roofed stone lanterns. Off to one side in a secluded, shady area, is a raised *kare sansui,* or "dry landscape," an abstract composition of rocks, raked sand, and moss, which draws from Zen Buddhist traditions.

Exotic as these features may be to the American eye, they are here experienced within a harmonious mix of native flora and Oriental species. Among the Korean firs, Japanese maples, and Siberian irises grow local pitch pines, sugar maples, Canadian hemlocks, American laurels, lupines, and such native ground covers as white-flowering bunchberry. Here, too, that quintessence of Maine's Down East barrens, the wild, low-bush blueberry, thrives on Mount Desert Island.

Mid-May to late June are Asticou's showiest weeks, when some 50 varieties of azaleas and 20 varieties of rhododendrons and laurels sequentially display their brilliant colors. Summer is a quieter, more contemplative time, when the tapestry of manicured green lawns, ferns and mosses, weeping hemlocks, and specimen conifers is seen in its fullness. In fall, the drama returns as deciduous leaves make their annual exits in bursts of fiery reds and yellows against a curtain of giant evergreens.

ASTICOU AZALEA GARDEN (175 miles northeast of Portland) Seal Harbor and Peabody Drive, Northeast Harbor, Mount Desert Island, ME 04662 **OPEN:** Daily dawn-dusk, June through Oct. **TOTAL ACRES:** 2.3 **SPECIAL COLLECTIONS:** Azaleas, rhododendrons, Japanese garden **ZONE 5** **H** **P**

THUYA LODGE AND GARDEN, ASTICOU TERRACES
NORTHEAST HARBOR, MOUNT DESERT ISLAND

Space limitations in the Asticou Azalea Garden, a half-mile away, proved to be a blessing for Asticou Terraces, a 200-acre woodland park and house complex bequeathed to the townspeople of Northeast Harbor by Joseph Henry Curtis. Curtis, a summer resident here from 1909 until his death in 1928, enjoyed a view of the picturesque harbor, below. When Charles Savage moved scores of Beatrix Farrand's shrubs and trees from Bar Harbor, some came here, to Curtis's home at the top of Eliot Mountain. What had been an apple orchard was transformed into Thuya Garden, named after Curtis's rustic lodge and the towering stands of *Thuya occidentalis* (American arborvitae or white cedar) that dominate the area.

Laid out in the form of a cross on 1.5 acres, Thuya features a double allée of lawn-bordered perennial beds running 128 feet along a central north-south axis. The upper (north) end culminates in a raised viewing pavilion while the lower (south) end is accented by a shallow reflecting pool, behind which rises a full-figured white cedar. The shorter cross axis traverses near the midpoint, taking its place between Thuya Lodge slightly downhill to the west and a majestic spruce to the east. A strolling path, strewn with crushed pink granite, winds through the lower third of the garden where a natural alpine glade features granite outcrops. Surrounding it all is a tall cedar fence, interrupted at the south entrance by a pair of handsome hand-carved gates designed by Savage himself.

Thuya's grand herbaceous borders reflect the influence of British designer Gertrude Jekyll, with a sweep of texture and warm and cool colors on either side of the green lawn carpet.

However, even the best-laid plans need updating from time to time, and in 1988, nine years after Savage died, a Thuya Garden trustee commissioned landscape architect Patrick Chasse to restore the overcrowded beds to their original vigor. Chasse reordered the best of the plants and, adding new ones, took advantage of the visual tricks of colors to present distinct perspectives dependent upon whether the garden is seen from below or above. Placing the

Stately spires of delphinium accent the cooler tones of this perennial border at Thuya Lodge Garden.

warmer yellows and corals at the lower end, Chasse followed with hot pinks toward the midpoint, grading into progressively cooler lavenders and blues toward the north end of the beds. The result, comprised of a dazzling 110 varieties in 60 genuses, is a sophisticated English-style garden. When visited at full bloom in summer, it is all the more delightful for being hidden away in its rustic setting.

THUYA LODGE AND GARDEN, ASTICOU TERRACES (175 miles northeast of Portland) Peabody Drive, Northeast Harbor, Mount Desert Island, ME 04662 **TEL:** (207) 276-5130 **OPEN:** Daily 9-5, mid-June to mid-Oct. **TOTAL ACRES:** Garden 1.5, grounds 150 **SPECIAL COLLECTIONS:** English-style perennial borders

ZONE 5 L   P WS

WILD GARDENS OF ACADIA, ACADIA NATIONAL PARK
BAR HARBOR, MOUNT DESERT ISLAND

Created in 1961 by the Bar Harbor Garden Club to display, preserve, and promote the conservation of native flora on Mount Desert Island, the Wild Gardens of Acadia offer more than 400 species planted in a dozen sections—all this on less than an acre within Acadia National Park. Here wildflowers flourish from spring to fall within the mixed woods, meadow, heath, pond, bog, and other areas, connected by paths lined with ferns and enclosed by a winding brook. A small beach created out of seaweed and stones displays the rare roseroot, sea lavender, and arctic beachhead iris, among many other plants and grasses. The choice of plants considered to be native to this area was carefully studied and selected, resulting in one of the most important native wildflower collections in the Northeast.

WILD GARDENS OF ACADIA (11 miles north of Northeast Harbor) Acadia National Park, Sieur De Monts Spring, Bar Harbor, Mount Desert Island, ME 04609 **TEL:** (207) 288-3338 **OPEN:** Daily dawn-dusk, May through Oct. **TOTAL ACRES:** Less than 1 **SPECIAL COLLECTIONS:** Wildflowers native to Maine

ZONE 5 F   H   P WS

HAMILTON HOUSE GARDEN
SOUTH BERWICK

In 1785, Col. Jonathan Hamilton built this dignified Georgian house high on a bluff overlooking his wharves on the Salmon Falls River. Hamilton House later was the setting for *The Tory Lover,* a popular historical romance by Maine author Sarah Orne Jewett. In 1898 Jewett persuaded her wealthy friend, Emily Tyson, to purchase and refurbish Hamilton House, which had fallen into disrepair. Tyson planted a garden combining formal ornamental elements from English and

Italian gardens with old-fashioned flowers blooming within boxwood hedges. In 1949, her daughter bequeathed the estate to the public. It was restored by the Society for the Preservation of New England Antiquities and today, in season, terraced flower gardens descend to the river's edge.

Here beds are planted with vibrant annuals and perennials, including phlox, poppies, and peonies from the original garden. Flowers line the paths and wildflowers thrive on the grounds. Everywhere this colorful garden offers panoramic vistas that evoke the romantic graciousness of a previous era. A stroll through the grounds allows the visitor to glimpse the original landscape of gardens, rolling hills, green lawns, and wonderful vistas that inspired Sarah Jewett to declare Hamilton House "unrivaled for the beauty of its surroundings and for a certain grand air which I find hard to match in any house I have ever seen."

HAMILTON HOUSE GARDEN (14 miles north of Portsmouth, NH) Vaughn's Lane, South Berwick, ME 03908 TEL: (207) 384-5269 OPEN: Tues., Thurs., Sat., and Sun., 12-5, June through Oct. TOTAL ACRES: 1.5 SPECIAL COLLECTIONS: Historic house garden   ZONE 5 F H HO P PA T

CELIA THAXTER'S GARDEN
APPLEDORE ISLAND, ISLES OF SHOALS

Visitors to the radiant cottage garden of poet Celia Thaxter walk in the footsteps of 19th-century luminaries. Immortalized in Childe Hassam's Impressionist paintings, the garden also drew the likes of Mark Twain, Ralph Waldo Emerson, James Lowell, and Sarah Orne Jewett to rocky Appledore Island, ten miles off the coast of Maine in the Atlantic Ocean.

Celia Thaxter's father was a lighthouse keeper on the Isles of Shoals. In 1948, when she was 12, the family moved permanently to Appledore, the largest of the nine isles, to open a summer hotel. In response to Appledore's off-season bleakness and isolation, Thaxter began her early gardening efforts. The whole island measures only 95 acres; within a remarkably small area—15-by-50 she planted a miniature Eden. Poppies (her favorite), sweet peas, hollyhocks, asters, marigolds, nasturtiums, and foxgloves flooded this informal cutting garden. She wanted as many bright colors as she could find and a garden she could pick. Her record book, *An Island Garden* (1894), illustrated by Childe Hassam, records more than 60 kinds of flowers—and her abundant joy in gardening.

After her death in 1894, the island's population slowly dwindled, and in 1914 fire destroyed the hotel and garden. In the 1970s, garden club volunteers joined forces with Dr. John M. Kingsley, founding director of the Shoals Marine Laboratory, a marine field station on the island run by Cornell University and the University of New Hampshire. They restored the garden using her book and Hassam's paintings as guides. Obtaining some of the old-fashioned garden flower varieties from the original garden proved difficult and some substitutions were made. Thaxter's clematis, called Traveler's Joy, now grows wild all over the island. Today, in a luminescent garden framed by sea and sky, Thaxter's legacy remains intact.

CELIA THAXTER'S GARDEN (10 miles off coast of Maine and NH) Appledore Island, Isles of Shoals, ME 03908 OPEN: July to Labor Day. Limited tours only, *reservations essential* FERRY: Sails at 7:30 AM and returns to Portsmouth, NH, by 1:30 PM TEL: (607) 255-3717 Shoals Marine Lab at Cornell University, Ithaca, NY TOTAL ACRES: 95 SPECIAL COLLECTIONS: Old-fashioned annuals

                                        ZONE 5 F G P PA T WS

A kaleidoscope of purple asters, yellow marigolds, and pink and red poppies are among the many old-fashioned flowers that inspired artists and writers on the Isles of Shoals, off the coast of Maine.

PRESCOTT PARK GARDENS
PORTSMOUTH

In the charming town of Portsmouth, a recreational park along the historic water-front features two distinctly different gardens. The Josie F. Prescott Memorial Garden is a small, lush retreat behind a white picket fence where visitors can find shade under Japanese crabapple canopies. Foliage plants decorate the garden's corners, and a profusion of annuals and perennials surround fountains with color from spring through fall.

Also flourishing within the 5 acres of Prescott Park, an All-America Selections Demonstration Garden presents more than 700 varieties of carefully labeled annuals organized into large rectangular beds. These include blocks of petunias, pansies, geraniums, stocks, and many others. Although their intent is mainly to be informative, these test and trial gardens, under the supervision of the University of New Hampshire, are a dramatic introduction to the rainbow palette of annuals available for any garden.

■ PRESCOTT PARK GARDENS (58 miles north of Boston, MA) Marcy Street, Portsmouth, NH 03801 OPEN: Daily dawn-dusk TOTAL ACRES: 5 SPECIAL COLLECTIONS: All-America Selections Demonstration Garden for annuals   ZONE 5 H P PA

STRAWBERY BANKE MUSEUM
PORTSMOUTH

Directly across from Prescott Park stands the restored historic community of Strawbery Banke, with houses and shops of merchants and sea captains from the 17th through 20th centuries. Named for the wild strawberries found in the area by the first settlers in 1630, the museum complex of 35 buildings on 10 acres also includes a few gardens. For example, some of the 17th-century houses are accompanied by small vegetable and herb gardens—but not in the pristine style of many restorations. With a refreshing realism, they reflect the hardships of daily life. Some, left overgrown and untidy, remain interesting for their content—the culinary and medicinal plants used by the early settlers.

An example of a garden from a 19th-century home is the Aldrich Memorial Garden. Within this small romantic setting, an unusual gatehouse stands covered in Virginia creeper and grapevines. Beyond a shaded nook under a grove of hemlocks, summer displays of lilies, liatrus, black hollyhocks, and phlox add color to this intimate setting.

The Goodwin House, the only building moved onto the site, belonged to New Hampshire's governor, Ichabod Goodwin, from 1859 to 1860. A Victorian garden was replanted according to the extensive garden diaries and sketches made by his wife, Sara Goodwin. Several rounded mounds, two feet high, are covered with annuals listed in her diary—cleome, perilla, and others—to form an unusual design feature.

■ STRAWBERY BANKE MUSEUM (58 miles north of Boston, MA) Marcy Street, Portsmouth, NH 03801 TEL: (603) 433-1100 OPEN: Daily 10-5, May through Oct. TOTAL ACRES: 10 SPECIAL COLLECTIONS: Colonial-era herbs and vegetables, Victorian-style flower gardens   ZONE 5 F G H HO P PA R T WS

In summer, the main garden on the first level below the Moffatt-Ladd House glows with golden coreopsis and daylilies among hollyhocks, phlox, campanula, and other floral accents.

Moffatt-Ladd House Garden
Portsmouth

Among the many stately homes in historic Portsmouth stands one of particular interest to the gardening enthusiast. John Moffatt, a wealthy sea captain, built this elegant Georgian mansion in 1763 as a wedding present for his son; descendants occupied it until 1900. On 1.5 acres behind the house, an exceptionally fine, old-fashioned garden reflects history, good design, and a wonderfully diverse display of flowers. Situated on a steep site and enclosed by fences and hedges of lilacs, the formal garden rises in a series of four terraces connected by grass steps.

On the first level, the main garden contains an abundant display of annuals and perennials, in full bloom in summer. Herbs, fruit trees, and ornamental shrubs grace the lower levels. Old brick walkways and decorated trellises add to the charm of this colonial garden. Historic plants include a damask rose, brought from England by the Moffatt's daughter-in-law, which grows near the steps of the middle terrace. On the eastern side of the house stands another point of interest, an enormous horse chestnut tree planted by John Moffatt's son-in-law upon his return to Portsmouth—after signing the Declaration of Independence.

Moffatt-Ladd House Garden (58 miles north of Boston, MA) 154 Market Street, Portsmouth, NH 03801 **Tel:** (603) 436-8221 **Open:** Mon.-Sat. 10-4, Sun. 2-5, mid-June to mid-Oct. **Total acres:** 1.5 **Special collections:** Old-fashioned flowers, historic house garden   ZONE 5 F HO P T WS

FULLER GARDENS
NORTH HAMPTON

Former Massachusetts Gov. Alvan T. Fuller chose the seaside town of North Hampton for his summer estate, and although the home no longer exists, his gardens remain. Occupying two acres, the gardens were designed in the 1920s by noted landscape architect Arthur Shurtleff, who was involved in the restoration of Colonial Williamsburg in Virginia. They feature perennial borders, a Japanese-style garden, and an All-America Rose Selection Garden of hybrid teas. The latter encircles a picturesque well in the first garden beyond the entrance.

A lavish display of colorful annuals surrounds an intimate conservatory holding a collection of tropical and desert plants. Nearby, the small Japanese-style garden offers visitors a shaded, secluded sanctuary. Here cedars, junipers, rhododendron, lantana, heliotrope, and wisteria enclose a pond filled with goldfish and koi. Beyond this cool enclave stretches a grand formal garden. Paths meander through more than a thousand rose bushes of hybrid teas, floribundas, and grandifloras that cover this central area, where elaborate perennial borders provide even more blooms along the walls. Sculpture, fountains, and tree standards add traditional formality to this gracious and richly colored setting.

■ **FULLER GARDENS** (9 miles south of Portsmouth) 10 Willow Avenue, North Hampton, NH 03862 **TEL:** (603) 964-5414 **OPEN:** Daily 10-6, mid-May to mid-Oct. **TOTAL ACRES:** 2 **SPECIAL COLLECTIONS:** Formal rose garden, perennial border, hostas, Japanese garden   **ZONE 5** C **F** G **H** P

SAINT-GAUDENS NATIONAL HISTORIC SITE
CORNISH

Just as Augustus Saint-Gaudens, sculptor of heroes and grand memorials, was about to begin his famous statue of Abraham Lincoln, a friend convinced him to purchase what seemed at first an unattractive property. His motivation: that he would find "many Lincoln-shaped men among the lean Yankee natives." Saint-Gaudens bought the 25 acres in 1885, transforming a former tavern on the grounds into a house that he called Aspet. As other artists followed him to settle in Cornish, the quaint New Hampshire town evolved into an active and vibrant artists' colony.

Saint-Gaudens became very involved in the design of his garden. While he may have had assistance from other landscape designers who were his neighbors, Saint-Gaudens' own classical approach is evident throughout the house and grounds. In a setting of panoramic vistas, he created a formal Italianate garden embellished with fountains, reflecting pools, columns, pergolas, and many of his own sculptures. Along with white fences, high hedges of pine and hemlock were used to enclose lavish flower gardens on terraces that connect the house and studio. Over a 20-year period, as his gardens grew to encompass 150 acres, Augustus Saint-Gaudens succeeded in creating a series of flowing, landscaped "garden rooms" that today continue to blend harmoniously with the surrounding bucolic countryside.

■ **SAINT-GAUDENS NATIONAL HISTORIC SITE** (120 miles north of Portsmouth) off N.H. 12A, Cornish, NH 03745 **TEL:** (603) 675-2175 **OPEN:** Daily dawn-dusk, Memorial Day through Oct. **TOTAL ACRES:** 150 **SPECIAL COLLECTIONS:** Sculpture and garden ornaments, Italianate-style garden, formal flower gardens
ZONE 4 **F** G **H** HO P **PA** WS

A grand arch of rhododendrons marks the way to a forest trail, one of the many attractions at Saint-Gaudens National Historic Site.

Vermont

Hildene
MANCHESTER

Until 1975, Abraham Lincoln's descendants summered at Hildene, a gracious Georgian Revival mansion surrounded by panoramic vistas of the Green and Taconic Mountain ranges. Jessie Lincoln, the President's granddaughter, designed the garden here in 1907. Having lived in England while her father, Robert Todd Lincoln, was U.S. ambassador there, she found inspiration for her garden in the stained-glass windows of Gothic cathedrals—she wanted her own garden to evoke leaded windows enclosing bright panes of glass. To achieve this, Jessie Lincoln used privet hedges to outline beds of flowers around rectangles of green lawn.

Each bed contains old-fashioned flowers in a single color. White, for example, dominates the center beds through daisies, cleomes, and baby's breath, while blue delphinium and bachelor buttons color another pane blue. Pink lupines, cosmos, and foxgloves tint still another area rose. Outer parterres display yellow primroses, coreopsis, and lilies. The garden ends in curved parterres of flowers, including a display of red roses named for President Lincoln and a yellow daylily named for his wife, Mary Todd.

In addition, the formal garden possesses an outstanding peony collection of more than a thousand plants. Here single and double blooms, tree peonies, and several specimens nearly a century old are particularly spectacular in June, but all seasons offer color in this historic parterre garden. Restoration of the gardens, ongoing since 1981, currently includes an elaborate cutting garden.

Hildene (99 miles south of Burlington) Historic Vt. 7A South, Manchester, VT 05254 **Tel:** (802) 362-1788 **Open:** Daily 9:30-4, mid-May through Sept. **Total acres:** Garden 4, estate 412 **Special collections:** Peonies, parterre gardens　　**ZONE 4** A F G H HO P PA R T V WS

Shelburne Museum Garden
SHELBURNE

Shelburne Museum, a major American folk art museum, is also home to one of the country's largest displays of lilacs. Every spring, more than 400 lilac plants representing 90 varieties burst into fragrant bloom amid the museum's historic buildings and along its connecting paths. Some bushes are old-fashioned, but most are hybrids, including the luxurious double blossoms of the white 'Mme. Casimir Perier'. Shelburne Museum also offers smaller gardens, showcasing medicinal and culinary herbs typical of late 18th-century households, and a circular perennial garden with simple plantings surrounded by fieldstone walls, herbs, and old-fashioned roses.

But each year, in the middle of May, the scene is best described in the poetry of Amy Lowell: "Heart-leaves of lilac all over New England/Roots of lilac under all the soil of New England."

Shelburne Museum Garden (7 miles south of Burlington) US 7, Shelburne, VT 05482 **Tel:** (802) 985-3344 **Open:** Daily 10-5, mid-May to mid-Oct. **Total acres:** 45 **Special collections:** Lilacs, historic herbs and vegetables, old-fashioned roses　　**ZONE 4** F G H HO P PA R T V WS

Lake Champlain and the Adirondack Mountains provide a spectacular backdrop for a lavish display of perennial flowers at Shelburne House's English-style cottage garden.

SHELBURNE HOUSE GARDENS
SHELBURNE

Turrets and gables adorn the castlelike Shelburne House along the shores of Lake Champlain. Originally the residence of a family of Webb and Vanderbilt heirs, Shelburne today is a luxurious inn on a thousand-acre experimental farm. The estate was planned with the advice of Frederick Law Olmsted, who went on to design Biltmore for other Vanderbilt family members, and Central Park in New York City. His parklike vistas of open meadows and stately trees remain integral to this majestic setting. Near the house, the main gardens along the lakeshore were designed by Lila Vanderbilt Webb, an avid gardener with imagination and income. Following the natural, colorful style advocated by horticulturist Gertrude Jekyll, she created a sophisticated English cottage garden within a classical framework of vistas and terraces. The gardens have been restored in part with modern cultivars replacing older varieties. Healthy herbaceous borders line the 70-foot central walkway. While peonies and poppies survive from the original garden, a rose garden has been replanted with modern tea varieties. An herb garden, a lily pond ringed in Siberian irises, and a cutting garden have also been redone. The original balustrade, reflecting pool, and pergola complete the restoration.

SHELBURNE HOUSE GARDENS (7 miles south of Burlington) Harbor Road, Shelburne, VT 05482 TEL: (802) 985-8686 OPEN: Daily dawn-dusk, mid-May to mid-Oct. TOTAL ACRES: Garden 1, farm 1,400 SPECIAL COLLECTIONS: Perennial borders, roses, cutting garden ZONE 4 F G H HO P R T V WS

Massachusetts

THE ARNOLD ARBORETUM
BOSTON

Located in the Jamaica Plain section of Boston, the Arnold Arboretum is a living museum of 7,000 hardy, woody plants collected from the highlands of the Himalayas, the hinterlands of the Orient, and the native habitats of Europe and the Americas. Since the late 19th century, intrepid plant explorers have built the arboretum's collection by selecting trees and shrubs that would survive transplant to New England's northern temperate climate. The resulting scientific institution is a delightful place to stroll, a showcase of dazzling seasonal changes, and a garden of the world's woodlands.

The oldest public arboretum in America, the Arnold Arboretum began in 1872 with a bequest to Harvard University from James Arnold, a New England merchant whose fortune, ironically, came from the timberlands of Michigan. The arboretum, which was established on 125 acres of farmland owned by the university, today comprises 265 acres and enjoys a worldwide reputation. Charles Sargent, a cousin of the painter John Singer Sargent, was chosen to be the arboretum's first director.

One of Sargent's first acts was to hire Frederick Law Olmsted, at the time involved in a pioneering plan to link Boston's public parks into a nine-mile "Emerald Necklace" encircling the city. Olmsted wanted to include the arboretum in the city's park system and, after ten years of stormy negotiations, an agreement to do so was reached in 1882. Olmsted skillfully designed a series of roads and paths to wind around the natural contours of the farmland, creating a landscape of simplicity and surprises that includes meadows, valleys, hills, and woodlands. Within this parklike scene, Sargent wanted to present every tree and shrub that would survive the New England climate. He ultimately achieved his goal—creating a woodland garden for Boston's residents and visitors alike.

Behind the dwarf conifer collection, a grove of sugar maples plays an autumn counterpoint to the evergreens at the Arnold Arboretum in Boston.

From a start of 125 species, Sargent began expanding the arboretum's collection, spending several years traveling to Europe, South America, China, Japan, and Korea to personally select new specimens. Later he engaged Ernest "Chinese" Wilson, an English plant explorer and part of a group of rugged and enthusiastic Victorian naturalists who traveled around the world in pursuit of rare plants. In Sargent's employ, he spent 15 years searching the remote corners of the Orient

This variety of European beech tree, with its twisted branches, is one of many interesting trees in the Arnold Arboretum. It came as a grafted specimen in 1888 from the Royal Botanic Gardens in England.

for exotic species, surviving landslides, malaria, and the Boxer Rebellion. He broke his leg while in pursuit of the regal lily, an injury that left him lame for life. Wilson described the conditions of this search, which involved 22 consecutive days of walking, in *Plant Hunting,* one of his many books:

> There in the narrow, semi-arid valleys down which torrents thunder, and encompassed by mountains composed of mud shales and granites whose peaks are clothed with snow eternal, the Regal Lily has her home. In summer the heat is terrific, in winter the cold is intense, and at all seasons these valleys are subject to sudden and violent wind storms against which neither man nor beast can make headway. There, in June by the wayside, in rock crevice, by the torrent's edge and high up on the mountainside and precipice, this Lily in full bloom greets the weary wayfarer. Not in twos and threes but in hundreds, in thousands, aye, in tens of thousands.... For a brief season this Lily transforms a lonely, semi-desert region into a veritable fairy land.

Daring and talented in selecting worthy species, Wilson introduced about a thousand plants to the United States from his expeditions. He went on to become a keeper of the arboretum in 1927. "Every garden great or small," he wrote, "owes more or less to this band of pioneers. Their bones lie scattered along the trails they blazed, but their work lives on in the garden beautiful." Many flowering trees and shrubs that are now common ornamentals in American gardens—such as Kousa dogwoods, mimosas, crabapples, and royal azaleas—were introduced through the perils and privations of Wilson and other Victorian plant hunters.

At the arboretum, this tradition of diligent searching has continued under new directors. In 1941, arboretum employees in China's Sichuan Province discovered the dawn redwood, previously thought to be extinct. Seeds were sent back to the arboretum and distributed to major gardens in America and Europe where, today, the redwood thrives as it did 200 million years ago. Visitors can see several at the entrance to the arboretum. One of the tallest, 90 feet high, is at Colonial Williamsburg in Virginia. Winterthur, in Delaware, and Sarah P. Duke Gardens, in North Carolina, also received seeds, and display wonderful specimens.

Within Frederick Law Olmsted's sensitive design, Charles Sargent chose to arrange the collection of native and exotic plants in groups by genus, whenever possible, to facilitate botanical comparisons and contrasts. Grouping plants that never occur together in nature was another of Sargent's creative approaches. An outstanding result of this aesthetic blending can be seen in the arboretum's maple collection. For the first time, Japanese, Chinese, and American maples became neighbors. The collection of 130 different maple species, one of the most comprehensive in the world, can be seen along Meadow Road just beyond the main entrance gate.

Across the way stands one of the arboretum's most popular attractions, the remains of an Amur cork tree. Its sweeping boughs have been polished by generations of children who are allowed to climb and slide along the low-slung limbs of this unusual tree. Beyond are grand collections of tulip trees, katsuras,

Bussey Brook meanders through an alpine scene of conifers, described as "a convention of Christmas trees for every taste."

In mid-May this hillside explodes with a panoply of more than 600 lilac bushes underplanted with bleeding-hearts. The lilac collection is one of the oldest and largest in North America.

and lindens. Trails spread in many different directions, leading to collections of rhododendrons, hawthorns, stewartias, hollies, conifers, and hemlocks.

In the midst of these towering trees, the Lars Anderson Bonsai Collection, housed in a wooden lath building, comes as a surprise. The collection, which contains rare specimens, some more than 200 years old, is one of the largest in the country after those at the Brooklyn Botanic Garden in New York and the National Arboretum in Washington, D.C. The Bonsai House is surrounded by an interesting variety of dwarf conifers.

The Arnold Arboretum offers splendors at every season. Spring begins in a dramatic blaze of color with one of the country's largest collections of forsythia, followed by outstanding displays of dogwoods, cherry trees, crabapples, magnolias, azaleas, and rhododendrons. In New England this season is also synonymous with lilacs, and Lilac Sunday has been a tradition at the arboretum since 1876. The luxuriant, fragrant array of purples, blues, burgundies, pinks, and white lilacs lasts for five weeks, peaking in mid-May.

During summer the arboretum's verdant canopies provide shade brightened by the blossoms of lindens and stewartias. Along the Chinese Path, exotic flowering trees provide a botanical bridge to Asia. These include golden-rain trees that once guarded the tombs of feudal princes in China and now bear clusters of fragrant gold in Boston; silk trees covered in clouds of pink blossoms; and the dove tree, named for its graceful, dangling brackets, each in the shape of a delicate white bird.

Summer-flowering shrubs include hydrangeas with their globes of blue; buckeyes with their white bottlebrushes; and buddleias, offering fragrant pink spires. Fall commences with the camellia-like white flowers of the rare Franklinia tree. The intense scarlet of maples, oaks, sourwoods, and tupelos complements the lustrous yellows of the ginkgo, golden larch, and katsuras. Winter snows heighten the quiet, year-round beauty of the arboretum's conifer collection. Then, ice slows the flow of Bussey Brook as it winds through groves of Korean firs, cedars of Lebanon, Serbian spruces, hemlocks, umbrella pines, and Douglas-fir.

As with any great collection, there is no quick way to truly see the Arnold Arboretum. This living museum is best experienced in many unhurried visits in all seasons. The arboretum also serves as a major international center for study and research, offering an important herbarium, library, and extensive educational programs for the public.

THE ARNOLD ARBORETUM 125 Arborway, Jamaica Plain, Boston, MA 02130 **TEL:** (617) 524-1718
OPEN: Daily dawn-dusk; Visitor Center Mon.-Fri. 9-4, Sat.-Sun. 10-4, except holidays **TOTAL ACRES:** 265
SPECIAL COLLECTIONS: Lilacs, bonsai, maple trees, conifers, major collection of native and exotic trees

ZONE 6 A C G **H** **L** P **T** V WS

ISABELLA STEWART GARDNER MUSEUM
BOSTON

On New Year's night in 1903, 150 of Boston's most prominent socialites were invited to a musicale performed by the Boston Symphony in the music room of a recently completed palace. Upon entering the room, adorned with Donatello's frieze of dancing boys, Boston aristocrats ascended a steep staircase to greet their hostess, Isabella Stewart Gardner. Dressed in severe black and wearing a diamond tiara, she was seated in a regal chair on the balcony above. The symphony played Mozart and Beethoven and, after the finale, the carefully kept secret of the building on the Fens was revealed.

When a mirrored wall was rolled back to present a magnificent courtyard, one of the guests recounted: "Here, in the very midst of winter, was a gorgeous vista of blossoming summer gardens…with the odor of flowers stealing toward one as though wafted on a southern breeze. There was intense silence for a moment broken only by the water trickling in the fountains; then came a growing murmur of delight, and one by one the guests pressed forward to make sure it was not all a dream."

Today, the austere, unembellished exterior of the Renaissance-style building in the Boston suburb of Brookline gives no hint of what awaits inside. The Isabella Stewart Gardner Museum, originally called Fenway Court, possesses one of the greatest private art collections in the world, including works of the great masters Botticelli, Titian, Rubens, and Rembrandt. Beyond the galleries, at the center of it all, is the museum's verdant inner sanctum—the courtyard garden, rising four stories to a multipaned glass skylight.

All the embellishments of this indoor garden reflect Mrs. Gardner's personal taste and sense of creative design, as well as her passion for Venice. Scouring Europe for artifacts to display in her pleasure palace, she returned with balconies, columns, arches, windows, and ironwork, mostly of 16th- and 17th-century Venetian origin.

Gardner meticulously planned the placement of all these diverse elements, down to the last detail. When the color of the stucco courtyard walls proved unsatisfactory, she climbed the ladder, dipped sponges into pails of white and pink paint, and smeared the walls until she achieved the desired effect, a marbleized pinkish hue that evoked the Venetian palaces she so much

In a time-honored tradition, Easter at the Gardner's Renaissance courtyard features traditional lilies, azaleas, and nasturtiums cascading from the second-floor balcony.

admired. The centerpiece, a Roman floor mosaic, depicts Medusa surrounded by colored scrolls of the four seasons.

Mrs. Gardner was known for her exuberant use of flowers as well as for her keen eye for artifacts. Her will stipulated simply that "Fenway Court always remain flowered," and her wishes are honored in lush displays that change monthly. Although this indoor garden is not subject to temperature changes, the potted plants are chosen to correspond to the seasons and holidays. As spring begins outdoors, narcissus, jasmine, and camellia are massed around sculptures and paths. The Easter holiday season culminates in an extravaganza of lilies, orchids, and nasturtiums. A special feature are the golden and scarlet nasturtium blossoms that cascade two stories down from the balconies.

The summer months are celebrated with Canterbury bells, hydrangeas, gloxinias, oleanders, cape primroses, and crape myrtle standards. Cool blues and soft pinks amid profuse ferns create a refreshing display. In

A Roman mosaic depicting Medusa dominates the center of the courtyard, decorated with palms and poinsettias in December.

fall there are bush and standard chrysanthemums in russets, yellows, and whites. At Christmas, the Gardner Museum's brilliant arrangement of poinsettias provides a cheerful contrast to the fragile blooms of heather and the healthy gloss of jade plants.

Although visitors are not permitted to enter the courtyard, the garden may be viewed from the archways of the surrounding cloisters and from the balconies above. The design of the courtyard allows all plants to be seen clearly from these varied vantage points. In addition to the famous courtyard garden, the museum has two modest outdoor walled gardens: the Monk's Garden, a charming, shaded area covered with ivy and evergreen shrubs and, in a sunnier location, a southern garden decorated with urns of flowers.

To keep the museum "flowered," thousands of plants are grown within six greenhouses that cover 8,000 square feet of land. These fascinating nurseries of traditional and exotic plants may be visited by special advance arrangement. Whatever the time of year, the Isabella Stewart Gardner Museum combines colorful flowers and delightful fragrances with timeless art and architecture to create a unique public garden.

ISABELLA STEWART GARDNER MUSEUM 280 The Fenway, Boston, MA 02115 **TEL:** (617) 566-1401 **OPEN:** Tues.-Sun. 11-5, except holidays. **SPECIAL COLLECTIONS:** Renaissance-style courtyard gardens, monthly displays of potted flowers, nasturtiums   C F G HO L P R WS

Japanese Garden at the Museum of Fine Arts
Boston

In Japan, a small group of garden masters are revered for their experience and talent. Their ranks include Kinsaku Nakane, creator of this walled garden on the north side of Boston's Museum of Fine Arts, as well as the Japanese garden at the Carter Library in Atlanta and the tea garden at the National Gallery in Washington, D.C. About 100 feet square, it is based on the dry landscapes of 15th-century Japanese Zen temples. Zen symbols are represented in the gravel sea, with islands of stone, boulders representing mountains, and beach stones for a waterfall. Thus are mountains, the center of the universe, connected by two large islands that represent prosperity and longevity. A stone path leads from a roofed gate made of Japanese cypress to a stone terrace that holds benches as well as stone lanterns from the museum's collection.

Seeking to blend the landscape of New England with the symbols of Japan, Nakane has departed somewhat from the established principles of Zen dry gardens by adding color and texture through some 600 perennials and hundreds of shrubs and trees. After two years of work, the garden was unveiled in 1988.

Japanese Garden at the Museum of Fine Arts 465 Huntington Avenue, Boston, MA 02115 **Tel:** (617) 267-9300 **Open:** Tues.-Sun. 10-4, April through Oct. **Total acres:** Less than 1 **Special Collections:** Japanese Zen garden   **ZONE 6** | F | G | H | HO | L | P | R | V | WS |

Called the Garden of the Heart of Heaven, the contemplative Japanese Garden at the Museum of Fine Arts in Boston uses gravel, stones, and boulders to represent water, islands, and mountains.

MOUNT AUBURN CEMETERY
CAMBRIDGE

A proper Bostonian attends elite schools, kneels in a privileged pew, and is buried in Mount Auburn Cemetery. Founded in 1831, Mount Auburn helped inspire the garden cemetery movement popular here and in England in the 19th century. Once known as "Sweet Auburn," it was a rural retreat for Harvard students and supposedly a favorite haunt of Ralph Waldo Emerson, Robert Frost, and many other literary figures. Among the graves to be discovered here are those of Amy Lowell, Oliver Wendell Holmes, and Henry Wadsworth Longfellow. Gen. Henry A.S. Dearborn, then president of the Massachusetts Horticultural Society, designed the grounds. Dr. Jacob Bigelow, a physician and founder of the Massachusetts Institute of Technology, was responsible for the Egyptian Revival entrance, the Gothic-style chapel, and the character of the sculpture.

This new version of Elysian Fields was landscaped on 174 acres of lakes and rolling terrain with more than 2,500 trees, including imposing beeches, oaks, birches, and maples. Tens of thousands of bulbs and summer annuals are planted throughout the grounds, resulting in swaths of blossoms each season. The grandeur of this parkland garden is further enhanced by numerous sculptures, intricate headstones, and architectural focal points, offering plenty for the contemplative visitor.

MOUNT AUBURN CEMETERY (4 miles west of Boston) 580 Mt. Auburn Street, Cambridge, MA 02138 TEL: (617) 547-7105 OPEN: Daily 8-5 TOTAL ACRES: 174 SPECIAL COLLECTIONS: Variety of rare trees and flowering shrubs   ZONE 6 H P T

LONGFELLOW NATIONAL HISTORIC SITE
CAMBRIDGE

Henry Wadsworth Longfellow received this gracious Georgian home as a wedding present after marrying his landlord's daughter. Historically important as George Washington's headquarters during the siege of Boston, the house's fame increased along with Longfellow's; he wrote most of his famous poems here and lived in the house from 1837 until his death in 1882.

Longfellow found inspiration in his garden and contributed to the layout and selection of flowers. In later years his daughter Alice hired Martha Hutcheson to restore and enlarge the garden. Subsequently, various other landscape designers, including Ellen Shipman and, in 1968, Diane Kostial McGuire, have been involved in the garden's interpretation.

Although Longfellow's original layout still prevails, today a combination of the garden's different designs is under consideration. The house sits on two acres surrounded by a splendid variety of mature oaks, maples, tulips, locusts, and elms with lawns, lilacs, rose bushes, and other ornamental shrubs and trees all about. The formal rear garden, on the property's western side, contains beds of annuals and perennials within scrolls of dwarf boxwood hedges. A view of the Charles River completes the elegant setting.

LONGFELLOW NATIONAL HISTORIC SITE (4 miles west of Boston) 105 Brattle Street, Cambridge, MA 02138 TEL: (617) 876-4491 OPEN: Daily 9-5, except holidays TOTAL ACRES: 2 SPECIAL COLLECTIONS: Poet's garden design, trees, ornamental shrubs   ZONE 6 H HO T WS

GARDEN IN THE WOODS
FRAMINGHAM

Strolling along the winding paths of Garden in the Woods revives childhood memories of fairy tales and their magical moments. Located near Framingham, Massachusetts, 25 miles southwest of Boston, Garden in the Woods offers the largest collection of wildflowers and native plants in the Northeast.

It all began in the 1920s with Will C. Curtis, a local landscape designer and nursery owner who dreamed of creating a garden to protect wildflowers and educate the public about plant conservation. One day an undeveloped site of glacial ridges and kettle holes caught his eye. These rolling hills, ponds, and streams, Curtis decided, would be the ideal setting for his garden dream. Along with partner Dick Stiles, he began clearing the difficult terrain in the early 1930s, an era before mechanized machinery eased such tasks. The garden expanded to include not only native New England flora but also plants from other parts of North America, the latter grown in re-created "ecological niches" to demonstrate the variety of North America's landscape. In 1965 Curtis and Stiles gave the garden to the New England Wildflower Society, which in turn raised the funds to rescue this showplace of northeastern flowers from encroaching urban development.

Today the garden encompasses 45 acres—17 acres of naturalistic gardens set within glacial contours and surrounded by 28 acres of cultivated wilderness. Three miles of trails lead through specially designed garden habitats: a woodland grove, a lily pond, a pine barren, a sunny meadow, bogs, a Western-style rock garden, and a rare plant garden. Unlike more formally designed gardens, the effect here is subtle. There are no large displays of color, no masses of blooms. Instead, the drama is in individual performances: lady's-slippers against backdrops of stately ferns, demure columbines silhouetted against amethyst phlox. The ever-changing light creates a play of quiet color, where different seasons present new botanical performers.

A tour of the garden begins in the woodland grove. Here, planners created the effect of a vaulted ceiling with limbing oak and beech trees that allow light to filter through to flowers and plants below. In the spring, before the leaves appear, hepatica and rare Oconee bells raise their heads, followed in April by Dutchman's breeches on tender stems. In May and June elegant lady's-slippers, slender spires of bowman's root, and graceful Mandarin lilies bloom. Summer brings exotic painted ferns from Japan to mingle with wild native geraniums on banks of Oriental hostas. Autumn begins with the soft hues of abundant rose mallows, pink asters, and blue gentians, continuing with the deep colors of ruby sourwoods and burgundy dogwoods.

Native flame azaleas line a path from the woodland garden to the lily pond, which is both a wetland garden and a habitat for small wildlife. The pond area, delicately colored in spring by blue flag iris and the rare witch alder, is in summer host to cardinal flowers, our only native red flower, and eight-foot Turk's-cap lilies that fringe the pond with a vivid mix of scarlet and orange.

Set in richer soil, slopes of rhododendron adorn a path leading to two rock gardens and an unusual collection of carnivorous plants native to the Southeast's savannahs. Here, visitors may see a pitcher plant capturing insects with its glowing lime green leaves and sweet secretions. An area of pine barrens, modeled after the southern New Jersey tract, contains a dry, sandy habitat for stunted pine trees. In June it is studded with turkeybeard spikes and meandering pyxie

*In early May, light filters through a canopy of trees beginn
to leaf above lady's-slippers and amethyst ph*

moss. In turn, the Western Rock Garden displays plants that grow west of the Mississippi River, including prickly pear cactuses and the glowing pink-and-white lewisia, discovered by Meriwether Lewis and William Clark. Nearby, the meadow blazes with sun-loving wildflowers. By midsummer black-eyed Susans, blazing stars, butterfly weed, and six-foot-tall purple ironweed attract many varieties of birds and flitting butterflies.

In July 1997, a new garden of rare and endangered plants opened here. Eventually, this two-acre garden will display more rare plants than most people see in a lifetime of searching New England habitats. Today the garden features 102 species—28 globally rare, 51 regionally rare, and 23 locally rare—from wetlands, woodlands, sandplains, and coastal shores.

Garden in the Woods offers several trails that wander alluringly off into the wilder woodland areas where oaks, white pines, beeches, hemlocks, and maples grow. Copses of spicebushes, witch hazels, and winterberries thrive in the moist, riparian conditions found along the banks of the nearby brook. Fiddleheads of cinnamon ferns and tapered horsetails, both species survivors from the age of dinosaurs, flourish here where they can keep their feet wet. As the weather chills, deciduous trees surge through their cycle of brilliance while crimson and golden berries appear on the boughs of wintergreens, winterberries, and spice-bush shrubs. In November, after this final performance, Garden in the Woods closes for the winter.

The garden's collection of trilliums, one of the largest in the country, includes

Floral vignettes appear throughout Garden in the Woods from spring to autumn. Within the native plant habitat, which features carnivorous plants, yellow pitcher plants (left) bloom in early June. Mid-May brings dwarf crested irises (below left) that blanket large areas with their purple hues in the woodland garden. In summer, red cardinal flowers fringe a lily pond in the garden's wetland area (below).

A golden trout lily nestles within a cluster of double bloodroot blossoms in the woodland garden in early May (above). The sunny part of Garden in the Woods's newer area features rare and endangered plants, including the New England blazing star (above, right). It can be found here in late summer. Red trilliums raise their starlike flowers in the woodlands by mid-May (right).

22 species out of 42 known to exist in North America. Their purple, pink, maroon, yellow, and white triple-petaled flowers bloom from April to June. Also of note is the lady's-slipper, one of this country's native orchids. Of the garden's three varieties, the largest, the fragrant yellow moccasin, is seen in clusters throughout the woodland area. It is also the easiest to grow. Experimental beds of large and small lady's-slippers, both yellow and the rare showy pink, teach visitors about optimum growing conditions and propagation. It's a slow process, as it can take three to six years for lady's-slipper seeds to develop into flowering plants in cultivation.

In all, more than 1,600 varieties of wildflowers and native plants thrive at Garden in the Woods. This important center for native plant conservation has joined with the National Center for Plant Conservation to protect selected endangered species. As the number of rare and endangered plant species grows, informing the public about their existence and their plight becomes essential to their survival. To that end, the garden offers programs of research, conservation, and education. A walk through this preserve is thus both a delight and an education, furthering Curtis's dream of saving our American wildflowers through respect and knowledge.

GARDEN IN THE WOODS (25 miles southwest of Boston) 180 Hemenway Road, Framingham, MA 01701 **TEL:** (508) 877-7630 **OPEN:** Tues.-Sun. 9-5, April and June through Oct.; Tues.-Sun. 9-7, May **TOTAL ACRES:** 45 **SPECIAL COLLECTIONS:** Wildflowers of New England, rare and endangered plant species, varied habitats, trilliums

ZONE 5 F G H L P T WS

Glen Magna Farms
Danvers

Glen Magna Farms was originally purchased by Capt. Joseph Peabody as a hiding place for valuable cargo stolen from British ships during the War of 1812. Seventy years later, the land was transformed by Joseph Chamberlain, landscape architect and father of the future British prime minister, into a garden for a stylish summer home. Aiding him in this task was legendary landscape architect Frederick Law Olmsted. Four generations of Peabodys and Endicotts lived on the estate before the Danvers Historical Society acquired it in 1963.

Each garden has it own personality—from a style of grandeur to a corner of intimate charm. The first garden was laid out in 1814 by an Alsatian gardener named George Huessler. Peabody Garden, the oldest, lies directly behind the house, a grand formal garden of hedges surrounding beds of annuals and perennials centered around a large, lovely tulip tree. Peonies and irises bloom in June, followed by hollyhocks, lilies, and many other old-fashioned flowers. At the end of this garden, a summer gazebo marks the entrance to another area, a long,

In the Chamberlain Garden, a wisteria-covered marble pergola and weeping trees add romantic grace to the perennial garden of the elegant and historic Glen Magna Farms estate.

walled Lover's Walk bordered in arborvitae. In the Chamberlain Garden, a stunning Italianate perennial garden, stone walls form a backdrop for lush flower beds of brilliant color, a central fountain, and a pergola of ten antique marble columns covered in wisteria.

Also of note, the shrub garden at Glen Magna features a monumental weeping birch tree amid a profusion of familiar and exotic plants. At the end of the rose garden, among hundreds of historic roses, lies one of the most important ornamental summer houses in garden architecture. A two-story Palladian structure of elegant proportions, the McIntire Tea House was built in 1793 by prominent cabinetmaker Samuel McIntire. His client was Elias Derby, one of Salem's wealthiest merchants. Now a National Historic Landmark, it was moved to this location in 1901, further enhancing Glen Magna Farms's striking setting. From spring to autumn, there is a luxurious display of color in the different garden rooms of this elegant estate.

GLEN MAGNA FARMS (20 miles northeast of Boston) Ingersoll Street, Danvers, MA 01923 TEL: (978) 774-9165 OPEN: Mon.-Fri. 9-dusk, Sat.-Sun. 9-12 (site hosts many private functions, so it is wise to call ahead) TOTAL ACRES: 11 SPECIAL COLLECTIONS: Formal gardens, roses, perennial border, McIntire Tea House

ZONE 6 **F** G **H** HO P T WS

SEDGWICK GARDENS, LONG HILL
BEVERLY

At the entrance to the Massachusetts mansion known as Long Hill, a tree-lined approach ending in a majestic copper beech tree marks the beginning of what might be a visit to an English country estate. Spacious and hidden, terraced garden rooms overlook dramatic vistas of the countryside. A circular pavilion from France rises in one garden room, a Chinese pagoda in another. Pathways through inviting arbors lead to natural and semi-formal gardens. At the back of the residence, the scene changes to the American South. The house, itself a reproduction of an antebellum Charleston mansion, features a decorative balcony accented by wisteria, hydrangeas, and boxwood. Here the garden features graceful weeping cherry trees, banks of multicolored azaleas, and a fine collection of tree peonies.

The estate's English and American influences blend the interests of the two Mrs. Sedgwicks. Ellery Sedgwick was editor of the *Atlantic Monthly;* his first wife, Mabel, was a talented horticulturist and accomplished garden writer. She laid out the original 5-acre garden on the 114-acre estate of forest, fields, and wetlands, purchased in 1916. Ellery Sedgwick's second wife, Marjorie Russell of England, was an accomplished gardener distinguished for propagating rare and exotic plants. She contributed to the estate's already outstanding array of plants, shrubs, and trees, working closely with the nearby Arnold Arboretum. She added oxydendrons, sophora, stewartias, and Japanese maple to prolong the flowering season.

With its brilliant array of flowering trees, rhododendrons, azaleas, lilacs, and peonies, spring is this garden's most outstanding season. However, summer and fall have their attractions, when floral displays highlight the estate's distinctive collection of shrubs and trees.

SEDGWICK GARDENS, LONG HILL (22 miles northeast of Boston) 572 Essex Street, Beverly, MA 01915 TEL: (508) 921-1944 OPEN: Daily 8-dusk TOTAL ACRES: 114 SPECIAL COLLECTIONS: Estate garden, tree peonies, flowering trees and shrubs, exotic plants

ZONE 6 **F** H P PA T WS

JOHN WHIPPLE HOUSE
IPSWICH

This abundant colonial garden presents a colorful introduction to the 17th-century home of the John Whipple family, Puritan settlers. One of the most authentic interpretations of a colonial dooryard garden, it was re-created in the 1980s by Ann Leighton, a leading historian of American gardens. Behind a low fence, raised beds contain close to one hundred different vegetables and herbs. This is far more than an average household would have raised, but representative of the range of culinary, medicinal, and aromatic herbs used in a typically self-sufficient household of the period. The garden's dense plantings, divided into six beds separated by crushed clam shells, offer a lush tapestry of texture, pattern, and subtle colors, aesthetic as well as utilitarian. A period trellis, covered with cascades of old-fashioned roses including Harison's Yellow, the Yellow Rose of Texas, and the pretty pink Seven-sisters, provides a romantic touch. This charming cottage garden is an American expression of the quaint and simple lifestyle of our early settlers.

JOHN WHIPPLE HOUSE (30 miles northeast of Boston) 1 South Village Green, Ipswich, MA 01938 **TEL:** (978) 356-2811 **OPEN:** Wed.-Sat. 10-4, Sun. 1-4, May through Sept. **TOTAL ACRES:** 2 **SPECIAL COLLECTIONS:** Colonial-era herbs and vegetables   **ZONE 6** HO

ADAMS NATIONAL HISTORIC SITE
QUINCY

While in London, Abigail Adams wrote to Thomas Jefferson that farming and gardening held more charms for her than life as the American ambassador's wife at the Court of St. James. But upon their return in 1788, public service called again, as John Adams went on to become the new nation's Vice President and then President. When John and Abigail were in residence at this "genteel dwelling," Abigail planted a garden of lilacs, nasturtiums, four o'clocks, and roses brought back from London. One, the Rose of York, still grows in the garden. Decades later, another Abigail Adams, wife of the first Abigail's grandson Charles (who was also an envoy to Britain), continued expanding the garden while her husband built a library for the family documents.

Today ivy, morning glory, trumpet vine, and honeysuckle climb in lush clusters on the walls of the house and library to unite buildings and garden. Visitors promenade the formal garden along corridors of color surrounded by rhododendrons, wisteria, specimen trees, and a fruit orchard. Large grass rectangles are lined with nine-inch-high English dwarf boxwood, and borders of beautiful flowers. Separated by gravel paths, three parallel borders more than 90 feet long are filled with seasonal splendor that begins with combinations of white peonies, bleeding hearts, oriental red poppies, and in late spring, white and blue irises. Summer follows, with coral bells, bachelor buttons, veronica, delphinium, larkspur, and many others. Blue, one of Abigail's favorite colors, is much in evidence.

ADAMS NATIONAL HISTORIC SITE (8 miles southeast of Boston) 135 Adams Street, Quincy, MA 02269 **TEL:** (617) 773-1177 **OPEN:** Daily 9-5, April through Nov. **TOTAL ACRES:** 4.7 **SPECIAL COLLECTIONS:** Historic house garden, annuals, perennial border   **ZONE 6** F H HO P T WS

Heritage Plantation
Sandwich

Heritage Plantation is an unusual and intriguing complex of Americana museums, but in June it belongs to rhododendrons. That month, thousands of Dexter hybrid rhododendrons fill the 76 acres of rolling woodlands with a spectacular display of pink, apricot, white, and lavender blooms.

After a successful career as a manufacturer, Charles O. Dexter purchased a farm along Shawme Lake, near Sandwich, the oldest village on Cape Cod. From 1921 to 1943, he pursued his hobby of hybridizing rhododendrons; his new cultivars were superior in color, size, and hardiness to the traditional "ironclads" developed in England in the 19th century from native American species. Dexter collaborated with Ernest Wilson and Charles Sargent at the Arnold Arboretum, generously distributing thousands of seedlings that he developed. Record keeping was not his forte, however, and where the plants went and how they fared often remained unknown. After his death, the American Rhododendron Society began the long process of researching, collecting, and evaluating Dexter hybrids.

In 1967 pharmaceutical magnate Josiah K. Lilly purchased the estate to create a museum for his family's collection of military miniatures, antique firearms, antique cars, and early American arts and crafts. In 1969 the Heritage Plantation of Sandwich was founded to administer the museums and continue the study of and search for Dexter rhododendrons. Today the estate grows 125 of the known 145 Dexter rhododendron varieties.

In June, Heritage Plantation is ablaze with blooms. Dexter's pink rhododendrons seen here are among the many hybrids he developed in his pursuit of hardier, more colorful plants.

Within the landscaped setting, trails wind around a lake banked with dense plantings of rhododendrons, through woods of azaleas and mountain laurel, and up hills of hollies and hostas. Though spring is the most striking season here, summer brings bursts of blooms from hedges of hydrangeas, carpets of annual flowers, and an important collection of 500 varieties of daylilies provided by the American Hemerocallis Society.

Heritage Plantation (58 miles southeast of Boston) Grove and Pine Streets, Sandwich, MA 02563 **Tel:** (508) 888-3300 **Open:** Daily 10-5, mid-May to mid-Oct. **Total acres:** 76 **Special collections:** Rhododendrons, daylilies   **ZONE 7** F G H HO P PA R T V WS

45

OLD STURBRIDGE VILLAGE
STURBRIDGE

Horticulture in the daily life of a 19th-century New England village is featured in the re-created gardens of this outdoor living history museum. Two flower gardens, at different houses, illustrate varying approaches to gardening in the early 1800s. The first, the Towne House Garden, presents a parterre enclosed by a hedge of Japanese quince. In spring, beds of tulips bloom here, followed in June by candytuft, gas plant, and false indigo framed by santolina borders. Annuals are planted in summer, with marigolds and amaranths dominant.

In contrast, the garden at Fitch House was influenced by the ideas of Joseph Breck, an important early horticulturist who thought "the flickering meteor called taste" was ruining country gardens. He espoused the educational value of gardening and the use of indigenous plants. Sweet violets, ox-eye daisies, and cranesbill grow alongside calliopsis brought back from early explorations of the prairies, as well as clarkia from Meriwether Lewis and George Clark's expeditions opening the West. In addition, two bountiful vegetable gardens offer grand displays of the staples of self-sufficient villages. An excellent herb garden, with more than 400 well-labeled varieties, gives the full range of culinary, medicinal, and fragrant plants. The gardens are carefully researched and excellent publications are available for purchase at various shops on the premises.

OLD STURBRIDGE VILLAGE (64 miles southwest of Boston) 1 Old Sturbridge Village Road, Sturbridge, MA 01566 **TEL:** (508) 347-3362 or (800) SEE-1830 **OPEN:** Daily 9-5, April through Oct.; Tues.-Sun. 9-5, Nov. through March **TOTAL ACRES:** Garden 1, village 200 **SPECIAL COLLECTIONS:** Colonial-era herbs and vegetables, historic house gardens   **ZONE 6** A F G H HO L P PA R T V WS

BERKSHIRE BOTANICAL GARDEN
STOCKBRIDGE

Inspired by the natural beauty of the Berkshire Mountains and their own pleasurable gardening endeavors, local and summer residents in the Stockbridge area organized a horticultural center in 1934 to share information about native flora and to encourage home gardening. Today the private, nonprofit Berkshire Botanical Garden, with eight acres of woodlands and another eight of informal flower gardens, features an old-fashioned rose garden, a daylily collection numbering over 200 varieties, a primrose meadow, perennial borders, a rock garden, and a woodland water garden.

Within an edible landscape of herbs, vegetables, and dwarf apple orchards are practical demonstration areas for homeowners, as well as greenhouses offering small displays of plants that can be grown indoors. The garden's strong focus on education, with informative and enjoyable workshops and lectures, is complemented by its aesthetic setting. It is this pervasive sense of beauty that contributes an additional inducement to visitors to protect the environment and to garden successfully.

BERKSHIRE BOTANICAL GARDEN (135 miles west of Boston) Mass. 102 and Mass. 183, P.O. Box 826, Stockbridge, MA 01262 **TEL:** (413) 298-3926 **OPEN:** Grounds: Daily 10-5, May through Oct.; Greenhouses: Daily **TOTAL ACRES:** 15 **SPECIAL COLLECTIONS:** Old-fashioned flowers, daylilies, primroses, perennial borders   **ZONE 5** A C F G H P PA T V WS

Naumkeag
Stockbridge

Stockbridge, Massachusetts, was the inland Newport of the Gilded Age. In 1885, Joseph Hodges Choate, New York lawyer and former ambassador to Great Britain, decided to build his summer retreat here. The 26-room shingled mansion he called Naumkeag was designed by eminent architect Stanford White. It would take two generations and two landscape architects to create the garden seen today. The result is not a garden of flowers, but rather a landscape of distinctly designed spaces that suggest the meaning of Naumkeag's Indian name: "Haven of Peace."

Nathaniel Barrett (1896-1905), the first landscape architect, laid out a two-tier garden divided by an evergreen walk of two rows of arborvitae shaped to look like Italian cypress trees in a Tuscan landscape. Though narrowed by the growth of trees, the allée remains impressive.

In the mid-1920s, following her father's death, Mabel Choate inherited the estate and devoted herself to creating a garden that would reflect those she had admired in her world travels. In 1926 she hired the innovative landscape designer Fletcher Steele to transform Naumkeag into one of the grand gardens of America; their collaboration lasted 30 years. Steele, uninterested in what he called "floricultural stunts," was impressed by the cubist movement in Europe and approached garden design as a landscape sculptor—but with a spirit of playfulness. His fusion of formal and informal elements of garden design, based upon abstract spatial principles popular in the art and architecture of the early 20th century, resulted in the interesting garden seen today.

Mabel Choate liked the then-novel California idea of "outdoor rooms." The first of a series of rooms Steele designed overlooking the Berkshire's serene valleys and mountains was the Afternoon Garden, positioned at the southwest corner of

Built in 1928, Naumkeag's Afternoon Garden features festive, Venetian-style gondola poles. It is one of many "garden rooms" in this sumptuous Berkshire estate.

Mabel Choate collected sculptures and objects during her travels to China and placed them in her garden at Naumkeag.

the house. Venetian-style gondola posts painted in red and blue and capped with gilded finials make up the fanciful walls of this room; festive garlands of clematis and Virginia creeper stretch across the columns. The colorful poles, originally oak pilings dredged from the bottom of Boston Harbor, frame a distant vista of seasonal color. At the center of this garden, a small oval pool, lined in black glass to simulate a mirror, is surrounded by rhythmic hedges of Japanese holly in the form of a French topiary knot. Delicate jets of water rise from four scalloped fountains within the green knots, creating a romantic and fanciful place for tea in the afternoon.

Below this area stretch great lawn terraces and a terrace featuring 42 Chinese tree peonies that bloom in late May, displaying large saucer-size flowers in white, yellow, magenta, and pink. On a nearby slope, Japanese red maples frame a Chinese pagoda with a spectacular view of Monument Mountain.

In Naumkeag's northeast corner, the Chinese Room re-creates an atmosphere reminiscent of the gardens Choate visited in the 1930s. A redbrick wall capped with blue tiles encloses the garden. The entrance is through a twisting "devil's screen" of brick and marble, leading to a Chinese-style temple framed by ginkgo trees and peony hedges. On display throughout this walled garden is Choate's collection of Buddhas, lions, and other Chinese statuary. One of the garden's last additions is the Moon Gate through which visitors exit.

What began as Mabel Choate's request for a simple path from the main entrance to a lower cutting garden resulted in Steele's most important and dramatic creation at Naumkeag. Completed in 1938, the Blue Stairs consists of a pyramid of steps formed by four tiers of blue concrete with water cascading down the center. Stair rails of white pipe curve elegantly into balustrades of concentric semicircles at the four landings, and dense groves of paperwhite birch trees of varying sizes are placed alongside. The result: water cascading amid graphic birch verticals and art nouveau horizontals, creating a striking effect.

Between 1955 and 1956 Fletcher Steele completed his last room, the Rose Garden. Here the series of serpentine curves of pink gravel punctuated by 16 beds of red, pink, and yellow floribunda roses is best viewed from the terrace above. Steele once posed the question, "Where will you sit to be with the stars?" In applying unconventional use of materials and arrangements of space, Naumkeag, the garden of many rooms with a view, became his answer.

■ NAUMKEAG (135 miles west of Boston) Prospect Hill, Stockbridge, MA 01262 TEL: (413) 298-3239 OPEN: Daily 10-5, Memorial Day weekend to Columbus Day TOTAL ACRES: 46 SPECIAL COLLECTIONS: Fletcher Steele design, garden rooms, birch walk, waterfall staircase, peonies   ZONE 5 F G HO P T WS

Sinuous white railings and an allée of white birches enclose the Blue Sta waterfall, considered Fletcher Steele's masterpie

GREEN ANIMALS
PORTSMOUTH

Topiary, the art of shaping plants, shrubs, and trees into fantastic forms by pruning and shearing, has been alternatively in and out of favor since Roman times. During the Renaissance, Italian and French nobility preferred geometric motifs in their formal and symmetrical parterres, while the Dutch and English were less restrained and drawn to fantasy rather than symmetry. The topiary "craze" reached its peak in 17th-century England, but by the 18th century, British landscape designers were scorning what they considered the contortions and constraints of topiary in favor of picturesque, naturalistic styles. With its artful, whimsical display of leafy animals, birds, and other fanciful forms, Green Animals, a topiary garden on the shores of Narragansett Bay, displays a healthy sense of humor on the subject. Whether visitors are tempted to sit on a plush green armchair in the shade of a 20-foot camel, or to step into the welcoming arms of a life-size bear, they cannot help but be enchanted by this menagerie of clipped and trimmed privet and yew.

Green Animals began in 1872 when Thomas Brayton, a successful textile merchant from Fall River, Massachusetts, acquired a seven-acre estate just outside of Newport. His modest summer house did not approach the extravagance of the Newport "cottages" soon to be built. Brayton was more intent on creating a distinguished garden.

Topiary captivated Brayton, but it is not clear where, if ever, he saw animals carved in evergreen. One story tells of his visit to a botanical garden in the Azores, another that he might have seen the famous topiary garden, Levens Hall, in England. Inspiration undoubtedly came from the young Portuguese mill worker he hired, Joseph Carreiro, whose family members had been gardeners on estates in the Azores. It was Carreiro's imagination and dexterity that helped create this beguiling garden. He was in charge from 1904 until 1945, when his son-in-law, George Medonca, took over. Medonca in turn continued the design and care of the topiary until 1985.

In 1939, Alice Brayton inherited her parents' summer estate, and made it her permanent residence. She named the collection of privet and yew sculptures Green Animals and used the garden to attract Newport society. According to author Mary McCarthy, who lived nearby and often visited Green Animals, "her social strategy, as carefully worked out as a Napoleonic battle plan, was based on reaching the child she counted on finding in every Newport dowager and tycoon." The plan succeeded. Invitations to her garden galas—which included the debutante party for future first lady Jacqueline Bouvier—were coveted. Alice went on to become one of the reigning matriarchs of Newport society until her death in 1972, at the age of 94.

Today visitors to Green Animals begin their tour in the main garden, where borders of English and Japanese boxwood are arranged in concentric circles and varied geometric patterns. Within these borders bloom lush displays of salvia, zinnias, verbena, snapdragons, cosmos, ageratum, dianthus, and many other colorful annuals—more than a hundred different species in all. Around this multicolored carpet, topiary animals perch atop shrub pedestals. There are 21 animals and birds carved in California privet and in yew. Many are life-size or

This life-size evergreen bear is one of many fanciful topiaries at the humorous, flower-filled Green Animals garden. Sheared out of slow-growing yew, it took ten years for the bear to grow to this size.

larger, and some appear quite realistic. Part of the fun is guessing the identity of some sculptures while marveling at the realistic shape and size of others. The senior stars in this verdant circus are the giraffe, the elephant, the camel, and the lion. More than 80 years old, they were the garden's first inhabitants. The main garden also boasts more than 50 abstract, architectural, and amusing forms sheared out of privet and boxwood. Towering corkscrew spirals, arched pavilions, globes, pyramids, and urns rise amid the animal kingdom.

Beyond this central display, borders of perennials and ornamental grasses are planted along paths leading to smaller beds of cutting flowers, a knot garden of santolina and germander, and a berry garden with red currants, gooseberries, and blueberries. Along the way hang trellises laden with grapevines, espaliered apple and pear trees, a lovely magnolia arbor, and even some fig trees and bamboo that have managed to survive New England's coastal climate. Nearby, a large vegetable garden provides a bounty that once filled the needs of a busy household. On the opposite side of the white clapboard house, a grand lawn sweeps down to the bay. The only area not covered with a profusion of plants, the lawn is simply surrounded by beautiful trees—sugar maple, copper beech, sycamores, and a tulip tree.

Traditionally, yew and boxwood are the preferred shrubs for topiary because they are slow growers. In the climate of New England, however, privet is a more durable semi-evergreen, faster growing and malleable although it needs to be trimmed more often. It is the preferred plant at Green Animals. Another variation in the topiary process here is that wire mesh is not used to form the animal

shapes. Instead, there is a metal skeletal structure for support within most shrubs. All the figures are actually planted and aren't portable.

The green and growing sculptures require extensive maintenance. Beginning in April each year, the California privet used in many of them is trimmed and sheared every three or four weeks, meticulous shaping done by hand, as power equipment does not allow for enough control and accuracy.

Dangers do lurk in this green zoo—for the animals, not the visitors. A hurricane once decapitated the giraffe, who now has a shortened neck. The elephant lost its trunk when a tourist collided with it. Inclement winters can often damage plant parts, and restoration is a slow process, sometimes requiring years for repairs to grow in.

Before her death in 1974, Alice Brayton

A senior member of this garden at almost 90 years old, the 20-foot camel looms over an armchair in the midst of parterres planted with an exuberance of summer annuals.

expressed concern about the fate of her unique topiary garden: "I couldn't bear the idea of seeing my giraffe leaving through the front gate." She rejected an offer from the New York Botanical Garden to transplant the topiary and instead left the estate to the Preservation Society of Newport County, which administers several historic houses and grand mansions in the Newport area. In keeping with the charm and spirit of the garden, the society created a toy museum within the house, collecting material from other sites that it administers. Green Animals has thus maintained its eclectic ambience, and continues to be carefully groomed. This family of whimsical animals delights visitors from May through October.

GREEN ANIMALS (10 miles north of Newport) 380 Cory's Lane, Portsmouth, RI 02871 TEL: (401) 683-1267 OPEN: Daily 10-5, May through Oct. TOTAL ACRES: 7 SPECIAL COLLECTIONS: Topiary, annuals, herbs, vegetables, ornamental grasses

ZONE 6 F G H HO P PA WS

Blithewold Gardens and Arboretum
Bristol

The gracious summer style that prevailed along Narragansett Bay in the early 1900s is well represented at Blithewold, named for an old English word meaning "happy woodlands." A landscape of seaside vistas, expansive lawns, majestic trees, and intimate gardens surrounds the English-style manor house built in 1907 for the Van Wickles mining family from Pennsylvania. John De Wolf, who was then supervising Frederick Law Olmsted's design for Prospect Park in Brooklyn, New York, was hired to design the grounds of this 33-acre estate. A tree that outgrew De Wolf's Brooklyn greenhouse is now one of Blithewold's outstanding specimens. The 85-foot giant sequoia, planted when it was 12 feet high, is today the largest sequoia east of the Rocky Mountains. It may be seen inside the enclosed garden, along with other impressive indigenous and exotic trees.

Nearby lies the "bosquet," a serene woodland of stately lindens, maples, and ash trees carpeted in lush foliage of vinca, ivy, myrtle, ferns and, in spring, drifts of daffodils. Smaller garden areas on either side of the 45-room mansion showcase roses and perennials. Along the shoreline, a Japanese-style garden presents rocks and stones artfully arranged with colorful flowers blooming in different seasons. A weeping willow and cherry tree decorate the water garden, where two small ponds are connected by a stone bridge. Summer brings a spectacular display of color in the cutting gardens. The Great Lawn, a sweep of ten acres down to the water's edge, completes this lovely tranquil scene.

The Van Wickles were extremely proud of their garden, and made it a family tradition to periodically open the grounds to the public. When they bequeathed Blithewold to the Heritage Trust of Rhode Island in 1976 they stipulated that, in funding, the gardens should take priority over the house.

Blithewold Gardens and Arboretum (15 miles north of Newport) 101 Ferry Road, Bristol, RI 02809 **Tel:** (401) 253-2707 **Open:** Daily 10-5 **Total acres:** 33 **Special collections:** Giant sequoia and other specimen trees, estate garden, cutting garden   **ZONE 6** **F** G **H** HO P PA **R** V

Newport Mansions: The Elms, The Breakers, Rosecliff
Newport

Newport was the summer capital for America's millionaires at the beginning of the 20th century. Sumptuous marble mansions publicized their owner's prodigious wealth and yachts and steamers drew up for champagne galas, garden parties, and racing during the short summer social season. Situated along the coast, these marble "cottages" had the sea as a backdrop for lawns, fountains, and sculpture. Most of the gardens—formal expressions of French, Italian, and English styles— were modest in scale compared with the grand architecture and interior treasures of the homes. They served as decorative settings for the mansions, not as attempts to re-create the great gardens of Europe.

Of the eight mansions that line Bellevue Avenue, three have gardens of special interest: The Elms, The Breakers, and Rosecliff. Although **The Elms** was never Newport's most lavish cottage, its grounds and gardens ranked among the most beautiful and today they are the finest gardens that remain from Newport's age of opulence. Owner Edwin Berwind, a mining magnate, commissioned Horace Trumbauer, then an unknown architect, to design a mansion in the style of a French château as well as the grounds. Trumbauer later went on to greater

Classical marble statues and flower-filled urns adorn the grandiose staircase at The Elms.

fame as designer of the Philadelphia Museum of Art, Duke University, and assorted Newport mansions. Bruce Butterton, the head gardener for many years, selected the plants and trees. In its heyday, The Elms had a staff of 12 gardeners for its 11 acres.

Although the house's namesake elms have disappeared, splendid specimens of weeping beeches, ginkgos, lindens, and Norwegian maples line the path leading to the mansion's entrance. Berwind collected exotic trees introduced by plant explorers at the Arnold Arboretum in Boston, and The Elms is considered to have Newport's finest tree collection. At the back of the mansion, overlooking manicured lawns, a grand terrace descends in three levels, landscaped with classical sculptures. The side terrace offers colorful flower beds arranged in Victorian parterres, including circular beds of begonias alternating with diamond-shaped beds of striking pink ageratum. Two marble teahouses mark the entrance to the Sunken Garden, which is more of an elegant retreat than a grand floral display. This small, formal parterre surrounded by lofty trees is distinguished by its formal architectural structures. At its center, a cistern decorated with dancing cherubs divides two large rectangular beds of hundreds of pink and white begonias edged in boxwood. From the Sunken Garden, a look back across the green expanse of lawn affords a dramatic view of the austere mansion rising above its terraced podium. Its elegant starkness is softened by shrubs planted below the balustrade, by rhythmic forms of terrace plantings, and by silhouettes of dramatic sculptures.

Newport's most elaborate "cottage," **The Breakers,** was designed in the Renaissance revival style by Richard Morris Hunt, family architect to the

Enclosed by a curtain of stately trees, statues overlook roundels of begonias and diamonds of ageratum set on a carpet of green lawn within the side terrace at The Elms.

Vanderbilts. Its owner, Cornelius Vanderbilt II, also hired Ernest Bowditch, a former student of Frederick Law Olmsted, to landscape the grounds. On the estate today, stately trees stand in isolated grandeur around an expansive lawn edged by clipped Japanese yew, Chinese junipers, and hemlocks. A small terrace on the house's western side displays a dense grouping of pink and white alyssum with blue ageratum in a colorful parterre—all minor elements in a prospect dominated by the huge mansion and set against sea, clouds, and sky.

Another of Newport's grand mansions, **Rosecliff,** belonged to Theresa Alice Fair, a Comstock silver lode heiress and a legendary hostess. She engaged one of the era's most fashionable architects, Stanford White, to design a modified version of the Grand Trianon at the Palace of Versailles in France. The resulting mansion, Rosecliff, was once surrounded by rose gardens.

At Rosecliff, garden ornaments are as important in the garden's design as flowers.

The ballroom opened on the western side to a French-style courtyard, a *cour d'amour* filled with overflowing urns of flowers and potted trees. On the eastern side, a terrace overlooked a circular fountain surrounded by rose beds framed by a background of lawn and sea. Today, one rose garden along the southern facade of the house has been restored to hold some 200 hybrid tea roses within boxwood borders. The mansions and their gardens are elegant reminders of past grandeur within boxwood borders connected by paths of marble chips.

NEWPORT MANSIONS: THE ELMS, ROSECLIFF Bellevue Avenue **THE BREAKERS** Ochre Point Avenue, Newport, RI 02840 **TEL:** (401) 847-1000 **OPEN:** Daily 10-5, May through Oct.; call for winter schedule **SPECIAL COLLECTIONS:** Estate gardens in Gilded Age design, sculpture, and ornaments

ZONE 6 **F** **G** **H** **HO** **P** **T** **V** **WS**

Sweeping lawns and majestic trees set the scene for the opulent life at Rosecliff. Flower beds are formal and discreet, while sumptuous balustrades, fountains, and sculpture accent the landscape.

Connecticut

Elizabeth Park Rose Garden
West Hartford

Cascades of crimson, pink, and white roses garland the arbors in this award-winning garden at Elizabeth Park in West Hartford. The number and size of its lushly draped trellises distinguish the garden. Red ramblers alternate with pink and white Dorothy Perkinses along the eight paths, each with ten arches fifteen feet high, radiating out from a central gazebo.

Surrounded by beds of hundreds of old and modern roses, the elevated trellises provide a dramatic perspective of radiant colors. Atop a mound in the center of this 2.5-acre garden, a Victorian gazebo rises in plush layers of Virginia creeper. The only solid green space in this brilliant array, the gazebo provides a shaded shelter from which to view vistas in all directions.

Lush pink clusters of the rose, 'Carefree Wonder', bloom under arches of 'Crimson Rambler' in the elaborate Elizabeth Park rose garden.

The nation's first municipal rose garden, Elizabeth Park opened in 1904 on a 100-acre estate bequeathed by local industrialist Charles Pond. Designed by Theodore Wirth, a Swiss-born horticulturist who was then superintendent of the city parks, the rose garden was a stunning success. It attracted thousands of visitors in its early years, and for nearly 60 years remained a leading showcase for roses, as well as being the first test garden of the American Rose Society. By the late 1960s, however, this historic rose garden was in decline. Fortunately, a volunteer organization, the Friends of Elizabeth Park, saved the garden in 1977 from residential development and it thrives today.

Restoration began in 1986, and in the difficult course of researching the garden's horticultural specifics a librarian discovered a list of "some French ladies who had contributed to the garden." The "French ladies" turned out to be roses in the original garden. Some still survive: Mme. Gabriel Luizet, Baronne Prevost, François Michelon, and their male companions, Henry Nevard, Paul Neyron, and Ulrich Brunner. These old garden roses are hybrid perpetuals, precursors to modern roses. Large, fragrant, and repeat bloomers, they were the most desirable exhibition roses of the Victorian era. At the peak of their popularity, there were close to 4,000 varieties. Most are lost or rare, except for the popular long-stemmed, red American Beauty—the flower of courtship and the florist's staple—

In this garden of endless rose-covered arches, 'Crimson Rambler' meets white 'Dorothy Perkins' (above, left), alternating with other ramblers.

and the white American Beauty called Frau Karl Druschki, one of the finest white roses available.

Today the garden has expanded beyond its original 108 beds to include some 15,000 rosebushes with more than 800 varieties, primarily modern roses. Most varieties are planted in separate beds, allowing color and form to be easily observed and appreciated. A circle of Chrystaline, Queen Elizabeth, Sarabande, and Mme. Caroline Testout surrounds the gazebo. Beyond fences of espaliered climbers and ramblers, a curtain of conifers leads into the recesses of the park. On the other side of the arbors, across the park path, several acres of smaller gardens await exploration. Among these are a heritage rose garden, boasting 250 varieties, an intriguing rock garden, and various displays of annuals and perennials, with ornamental grasses adding texture. Although overshadowed by the major rose garden, these attractive plantings offer colorful blooms from June through September. Since 1992 Elizabeth Park has served as an All-America Rose Selections Test Garden, one of 23 in the United States. In addition, the site offers three greenhouses dating from 1898, designed by the well-known firm of Lord and Burnham. Inside are displays of exotic plants as well as exhibits that explain the process of plant propagation.

ELIZABETH PARK ROSE GARDEN (5 miles from downtown Hartford) Prospect and Asylum Avenues, West Hartford, CT 06119 **TEL:** (860) 242-0017 **OPEN:** Daily dawn-dusk **TOTAL ACRES:** Garden 2.5, park 100 **SPECIAL COLLECTIONS:** Climbing roses, ramblers, hybrid perpetuals, heritage roses

ZONE 5 A C G H P P PA R T V

ROSELAND COTTAGE (BOWEN HOUSE)
WOODSTOCK

A lipstick-pink house with thrusting Gothic gables surprises visitors to the typically conservative New England colonial village of Woodstock. It is Roseland, summer house of silk merchant Henry C. Bowen, which attracted celebrity visitors following it completion in 1846. Presidents Grant, Hayes, Harrison, and McKinley all attended lavish Fourth of July celebrations here—just when Roseland's extravagant Victorian garden was in full bloom. Joseph C. Wells, a church architect, designed the house and New York landscaper Henry A. Dyer designed the garden in the popular style of its era. Both were influenced by the design philosophy of Andrew Downing, the period's leading landscape authority who promoted Gothic Revival architecture and formal beds of flowers set in a natural landscape for country retreats. Roseland Cottage is a good example of both.

Bowen bought his boxwood by the yard and flowers by the thousands. His plant lists read like a major nursery catalog. The Society for the Preservation of New England Antiquities, which purchased the property in 1970, used these lists, as well as old photographs, during its restoration. The parterre garden, with its 600 yards of dwarf boxwood edging, is thought to be one of the oldest boxwood gardens in the country. When Rudy Favretti, a prominent restorer of historic gardens, recommended cutting back the much overgrown boxwood, an outcry arose in the village. However, the boxwood was radically pruned to historic standards and, under Favretti's direction, the garden returned to its brilliant Victorian prodigality. Today nearly 5,000 annual and perennial plants thrive in 21 geometric boxwood borders, each displaying two or three different flowers. Nineteenth-century varieties such as the small single blue "pearl" petunia dominate. Elsewhere, displays of snapdragons, geraniums, salvia, and verbena showcase the Victorian carpet-bed style of design, while old shrub roses, rugosas, and hybrid perpetuals dating from the original garden honor the house's name and color.

ROSELAND COTTAGE (BOWEN HOUSE) (47 miles east of Hartford) 556 Route 169, Woodstock, CT 06281 **TEL:** (860) 928-4074 **OPEN:** Wed.-Sun. 11-5, June to mid-Oct. **TOTAL ACRES:** 3 **SPECIAL COLLECTIONS:** Boxwood borders, Victorian-style parterres with annuals and perennials **ZONE 6 G HO P R T WS**

THE SUNDIAL HERB GARDEN
HIGGANUM

In the 1970s in the course of restoring an 18th-century farmhouse and decorating its outdoor "rooms" with fountains, sundials, planters, trellises, and benches, Tom and Ragna Goddard found themselves in the garden business. Much more than just a retail operation, Sundial features picturesque herb gardens, lushly planted around a sundial, as well as a 16th-century-style raised knot garden and a topiary garden. A 100-year-old pear arbor marks the garden's entrance, wherein a vast array of culinary, medicinal, and household herbs are grown as small hedges, bedding plants, and standards. Flowers add colored accents. For a particularly personal look at this garden, visitors are advised to call ahead and reserve tea and a guided tour, with Ragna Goddard as guide. An extensive collection of herbs is for sale.

THE SUNDIAL HERB GARDEN (24 miles south of Hartford) 59 Hidden Lake Road, Higganum, CT 06441 **TEL:** (860) 345-4290 **OPEN:** Sat.-Sun. 10-5, except holidays; other days by appointment. **TOTAL ACRES:** 1 **SPECIAL COLLECTIONS:** Herbs in historic design setting **ZONE 6 F G H P R T WS**

Caprilands Herb Farm
North Coventry

What began as a pastime became a consuming passion for Adelma Simmons, an early champion of herbs and their multiple uses. She started about 60 years ago with a small dooryard garden on a rock-strewn farm that her family purchased in 1929. When their goat farm failed, the family explored the herb business. Simmons researched the lore and legend of herbs, writing some 50 publications on the subject. Today, her five-acre garden ranks as one of the oldest and largest herb gardens in the country. It is also a successful commercial venture.

A maze of gravel and brick paths connects a series of 31 plots organized around themes and single plants. Her first theme garden, the Butterfly Garden, was named for its shape. Others include a Shakespeare Garden; a Bride's Garden, with heart-shaped foliage and plants traditionally linked to love; and more standard culinary and medicinal gardens. In all, 360 varieties of plants are arranged in formal and informal beds reflecting Simmons's distinct personal style. This popular, colorful emporium also offers plants, dried herbs, books, and a luncheon lecture.

Caprilands Herb Farm (40 miles east of Hartford) 534 Silver Street, North Coventry, CT 06238 **Tel:** (860) 742-7244 **Open:** Daily 9-5, except holidays **Total acres:** 5 **Special collections:** Great variety of herbs   **ZONE 6** C G P PA R T

At Sundial Herb Gardens, a brass-and-copper sundial sits within a bed of lamb's ears surrounded by dwarf boxwood and beds of lavender, germander, southernwood, and other herbs.

Harkness Memorial State Park
Waterford

Panoramic ocean vistas, formal gardens, terraces, porticoes, and magnificent trees surround this Italian-style villa, making it an enticing place to visit. The Harkness family, known for its Standard Oil fortune and philanthropic largesse, placed a 42-room summer home on 234 acres overlooking Long Island Sound. While the gardens are not large, their design, flowers, and seaside setting are delightful. One area includes a romantic Italian garden, another holds an Oriental garden, and still others, a cutting garden and a rockery.

Two prominent American landscape artists helped plan the estate's gardens. In 1919, Beatrix Farrand, a frequent visitor, designed the Italian garden with plantings of elaborate parterres and an Oriental garden of stones, statues, and water. In 1949, Marian Coffin, known for her work at Winterthur and other estate gardens, was commissioned to redesign several garden areas. A blending of their talents and more recent changes have resulted in this pleasant retreat.

The estate was bequeathed to the state of Connecticut in 1950 and half of it was set aside as a recreation center for the handicapped. Restoration of the house and gardens are in process, scheduled for completion in 1999.

Harkness Memorial State Park (60 miles southeast of Hartford) 275 Great Neck Road, Conn. 213, Waterford, CT 06385 **Tel:** (860) 443-5725 **Open:** Daily 8-dusk **Total acres:** 134 **Special collections:** Estate garden, designs by Beatrix Farrand and Marian Coffin, rock garden, cutting garden

ZONE 6 A H HO P PA

The Gertrude Jekyll Garden at the Glebe House Museum
Woodbury

Renowned British designer Gertrude Jekyll has influenced many gardens in America, but Glebe House, birthplace of the Episcopal Church in America, has the only extant garden of the three in this country actually designed by her. When Glebe House was being converted into a museum in 1927, the small local historic society commissioned Jekyll to design an old-fashioned garden, sending her photographs and descriptions of the site. On that basis she contributed a scheme and plant list suitable for a cottage garden, but it was never installed.

Sixty years later, the plans were found in Beatrix Farrand's archives at the University of California at Berkeley and today the garden is laid out according to her original concepts. Her advice was clear: "I think this simple treatment of flower borders in front of sheltering shrubs and green spaces of plain grass will be best for the main front and side part. For the flowers I have proposed some of those best known in old gardens...." A lush perennial border some 300 feet long and 12 feet deep runs along the front and sides of the lawn, against yew hedges. Some of the borders are planted with delphinium, dahlias, lilies, cleomes, holly-hocks, and many other cottage flowers. In addition, a charming rose allée leads to a rose garden and a small kitchen herb garden.

The Gertrude Jekyll Garden at the Glebe House Museum (49 miles southwest of Hartford) Hollow Road, Woodbury, CT 06798 **Tel:** (203) 263-2855 **Open:** Wed-Sun 1-4, April through Dec. **Total acres:** Less than 1 **Special collections:** Only extant Gertrude Jekyll–designed garden in U.S., perennial borders

ZONE 6 F G H HO

The herbaceous borders at Glebe House feature plants favored by Gertrude Jekyll, including foxgloves and irises (shown opposite).

Hill-Stead Museum Garden
Farmington

A grand Colonial Revival mansion, Hill-Stead was completed in 1901 for industrialist Alfred Pope. His only child, Theodate, became one of the first female architects in America and collaborated with Stanford White in the design of the house. Pope had a passion for Impressionist art and his collection, including works by Monet, Degas, Manet, and Mary Cassatt, adorns the walls inside his former residence, now a house museum.

Warren Manning, a pioneer landscape architect in the early 20th century, created for Hill-Stead a "gentleman's farm" of 150 acres of rolling hills, open fields, and woodlands. Manning, a former associate of Frederick Law Olmsted and a leader in the natural landscape movement, is also credited with suggesting horticulturist Beatrix Farrand for the design of the estate's flower gardens. Farrand's archives revealed an unexecuted design for a sunken garden near the mansion, a proposal that became reality in 1988.

A summer garden house surrounded by thousands of perennials, bulbs, and roses stands within an octagonal evergreen hedge. Today, the selection of plants follows Farrand's list, with some contemporary hybrids substituted for older varieties. Delicate pastel hues of pink, blue, and lavender predominate in beds of peonies, irises, lilies, dahlias, delphiniums, damask roses, and many other flowering plants. While June is the peak month for blooms, vivid colors persist through summer and fall.

Hill-Stead Museum Garden (10 miles west of Hartford) 35 Mountain Road, Farmington, CT 06032 **Tel:** (860) 677-4787 **Open:** Daily dawn-dusk **Total acres:** Garden less than 1, grounds 150 **Special collections:** Estate garden, sunken garden designed by Beatrix Farrand

ZONE 6 H HO P T V

Bellamy-Ferriday Garden
Bethlehem

In the little town of Bethlehem, hidden behind a picket fence and a dense evergreen screen of hemlocks and white pine, lies a charming family garden designed by a mother-daughter team. Purchased in 1912, the Ferriday family's handsome four-acre summer estate consisted of an 18th-century house and farm property. Eliza Ferriday soon began the collection of trees, shrubs, and flowers that form the foundation of the garden today. Inspired by the pattern of her Aubusson carpet, she designed the formal garden in the traditional parterre style. Her daughter, Caroline, continued the tradition, bequeathing the estate to the Antiquarian and Landmarks Society in 1990. Peonies, irises, old roses, and newer varieties of perennials and annuals are planted in serpentine and geometric shaped beds edged with yew shrubs.

Although this garden is shielded on all sides by woods, an orchard, and the house, visitors can still glimpse open, distant fields. These vistas will remain, protected as part of 80 acres of fields given by Miss Ferriday to the Bethlehem Land Trust.

Bellamy-Ferriday Garden (38 miles southwest of Hartford) 9 Main Street, Bethlehem, CT 06751 **Tel:** (203) 266-7596 **Open:** Wed., Sat., Sun. 11-4, May through Oct. **Total Acres:** 10 **Special collections:** Estate garden, parterres, roses, magnolias, lilacs, peonies, shrubs **ZONE 6 F G H HO P PA T**

Hillside Gardens and Nursery
Norfolk

The country garden of Mary Ann and Fred McGourty, who are authorities on perennials and authors of many books on gardening, may seem surprisingly small. But it is very special. These five acres are considered by many plant experts to constitute one of the best perennial gardens in the Northeast. Alongside typical Connecticut stone walls, perennial borders bloom with a profusion of color starting in mid-June and ending in an array of brilliant foliage in fall. Rare plants and well-known flora are arranged in unusual places and combinations, many flourishing in abundance.

This personal garden in the northern part of Connecticut is also a selective nursery. Perennials are tested in its trial gardens and offered for sale after a successful period in the New England climate. The varied collection is based upon the McGourtys' experience and ingenuity in pursuing remote sources. Displays also showcase their talent in designing with perennials in borders, on berms, or casually along a path.

Hillside Gardens and Nursery (38 miles west of Hartford) 515 Litchfield Road, Norfolk, CT 06058 **Tel:** (860) 542-5345 **Open:** Daily 9-5, May through Sept., except holidays **Total acres:** 5 **Special collections:** Unusual perennials   **ZONE 6** A G P T WS

Rounded yew hedges give the parterres at the Bellamy-Ferriday Garden a distinctive design. The beds are filled with more than 50 different kinds of old-fashioned flowers from May to November.

CHAPTER 2

MID-ATLANTIC

■

New York

New Jersey

Pennsylvania

Delaware

Maryland

Washington, D.C.

This geometrical topiary, formed from Canadian hemlock, is one of the fine examples of "living sculpture" at the Ladew Topiary Gardens in Maryland.

NEW YORK BOTANICAL GARDEN
THE BRONX, NEW YORK CITY

Ten miles north of the skyscrapers of midtown Manhattan, the New York Botanical Garden presents another skyline—virgin forests and crystal pavilions within a naturalistic landscape of 250 acres. Located in the Bronx, New York City's northern borough, this is one of the largest and most important botanical gardens in the country. Renowned for its Victorian conservatory, plant collections, and specialized gardens, it is also an important research and educational institution behind the scenes.

The idea for this garden dates from 1889, when Nathaniel and Elizabeth Britton, young botanists on their honeymoon, visited the Royal Botanic Gardens at Kew outside of London. Upon their return, they campaigned and gained the financial support of Andrew Carnegie, Cornelius Vanderbilt II, and J.P. Morgan to create a similar garden in the United States. New York City provided the land, formerly the lavish estate of the Lorillard tobacco family.

In 1896 Nathaniel Britton became the garden's first director, and within 15 years he created a major botanical garden, as well as the largest conservatory in America, and the most comprehensive herbarium of North American specimens anywhere. The decades that followed saw the addition of important rock and rose gardens, and outstanding collections of decorative shrubs, flowering trees, and exotic specimens. Today they decorate the garden's rolling hills, open lawns, and winding paths. At the center of this parklike landscape stands 40 acres of one of the few uncut forests in New York City, here preserved as a natural woodland of red oak, white ash, hemlocks, and tulip trees.

Every April, tens of thousands of daffodils blanket the slopes of Daffodil Hill, one of the New York Botanical Garden's many areas with prolific spring blooms.

Beyond the garden's main entrance, the grandeur of the Victorian era is apparent in two majestic architectural landmarks, the beaux arts museum building and the Enid A. Haupt Conservatory. A grand allée of tulip trees leads to the museum building which now houses an orchid terrarium, a distinguished reference library, and a herbarium. On a nearby hillside stands the Haupt Conservatory, a stately garden under an acre of glistening glass. It opened in 1902, and was refurbished in 1997. Larger than its model at Kew Gardens, today it is an official New York City Landmark and one of the world's great conservatories.

Eleven glass galleries are arranged around an exterior rectangular courtyard with two large reflecting pools filled in summer with waterlilies, including the giant lily platters. Inside, the Victorian Palm Court's dome soars 90 feet above a luxurious collection of

In a recent renovation of the Haupt Conservatory, 17,000 panes of glass were replaced by hand. Exhibitions of exotic rain forest and desert plants, as well as spectacular floral shows, thrive under the glistening 90-foot dome (shown above) and in ten connected galleries.

palms native to tropical and subtropical climates. Massive royal palms found in Central and South America, an everglade palm from Florida, and a beautifully plumed queen palm from Brazil stand guard above a reflecting pool. The Lowland Tropical Rain Forest Gallery exhibits a large diversity of plants in various sizes and shapes, growing as they do in nature. Likewise, the Upland Tropical Rain Forest Gallery abounds with plants from higher elevations. Here an extravagant display of ferns surrounds and covers a simulated volcanic crater-turned-waterfall. Exotic orchids are scattered among the moss covers and clusters of foliage and an ingenious elevated skywalk winds unobtrusively around the different levels, providing unusual perspectives of this important collection.

The Deserts of America Gallery (from California to Argentina) features a fine collection of cactuses, including the massive saguaro from the Sonoran Desert. The Deserts of Africa Gallery displays a collection of succulents including the aloe tree that grows upwards of 60 feet in its native African habitat, to the small and inconspicuous stone plants. Other galleries focus on dramatic seasonal displays and interesting thematic shows. For example, a lavish chrysanthemum and bonsai festival in autumn is followed by a Christmas display of miniature railways running through a wondrous landscape of plants and flowers.

Outside the conservatory, newer gardens represent diverse horticultural and design ideas for the home gardener. The Jane Watson Irwin Perennial Garden opened in 1982 to present ensembles of color, pattern, and texture in the English style of Gertrude Jekyll, the renowned garden designer. Yew hedges divide an acre of herbaceous plants into a "cool" garden in varied shades of pink, blue, and white flowers and a "hot" garden of red, yellow, and orange blooms. These are set against a background of decorative shrubs, dwarf evergreens, and ornamental grasses. In summer more than sixty species of clematis cascade over arbors with pastel and deep purple blooms.

The 170-foot Seasonal Walk provides a kaleidoscopic array of color throughout the year. Masses of spring tulips in April and May are followed by dazzling summer annuals. Here nicotiana and cleomes frame clusters of marigolds, daisies, zinnias, and ageratum along the walk. Beyond, demonstration gardens for the home gardener are organized into separate thematic displays including vegetable, herb, fragrance, cutting, shade, and country gardens. Two distinguished lily collections include the Daylily Walk, where some 200 varieties of daylilies peak in July in colors ranging from tints of yellow to deep black-reds. In addition, the Arlow B. Stout Daylily Garden at the garden's far eastern end offers species lilies native to Siberia, China, and Japan, along with an outstanding collection of hybrids.

Wildflowers, shrubs, ferns, grasses, and trees found within a hundred-mile radius of New York City flourish in the naturalistic setting of the Native Plant Garden. Surprisingly secluded on the fringes of the natural forest, the Thomas H. Everett Rock Garden, designed by and named for the garden's former director of horticulture, is one of the largest and finest public rock gardens in America. Jagged ledges, crooks and crannies, screes and streams, alpine meadows, and a picturesque waterfall provide varied habitats for an impressive array of dwarf shrubs, heath, heather, and such mountain perennials as rock jasmine, alpine pinks, and many others. Striking boulders bisect the garden and divide planted areas into terraces of sweeping colors and textures. April through June are the

Flowers on a summer day flaunt their colors in the country garden next to the Haupt Conservatory. Displays are designed to provide both pleasure and education.

best months for the delicate blossoms in this fascinating terrain.

In 1916 Beatrix Farrand, one of America's most outstanding landscape designers, was commissioned to design a rose garden, but the design was never executed. Her conceptual drawings were rediscovered at the University of California at Berkeley and adapted by the New York Botanical Garden in a restoration funded by David Rockefeller in honor of his wife. The result, the Peggy Rockefeller Rose Garden, was dedicated in 1988. Situated at the bottom of a slope, the two-acre triangular plot is edged by a dramatic perimeter of dark green metal lattices joined by arches. The domed gazebo at its center is encircled by posts and chains garlanded with climbing roses, a design feature favored by Beatrix Farrand. From this central point more than 80 rosebeds radiate outward, arranged according to variety; modern roses, including hybrid teas, grandifloras, and floribundas are planted in the interior beds and along the walkways. More than a hundred kinds of old garden and shrub roses grow in the wide perimeter beds. Paths of crushed blue stone connect the display of 2,700 roses. This elegant garden, ablaze with color in June and September, is subdued but lovely in the months in between.

Distances from one area to another are often quite far, however a tram tour covering key sites is available. In any case, visitors should expect a full day's excursion to the conservatory and its surrounding gardens. If time here is limited, the Visitor Center offers an excellent map and informative brochures for careful planning.

NEW YORK BOTANICAL GARDEN (10 miles north of midtown Manhattan) 200th Street and Southern Boulevard, The Bronx, NY 10458. **TEL:** (718) 817-8700 **OPEN:** Tues.-Fri. 8-6, April through Sept.; Sat.-Sun. and holidays 10-6, Oct. through March **TOTAL ACRES:** 250 **SPECIAL COLLECTIONS:** Conservatory, roses, perennials, rock garden, trees, daylilies, native plants   **ZONE 6** C F G H P PA R T V WS

Situated along the Bronx River, this grove in the center of the New York Botanical Garden is the only major uncut woodland remaining from a forest that once covered all of New York City.

Wave Hill
The Bronx, New York City

A spectacular panorama of the Hudson River and Palisades frames the gardens of Wave Hill. A surprising haven in Riverdale, in the northwest corner of the Bronx, this grand estate housed such luminaries as Theodore Roosevelt, Mark Twain, and Arturo Toscanini. Wave Hill's last occupants, the Perkins-Freeman family, donated the estate to New York City. An ardent conservationist, George W. Perkins was active in protecting the Palisades on the opposite side of the Hudson River as an interstate park. In 1965, Wave Hill opened to the public, and today its 28 acres of quiet woodland walks and glorious gardens is a major attraction for all serious gardeners.

Initially, however, the gift consisted mainly of a beautiful site, two museums, and the outlines of neglected gardens and greenhouses. The distinct and diverse gardens began in 1967 with the appointment of Marco Polo Stufano as director. Stufano, an art history major, was joined by curator John Nally, a printmaker. Their innovative approach to gardening fused a sense of tradition with the excitement of experimentation. In so doing they maintained the ambience of a personal, intimate garden within the grandeur of its setting.

A main feature at Wave Hill remains the luxuriant old-fashioned flower garden, filled with cultivars popular in the early 20th century as well as modern varieties of perennials and annuals. Masses of color mix everywhere in carefree and imaginative combinations, creating what Stufano liked to call "plant pictures." Without preconceived ideas about garden styles and correct plants, this garden's design is in constant flux. In the background, an ornate Victorian conservatory is filled with a small but select collection of tropical and semitropical plants.

At the estate's highest point a wild garden holds plant species from five continents, combined in casual, naturalistic settings. More than a typical native plant garden, drifts of brilliant red and orange flowers here mingle with different ornamental vegetables. Other gardens include an aquatic garden of large water-lilies and lotuses; an herb garden with more than a hundred plants; a dry garden of Mediterranean plants; and a monocot garden of ornamental grasses. Also of interest is the T.H. Everett Alpine House, the only public collection of alpine plants under glass in the Northeast. Display areas on the hillsides are separated by rustic cedar fences and surrounded by lawn terraces and shady pergolas.

As is readily apparent to even a casual visitor, Wave Hill's main emphasis is on knowledge of plants and the aesthetics of gardening. An enormous variety of plants are used in creative and interesting combinations to highlight their individual characteristics. And still the pleasures of a country estate permeate this urban yet tranquil corner. The two mansions on the grounds contain changing exhibitions related to art, horticulture, and the environment.

Wave Hill is attractive in all seasons, but autumn offers particularly spectacular gardens specifically planted to maximize texture and color compositions—all against a backdrop of the Palisade's autumnal color, across the Hudson River.

Wave Hill (12 miles north of midtown Manhattan) West 249th Street and Independence Avenue, The Bronx, NY 10471 **Tel:** (718) 549-3200 **Open:** Tues.-Sun. 9-5:30 and until dusk Fri., mid-May to mid-Oct.; Tues.-Sun. 9-4:30, mid-Oct. to mid-May; closed holidays **Total acres:** 28 **Special collections:** Variety of perennials in formal and informal scenic settings, alpine plants

ZONE 6 C F G H HO P PA R T WS

The Hudson River and the cliffs of the Palisades on the New Jersey shore are dramatic backdrops for the rainbow of irises and potted boxwood on the main terrace at Wave Hill.

THE CLOISTERS
MANHATTAN, NEW YORK CITY

High above the Hudson River in northwest Manhattan, a re-created 12th-century French monastery houses the Metropolitan Museum of Art's outstanding medieval collection. Renowned for its sacred and secular art collections and the drama of its setting, the Cloisters also features four small, exquisite courtyard gardens with a unique display of medieval horticulture. The largest and most formal of these is the open courtyard of the Cuxa Cloister, where capitals from a Benedictine monastery form an arcade around quadrants of flowers and fruit trees. At the center of this medieval pleasure garden, a lion fountain spews water. Fig, lemon, and lime trees stand among jasmine, oleander, foxgloves, and johnny-jump-ups. In winter, the open arcades are glazed and the walkways filled with pots of rosemary, jasmine, citrus, and spring bulbs.

The Bonnefont Cloister holds the herb garden of a monastic kitchen. Here more than 250 species of culinary and medicinal plants are contained in raised beds among the characteristic wattle fences, espaliered fruit trees, and a central wellhead. Nearby, the Trie Cloister displays all the identifiable plants depicted in the hunt scene of the famous Unicorn Tapestries. Such "tapestry trees" as oak, orange, hazelnut, pomegranate, and holly are surrounded by a flourishing display of Madonna lilies, violets, primroses, carnations, and dandelions. The final, smallest garden is situated under a skylight in the Saint-Guilhem Cloister, and offers displays from Christmas to Easter of fragrant paper whites, hyacinths, lilies-of-the-valley, and other blooms. Together, this surprising combination of art, gardens, and vistas makes the Cloisters one of New York's most magical experiences.

■ THE CLOISTERS (12 miles north of midtown Manhattan) Fort Tyron Park, New York, NY 10040 TEL: (212) 923-3700 OPEN: Tues.-Sun. 9:30-5, except holidays TOTAL ACRES: Less than 1 SPECIAL COLLECTIONS: Courtyard gardens; medieval-era herbs, fruits, vegetables ZONE 6 F G H P T WS

CONSERVATORY GARDEN IN CENTRAL PARK
MANHATTAN, NEW YORK CITY

The entrance to the only formal gardens in New York City's Central Park, at Fifth Avenue and 105th Street, is marked by massive iron gates that once guarded a Vanderbilt mansion. Inside, six acres divided into three gardens host sumptuous displays of fountains and flowers reminiscent of elegant European gardens. Facing the gate, the Central Garden's large green rectangle of lawn is flanked by double allées of pink-and-white blooming crabapple trees. At the lawn's end, rising dramatically above a fountain, semicircular tiers of evergreen and deciduous shrubs are crowned by a latticed pergola covered in wisteria vines half a century old.

To the right of the entrance lies the North Garden, a classical garden in the French style. Within, parterres of annuals and santolina form a scroll pattern around a central bronze fountain of dancing maidens. Circles of blazing colors sweep the inner parterres, the result of a spring planting of 20,000 tulips and, in fall, 5,000 chrysanthemums. In addition, flowering shrubs and roses decorate the outer ring of archways. Alongside the central garden, the South Garden

Within Central Park's Conservatory Garden lies the South Garden, designed in English style with drifts of perennials, lush roses, and flowering trees and shrubs. It offers a serene retreat from the

provides a lush, more naturalistic setting of bulbs, annuals, and perennials. A horseshoe of five large, English-style borders displays more than 3,500 perennial plants among flourishing roses and such long-blooming annuals as snapdragons, nicotiana, blue salvia, and many others—an arrangement designed by the garden's current director, Lynden Miller. Sometimes called the Secret Garden after the famous children's book by Frances Hodges Burnett, bronze sculptures of the story's main characters, Mary and Dickon, stand in the middle of the lily pond.

From 1899 to 1934 the conservatory's elaborate Victorian glass houses provided plants for all the city parks. In 1937, during the Depression and under the stewardship of Park Commissioner Robert Moses, a new garden designed by M. Betty Sprout and Gilmore D. Clark was built as a Works Progress Administration project. The gardens were restored in the 1980s thanks to the enthusiastic fundraising efforts of the New York Garden Club.

CONSERVATORY GARDEN IN CENTRAL PARK Fifth Avenue at 105th Street, New York, NY 10021 **TEL:** (212) 360-2766 **OPEN:** Daily dawn-dusk **TOTAL ACRES:** 6 **SPECIAL COLLECTIONS:** Parterres, perennial borders, crabapple allées   **ZONE 6** A H T WS

hectic city. In a pool at its center, a bronze statue immortalizes two fictional children, Mary and Dickon, from the beloved children's classic The Secret Garden, *by Frances Hodges Burnett.*

Considered one of the most outstanding in America, the Brooklyn Botanic Garden's Japanese Hill and Pond Garden offers harmonious plant arrangements—spiritual symbols that you may enter.

BROOKLYN BOTANIC GARDEN
BROOKLYN, NEW YORK CITY

The Brooklyn Botanic Garden is a remarkable sanctuary of gardens within a garden in the midst of the stark urban setting of New York City's largest borough. Enclosed within 52 acres, this diverse pageant of formal and informal landscapes includes a distinguished Japanese garden, outstanding collections of cherry and magnolia trees, and the largest rose garden on the East Coast.

Brooklyn entered the 20th century with some of New York City's grandest cultural and recreational institutions: the massive Brooklyn Museum had recently been completed, and the Brooklyn Public Library, Prospect Park, and the Brooklyn Botanic Garden were in the planning stages. On the site of a city dump, purchased in 1910, a glorious garden emerged. Credit for this achievement belongs mainly to the garden's talented first director, Dr. C. Stuart Gager, a professor of botany from the University of Missouri. For 33 years, Dr. Gager guided the design, plant collections, and innovative educational programs for which the garden remains renowned worldwide.

The Olmsted Brothers firm's general plan placed key architectural structures —the McKim, Mead and White-designed Victorian Palm Conservatory and beaux arts administration building—along the garden's eastern perimeter (Washington Avenue). But it was in designing many of the garden areas that Harold Caparn, a landscape architect, and Montague Free, the garden's horticulturist, together combined botany with beauty. By 1945, the garden's popularity rated the local headline: "Botanic Garden Outdraws Dodgers with 1,250,000 Visitors Annually."

The marvel is how much is achieved in such a small area. Beginning at the main entrance, visitors are greeted by an herb garden filled with more than 50 culinary and nearly a hundred medicinal plants; a lovely Elizabethan knot garden with rows of intertwined germander and santolina against a background of crushed white and coral gravel; and a cottage garden containing plants mentioned in Shakespeare's plays and sonnets.

Nearby is the Japanese Hill and Pond Garden, considered one of the best examples of this style in America. One of the Brooklyn Botanic Garden's earliest areas, it was designed in 1914 by Takeo Shiota, a Japanese artist living in New York. A strategically positioned viewing pavilion affords the best view of this garden's "mirror of nature," the sinuous pond. Shaped in the form of the Chinese symbol for the heart, or "meditating center," the pond surrounds a towering red torii that rises from the water as the "gateway to heaven." Above the pond, a shrine dedicated to the Shinto god of harvest overlooks the "evergreens of eternity," pines trained to look windswept and shrubs artfully sheared to resemble hillocks and clouds. The soft sound of a cascading waterfall induces a sense of tranquility, while carefully placed rocks convey strength and stability. Stepping stones, arranged for both pattern and practicality, lead to an arched bridge, its shape completed by its reflection in the water. A stone snow-view lantern symbolizes the importance of all seasons in a Japanese garden. In this traditional hill-and-pond garden, flowers are used with restraint. In early spring graceful weeping cherry trees, blossoming apricots, and delicate irises decorate the banks of the pond. Later, the blossoms of azaleas, wisteria, and peonies punctuate the greens and grays.

Beyond lies the large rectangular Cherry Esplanade. Flanked by double rows of 'Kwanzan' cherry trees that burst into parachutes of pink blossoms in early May, the lawn becomes a beautiful pastel carpet of fallen petals as the month progresses. These trees were a generous gift from Japan, as were the famous Yoshino cherry trees in Washington, D.C.

A stroll along Ginkgo Walk, named for the trees bordering its raised path, leads to an overlook of the spectacular Cranford Rose Garden. Incredible colors seem to explode within this acre of formal rose beds, where graceful arches draped in lush mantles of blossoms end in an elaborate rose-adorned pavilion. The garden perimeter is enclosed by white wooden trellises

Near the end of the Japanese Hill and Pond Garden, a weeping cherry tree adds its graceful shape and delicate color to a contemplative scene.

covered with robust ramblers and climbers and, below, beds of wild species and old garden roses. Species roses include the Wild Irish Rose and the Yellow Rose of Texas—also called Harison's Yellow—which was first discovered in Manhattan in 1830 and taken west by the pioneers. From June to September, 15 center beds glow with hundreds of varieties of modern roses. Just outside the main rose garden, opposite the pavilion, lies the Rose Arc. Within this separate enclave lovely ramblers, modern roses, and a rare hybrid musk called 'Clytemnestra' surround a semicircular reflecting pool. The Cranford Rose Garden opened in 1928 on a grand scale, with 3,000 plants. Today its 5,000 plants, representing 1,500 species and cultivars, make it the third-largest public rose garden in America.

Ginkgo Walk continues to the Osborne Garden, the most formal of all the gardens. From an impressive staircase visitors descend into a landscape of expansive lawns and terraces punctuated with stately trees, decorative columns, fountains, and pergolas engulfed in wisteria. To the west, an area for native flora provides a naturalistic counterpoint, with two acres of woodland micro-habitats of the trees, shrubs, and wildflowers found within a hundred-mile radius of New York City.

Throughout the Brooklyn Botanic Garden thrive other, smaller, specialized gardens; the Rock Garden, restored in 1992 for its 75th anniversary, was the first public rock garden in the country. Masses of alpine blossoms appear in May, tucked into rugged niches and surrounded by the greenery of mosses and diminutive shrubs. The Children's Garden began as an educational experiment in 1914 and became the prototype for children's gardens around the world. The Fragrance Garden for the Blind, the first of its kind, contains raised beds of scented and unusually textured plants meant to be touched and smelled. Such areas have now become popular features in many public gardens.

The garden's most recent addition, the Steinhardt Conservatory complex, opened in 1988. The original Victorian Palm Conservatory was reproduced and three striking contemporary pavilions of varying heights added. Dubbed "ornaments in the garden," these glass octagonal pyramids positioned around ponds of waterlilies contribute a sparkling and dramatic presence. The Palm Conservatory is used for special events while the newer pavilions house the tropical, temperate, and desert exhibitions. Of particular note, the conservatory's C.V. Starr Bonsai Museum is the finest and largest display of bonsai outside of Japan. Its more than 750 specimens, some more than a century old, are beautifully arranged against facets of glass to set off their miniature grandeur.

From its beginning in 1910, the Brooklyn Botanic Garden has made education a priority. This private institution receives 30 percent of its funding from New York City and is deservedly one of the region's most popular attractions. Approximately half of the garden's 52 acres are devoted to the Plant Family Collection, where plants are arranged scientifically by plant families and in an evolutionary sequence from the simpler ferns and conifers to the more complex olive, heath, rose, and daisy families. This living textbook provides botanical instruction for students and gardeners in a lovely naturalistic landscape designed around a winding brook.

BROOKLYN BOTANIC GARDEN (10 miles southeast of midtown Manhattan) 1000 Washington Avenue, Brooklyn, NY 11225 **TEL:** (718) 622-4433 **OPEN:** Tues.-Fri. 8-6, Sat.-Sun. and holidays 10-6, April through Sept.; Tues.-Fri. 8-4:30, Sat.-Sun. and holidays 10-4:30, Oct. through March **TOTAL ACRES:** 52 **SPECIAL COLLECTIONS:** Roses, Japanese garden, bonsai, cherry trees, rock garden, children's garden

ZONE 6 C F G H L P R T V WS

The entrance to the Brooklyn Botanic Garden's Cranford Rose Garden, above, is but a hint of the profusion of roses to be seen beyond the pergola.

QUEENS BOTANICAL GARDEN
QUEENS, NEW YORK CITY

In the bustling, ethnically diverse section of the borough of Queens called Flushing, the Queens Botanical Garden forms an educational and horticultural center on 38 acres of woodland and flower gardens. More of a community park than its grander counterparts in Brooklyn and the Bronx, this garden offers a practical selection of horticultural ideas and an impressive rose garden. The 4,000 plants of the Charles N. Perkins Memorial Rose Garden make it one of the largest in the Northeast, concentrating on modern roses. Jackson & Perkins, the large, Oregon-based rose nursery, began its business in Queens and was the original donor of this garden. They continue to test roses here.

Beyond a white picket fence, a Victorian-style gazebo surrounded by flowers forms the focal point of the Wedding Garden, a popular setting for wedding photographs. Other small demonstration areas feature gardens designed to attract birds and bees, an herb garden, and an All-America Selections display of flowers and vegetables. Other plots created with backyards in mind offer selections of shade plants for dark areas, dwarf conifers and ornamental grasses for rock gardens, and plants for patios. The Ethnic Garden organizes plants according to the different countries represented in the community. In spring, thousands of tulips and other bulbs are complemented by flowering orchards of 'Kwanzan' cherry trees and crabapples. A brilliant array of annuals follows in summer, ending with dahlias and chrysanthemums in autumn.

QUEENS BOTANICAL GARDEN (10 miles east of midtown Manhattan) 43-50 Main Street and Dahlia Avenue, Queens, NY 11355 TEL: (718) 886-3800 OPEN: Daily dawn-dusk TOTAL ACRES: 38 SPECIAL COLLECTIONS: Roses, annuals, vegetables, ethnic garden ZONE 7 G P PA T

OLD WESTBURY GARDENS
OLD WESTBURY, LONG ISLAND

Majestic linden and beech trees line the mile-long entrance to Old Westbury Gardens. The drive leads to a sumptuous Charles II-style mansion surrounded by lavishly landscaped gardens. The epitome of what Mark Twain dubbed the Gilded Age, this estate has often been used as a setting for the scenes of opulence we associate with the beginning of the 20th century, most memorably by author F. Scott Fitzgerald and Hollywood filmmakers. Open to the public since 1959, this 150-acre estate possesses one of America's great gardens.

Financier and sportsman John Jay Phipps, heir to a steel fortune made by his father in partnership with Andrew Carnegie and Henry Clay Frick, promised his patrician English bride a summer mansion reminiscent of her stately home in Sussex. For the site he chose Old Westbury, and in 1907 built a country house and garden in the aristocratic British tradition. He commissioned Englishman George Crawley, at the time working on the interior of his father's town house, to design his estate.

Old Westbury was a secluded Quaker community, 25 miles from the frenzy of New York City. This bucolic area attracted the hunting set of New York society and soon became a major center of hunting, polo, yachting, and parties. Following Phipps's lead, a surge of building began as Long Island's north shore became

One of the grandest herbaceous borders in the United States, the Walled Garden at Old Westbury displays a sumptuous array of diverse flowers and brilliant color from spring to autumn.

Gatsby's Gold Coast. The Morgans, Vanderbilts, Woolworths, and other tycoons of industry were joined by movie moguls and European royalty in creating grandiose castles, villas, and châteaux. While most estates have succumbed to residential development, the Old Westbury mansion and gardens remain as an elegant example of that legendary era.

The estate's suggested tour begins on the western terrace, overlooking the classical prospect of the Boxwood Garden before descending a grand staircase flanked in June by massive banks of blooming rhododendrons. Farther on, a natural pond lies shaded by stately willows, sycamores, and maples, some of the oldest and largest specimens on Long Island. A whimsical swan boat, once used to cross the pond, rests on the bank amid rushes.

A subtle enclave in green, the Boxwood Garden holds large mounds of boxwood so typical of English gardens but difficult to grow in this climate. They were brought here from Virginia in 1928, already more than a century old. Behind them, mature beech trees and graceful weeping beeches meet an arc of Corinthian columns, enclosing a statue of Diana, goddess of the hunt.

The glory of Old Westbury is its Walled Garden, possessing some of the best herbaceous borders on the east coast. Hidden behind eight-foot redbrick walls punctuated by handsome filigreed gates, corner alcoves, and slender cypress trees, this garden is Italianate in its architectural details. The ebullient display of floral color and texture follows the style of Gertrude Jekyll, the famous English gardener. The ambience remains both romantic and intimate as paths lead from one tableau to another across the garden's two acres, engulfed by

The dramatic south facade of the Old Westbury mansion features a terrace and ceremonial staircases. Along these, accents of sculpture and topiary adorn the scene.

Impressionistic hues, subtle fragrances, and a tapestry of textures.

At the garden's northern end, a central path divides the upper level into wide borders of mellow colors. These lead to a balustrade and the only overview of the entire garden. Stepping down into the main part of the garden, four large rectangles of richer colors converge at a central Florentine fountain decorated with dense plantings of white flowers. The garden's southern end curves into a lavishly ornate blue-green pergola encircling a pond of stately lotus and sparkling waterlilies. Views from the pergola's latticed arches and portholes, covered in mantles of wisteria, present beautifully framed floral vignettes.

Originally planned as a garden for spring and fall, the two seasons that the family would be present, the Walled Garden has been redesigned for continuous seasonal drama, with annuals and perennials arranged in subtle and dazzling color constellations. May begins with more than 2,000 boldly colored tulips underplanted with pansies, forget-me-nots, and English daisies. June, the most beautiful month here, unveils bearded irises, peonies, astilbes, poppies, foxgloves, and the garden's famous display of some 300 giant delphiniums in shades of blue

White wisteria softly cascades around a bust decoratively tucked into a niche of the brick wall surrounding the manor.

and pink. Garlands of roses cascade behind this radiant display. In summer, colors intensify with vibrant annuals, including hardy fuschias, snapdragons, and phlox. The walls are adorned in espaliered viburnum, plumbago, and a dozen varieties of clematis. Fall ends with a blaze of 26 kinds of chrysanthemums, dahlias, and asters, echoing the fiery colors of the surrounding autumnal trees.

Beyond the gates awaits a mysterious verdant reprieve from the color of the Walled Garden: a Ghost Walk of mournful hemlocks representing the souls of deceased monks, reminiscent of an English garden. Margarita Phipps's interests and influence are evident throughout the gardens, especially in the lovely Rose Garden, one of her favorite areas. Here, clouds of pink and white climbing roses cling to an arbor surrounding a 17th-century parterre-style garden as moss-covered paths wind around beds of floribunda and hybrid tea roses edged in Japanese ilex.

Under a rustic rose arbor, the Primrose Walk leads to one of Old Westbury's most charming reminders of its luxurious past—a Tudor-style playhouse, given as a birthday present to the Phipps's 10-year-old daughter, Peggie. Shaded by the silver boughs of a towering maple tree and lower dogwood trees, the miniature thatched cottage nestles behind a white picket fence in the midst of its own garden of fairy roses, lacecap hydrangeas, and miniature flowers. As Peggie later wrote, "This magical setting recalls the halcyon days with boys and girls in merry play."

After crossing the main axis, a grand allée of lofty European lindens and hemlock hedges, the southern facade of the 17th-century-style mansion rises above the great lawn in imposing splendor. Elegant and symmetrical, it sits like a crown on an elaborate terrace decorated with niches for sculpture, veils of wisteria, and roundels of yew topiary. A panoramic view from the top of the splendid double staircase showcases the picturesque landscape.

The eastern part of the estate contains newer areas designed to inform the public. In the Demonstration Gardens grow herbs, shade plants, vegetables, Japanese-style arrangements, and an All-America Rose Selection Garden. Beyond this practical area flow a wildflower meadow, woodlands, and East Lake, the largest lake on the estate and site of thousands of naturalized daffodils, daylilies, and irises. At the end of the lake stands the Temple of Love, an ornamental rotunda popular in 18th-century landscape design. From here vistas of natural beauty provide a pastoral climax to the formal grandeur.

In the tradition of the British National Trust, Old Westbury was one of the first private estates in America to establish a nonprofit foundation to administer the property for the benefit of the public.

◼ **OLD WESTBURY GARDENS** (25 miles east of New York City) 71 Old Westbury Road, Old Westbury, NY 11568 **TEL:** (516) 333-0048 **OPEN:** Wed.-Mon. 10-5, May through Dec. except Christmas **TOTAL ACRES:** 150 **SPECIAL COLLECTIONS:** Estate Garden, English walled garden, children's cottage garden, roses, delphiniums, lily pond, specimen trees   **ZONE 7** **F** G **H** HO P PA T WS

*The Walled Garden ends in a grand pergola where connect
arches enclose a luxurious pool of lotus and waterlil*

Planting Fields Arboretum State Historic Park
Oyster Bay, Long Island

The north shore of Long Island—fertile land that local Matinecock Indians dubbed their "planting fields"—became the Gold Coast of millionaire mansions in the 20th century. One such estate, that of insurance executive William Coe, was inspired by the architecture and landscape of Coe's native England. Completed in 1921, his imposing Elizabethan-style manor house is set in a magnificent scene of sweeping lawns and vistas with dramatic specimen trees and massive plantings of rhododendrons. The landscape is the work of talented landscape designers with close ties to Boston's Arnold Arboretum, including the prestigious landscape design firm of the Olmsted Brothers.

Rhododendrons, the so-called king of shrubs, were a favorite in the panorama of English estates. Coe imported thousands of 'ironclads' from an English nursery famous for hybridizing this hardy variety of native American species from the Carolinas with the clearer color of Asiatic species. Coe gathered fine specimens of rhododendrons and azaleas throughout his lifetime, a collection added to since his death in 1955. Today, Planting Fields contains more than 600 species. In spring, its banks of beautiful blossoms are part of a grand display of weeping cherries, crabapples, magnolias, and lilacs.

From the entrance drive lined with stately European beeches, handsome trees abound on this 409-acre estate. Majestic 80-foot specimens of cedar of Lebanon and atlas cedar stand near the mansion, while farther down the greensward a regal copper beech faces a weeping silver linden whose branches have rooted, creating an arboreal crinoline. In addition, an excellent collection of more than 160 American, English, and Japanese varieties of hollies makes Planting Fields an official holly arboretum.

The small conservatory offers orchids and interesting seasonal floral displays while a nearby greenhouse contains a luxurious collection of camellias. With more than 300 plants representing a hundred different varieties, this is the largest collection of camellias under glass in the country. *Camellia sasanqua* blooms in October, followed by others in January and February. *Camellia japonica*, the main collection, peaks in February.

Other specialized gardens include roses, perennials, demonstration gardens, heath and heather gardens, dwarf conifers, and an Italian pool garden. Of particular interest is one of the first Synoptic Gardens—400 species and cultivars of deciduous and evergreen plants arranged alphabetically according to their botanical name. These are displayed decoratively on five acres to show local residents what grows best in the area. This innovative and educational service has spread to many other horticultural institutions around the country.

Colorful in all seasons, Planting Fields is unusually splendid in winter, when poinsettias, cyclamen, and orchids flourish in one conservatory, and the colors of furled, scalloped, and striped camellias glow in another. Outdoors, rich green and variegated hollies with their decorative berries complement the architectural splendor of stately trees silhouetted on the expansive lawns. Snow often adds a decorative layer to the grandeur of this garden.

Planting Fields Arboretum State Historic Park (35 miles east of New York City) Planting Fields Road, P.O. Box 58, Oyster Bay, NY 11771 **Tel:** (516) 922-9200 **Open:** Daily 9-5 **Total acres:** 409 **Special collections:** English-style estate garden, synoptic garden, rhododendrons, azaleas, specimen trees, hollies, camellia conservatory

ZONE 7 C F G H HO L P T V WS

Towering trees, such as the red horse chestnut tree shown above, add a majestic touch to the expansive lawns of the Planting Fields Arboretum. Hundreds of rhododendrons and azalea species bloom profusely in spring, adding dazzling color to the landscape.

MADOO—THE ROBERT DASH GARDEN
SAGAPONACK, LONG ISLAND

In 1966, noted landscape painter Robert Dash moved to the eastern end of Long Island to live and paint. In the midst of potato fields, near the ocean, he began creating a garden as a form of autobiography and fine art. The garden's impromptu, casual style belies its complexity and originality while following Dash's aesthetic— that gardening must appear effortless to succeed. It is readily apparent, however, that imagination and hard work are the essence of this interesting garden. The lush and Impressionistic design uses a wide variety of plants to create forms and textures, presenting a subtle palette of colors in all seasons. While Dash avoided strong floral colors, he used vibrant tones in his fences, gates, and benches, such as the sunshine-yellow arc and plum-purple gazebo. Abundant grasses and masses of perennials and annuals enclose some areas around the house and studio. Clipped allées of privet lead to vistas and ponds, creating a sense of space larger than the existing two acres. Madoo is a sponsored project of the Garden Conservancy.

MADOO—THE ROBERT DASH GARDEN (96 miles east of New York City) 618 Main Street, Sagaponack, NY 11962 **TEL:** (516) 537-8200 **OPEN:** Wed. and Sat. 1-5, May through Sept.; telephone ahead **TOTAL ACRES:** 2 **SPECIAL COLLECTIONS:** Country-style oceanside garden, vegetables, ornamental grasses, roses, old-fashioned flowers

ZONE 7 **F** **P** **T**

LYNDHURST
TARRYTOWN

The grandeur of the Hudson River Valley has historically attracted both artists and the affluent tycoons of American industry. Lyndhurst, one of the country's finest Gothic Revival mansions, was a summer home to a string of millionaires ending with railroad magnate Jay Gould. Today its grounds present an outstanding example of the picturesque landscape popularized by Andrew Jackson Downing in the 1840s. Overlooking the majestic Hudson River (somewhat obscured today), Lyndhurst's 67 acres of sweeping lawns are accented with shrubs, specimen trees, surprise views, and what in 1881 was the largest conservatory in the country. Predating the renowned New York Botanical Garden conservatory, it was the first to use metal framing. Although nothing blooms inside the impressive skeletal structure today, the grounds offer a 500-plant rose garden where profuse blooms surround a Victorian gazebo, arranged in garlanded trellises. In addition, an extensive collection of more than 300 ferns popular in Victorian times line the entrance drive, including native plants and such exotics as a rare wood fern from the mountains of Oaxaca, Mexico; crested European lady fern; and Himalayan maidenhair fern.

LYNDHURST (28 miles north of New York City) 635 South Broadway, Tarrytown, NY 10591 **TEL:** (914) 631-4481 **OPEN:** Tues.-Fri. 10-5, May through Oct.; Sat.-Sun. 10-4, Nov. through April **TOTAL ACRES:** 67 **SPECIAL COLLECTIONS:** Historic design, roses, ferns   ZONE 6 F G H HO P PA R T WS

KYKUIT, THE ROCKEFELLER ESTATE
POCANTICO HILLS

Kykuit was completed in 1913 as the summer residence for John D. Rockefeller, founder of the Rockefeller empire. Four generations of the family lived here until 1991, when it became part of the National Trust and the Sleepy Hollow Restoration, a network of historic house museums. Surrounded by 87 acres in Westchester County, the neoclassic 40-room mansion commands a panoramic view of the Hudson River, thus the name Kykuit—"lookout" in Dutch. The grounds were designed by William Wells Bosworth, a former associate of Frederick Law Olmsted, who combined Italian, French, and English ideas in a series of dramatic terraces featuring formal gardens, fountains, and sculptures.

Although trees, shrubs, and flower beds display their colors in different seasons, they are but accessories here. The garden's main features are classical sculpture; terraces with flowing fountains, pavilions, and elaborate urns; and, most importantly, Governor Nelson Rockefeller's impressive collection of 20th-century sculpture. Works by Brancusi, Moore, Picasso, Matisse, Maillol, and Calder, 70 pieces in all, are strategically placed to enhance the art and landscape of this memorable estate. In a striking setting, Maillol's bronze, "Bather Putting Up Her Hair" (1930), stands in the middle of a fountain designed as a long channel of water bordered by hedges, colorful potted plants, and other works of contemporary sculpture.

KYKUIT, THE ROCKEFELLER ESTATE (30 miles north of New York City) Pocantico Hills, NY 10591; Visitor Center and facilities at Philipsburg Manor, US 9, Sleepy Hollow, NY **TEL:** (914) 631-9491 **OPEN:** By reservation only, Wed.-Mon. 10-4, May through Oct. **TOTAL ACRES:** 87 **SPECIAL COLLECTIONS:** Estate garden, 20th-century sculpture, fountains, roses   ZONE 6 F G H HO P PA R T V WS

Rockefellers placed their rose garden (opposite), one of the main flowering gardens at Kykuit, on a crest overlooking the Hudson River.

Donald M. Kendall Sculpture Gardens at Pepsico
Purchase

A distinguished landmark in corporate art patronage, the headquarters of the Pepsi-Cola Company displays more than 40 works by outstanding international sculptors on 120 acres of landscaped grounds. This is the brainchild of Donald M. Kendall, a former CEO of the company, who hired architect Edward Durrell Stone, Sr., and his son, landscape designer Edward, Jr., to execute it. The building and grounds opened in 1970, and ten years later leading garden designer Russell Page was asked to reshape the landscape. Page's design reflects his elegant and subdued style—sculptures silhouetted against trees and placed amid rolling lawns, lakes, and groves. Clusters of weeping hemlocks form a textured backdrop for the rounded granite quadrangle of Noguchi's "Energy Void"; and in the distance, stately blue spruces contrast with the vibrant Calder stabile, "Hats Off." A sinuous walkway called the Golden Path joins the various parts of the garden. The abundant display of perennials running along the building's edge contains potentilla, columbines, achillea, and billowing Russian sage. Pastel daylilies adorn the wall below and, at the base of the slope lies an exquisite waterlily garden. Seen from the terrace above, the design, a simple linking of rectangles of water and grass fringed with cattails and changing flowers, epitomizes Page's sophisticated approach. An allée of Mount Fuji cherry trees and a few topiaries frame the formal area.

Donald M. Kendall Sculpture Gardens at Pepsico (31 miles north of New York City) 700 Anderson Hill Road, Purchase, NY 10577 **Tel:** (914) 253-2000 **Open:** Daily dawn-dusk **Total acres:** 120 **Special collections:** Landscape design by Russell Page, sculpture, waterlily garden   **ZONE 6** P V

Boscobel
Garrison-on-Hudson

The splendor of this federal-style mansion overlooking the Hudson River is the result of a remarkable restoration effort. Formerly located 15 miles downriver in the village of Peekskill, the ramshackle house was sold for $35 in 1955. Its restoration was taken up by Lila Acheson Wallace, co-founder of *Reader's Digest,* who had Boscobel relocated piece by piece, restored to its stately condition, and set within 16 acres graciously landscaped by the noted firm of Innocenti and Webel. Since 1961 the house has served as an elegant museum of decorative arts of the federal period. Although the original garden was not reproduced, the current design reflects elements of 19th-century taste.

Handsome trees line the entrance drive, bordered to the south by a pond and wildflower meadow. An orchard to the north gives way to the octagonal main garden close to the house. Here some 700 roses are arranged in beds of red, pink, yellow, and white blooms set against boxwood and candytuft. In May, before the roses bloom, the beds are filled with thousands of yellow and white Darwin tulips underplanted with blue pansies. Nearby, an herb and vegetable garden represents a practical garden of the 18th century. In winter the adjacent orangerie is filled with orchids, herbs, and potted plants.

Boscobel (52 miles north of New York City) RD2, N.Y. 9D, Garrison-on-Hudson, NY 10524 **Tel:** (914) 265-3638 **Open:** Wed.-Mon. 9:30-5, April through Oct.; Sat.-Sun. 9:30-5 in March; closed holidays **Total acres:** Garden 16, estate 45 **Special collections:** Estate garden, roses, herbs, tulips

ZONE 6 C F G H HO P PA T V WS

Stonecrop Gardens
Cold Spring

On a windswept hilltop filled with rocks and boulders, Frank and Anne Cabot created a distinctive garden appropriately called Stonecrop. They began in 1959 with a small rock garden, expanding their 40-acre estate into a series of enchanting gardens, some with panoramic vistas of the Hudson Highlands. Alongside their French Provincial house, an enclosed English-style flower garden was created by Caroline Burgess, now the garden's director. Within, square beds overflow with masses of flowers and vegetables, while clematis and espaliered fruit trees cover the walls. Beyond the house are raised alpine beds, a woodland garden, a grass garden, and, most dramatic of all, a cliffside rock garden. Here additional boulders were added to an already rocky terrain, along with hundreds of different alpine plants, grasses, and dwarf conifers. Man-made streams flow through the garden into pools and a small lake. A striking new conservatory showcases rare miniature alpine plants and bulbs, and a limited selection of unusual alpine species and perennials are for sale. The garden opened to the public in 1992. The Cabots, leading authorities on rock gardening, are also the founders of the Garden Conservancy movement, dedicated to the preservation of gardens.

Stonecrop Gardens (56 miles north of New York City) N.Y. 301, RR2, Box 371, Cold Spring, NY 10516 **Tel:** (914) 265-2000 **Open:** By appointment only, Tues., Wed., Fri., mid-April through Oct. **Total acres:** Garden 9, estate 40 **Special collections:** Alpine plants, rock gardens

ZONE 5   C   **F**   G   P   **T**   V   **WS**

Stonecrop's garden, overflowing with fragrant herbs, flowers, and shrubs, is reminiscent of an English country garden. Here, dark purple alliums, clusters of roses, yarrow, and the drifts of many other plants give this garden its subtle palette and texture.

Mohonk Mountain House Gardens
New Paltz

One of the most splendid Victorian resorts still in existence, Mohonk offers an alpine setting of craggy mountains, lakes, gardens, and woodland paths with over a hundred gazebos from which to view picturesque vistas. Built from 1879 to 1910 by twin brothers Albert and Alfred Smiley as a Quaker sanctuary, the resort soon expanded, as did Albert's passion for gardens. The hotel's grounds followed garden fashions of the day, with formal carpet gardens, perennial borders, rose gardens, arbors, a croquet lawn, and rustic garden ornaments set within the dramatic natural landscape. To sustain formal plantings on such an inhospitable terrain required a massive effort, and today the gardens cover some 15 acres within a grand 24,000-acre setting. The Show Garden is the quintessential Victorian "oriental carpet" with almost every annual in a seed catalog arranged in geometric beds; it offers a wonderful opportunity to see old-fashioned flowers intermingled with more recent varieties. Enclosed by twig lattices, the Rose Garden features hybrid teas and old species as well as arbors and trellises covered with roses, wisteria, honeysuckle, and other vines. In other areas, peony and lilac shrubs bloom in spring along with many other flowering trees and bulbs. Perennial borders and an herb garden display add to this garden's diversity. The greenhouse produces some 30,000 plants a year that are rare, unusual, common, or new. Wildflower and fern trails are part of an extensive network of spectacular woodland walks that wind through the thousand acres of this mountain resort.

Mohonk Mountain House Gardens (90 miles northwest of New York City) 100 Mountain Rest Road, New Paltz, NY 12561 **Tel:** (914) 255-1000 **Open:** Daily dawn-dusk **Total acres:** 15 **Special collections:** Carpet beds of annuals, peonies, roses, gazebos   **ZONE 6** C F G HO P PA R T WS

One of the formal garden areas at the Mohonk Mountain House resort displays an abundance of old-fashioned flowers in bedded geometric arrangements.

THE ITALIAN GARDENS AT VANDERBILT HISTORIC SITE
HYDE PARK

Vanderbilts and baronial estates seem synonymous. At the turn of the century, the splendid Hudson River provided the setting for a sumptuous mansion built for Frederick W. Vanderbilt, grandson of the famous commodore. Designed by McKim, Mead and White, the glittering 40-room house surrounded by more than 200 acres remains perhaps the grandest of the many interesting historic houses along the Hudson. The estate formerly belonged to the Astor family and even earlier, in 1799, to David Hosack, who established America's first botanical garden on the site of New York City's Rockefeller Center. Hosack hired André Parmentier, one of the first important landscape architects in the United States, and together they designed the picturesque parklike setting and smaller walled garden.

After purchasing the estate in 1895, Vanderbilt, who majored in horticulture at Yale University, devoted himself to the creation of what was then becoming the height of aristocratic fashion in the U.S.: the Italianate garden. Designed by James Greenleaf, the Vanderbilt garden provides a distinguished example of this splendid style. Within century-old redbrick walls, five acres of elaborate formal gardens include terraces on eight levels planted with a prodigious array of annuals, perennials, and roses surrounded by pools, ornamental fountains, trellises, pergolas, and classical statuary. The estate, given to the National Park Service in 1940, has undergone a reconstruction of its gardens, completed in 1984. In addition, the volunteer Vanderbilt Garden Association has been responsible for replanting the gardens, closely following Vanderbilt's records.

THE ITALIAN GARDENS AT VANDERBILT HISTORIC SITE (98 miles north of New York City) US 9, Hyde Park, NY 12538 TEL: (914) 229-6432 OPEN: Daily 9-dusk TOTAL ACRES: Garden 3, estate 240 SPECIAL COLLECTIONS: Formal Italian gardens, roses, perennials   ZONE 6 H HO P T WS

MARY FLAGLER CARY ARBORETUM
MILLBROOK

One of the Northeast's largest collections of perennial plants open to the public is part of the research and educational center at the Mary Flagler Cary Arboretum. Located near the picturesque town of Millbrook, the arboretum's more than 800 different species and cultivars of perennials demonstrate the relationship between good horticulture and sound ecology. Almost 5,000 plants have been arranged around the 19th-century Gifford House, now the Visitor Center. These informal beds of harmonious color schemes and interesting textural combinations focus on seasonal variations and low maintenance. An extensive lilac collection is also on display, along with peonies, lilies, roses, and ornamental grasses. The arboretum encompasses some 600 acres of forests, swamps, meadows, and special collections of pines, birches, and willows. A fern glen is especially charming, containing more than 125 varieties from all over the world. A small greenhouse on the far side of the arboretum displays tropical plants and ecological research projects.

MARY FLAGLER CARY ARBORETUM/INSTITUTE OF ECOSYSTEM STUDIES (97 miles north of New York City) N.Y. 44A, Millbrook, NY 12545 TEL: (914) 677-5359 OPEN: Mon.-Sat. 9-6, Sun. 1-6, May through Sept.; Mon.-Sat. 9-4, Sun 1-4, Oct. through April; closed holidays TOTAL ACRES: Garden 3, arboretum 600 SPECIAL COLLECTIONS: Lilacs, perennials, ferns, ecological gardens   ZONE 6 C G H P PA T V WS

INNISFREE GARDEN
MILLBROOK

From the crest of a hill overlooking a sylvan lake in Millbrook spreads a garden scene unlike any other. Familiar garden elements of water, lilies, tree islands, stones, and hills are combined in a distinctly different tableau, composed over a half century. Sculptured and etched from the wilderness of northern Westchester County, granite cliffs, mysterious boulders, and sentinel stones stand poised on the lakeshore, evoking images of enigmatic Easter Island monoliths or Noguchi sculptures. Islands of willows float in the midst of massive beds of waterlilies, and jets of water rise and fall within distant woodlands. Although some flowers such as naturalized daylilies, white satin lotus blossoms, and a sprinkle of delicate wildflowers do bloom here, the garden's colors come from the subtle tones of a simplified landscape.

Innisfree explores a Chinese garden design concept called a "cup garden." The garden's original owner and early designer, Walter Beck, was a painter and teacher influenced by Chinese scroll paintings in which scenes unfold in separate, enclosed pictures for pleasure and contemplation. In this progression, the first "picture" forms the largest cup on the horizon, surrounded by others. Strolling from one three-dimensional picture to another, cups are self-contained garden experiences.

Separate areas have their centers of natural beauty, be it a single stone covered in plush mosses or the stately array of Turtle Rock, Dragon Rock, and Owl Rock standing watch by the lake. The freedom in the arrangement and discovery of these garden pictures is distinguished from the formality of Japanese gardens.

Beginning in 1929, this natural and seemingly effortless garden was carefully designed by Walter Beck and Lester Collins, who later became

Monoliths of stone sculpture add to the mysterious ambience of this Chinese-influenced garden. Rocks and plants are often arranged to reflect scenes from Chinese scroll paintings.

the chairman of the Department of Landscape Architecture at Harvard University. After Beck's death in 1954, Collins continued shaping and redesigning this garden, planting islands of willows in the 40-acre lake, bulldozing mounds and hills, and carving streams and miniature waterfalls out of aesthetically placed boulders. In 1960, this hundred-acre garden opened to the public. The garden's name comes from a poem by William Butler Yeats, which begins: "I will arise and go now, and go to Innisfree."

INNISFREE GARDEN (97 miles north of New York City) Tyrrel Road, off US 44, Millbrook, NY 12545 TEL: (914) 677-8000 OPEN: Wed.-Fri. 10-4, Sat.-Sun. and holidays 11-5, May to mid-Oct. TOTAL ACRES: 100 SPECIAL COLLECTIONS: Landscape design with Chinese influences ZONE 6 F P PA

Flowers are not central to the landscape at Innisfree. The color of shrubs and trees give garden its subtlety in spring, intensity in summer, and brilliance in aut

CORNELL PLANTATIONS
ITHACA

Since its founding in 1868, Cornell University has had a tradition of innovative commitment to the study of the natural sciences, establishing one of the first and most outstanding schools of agriculture. When world-renowned horticulturist Dr. Liberty Hyde Bailey directed the school, he created the Cornell Plantations as outdoor study centers adjacent to the university's campus above Cayuga Lake. In recent years, the grounds have been expanded and redesigned and today the Plantations encompass 200 acres devoted to botanical gardens. In addition, 3,000 acres of natural areas surround an arboretum.

In the center of the flower gardens, the Field House offers the American Peony Society Garden's collection of more than 75 species and cultivars. Here in early spring, tree peonies flower under blooming cherry trees as rhododendrons and azaleas grow nearby. Another unusual garden displays heritage crops, some hundred vegetable varieties grown in this country during the 19th century. Other specialty gardens feature herbs, cutting flowers, rock garden plants, wild-flowers, poisonous plants, and an international crop and weed garden. An extensive network of trails wanders through the F. R. Newman Arboretum, which specializes in trees and shrubs native to New York State, and into the beautiful natural woodlands with dramatic gorges, waterfalls, ponds, and lakes beyond.

■ CORNELL PLANTATIONS (230 miles northwest of New York City) One Plantations Road, Ithaca, NY 14850 TEL: (607) 255-3020 OPEN: Daily dawn-dusk TOTAL ACRES: Garden 50, arboretum 150 SPECIAL COLLECTIONS: Peonies, herbs, wildflowers, heritage crops   ZONE 5 A G H P PA T WS

THE GARDENS AT GEORGE EASTMAN HOUSE
ROCHESTER

Famous for developing the Kodak camera, George Eastman was the son of a nurseryman, and inherited his father's passion for flowers and gardens. Eastman's travel albums are filled with photographs of European gardens, undoubtably a source of inspiration in building his dream house in the city of Rochester. His Georgian Revival mansion was complemented by eight individual gardens skill-fully designed to create the effect of a country estate. Spacious lawns, flower gardens, orchards, a poultry yard, and pastures for cows once covered the 12 acres. Many of the gardens were formally designed in 1902 (and blooming by 1905) by Alling DeForest, a Rochester landscape architect. Eastman's own photographs of his gardens, taken from 1902 to 1932, aided the million-dollar adaptive restoration now in process. While buildings for the University of Rochester and the new International Museum of Photography, the world's largest collection of photographs, occupy some of the former garden sites, four gardens have been completely restored.

Eastman's favorite retreat was the Terrace Garden, a formal flower garden with 23 beds edged in boxwood and filled throughout the seasons with nearly 6,000 bulbs, annuals, and perennials. Eastman loved a riot of color, and his taste is reflected in some of the unusual combinations found here. Strong colors and tall flowers such as sunflowers and hollyhocks thrive in formal beds. A grand pergola covered in wisteria runs almost the length of the terrace. It frames an oval waterlily pool discovered during the reconstruction. Adjacent to the terrace and museum's library, the Library Garden was originally the cutting garden. Now a simple arrangement of geometric beds, its flower displays are carefully designed to protect the museum archives housed two feet below, as space-age fabrics provide the foundation below the soil. At the estate's northern end, a refurbished grape arbor designed by DeForest as a horseshoe-shaped pergola leads to a rock garden.

THE GARDENS AT GEORGE EASTMAN HOUSE 900 East Avenue, Rochester, NY 14607 **TEL:** (716) 271-3361 **OPEN:** Tues.-Sat. 10-4:30, Sun. 1-4:30, May through Sept. **TOTAL ACRES:** 12.5 **SPECIAL COLLECTIONS:** Formal flower gardens, old-fashioned flowers, lily pond, rock garden

ZONE 6 F G H HO P PA R T WS

HIGHLAND PARK
ROCHESTER

In the late 19th century, Rochester was dubbed America's Flower City after the numbers of nurseries that flourished there. In the 1880s, two of the most prominent nurserymen, George Ellwanger and Patrick Barry, donated 20 acres and a plant of everything they stocked to create a public park in a city quickly extending its urban boundaries. Frederick Law Olmsted laid out the greenwards, majestic trees, and winding paths in gracious naturalistic settings.

Talented horticulturists expanded the botanical collections, establishing its now famous collection of lilacs. The first lilacs were planted in 1892 and eventually many new varieties were introduced here—now 22 acres hold 1,200 shrubs representing 500 varieties. This is the largest collection of lilacs in the country, and possibly the world. Every May there is a week-long lilac festival celebrated with an array of events. Another tradition, established in 1902, occurs at the same time—the Pansy Bed, a floral carpet of over 10,000 plants in changing patterns. Magnolias, horse chestnuts, rhododendrons, and many interesting and rare trees spread across the 150 acres. A conservatory of 8,000 square feet presents five seasonal floral shows with permanent desert and tropical exhibits. Small display gardens of roses, ferns, herbs, and daylilies, and a recently restored sunken garden designed by Alling De Forest, encircle the Gothic mansion, now the Garden Center.

HIGHLAND PARK 180 Reservoir Avenue, Rochester, NY 14620 **TEL:** (716) 244-8079 **OPEN:** Daily dawn-dusk **TOTAL ACRES:** 150 **SPECIAL COLLECTIONS:** Lilacs, pansies   **ZONE 6** A C G H P PA T WS

SONNENBERG GARDENS
CANANDAIGUA

Sonnenberg's nine magnificent, yet small gardens surround a 40-room Queen Anne-style summer "cottage," the consummate expression of gardening taste in the Gilded Age. Begun in the 1860s, the Victorian estate's German name translates as "Sunny Hill." It was the summer home of Frederick F. Thompson, a wealthy New York financier, and his wife, Mary, who was raised in Canandaigua in the Finger Lakes region. They were famous for their hospitality and their gardens. Spacious lawns with handsome shade trees and resplendent, patterned plantings were admired and enjoyed by their many visitors.

In the fashion of the day, many of Sonnenberg's original gardens were "bedded out" with an unending supply of brilliantly colored annuals arranged in geometric patterns. But even these bright embellishments were not enough for Mary Thompson. In 1900, when she found herself a widow at 67, she decided to redesign and enlarge the gardens. Though the tradition of patterned beds was preserved, many new features were introduced. Like many affluent gardeners of her era, Mrs. Thompson had the imagination and knowledge of a horticultural amateur. With landscape architect John Handrahan of the leading Boston firm of Ernest Bowditch & Co., she set about translating a lifetime of garden experience into a distinguished horticultural "museum." Constantly working to improve, she kept as many as 90 gardeners employed year-round. She opened her gardens to the public several days annually, with up to 7,000 eager visitors enjoying the sights, which also included a deer park and an aviary complex. A lover of trees, Mrs. Thompson continued her husband's practice of asking distinguished house guests to plant a tree. As a result, Thomas Edison, several governors, and a number of Civil War generals, among others, are memorialized by such specimen trees as maples, oaks, ashes, and pines bordering the parklike South Lawn. After Thompson died, the house and grounds became a hospital complex and fell victim to age and neglect. In the late 1960s the citizens of Canandaigua began a campaign to restore the property. Sonnenberg Gardens have gradually been brought back to the showplace glory of Mrs. Thompson's era.

A tour of the modern-day gardens begins with a visit to the conservatory. Fabricated of glass and cast iron in the early 1900s by Lord & Burnham, it is a fine example of Victorian greenhouse construction. In Mary Thompson's time the central Palm House contained numerous tropical exotics, including palm, banana, and lemon trees. Adjoining wings were devoted to the raising of grapes, peaches, melons, and a variety of vegetables and cut flowers through the colder months, and bedding plants in spring. Today, exotics once again flourish in the conservatory, along with over 200 types of orchids.

A short stroll north leads to the first of the nine theme gardens, the Japanese Garden. Secluded and tranquil, this garden draws its inspiration from Japanese garden aesthetics, in which a relatively small space becomes a microcosm of the natural landscape and all the elements—rocks, flowing water, earth, sun and shade, paths and plant materials—have symbolic meaning. Designed originally by the Japanese landscape designer K. Wadamori, this naturalistic garden with its irregular terrain, pools, and watercourses was built on what had been smooth, sloping lawn. Its most impressive accents are the reproduction of a venerable Kyoto teahouse and the large bronze Buddha overseeing the scene. Choice conifers, Japanese maples, and an umbrella pine grow near the arched red bridge adjacent to the teahouse. In another secluded location, the Secret Garden is a green and white sanctuary hemmed with a dense green hedge of boxwood and swags of cathedral bell vine. Benches, incorporated in a classical marble wall fountain of Zeus with Diana and Apollo, invite the visitor to rest.

The spectacular Rose Garden is one of the three gardens that still preserve the geometric floral display so popular in the Victorian era. Its more than 5,000 red, pink, and white roses are planted in a cascade of curved formal beds, including among its mainstays such favorites as the pink floribunda 'Gene Boerner' and the white floribunda 'Iceberg.' As the original rose stock had all but disappeared by the 1970s, the Sonnenberg gardens were especially fortunate to obtain 4,000 rosebushes from the well-known Jackson & Perkins Rose Gardens, when they moved their nurseries to Oregon. All-America Rose Selections are also displayed.

The Italian Garden, close to the mansion on axis with the library, was Mrs. Thompson's grandest revision. Reminiscent of Italian and French château gardens but with a Victorian exuberance all its own, this garden consists of a crisscross of wide allées for strolling, as well as four square, sunken lawns. Each contains a

A view of the swirling fleur-de-lis and scimitar patterns in the Italian Garden at Sonnenberg. Richly colored annuals are planted and maintained throughout the season. Small conical-shaped yews are evenly spaced along the paths between the slightly sunken parterres.

bed shaped in the form of a fleur-de-lis and scimitar, filled with brilliant-colored annuals. Beginning in June, as many as 15,000 plants from the greenhouses are bedded to create these floral tapestries. By contrast, the Colonial Garden takes its inspiration from the 18th-century American gardens of Williamsburg and Mount Vernon. Laid out in the traditional pattern of five interlocking circles, it shows off the gardener's palette in full glory, with more than 150 varieties of old-fashioned annuals and perennials.

The Rock Garden, the last to be created, is a rambling three-acre enchanted glen to the east of the house, designed and meticulously engineered by Handrahan. Several tons of Onondaga limestone, a type of naturally pocketed aggregate, were brought in to transform level ground into a multilevel terrain punctuated by canyons, waterfalls, and stream beds. Nestled in the stone's multitude of nooks is a wonderful array of dainty rock plants, including coral bells and cornflowers.

Still other delightful gardens include Thompson's personal favorite, the intimate Blue and White Garden, displaying peonies, snapdragons, delphinium, and blue and white irises. Here also are the Pansy Garden, devoted to her favorite flower, and the Moonlight Garden, a romantic and uncommonly fragrant Victorian garden, whose assorted white flowers—nicotiana and cimicifuga, among others—take on a magical glow on moonlit summer nights. The last of the nine gardens to be restored, the Moonlight Garden glows once again.

SONNENBERG GARDENS (25 miles east of Rochester) 151 Charlotte Street, Canandaigua, NY 14424 TEL: (716) 394-4922 OPEN: Daily 9:30-5:30, mid-May to mid-Oct. TOTAL ACRES: Garden 20, estate 50 SPECIAL COLLECTIONS: Estate garden, Victorian carpet bed design, orchids, Japanese garden, Italian garden, rose garden, rock garden   ZONE 6 C F G H HO P PA R T WS

Duke Gardens
Somerville

The grand horticultural traditions of many different civilizations are on display in the 11 glass galleries of Doris Duke's ingenious and imaginative garden conservatory. Remarkably, Duke Gardens, the United States' most distinctive indoor garden, is only one acre in size.

Opened to the public on a limited schedule in 1964, each gallery displays a microcosm of a great gardening legacy within faceted crystal-like enclosures. This miniaturization captures the spirit of some of the world's great gardening styles with artistry, meticulous skill, and a sensitivity to scale that is reminiscent of a Faberge egg. Whatever the climate outdoors, Duke Gardens is filled with the lush abandon of an Italian garden, the cheerful abundance of a British spring garden, the elegance of French parterres, and the cool, abstract perfection of a Persian paradise. Lord & Burnham, distinguished builders of New York City's great botanical conservatories, designed this private greenhouse in 1908 for tobacco tycoon James B. Duke. His grand estate, 2,300 acres on the Raritan River in central New Jersey, was inherited by his only child, Doris, who began designing this visionary garden in 1958. Miss Duke knew what she wanted and she could afford it—refurbishing structures, adding rooms, directing the design, and selecting the plants. She lived on the estate until her death in 1996.

Each area at Duke Gardens has its own designed path.

The tour begins in the Italian Garden, one of the largest galleries, entered under a cascade of billowing magenta bougainvillea and yellow hibiscus. Inside awaits a romantic scene of languid lushness filled with classical touches—a stone balustrade, sculptures, urns, and fountains. Charming, semi-clad stone maidens nestle under the soft touch of vines. A serene patina of the past is created by the subtle and casual blending of colors, textures, and statuary. This is not a formal re-creation of an Italian garden, but rather a Mediterranean memory.

In the next gallery, the Colonial Garden evokes the ambience of a small southern Eden. Commanding its center, a lustrous *Magnolia grandiflora* stands encircled by flowers. Against latticed brick walls, camellias and crape myrtles are underplanted with a profusion of colorful seasonal plants—masses of tulips in spring and cyclamens in winter. In addition, oleander, fuchsia, and star jasmine perfume the room and decorate the walls. The Edwardian Room, typical of private greenhouses of the English gentry, is filled with exotic plants, a vogue that began when plant explorers introduced their new discoveries. Giant palms, elephant's ear, and elk's horn ferns overlook bromeliads and fiddle-leaf figs. Hanging asparagus ferns lend their delicate

The first of Duke's many gardens is the romantic Italian Garden, overflowing with bougainvillea, acacias, and hibiscus trees. Within, a pebble-covered path lined with daffodils leads to an ivy-covered stone balustrade, Renaissance-style sculpture, and fountains.

filigree accents while sensuous orchids float above the surface of the patterned foliage. Some 40 varieties of orchids are also displayed.

After this luxurious, intimate setting, the French Garden provides a stunning surprise—an entire room covered with a remarkable combination of *parterre broderie,* where low beds of flowers are planted in intricate designs resembling embroidery or brocade, and trelliage, the highly developed art of decorating with lattice. Both are important design elements in formal French gardens. Dark green latticework completely covers the barrel-vaulted ceiling, alcoves, walls, pillars, doors, and windows. Hundreds of flowers fill the beds, changing with the seasons and creating a dramatic tapestry of color amid the points of light filtering through intricate lattice.

Leaving the formality of the French, visitors cross a stylistic channel to the free-flowing borders of the traditional English herbaceous garden. Here a radiant panoply of color fills wide borders, 75 feet long, enclosed by wattle fences and grass paths. Perennials and a profusion of annuals are planted together at the perfect stage of peak bloom. Marigolds, snapdragons, dahlias, asters, zinnias, delphinium, and blue Queen Anne's lace are planted in spring for the summer display, and spring bulbs fill the garden in winter. At either end of this exuberant array lie small areas devoted to topiary, an Elizabethan knot garden, and an interesting sunburst of succulents. Handsome sentries of the American Southwest, a saguaro and a century plant, tower above lower cactuses and succulents in the Desert Gallery. Many of these plants, popular in larger conservatories, are seen here in a smaller space, resulting in a heightened sense of scale and texture.

At the entrance to the Chinese Garden stands a grove of variegated bamboo. Symbols of longevity, they lead to a bridge arched over a pool filled with papyrus, lotus blossoms, and a rock island said to contain ancestral spirits. Weeping willows, wisteria, azaleas, and jasmine flank the banks of a stream leading to a second bridge, this one zigzagging to avoid evil spirits, which, according to legend, can only follow a straight line. A mysterious grotto created with mirrors adds to the evocative setting of this garden. A moon gate leads to the Japanese Garden. Here traditional Japanese motifs of water, stones, and sculptured shrubs are arranged around a teahouse, with camellias, dwarf maples, irises, and azaleas adding color to this tranquil setting.

Enclosed, cool, and colorful, the Indo-Persian Garden offers a striking and unusual sight rarely seen in the U.S. Paradise, the Persian word for a walled garden, is here re-created in a miniature version of the gardens of the Mogul emperors of the 16th century. Reacting to the barren and arid land they lived in, Persians enclosed private areas to contain water, shade, order, and beauty. Within the Indo-Persian Garden, white latticed walls and filigreed screens surround a dramatic, narrow, 70-foot-long channel of water, flowing down three subtly graduated levels between two raised redbrick paths. Elegantly arched screens intersect the brick paths, enclosing symbolic plantings. At the channel's

An abundance of colorful flowers, such as the tulips, grape hyacinths, and daisies seen here, fill the wide borders of the English Garden. The typically British wattle fence in the background gives this winter garden an authentic feeling.

end, a raised platform showcases a fountain surrounded by four square beds of hybrid tea roses in satiny white and delicate pastels, contributing to this garden's graceful Indo-Persian design. The tour ends in the rain forest and jungle atmosphere of the Tropical and Semitropical Gardens. An earthen path winds past overflowing vines mixed with flourishing plants and trees; tropical orchids and unusual blue-flowering ginger can be seen near a cascading waterfall. Noteworthy plants in the semitropical garden include tree ferns from the volcanic plateaus of New Zealand and Hawaii, and the delicate, lacy jacaranda tree from South America. The giant bird of paradise tree, with its black-and-white flowers, is one of the oldest in the conservatory.

The gardens close in summer, due to the intense humidity and heat within the conservatory environment. Visitors should take note that seasonal displays indoors do not necessarily follow the outdoor calendar, as all the plants are grown and forced in greenhouses behind the scenes. The result—impeccable displays fulfilling the garden's motto, "Perfection Under Glass."

DUKE GARDENS (37 miles southwest of Newark) US 206 South, Somerville, NJ 08876 **TEL:** (908) 722-3700 **OPEN:** By reservation only, Daily 12-4, October through May, except holidays **TOTAL ACRES:** 1 **SPECIAL COLLECTIONS:** Historic and international garden styles, orchids, parterres, trellises   **C F P T**

Green latticework covers the walls, ceilings, and alcoves of the French Garden. Formal parterres, shown here planted in geometric designs with white, yellow, and red tulips, change flowers with the seasons.

Leonard J. Buck Garden
Far Hills

Rugged boulders softened by mantles of color and texture dominate this dramatic, spectacular rock-and-woodland garden. Leonard J. Buck, a wealthy mining engineer, traveled worldwide over a period of 40 years collecting rare and exotic alpine treasures. When selecting a site for his estate, he was attracted to the glacial geology of Moggy Hollow, one of many gorges in north-central New Jersey. Eventually Buck became a proficient horticulturist, working with Swiss-born rock garden designer Zenon Schreiber to create a rock garden that would be both ecologically correct and visually appealing. Together, they developed one of the most interesting rock gardens in the Northeast.

The team began work in the late 1930s, and it took a decade of massive construction—clearing rocks, moving trees, simulating alpine soils, and damming brooks—to implement Schreiber's plan. Winding woodland trails lined with wildflowers connect streams, brooks, meadows, and overlooks. Each rock formation serves as a pivotal point, visible from the paths, bridges, and lawn areas. In addition to a great variety of alpine plants, outstanding collections of ferns, azaleas, rhododendrons, and primulas grow in a naturalistic setting. The rock garden, studded with alpine blossoms, provides a distinctive display from late April through June.

Leonard J. Buck Garden (35 miles southwest of Newark) 11 Layton Road, Far Hills, NJ 07931 **Tel:** (908) 234-2677 **Open:** Mon.-Fri. 10-4, Sat. 10-5, Sun. 12-5, March through Nov.; Mon.-Fri. 10-4, Dec. through Feb. **Total acres:** Garden 13, grounds 33 **Special collections:** Rock garden, primulas

ZONE 6 G P T V WS

Rudolf W. van der Goot Rose Garden
Colonial Park, East Millstone

An elegant vista providing a preview of three formal gardens is visible from the gazebo at the entrance to this outstanding rose garden. It is dedicated to horticulturist Rudolf W. van der Goot, who spent seven years designing and planting this one-acre garden. An official All-America Rose Selections Garden since 1973, its more than 3,000 rosebushes, encompassing 275 varieties, are displayed within graceful geometric gardens. The rectangular Mettler Garden, named after the estate's original owner, features a central fountain surrounded by miniature roses and modern hybrid tea roses. Nearby, Grandmother's Garden contains old hybrid perpetuals, some dating from the 1820s. A second formal garden, framed by a redwood trellis, offers a circle of hybrid tea, grandiflora, and floribunda roses radiating from its center. On the outer edges of this garden, an outstanding collection of heritage roses includes Bourbons, Damask, Gallica, Moss, and Cabbage varieties. A third garden area copies the style of a formal rose garden in Holland, with compact beds edged in candytuft displaying modern and heritage roses.

Colonial Park also has a fragrance and sensory garden, a four-acre perennial garden, and an arboretum of 144 acres where fine specimen trees, dwarf conifers, flowering shrubs, and a collection of some 200 lilacs thrive.

Rudolf W. van der Goot Rose Garden (35 miles southwest of Newark) Colonial Park, Mettler's Road, East Millstone, NJ 08873 **Tel:** (908) 234-2677 **Open:** Tues.-Sun. dawn-dusk, Mon. 12-dusk **Total acres:** Garden 5, arboretum 144 **Special collections:** Roses, lilacs, specimen trees

ZONE 6 F H P PA T WS

Thousands of varieties of irises, from recently introduced hybrids to species dating as far back as the 1500s, bloom in almost every color of the rainbow at Presby Memorial Iris Gardens. This suburban New Jersey garden is tended by volunteers.

Presby Memorial Iris Gardens
Upper Montclair

Iris, the Greek goddess of the rainbow, would have approved of this memorial garden celebrating more than 4,000 varieties of her namesake flower. Established in 1927 in honor of Frank H. Presby of Montclair, an eminent horticulturist and founder of the American Iris Society, this garden is distinguished more for its comprehensive collection than its basic, rainbow-curve design. One of the grandest displays on the East Coast, its masses of irises are arranged in sections, beginning to the north with the oldest plants. Hundreds of antique varieties follow in chronological rows, including the blue and white florentina from the 16th century and the honorabile, a 19th-century hybrid that crossed America in pioneer wagons.

Central triangle beds display the almost psychedelic colors of the newest hybrids. Here, bearded irises predominate with colors ranging from blue-black to myriad color combinations. Surprisingly, red is missing from the iris palette, which includes more colors than any other flower. A variety of beardless irises, Siberian, Louisiana, and the later-blooming Japanese iris, grow along the damp banks of a small brook. On a hillside at the garden's southern end, wild irises from all over the world face beds of dwarf and medium bearded irises, including the fleur-de-lis, the "yellow flags" that became the symbol on the French flag during the Crusades. June is the best month for blooms here, but visitors should call ahead as there are no other horticultural features in this garden.

■ **Presby Memorial Iris Gardens** (16 miles north of Newark) 474 Upper Mountain Avenue, Upper Montclair, NJ 07043 **Tel:** (973) 783-5974 **Open:** Daily 10-8, mid-May to mid-June **Total acres:** 4 **Special collections:** 4,000 varieties of irises   **ZONE 6** G H HO P PA T WS

Skylands Botanical Garden
Ringwood

This botanical showcase of close to 5,000 species and varieties of plants has been New Jersey's official botanical garden since the state acquired it in 1966. The estate belonged at various times to garden enthusiasts—Francis Stetson, a distinguished New York lawyer, and later, Clarence Lewis, an investment banker and notable amateur horticulturist, were both trustees of the New York Botanical Garden. Prominent landscape architects contributed to the design, including Samuel Parsons, a protégé of Frederick Law Olmsted and author of an important text on landscape design. Parsons began to lay out the grounds for Stetson at the turn of the century. In 1922, when Lewis bought the estate, he commissioned the firm of Vitale and Geiffert, designers of the gardens at Rockefeller Center and the grounds of Princeton University, to create the formal gardens within the picturesque landscape seen today. Lewis was a zealous plant collector, dauntless

At Skylands Botanical Garden, a rich display of azaleas and rhododendrons are planted alongside a reflecting pool. Large evergreen trees provide a contrast in color and texture while enhancing the landscape behind the mansion.

in experimenting with plants from such exotic locales as the Belgian Congo and Kashmir. In peak season as many as 60 gardeners worked on his estate, which eventually had one of the finest collections of plants in the state of New Jersey.

Today, the garden retains its original grandeur on 96 acres within a larger state park in the foothills of the Ramapo Mountains. Outstanding specimen trees, small formal gardens, sweeping lawns, and wildflower meadows surround the 45-room Tudor Revival mansion, designed by John Russell Pope. Descending behind the house, a series of terraced garden rooms gradually form a long narrow axis. At its top, low rock walls studded with flowering dwarf plants enclose the Octagonal Garden, named for the so-shaped pool in the center. Fragrant southern magnolias line the long walk leading to the Azalea Garden, where evergreens provide a backdrop to banks of vibrant azaleas and rhododendrons on both sides of a reflecting pool. At the end of the axis, tree peonies give way to a quiet circle of hemlocks surrounding an impressive stone bench. In addition, an extensive lilac collection with more than 400 varieties of eight different species adjoins the terraces.

The Crabapple Vista, 166 trees in double rows, divides the formal landscape from the naturalized areas on the eastern side of the estate. A major attraction in May, this parade of billowing pink blossoms extends for a half mile, ending in meadows of bog plants and wildflowers.

SKYLANDS BOTANICAL GARDEN (50 miles north of Newark) Ringwood State Park, Ringwood, NJ 07456 **TEL:** (973) 962-7527 **OPEN:** Daily 8-8 **TOTAL ACRES:** 96 **SPECIAL COLLECTIONS:** Estate garden, azaleas, lilacs, crabapples, rhododendrons, wildflowers, pinetum **ZONE 6** **F** **G** **H** **HO** **P** **T** **V** **WS**

LEAMING'S RUN GARDENS
SWAINTON

Located between the Victorian seaside resort of Cape May and the famous New Jersey coastal pine barrens, Leaming's Run Gardens is a curious and surprising summer garden devoted entirely to annual flowers. Within 20 acres of pine and oak woodlands, forest and flowers alternate along a mile-long path filled with thousands of annuals in striking color combinations and beds of single colors in 26 separate gardens. Cool glades of cinnamon ferns lead to the Serpentine Garden, so named for the sinuous curve of red salvia flowing toward a gazebo picturesquely situated above a pond, itself fringed with giant hibiscus.

The Yellow Garden features five kinds of marigolds amid nasturtiums, zinnias, dahlias, and gladioluses. A Red and Blue Garden holds scarlet sage, ageratum, lobelia, and ornamental peppers. In one of the larger areas, the English Cottage Garden, dense plantings of 150 different annuals in intense colors and contrasting textures create an almost tropical intensity in the flamboyant display of red clashing with orange and purple.

Owners Jack and Emily Aprill spent many years creating this garden, opening it to the public in 1978. Each year begins with seeds, as they select new varieties and old favorites for their exuberant showcase of annuals.

LEAMING'S RUN GARDENS (5 miles north of Cape May Courthouse; 80 miles southeast of Philadelphia) 1845 Route 9 North, Swainton, NJ 08210 **TEL:** (609) 465-5871 **OPEN:** Daily 9:30-5, mid-May to mid-Oct. **TOTAL ACRES:** 20 **SPECIAL COLLECTIONS:** One of the largest collections of annuals in the U.S. **ZONE 7** **F** **G** **H** **P** **T**

Pennsylvania

LONGWOOD GARDENS
KENNETT SQUARE

The du Pont dynasty, famous for its chemical empire, also created some of the most elaborate gardens in the United States. Longwood, Nemours, and Winterthur are all within about 10 miles of each other in the lovely Brandywine Valley of Pennsylvania and Delaware. The du Pont fortune began when this aristocratic French family emigrated to America and in 1802, encouraged by Thomas Jefferson, built a gunpowder mill on the banks of the Brandywine River. At the family's nearby first home, Eleutherian Mills, flourished a kitchen garden with espaliered fruit trees and a garden of exotic flowers grown from seeds imported from France. A century later Pierre S. du Pont, a great-grandson of the original emigrating family, built a modern industrial conglomerate and began the creation of Longwood Gardens.

Today Longwood is a spectacular pleasure garden combining European grandeur and American ingenuity. The ornate fountains and opulent conservatories here are among the largest in the U.S., rivaling those of Europe with their aquatic and floral dramas. The surrounding 1,050 acres of natural woodlands, wildflower meadows, lakes, and formal flower gardens reflect the beauty and serenity of the English landscape tradition. In season, more than 11,000 different plants offer millions of blooms.

Pierre du Pont acquired co-ownership of the DuPont Company in 1902. He was 32 years old and a bachelor. Three years later he bought Peirce's Park,

In May, the gossamer, pink-purple blooms of the paulownia trees frame the geometric silhouettes of the evergreen shrubs in Longwood's Topiary Garden.

a 202-acre farm and distinguished arboretum in Kennett Square, for about $16,000. He expanded the property to 1,000 acres of rolling hills and woodlands and named it for the nearby Longwood Quaker Meetinghouse, once an active station on the underground railroad. Notoriously meticulous, Pierre took a personal interest in virtually every detail of Longwood's development, trusting no one's judgment but his own. After reading a few popular books on home gardening (*How to Plan the Home Grounds* by Samuel Parsons was one) he felt competent to proceed, acting on ideas as they came to him rather than creating a master plan. He once said a great garden should be like Wanamaker's (the dry goods store of Philadelphia), to be experienced department after department. And while some traditionalists may find this eccentric, the description fits Longwood to this day.

Pierre du Pont designed his first garden in 1907, a 600-foot Flower Garden Walk that he described as "the old-fashioned plan of straight walks and boxwood

Recalling the majestic fountains of Europe, Longwood's Main Fountain Garden combines theatrical drama, architecture, and technology to achieve its dazzling effects. At night, fireworks and multi-colored lights add to the magic of this spectacle.

borders at the edge of flower beds." Planted at first with the family's favorite annuals and perennials, the garden was filled with continuous blooms from April until frost. Sweeps of vibrant bulbs underplanted with carpets of purple pansies changed to a brilliant arrangement of annuals in summer and chrysanthemums in autumn. He then added other specialized garden "departments," including the Sundial Garden, the Rose Garden, and the Rose Arbor. But it was shortly after marrying his cousin Alicia Belin in 1915 that Pierre began his masterpieces, the fountains and conservatories at Longwood. At this time he was regarded as one of the richest men in the world, having become chairman of DuPont and of General Motors.

An engineer by training and instinct, Pierre du Pont took particular delight in fountains. A boyhood visit to the Philadelphia Centennial of 1876, where he saw indoor water pump systems, impressed him with what technology could achieve. Later travels revealed the hydraulic marvels of France and Italy. As wealthy as any European royalty, du Pont thought nothing of rivaling the scale of Versailles' waterworks and, with the advent of modern technology, he built some of the finest and most spectacular ornamental waterworks in the world.

The first of Longwood's famous fountains were the Theater Fountains, an integral part of the Open Air Theater. Here du Pont held musicales for his friends, and today audiences of close to 2,100 people can gather for alfresco musical and theatrical performances. As a grand finale to such events a 10-foot-high water curtain, lit with a rainbow of colors, rises at the front of the stage

while 50-foot jets of water shoot skyward at the rear. Also installed in 1927, the Italian Water Garden is modeled after the gardens of Villa Gamberaia near Florence. Bordered by an allée of lindens, this water garden is a tranquil, refreshing scene in sharp contrast to the next fountain.

Borrowing from the Avenue of One Hundred Fountains at the Villa D'Este in Italy and the French château, Vaux-le-Vicomte, the model for Versailles, in 1931 du Pont created his masterpiece, the monumental Main Fountain Garden, in front of the conservatory. He added to five acres of boxwood and Norway maples two long canals, two circular pools, and a huge rectangular basin. Filled with 380 fountainheads and 674 colored floodlights, the Main Fountain Garden is designed to send its "liquid fireworks" as high as 130 feet. Three times a day, all summer long, 10,000 gallons of water are thrust into the air. To ensure the proper framework for his hydraulic extravaganza, du Pont had the surrounding cornfields turned into a forested landscape almost overnight, transplanting 500 mature specimen trees and shrubs gathered from as far away as Massachusetts, Michigan, and Georgia. Delightful from spring to fall, the waterworks are especially magical during the summer Festival of Fountains, when visitors can enjoy them set to music and occasionally in combination with extravagant fireworks displays.

Du Pont's ability to harness technology to support his gardens is also apparent in Longwood's heated conservatory buildings, which together house 20 distinct gardens under nearly four acres of glass. The first conservatory, the Orangery and its adjoining Exhibition Hall, opened in 1921. Vine-clad, treelike pillars, 40-foot-high glass ceilings, and fenestrated walls create a stunning showcase for the lavish floral displays. Additional greenhouses were added later.

The Orangery and the newer East Conservatory are famous for the country's largest indoor flower shows. Inside, emerald green lawns are decorated with massive displays year-round. From January through April, the annual Welcome Spring display features 45,000 flowers, including daffodils, hyacinths, and tulips, ending with thousands of Easter lilies. In summer, bougainvilleas, fuschias, crape myrtles, impatiens, and other annuals fill the stately rooms with radiant colors. November brings Longwood's famous Chrysanthemum Festival, featuring some 15,000 mums. The gardeners here have perfected techniques for training and shaping these flowers, from traditional mounded shapes, to bonsai and topiary styles, to spectacular hanging baskets, each nearly five feet in diameter. After Thanksgiving, cream and red poinsettia plants fill the rooms in celebration of the Christmas season. Other greenhouses host special collections, including orchids, bonsai, ferns, palms, a silver garden, a Mediterranean garden, and an indoor children's garden with a maze. The Cascade Garden, the only realized garden in America designed by Roberto Burle Marx, opened in 1993 with plants from the Brazilian rain forest.

The large courtyard outside the conservatory holds the waterlily garden, with five pools displaying a dramatic variety of aquatic plants, including the six-foot-wide Victoria hybrid waterplatter. Distinctive for its size and weight, the leaves can bear up to 150 pounds. Plant research and education remain critical activities at Longwood, thanks to Pierre du Pont's generous bequest.

LONGWOOD GARDENS (40 miles west of Philadelphia) US 1, Kennett Square, PA 19348 **TEL:** (610) 388-1000 **OPEN:** Daily 9-6, April through Oct.; daily 9-5, Nov. through March; open some evenings for special events **TOTAL ACRES:** 1,050 **SPECIAL COLLECTIONS:** Conservatory exhibits, fountains, roses, formal gardens, topiary, water gardens, specimen trees   **ZONE 6** C F H P PA R T V WS

East Conservatory, renowned for its huge indoor flower shows, has appealing year-round
: Here, thousands of cymbidium orchids create a rainbow of pastels in late spring.

Historic Bartram's Garden
Philadelphia

Appointed royal botanist by King George III and complimented by scientific scholars abroad, John Bartram (1699-1777) was the greatest botanist and plant explorer of 18th-century colonial America. This self-taught Quaker farmer and father of nine children achieved outstanding recognition by pursuing his intense

interest in the plants around him over a period of 40 years. One of many dignitaries to visit Bartram's garden was George Washington, who took away some seeds for Mount Vernon. He described the garden as "stored with many curious Trees, Shrubs, and Flowers...neither large nor laid out with much taste." Designing or copying gardens of the period did not interest Bartram, whose scientific curiosity fueled his travels throughout the colonies, where he explored and collected the native seeds and plants of the New World. His correspondence with European naturalists eventually led to the introduction of more than 200 varieties of American native plants to Europe. The European enthusiasm for exotics began in this period, and Bartram's seeds and plants were eagerly sought.

One of his greatest finds was in Florida, the *Franklinia alatamaha* tree, named for his good friend Benjamin Franklin. Extinct in the wild since 1803, all the trees found today are descendants of Bartram's collection. Plant collection and distribution was carried on by his son, William, a famous botanical illustrator, and other members of the family, whose successful commercial nursery lasted until the year 1850.

Towering above the flowers of summer, the tall yellowwood tree, collected in the 1780s, is one of the oldest in Bartram's Garden.

The first botanical garden of the United States, this 44-acre National Historic Landmark on the banks of the Schuylkill River features more than a hundred native trees and shrubs identified by Bartram, as well as an expansive wildflower meadow, a kitchen garden, and a butterfly and hummingbird garden. His original stone house also stands on the property.

Historic Bartram's Garden 54th Street and Lindbergh Boulevard, Philadelphia, PA 19143 Tel: (215) 729-5281 Open: Daily dawn-dusk Total acres: 44 Special collections: Historic trees, native plants, butterfly garden, azaleas, rhododendrons   ZONE 6 G HO P PA T WS

Wyck
PHILADELPHIA

A pleasurable oasis of roses, shady lawns, orchards, and kitchen gardens surround one of the oldest houses in Germantown, a section of Philadelphia with a strong tradition of gardening. In the 18th and 19th centuries the area was a popular summer retreat and later an affluent suburb. From 1690 from 1973, nine generations of the Quaker Wistar and Haines families lived and gardened in this charming colonial setting. The Haines family created this garden in 1820, continuing its cultivation until the house and gardens were opened to the public in 1973. The family also founded the original school of horticulture at Temple University and the Pennsylvania Horticultural Society. The rose garden is particularly notable. Between 1814 and 1829, prior to the introduction of modern roses, Jane Bowne Haines planted parterres of boxwood borders enclosing beds of roses. Today, the garden holds some 30 varieties of roses, some possibly dating to the 1750s, others to her original garden. This rose "museum" includes the beautiful 'Tuscany' and other gallicas, with damasks, hybrid perpetuals, and others at peak bloom in June. Small vegetable and herb gardens along with some original outbuildings evoke a strong sense of the past within this modern metropolis.

Wyck 6026 Germantown Avenue, Philadelphia, PA 19144 **TEL:** (215) 848-1690 **OPEN:** Tues., Thurs., Sat. 1-4, April to mid-Dec., and by appointment **TOTAL ACRES:** 2.5 **SPECIAL COLLECTIONS:** Historic design, roses, boxwood **ZONE 6** C F G HO L P PA T WS

Morris Arboretum
PHILADELPHIA

One of the largest collections of Asiatic trees and shrubs in the United States forms the nucleus of this 19th-century landscaped garden. John and Lydia Morris, wealthy Quaker siblings, shared a passion for collecting the ornamental and exotic trees being introduced by plant explorers at Boston's Arnold Arboretum and elsewhere. These worldwide travelers borrowed romantic ideas of the English Victorian landscape movement, added their own eclectic notions and created a pastoral setting for their outstanding collection of plants in the rolling countryside of Chestnut Hill, now an affluent section of Philadelphia.

The garden's bucolic landscape includes lush expanses of lawn decorated with dramatic specimen trees, streams bordered by a copse of dawn redwoods from China, a Japanese rock garden, and a Tuscan love temple at the edge of a swan pond. The estate's only formal garden is an All-America Rose Selections Garden. Instead, free-form areas lend grace, such as the hillside of holly that ends in an azalea meadow, where two whimsical bronze sculptures of John and Lydia stand one behind the other in the Quaker tradition of the unmarried. Other sculptures, traditional and contemporary, are displayed on the grounds. The newly restored Fernery, devoted exclusively to tropical ferns, provides a rare example of this Victorian fad. In 1932, the estate became the Morris Arboretum of the University of Pennsylvania and today exhibits more than 5,000 trees and shrubs.

MORRIS ARBORETUM OF THE UNIVERSITY OF PENNSYLVANIA, CHESTNUT HILL 100 Northwestern Avenue, Philadelphia, PA 19118 **TEL:** (215) 247-5777 **OPEN:** Daily 10-4, and until 5 Sat.-Sun., April through Oct. **TOTAL ACRES:** 92 **SPECIAL COLLECTIONS:** Estate garden, ornamental and exotic trees, azaleas, roses, magnolias, ferns, rock wall garden **ZONE 6** C F G H P PA T V WS

Meadowbrook Farm
Meadowbrook

Meadowbrook Farm, set on a hillside surrounded by woodlands in a Philadelphia suburb, is a sophisticated garden on less than two acres. Reminiscent of the meticulous miniatures of villa gardens in Renaissance paintings, the lovely terraced gardens of this private estate are decorated as intimate, elegant "rooms," arranged with flowers and architectural furniture. They are designed by J. Liddon Pennock, an important influence in the Pennsylvania horticultural world and a designer of White House gardens.

Twelve thematic gardens present an eclectic architectural emphasis. Gazebos, classical columns, statues, fountains, pedestals, and urns dominate separate areas filled with arrangements of flowers, shrubs, vines, and trees. The scale of ornaments and plantings within the gardens combines grace and elegance while providing a unique focus. The Round Garden, enclosed by a circle of low stone walls, features a fountain and a columned belvedere. In spring, masses of azaleas are followed by blazes of annual flowers. A cast-iron eagle flanked by clipped weeping hemlocks overlooks steep meadow banks within the woodlands, and stairways, stone paths, and allées connect terrace rooms positioned to maximize the perspective of vistas. Adjacent to the garden, Pennock's commercial nursery offers a fine selection of plants and garden ornaments.

■ **Meadowbrook Farm** (20 miles north of Philadelphia) 1633 Washington Lane, Meadowbrook, PA 19046 **Tel:** (215) 887-5900 **Open:** Mon.-Sat. 10-5, except holidays **Total Acres:** 1.5 **Special collections:** Thematic gardens, topiary, garden ornaments   **ZONE 6** C **F** G P

The Henry Foundation for Botanical Research
Gladwyne

Dramatic boulders and exotic plants characterize this idiosyncratic botanical research center. Down a winding road on a rustic estate in the Main Line area outside of Philadelphia, Mary G. Henry, a pioneer in the collection and preservation of American native plants, created an unusual garden. She spent some 40 years traveling the entire continent of North America gathering rare and endangered species. They were planted around her estate, within a naturalistic setting of rolling hills and enormous rocks and in 1948 a foundation for research was founded. She died in 1967, and her daughter, Josephine de N. Henry, also a dedicated field botanist and pursuer of plants around the world, continues her work. This connoisseur's garden on 50 acres features unusual collections of rhododendron, styrax, halesia, magnolia, and lilium; plants from Texas and the Yucatan grow in this garden with plants from Canada. Vast outcroppings of rocks provide striking settings for smaller plants, such as phlox and hespealoe from New Mexico, artemisia from Nova Scotia, and penstemon from the Rockies. A charming and casual landscape of undulating hills, lovely vistas, flower meadows, rock gardens, and woodlands makes this a pleasurable learning center. Plants are also propagated and distributed to botanic gardens here and abroad.

■ **The Henry Foundation for Botanical Research** (13 miles northwest of Philadelphia) 801 Stony Lane, Gladwyne, PA 19035 **Tel:** (610) 525-2037 **Open:** Mon.-Fri. 10-4, and weekends by appointment **Total Acres:** 50 **Special collections:** Rock gardens, rare and endangered American native plants, exotic trees and shrubs   **ZONE 6** P T

The slopes of the hillside at Chanticleer, swathed in flower drifts of texture and color, end in a pergola at the bottom covered by a cloud of roses.

CHANTICLEER
WAYNE

In the 1970s Adolph Rosengarten, a wealthy chemical executive, formed the Chanticleer Foundation to develop his 30-acre estate into a public garden. The family's original garden has expanded into a major garden displaying the art of horticulture. Those working here describe themselves as "plant passionate," desiring to present a pleasure garden with intoxicating colors. This new addition to the lovely gardens in the Philadelphia area opened in 1993.

Adjacent to the imposing stone house, hemlock hedges surround a formal courtyard garden. Within, flowering trees, shrubs, perennials, and roses bloom in their seasons. From a terrace on the other side of the house, a hillside meadow slopes down to colorful perennial gardens dotted with trellises covered in blooms. In spring, the hillside is covered with flowering bulbs, followed by sun-loving wildflowers in summer. As part of the garden's expansion, a crabapple orchard has been planted and an Asian woods is in progress. Throughout the garden, ponds and streams display ornamental grasses and herbs. The presence of an English cutting garden and bountiful vegetable garden complete the horticultural diversity within this estate.

CHANTICLEER (22 miles west of Philadelphia) 786 Church Road, Wayne, PA 19087 **TEL:** (610) 687-4163 **OPEN:** Wed.-Sat. 10-3:30, April through Oct. **TOTAL ACRES:** 30 **SPECIAL COLLECTIONS:** Perennials, native plants, cutting garden, roses, ornamental grasses   **ZONE 6** F H HO P T WS

Hershey Gardens
Hershey

Within the lush farmland area of central Pennsylvania, the Hershey chocolate factory and entertainment complex includes an elaborate garden of 23 acres. Hershey Gardens, famous for its thousands of roses, is designed in a traditional parklike setting with outstanding specimen trees, ornamental shrubs, and theme gardens.

The garden began in 1937 when Milton Hershey wanted a "nice garden of roses" near his new hotel. The rose garden opened in June 1937, and, according to Hershey's records, attracted 20,000 visitors in one day. His three acres of roses expanded into a major award-winning collection of 7,000 roses with over 275 varieties of hybrid teas, floribundas, grandifloras, climbing roses, miniatures, shrub roses, and old-world roses arranged in geometric beds around a pond and gazebo. A major restoration of the rose garden was completed in 1997 to celebrate the garden's 60th anniversary.

Across from the rose garden, the annual display garden provides a striking succession of massive blooms in staggering numbers: 30,000 tulips in spring, followed by 10,000 annuals in summer, and 2,500 chrysanthemums in autumn. Other gardens include Mrs. Hershey's original rose garden, transplanted from the private residence in 1942; a Japanese garden; a perennial garden; ornamental grasses; a geranium test garden with more than a hundred varieties; and an attractive butterfly garden.

Spectacular specimen trees decorate the grounds, such as a giant sequoia, atlas cedar, sourwood, bald cypress, and others. The Hohman Garden, donated by a noted plant collector, contains an impressive display of dwarf evergreens and English and American hollies. This is an especially pleasant spot in spring, when rhododendrons, azaleas, and flowering fruit trees provide vistas of color.

Hershey Gardens (15 miles east of Harrisburg) 170 Hotel Road, Hershey, PA 17033 **Tel:** (717) 534-3492 **Open:** Daily 9-5, mid-May through Oct. **Total acres:** 23 **Special collections:** Roses, tulips, annuals, perennials, dwarf evergreens, hollies   **ZONE 6** F G P PA R T V WS

Pittsburgh Civic Garden Center, Mellon Park
Pittsburgh

In 1940, the millionaire Mellons donated their estate to the city of Pittsburgh as a memorial to their family. The gracious grounds, now called Mellon Park, feature a series of gardens created over the years by dedicated volunteers intent on showing what plants grow best in the area. Educational in design and purpose, the attractive gardens include a rock garden with alpine plants amid small boulders; a herb garden featuring the traditional plants mentioned in Shakespeare's works; a knot garden; a ground cover garden showcasing more than 50 varieties and some ornamental grasses; a dogwood area; and a native plant garden. Although the mansion is gone, tall, mature trees and the family's original carriage house and stable enhance the grounds and add character to this urban Pennsylvania park.

Pittsburgh Civic Garden Center, Mellon Park 1059 Shady Avenue, Pittsburgh, PA 15232 **Tel:** (412) 441-4442 **Open:** Mon.-Sat. 10-4 **Total acres:** 17 **Special collections:** Rock garden, herb garden, ground cover, native plants   **ZONE 6** G H L P PA T V

Phipps Conservatory, Schenley Park
Pittsburgh

Crystal conservatories were fashionable and formidable parts of public gardens at the turn of the century when steel magnate Henry Phipps offered the city of Pittsburgh the funds to build such a structure in Schenley Park. Designed by the firm of Lord & Burnham with the traditional central Palm Court, 12 large exhibition galleries, and 9 growing houses, the conservatory opened in 1893 as the largest in the United States. That year, when Chicago's World Colombian Exposition closed, most of its rare plants were purchased for the 2.5-acre Phipps Conservatory. Some of these palms and cycads remain today, augmented by major collections of tropical plants including an impressive grouping of orchids, mostly from Thailand. Specialized French, Japanese, and English gardens illustrate the major design elements of these important historic styles. In addition, seasonal flower extravaganzas are created by the conservatory's staff from plants grown on site. In spring, close to 30,000 tulips, hyacinths, daffodils, lilies, azaleas, cineraria, primroses, and many others are planted throughout the galleries. In autumn, seven galleries concentrate on more than 400 varieties of chrysanthemums, staged in interesting and intricate designs. Another elaborate show follows at Christmas. Outdoor gardens adjacent to the conservatory include a waterlily pond, a medieval herb garden, and large demonstration gardens of annuals and perennials.

Phipps Conservatory, Schenley Park, Frank Curto Drive, Pittsburgh, PA 15213 **Tel:** (412) 622-6914 **Open:** Tues.-Sun 9-5, except Thanksgiving and Christmas **Total acres:** 2.5 **Special collections:** Seasonal floral exhibitions, tropical plants, orchids, bonsai

C F H T WS

Victorian conservatories such as the Phipps continue to be popular flower houses in the United States and England. Seasonal spectacles take place indoors throughout the year.

Delaware

Winterthur Museum, Garden and Library
Wilmington

Admired internationally as one of the great naturalistic gardens in the world, Winterthur showcases an important collection of rare woodland plants in a carefully conceived landscape setting. Credit for these achievements goes to Henry Francis du Pont who was born at Winterthur in 1880 and worked, as he often liked to say, as "head gardener" on the family estate for virtually all of his life. A connoisseur of art, antiques, and plants, du Pont, called Harry, created and designed most of the beautiful grounds of this country estate in the English tradition of park and woodlands. At the same time, within a 10-mile radius, cousins Pierre at Longwood and Alfred at Nemours were creating their lavish, formal gardens.

Winterthur itself began in 1839 when Evelina du Pont, daughter of the founder of the du Pont dynasty, and her wealthy husband, James Antoine Biedermann, bought land near the gunpowder mills that brought her father fortune. Named for Biedermann's village in Switzerland, the estate in the bucolic Brandywine Valley was surrounded by rolling hills, woodlands, and sprawling meadows punctuated by rocky outcrops and meandering streams. The couple built a small sunken garden near the house, but it was Col. Henry A. du Pont who began the era of gardening when he bought the land from his sister in 1875. He enlarged the gardens, adding terraces, a rose garden, and more foundation plantings.

His son Harry followed the family tradition. While at Harvard University, he studied with America's leading horticulturists Charles Sargent and E.H. "Chinese" Wilson at the Arnold Arboretum and remained involved with them. His philosophy of gardening differed radically from the grandiose European schemes of the other du Ponts gardening nearby. For him, the site was everything: "It determines both the form and content of the garden...even the placement of walks and paths, the lines of massed shrubs or trees, the forms of beds."

He never changed existing grades, choosing instead to work around the natural contours, preserving as much of the indigenous vegetation as possible. He also avoided

Clenny Run flows through the center of Winterthur, filling ponds on its way to the Brandywine River. It is an attraction for wildlife and a source of irrigation in times of drought.

A variety of azaleas and rhododendrons, each a different color, carpet the grounds of Winterthur's Azalea Woods. Each year, this stunning display of multicolored shrubs planted among towering trees heralds the arrival of spring.

removing trees, instead planting his newly acquired exotics around them. Yet for all his insistence on naturalism, Harry could be a surprisingly exacting taskmaster, having plants moved constantly until the colors, shapes, heights, vistas, and sense of space looked as they did in his mind's eye. The older he became, the greater grew his ambitions for Winterthur. While in his eighties, he decided to bring in an additional 2,367 species and varieties of plants for field testing and planting; in those days, Winterthur kept a hundred gardeners busy on the estate.

Henry Francis du Pont's first contribution to Winterthur's gardening history was along the March Walk. This lovely path extends northward from the house to an area called Magnolia Bend, marked by a grand old saucer magnolia planted by the colonel in 1875. Where his father had established daffodils and other old-fashioned flowers near the north side of the house, Harry began naturalizing many small bulbs until the embankment along the entire west side of the walk was carpeted with snowdrops, winter aconite, snowflake adonis, glory-of-the-snow, Italian windflowers, miniature daffodils, crocuses, and other cheery harbingers of spring. True to its name, the March Walk is at its most spectacular at the end of that month, although violets, bluebells, and other favorites carry on the colorful show until late summer.

Col. du Pont and his son laid out a pinetum in 1914, planting more than 50 species and varieties of rare and native conifers. The younger du Pont continued to add trees in later years, and as a result Winterthur's pinetum is considered one of the finest collections in the eastern United States. Included among its many noteworthy specimens are two magnificent atlas cedars, several giant arborvitaes, a dawn redwood, and a dragon spruce.

The Azalea Woods, the heart of Winterthur's garden, date from 1917, the decade in which Harry du Pont inherited Winterthur. It began to take shape serendipitously when, as the result of a chestnut blight sweeping the eastern United States, large open spaces appeared in a previously thickly wooded area near the March Walk. Du Pont decided to use this eight-acre area as an azalea nursery. He acquired 17 Kurume azaleas introduced from Japan for the first time at San Francisco's Panama-Pacific International Exhibition in 1915 and was among the first to recognize the particular value of the Kurume hybrids— distinguished by small shiny leaves, dense growth habit, and abundance of tiny flowers. In addition, he planted more than 250 other species and varieties here. In the 1930s some 60 hybrid Asiatic rhododendrons developed by noted Massachusetts hybridizer, Charles Dexter, arrived to further enrich the collection. The Azalea Woods is spectacular throughout May, beginning with the Kurume and torch azaleas and ending with the Dexter hybrid rhododendrons.

The Peony Garden, begun in 1946, is one of only two Winterthur gardens that are somewhat formal. Once Harry decided peonies did not lend themselves to naturalizing, he laid out his outstanding collection along a terraced path in eight separate beds. There are uncommon single and semidouble Japanese, Chinese, and French hybrid herbaceous peonies, as well as the rarer tree peonies. Steps lead down to the Reflecting Pool Garden, formerly the Sunken Garden, one of the only areas with garden sculpture and furniture.

The second formal garden at Winterthur, called the Sundial Garden, was created in 1957 on the site of the tennis and croquet courts from a design by Marian Coffin, a noted landscape architect. Four curved beds of early white spireas, star magnolias, pink flowering almonds, and quinces surround the armillary sundial at its center.

Of a very different style is the Quarry Garden, begun in 1961 in an old quarry on the estate. Du Pont selected for this unusual, boglike site various species of hybrid primulas, which are somewhat difficult to grow. In late March, a Himalayan variety with mauve and white globes emerges, growing a foot high by the end of April. In late spring and summer, other tall candelabra primulas in many colors decorate the boggy site. Here, too, tall oaks and beeches cast their shade over the ridged and rocky crevasses of the quarry, where shrubs, ferns, and wildflowers cling. Spring-fed streams create the cool, wet ground that nurtures marsh marigolds, dwarf bearded irises, cyclamen, and masses of primulas.

Du Pont's passion for horticulture was matched by his interest in antiques— the forms, colors, and textures of the natural world influenced his selection of decorative objects at home. He eventually acquired the largest collection of American decorative arts in the world, transforming his country house into a 196-room mansion to accommodate his treasures. In order to share his trees and other beautiful treasures with the public, he deeded the whole of Winterthur to an educational and charitable foundation in 1951, continuing his involvement until his death in 1969.

WINTERTHUR MUSEUM, GARDEN AND LIBRARY (6 miles northwest of Wilmington) Del. 52, Winterthur, DE 19735 **TEL:** (302) 888-4600 or (800) 448-3883; TTY (302) 888-4907 **OPEN:** Mon.-Sat. 9-5, Sun. 12-5 **TOTAL ACRES:** 985 **SPECIAL COLLECTIONS:** Azaleas, rhododendrons, peonies, primulas

ZONE 7 F G H HO L P PA R T V WS

Softly colored flowering shrubs line Winterthur's Azalea Woods. A dense stand massive trees helps transform the landscape into a colorful, textured tapes

Nemours Gardens
Wilmington

Generations of America's powerful du Pont family have been avid gardeners. In what amounts to internecine rivalry, these descendants have created extraordinary gardens, both private and public, intimate and grand, in the Wilmington area. Just north of the city lies Nemours, the 300-acre estate of scion Alfred Irénée du Pont. Alfred began his great estate in 1909 on land left to him by his father, naming it Nemours in honor of the family's ancestral seat in northern France. Its lavishness was perhaps an act of revenge—Alfred's reputation as a maverick placed him outside of family society, and he showed his disdain by building something truly spectacular.

Designed by Carrère & Hastings, the famed beaux arts architects of the equally imposing New York Public Library, Nemours is often described as a mini-Versaille. Though speculation about Nemours's grandeur circulated constantly during the construction, Alfred kept the curious away by surrounding the property with a nine-foot-high wall studded with glass. Some years later, when Nemours was perfected to his satisfaction, he held a one-day public open house, charging a dollar for admittance. Among the throngs touring the 102-room mansion were a good many curiosity driven du Ponts. Watching them, and eavesdropping freely in his disguise as a uniformed parking attendant, was Alfred du Pont.

The gardens were completed over nearly two decades, taking their inspiration from the era of Louis XIV and the design concepts of the French garden master André LeNôtre. Alfred's son, Alfred Victor du Pont, is credited with the overall planning of Nemours's landscaping, having studied garden design in Paris and Versailles in preparation for the project.

Beginning from the mansion's west terrace, the gardens descend in gentle stages. The vista extends in a dramatic sweep from the mansion to the Temple of Love, a straight axis lined with Japanese cedars, pink-flowering horse chestnuts, and pin oaks. The first garden, called the Main Vista, features a 100-foot-long greensward punctuated by six landings where giant urns are filled with seasonal flowers. At the end of the grass landings lies an acre-long reflecting pool, sometimes animated by the displays of 157 water jets. White Carrara marble statues representing the four seasons stand guard above the pool.

A maze garden is slightly raised at the pool's lower end, to better the view from the mansion of the geometric patterns of shrubs. Inspired by French parterres, the maze is formed by two kinds of dwarf evergreens: Canadian hemlock on the outer beds and Japanese holly on the inner beds. At the center a large golden statue symbolizing achievement looms above a small, circular pool.

Farther down the row of gardens stands a memorial to the du Pont's ancestors in the form of a monumental limestone colonnade. Before it lies the elaborate Sunken Garden. Here, sumptuous marble staircases encircle and lead to an outdoor room where the focal point, a grand fountain wall, is decorated with mythological sculptures. Wall basins overflow and water spouts from cherubs and beasts into large pools below. Beyond the pools a luxurious display of flowers is presented in a large rectangular parterre. Here masses of blossoms are in bloom for much of the year—thousands of tulips each spring, begonias in summer, and chrysanthemums in fall.

Nemours's grand progression of French-inspired formal gardens and garden architecture ends finally at a small, still pond and the raised rotunda known as

aerial view captures the splendor of Nemours. The architectural aspects of this
nch-style garden are clearly depicted in this autumnal view.

the Temple of Love. Within stands a life-size statue of Diana the Huntress, cast in bronze in 1780 by the noted sculptor Jean Antoine Houdon.

Another group of fine gardens extends on the south side of the mansion and features a formal parterre of English boxwood and an English-style pleasure garden. Named the Four Borders, this 800-foot-long garden contains four flower beds planted with a great variety of summer annuals and perennials. A specimen tulip poplar, one of the trees so admired by Alfred's father, stills casts its shade here. There are also the original greenhouses, somewhat expanded in recent years, and two acres of cutting gardens, trial gardens, and nurseries.

The austere geometrical arrangements of trees, shrubs, and parterres; the precise plotting of main and subsidiary axes; the extravagant use of fountains, reflecting pools, and classical sculpture; and the creation of artificial terraces all combine to make the gardens of Nemours another remarkable du Pont family contribution. In January 1935, at the age of 71, Alfred created the Alfred I. du Pont Institute, a charitable children's hospital north of the mansion. The house and gardens were opened to the public in the mid-1970s, and have proven to be a popular destination.

NEMOURS GARDENS (3.5 miles northwest of Wilmington) Rockland Road, Wilmington, DE 19803 **TEL:** (302) 651-6912 **OPEN:** Tues.-Sat. 9-3, Sun. 11-3, May through Nov. **TOTAL ACRES:** 300 **SPECIAL COLLECTIONS:** 17th-century French design, sunken garden, fountains, parterres

ZONE 7 F G HO P T V WS

HAGLEY MUSEUM'S E.I. DU PONT RESTORED GARDEN
WILMINGTON

"Being without a garden was the greatest deprivation; and it is the first thing that occupied my time." So wrote Eleuthère Irénée du Pont de Nemours, a French émigré to the banks of the Brandywine in 1801. To fulfill his need, he built with his residence a modest French-style garden overlooking the gunpowder mills that created the du Pont fortune. Gunpowder explosions eventually destroyed the house, gardens, and mills in 1890.

Today the gardens are part of a 230-acre restoration project on the life and work of the du Ponts in the 19th century. Reconstructed by landscape architect William H. Frederick in 1972, the present two-acre garden is laid out opposite the house in quadrants of alternating heirloom varieties of vegetables and flowers, all surrounded by low fences of espaliered fruit trees. Violets and primulas grow with asparagus and garlic, and fruit trees are trained into dwarf-size tent, fan, and conical shapes—a time-intensive style popular during the Napoleonic era that is rarely seen today.

In the 1920s a great-granddaughter, Louise Crowninshield, inherited the property and became the last du Pont to live here. Her husband, Frank, created the second garden on the estate, a romantic folly styled after the Villa d'Este in Italy. Using the ruins of the mill as a backdrop, he placed statues, columns, and courtyards in the midst of lush plantings of azaleas, rhododendrons, lilacs, and magnolias within a woodland landscape.

HAGLEY MUSEUM'S E. I. DU PONT RESTORED GARDEN (3 miles north of Wilmington) Del. 141, Wilmington, DE 19803 **TEL:** (302) 658-2400 **OPEN:** Daily 9:30-4:30, mid-March through Dec.; call for winter hours **TOTAL ACRES:** 3 **SPECIAL COLLECTIONS:** Historic vegetables and fruit trees, native plants, azaleas

ZONE 7 F G H HO L P PA R T V WS

Mount Cuba Center for the Study of Piedmont Flora
Greenville

Noted for its exceptionally rich horticulture, the Piedmont region extends a thousand miles from the Hudson River west to the Blue Ridge and Appalachian Mountains, to the Atlantic coastal plain on the east, and south to central Alabama. Over 3,000 species of plants have been identified as native to the Piedmont and today Greenville's Mount Cuba Center, established in 1983, focuses on research and conservation of Piedmont flora. The estate garden of Mrs. Lammont du Pont Copeland, it is open to the public by appointment.

The property acquired by the Copelands in 1935 provided a backdrop of forests, rolling hills, and farmlands for the formal gardens created and embellished by various designers including Marian Coffin, a designer of nearby Winterthur. Majestic trees, terraces of azaleas and crimson barberry, and circular borders of seasonal flowers surround the elegant Georgian residence. Beyond, woodland gardens reflect Mrs. Copeland's lifelong interest in native flora. For more than 30 years, she has been involved in the selection of native plants and their use in the landscape, gathering an important collection of wildflowers, shrubs, and trees native to the Piedmont. In spring, the forest floor is filled with Dutchman's breeches, rue anemones, and different varieties of trillium, followed by many other wildflowers in summer and autumn.

Mount Cuba Center for the Study of Piedmont Flora (5 miles northwest of Wilmington) Barley Mill Road, Greenville, DE 19807 **Tel:** (302) 239-4244 **Open:** Private estate, by appointment only, Wed.-Fri., May **Total acres:** 20 **Special collections:** Native plants of the Piedmont region   **ZONE 7** **P** **T**

This delicate woodland scene showcases the variety of native flora collected at Mount Cuba, which preserves plants of the Piedmont region.

Maryland

LADEW TOPIARY GARDENS
MONKTON

Millionaire adventurer Harvey Ladew claimed that by the time he was 15, he had sat on more thrones in Europe than all of Queen Victoria's vast clan put together. His family's leather business fortune supported an aristocratic lifestyle of good hunting, grand houses, and glorious gardens. An international equestrian and a master of the hounds in the elite fox-hunting set near Baltimore, Ladew also became a skillful master of the art of topiary and spent more than 40 years creating the finest topiary garden in America. Although architectural and sculptural topiary forms the central focus in Ladew's 22 acres of formal gardens, 15 other "outdoor living rooms" present varied floral themes within a stately setting of vistas, emerald allées, and intimate enclosures.

Ladew began creating the elaborately designed gardens in 1929 at the age of 43 without any professional assistance. He combined his sense of whimsy with an elegant style reminiscent of the gardens of England and Europe he knew so well. Fascinated by the art of topiary, Ladew studied the process, built his own frames, and developed his own methods. One of his early designs was the charming life-size fox hunt scene that still greets visitors at the entrance to the house and gardens. Intrigued by a topiary hedge of fox hunting while on a hunt in England, he ordered wire frames and created a more elaborate free-standing version of horse, rider, and hounds in pursuit of a fox. Ladew started with large plants, training and trimming them to fit the frame, rather than waiting for the plant to grow around it, as was the more traditional method.

On the north side of the house, a graceful panorama unfolds in stages. The main axis flows over 1,000 feet from the terrace adjacent to the house down to a classical temple at the opposite end. A circular greensward and allée of hemlocks dominate the center, while on both sides a magical array of sculptured and colored gardens await the visitor along parallel borders.

Beginning at the house, a dark-green terraced garden supports three tiers of imposing geometrical forms sculptured from Canadian hemlocks; high obelisks alternate with smaller conical shapes and perky cockatoos perched on rectangular nests. The terrace is enclosed on two sides by stately walls of crenelated hemlock, complete with graceful garlands carved from the smooth surface of the hedges. Between their decorative folds rectangular windows have been cut into the hedge, framing intimate views beyond.

The terrace's last tier leads to a vast bowl of manicured lawn with a large oval fountain in the center, formerly the swimming pool. The Great Bowl is bordered to the east by a delightful hedge where topiary swans glide on green waves of undulating yew hedges parting and leading to the Iris Garden. In this Oriental garden, bearded, Siberian, and Japanese irises are interplanted with other seasonal flowers along a central stream. In addition, bamboo, weeping crabapple, a superb split-leaf dwarf Japanese maple, and tree peonies line the grassy walkways along with some more interesting topiary.

From the central fountain, a grand architectural allée of hemlocks leads to the topiary sculpture garden and the Temple of Venus beyond. The most elaborate green sculptures here include some of Ladew's first and favorite topiaries: a unicorn, a sea horse, a lyrebird (a pheasantlike bird with a lyre-shaped tail,

This whimsical fox-hunting scene adorns the entrance to the Ladew Topiary Gardens. The display depicts a horseback rider jumping over a fence, with accompanying hounds chasing a fox.

found in Australia), a heart pierced with Cupid's arrow, and a butterfly. In the playful spirit of Ladew's anglophilia, other topiary forms represent Churchill's famous 'V' for Victory, and his top hat. Placed on circular pedestals of Japanese yew, they are all surrounded by broad swaths of color beginning with tulips in spring, annuals and perennials in summer, and chrysanthemums in fall.

Ladew used some boxwood and privet for his topiary, but preferred Canadian hemlock for the hedges and larger geometrical shapes and English and Japanese yew for the sculptures. He personally pruned and trimmed much of the topiary throughout the garden.

Next to this menagerie, the Tivoli Teahouse and Garden offers a large border of lilies, peonies, spirea, viburnum, bridal wreath, and lilacs. The teahouse facade was once the ticket office of the Tivoli Theater in London. From here, the imposing allée continues through an English park setting to the remote colonnaded Roman Temple of Venus on a hill, the focal point of the long view from the terraced garden. A stroll back along the opposite side of the allée leads through a series of interconnecting smaller theme gardens. These reflect Ladew's sophisticated horticultural interests beyond his fascination with topiary. A golden chain tunnel of laburnum forms a brilliant arcade in May and leads to the Yellow Garden, a lovely delicate display of tints and shades of yellow flowers and shrubs bisected by a stream. Spring-blooming *Kerria japonica* and Exbury azaleas among the ever-golden arborvitae and juniper intensify the yellows of spring bulbs, water irises, pansies, andromeda, potentilla, daylilies, and many others.

Impressed by Vita Sackville West's white garden at Sissinghurst Castle in

England, Ladew designed his own white garden using more than 35 different kinds of flowers that bloom from spring through fall. Next, a waterlily garden presents an unusual collection of hostas and tree hydrangeas, followed by the Keyhole Garden. Named for the shape of the entrance cut into the hedge, this garden provides an intimate conversational setting decorated in red-flowering plants such as tulips, astilbe, and dahlias.

In one of Ladew's most fanciful gardens, the Garden of Eden, a statue of Eve handing an apple to Adam stands among a dense thicket of blushing pink azaleas and under a canopy of apple and crabapple trees.

Along the estate's western side, a circular, walled rose garden blooms with a large collection of floribundas, grandifloras, climbers, ramblers, and hybrid teas underplanted with blue pansies. Espaliered pear and apple trees line the outside of the garden wall, and climbers and clematis, edged with lavender, line the inner wall. Smaller gardens closer to the house include a pink garden of 'Fairy' and 'Carefree Beauty' roses, astilbe, weigela, rhododendrons, and many different annuals. The Berry Garden, strictly for the birds, is patterned after a formal Italian garden with a variety of nandina, snowberry, hawthorn, callicarpa, and much more. Of additional interest, next to the manor house visitors may explore a small wildflower garden, filled with ferns and native Maryland wildflowers, as well as a colorful Victorian garden.

In Ladew's Garden of Eden, a statue of Adam and Eve stands nestled between several soft pink azaleas. The azaleas are shaded by a cover of tempting apple and crabapple trees.

Ladew's sumptuous lifestyle included balls, hunts, and lavish possessions. Yet he had a simpler side, as expressed and engraved on the stepping stones leading to his garden. The words are from a Chinese proverb: "But if you would be happy all your life, plant a garden." Along with his staff, this amazing talent worked in the gardens until 1971, when he was 84. And because of his dedication, we have his legacy of a beautiful garden of dramatic and amusing topiary, a gorgeous bounty of flowers and shrubs, and a medley of grand and intimate designs that will long be remembered.

LADEW TOPIARY GARDENS (28 miles north of Baltimore) 3535 Jarretsville Pike, Monkton, MD 21111 **TEL:** (410) 557-9570 **OPEN:** Mon.-Fri. 10-4, Sat.-Sun. 10:30-5, mid-April through Oct. **TOTAL ACRES:** 22 **SPECIAL COLLECTIONS:** Topiary, annuals, perennials, irises, roses

ZONE 7 F G H HO P PA R T WS

Among the elaborate and elegant topiary designs found in Ladew's Sculp Garden are lyrebirds perched atop circular stands of Japanese yew (oppos

LILYPONS WATER GARDENS
BUCKEYSTOWN

Lilypons, the largest retail nursery of aquatic plants in the United States, is a water garden wonderland. Some 200 types of aquatic plants, including a hundred varieties of waterlilies and exotic fish, are grown within more than a hundred acres of marshy lands and 500 man-made ponds. This patchwork of color is not a formal landscaped water garden, but a series of "production ponds" filled with plants that bloom from late May to September. Dikes separating the ponds provide footpaths from which to view the beautiful flowers as they vary from day to day and season to season. A major Lotus Festival is held in mid-July and the season ends with a Koi Festival in September. George Thomas started it all in 1917 with a goldfish business and a waterlily hobby. By 1935, the enterprise was so successful he was granted his own post office in his farmhouse and named it for Lily Pons, the famous opera singer. The Thomas family remains involved and has expanded the enterprise to Texas and California.

LILYPONS WATER GARDENS (50 miles west of Baltimore) 6800 Lilypons Road, Buckeystown, MD 21717 **TEL:** (301) 874-5133 or (800) 999-5459 **OPEN:** Daily 9:30-5:30, March through Oct.; Mon.-Sat. 9:30-4:30, Nov. through Feb. **TOTAL ACRES:** 287 **SPECIAL COLLECTIONS:** Waterlilies   ZONE 7 A G **H** P **T** WS

BROOKSIDE GARDENS
WHEATON

Brookside Gardens opened in 1969 as a public display garden, arboretum, and conservatory in Wheaton Regional Park. Hans Hanses, educated in Germany and Switzerland, designed the grounds based upon his European aesthetic of what would please the public, rather than using a particular historic style. An outstanding collection of trees, shrubs, and flowers around large and small ponds fringed with blossoms divide the formal and informal areas into 11 specialty gardens. Under a canopy of native trees, hundreds of varieties of azaleas and rhododendrons bloom between March and June. Some 15,000 tulips and other spring-flowering bulbs burst forth each spring in the Trial Garden, designed to offer ideas for the home gardener. Perennials begin to bloom in May and last until October throughout the garden. In June on a grassy hillside decorated with fountains and a wisteria-covered pergola, an All-America Rose Selections Garden displays the newest roses. Conifers and ornamental grasses surround the rose garden and supply year-round interest. The nine-acre Gude Garden, named for Adolph Gude, Sr., a prominent local nurseryman, is a Japanese-style garden of gentle hills, ponds, flowering trees, shrubs, and a teahouse designed by Hanses. Other areas include a fine collection of viburnum; a water garden filled with delicate pink lotus; a fragrance garden with herbs selected for taste, smell, and touch; and a winter garden with a display of trees and shrubs that have colorful barks and berries when nothing else is in bloom. Picturesque even in winter, the garden is a treat indoors and outdoors. Two conservatories provide attractive displays of seasonal flowers throughout the year.

BROOKSIDE GARDENS (39 miles south of Baltimore; 12 miles north of Washington, DC) 1500 Glenallan Avenue, Wheaton, MD 20902 **TEL:** (301) 949-8230 **OPEN:** Daily 10-5 **TOTAL ACRES:** 50 **SPECIAL COLLECTIONS:** Conservatory displays, azaleas, rhododendrons, spring bulbs, roses, Japanese-style garden   ZONE 7 C **G** **H** L **P** **T** V

McCRILLIS GARDENS
BETHESDA

Azaleas dominate the five-acre shade garden that surrounds the lovely stone house that belonged to William McCrillis, an Assistant Secretary of the Interior under Presidents Roosevelt, Truman, and Eisenhower. McCrillis's initial collection of azaleas, rhododendrons, and exotic plants and trees was augmented in 1981 when Brookside Gardens took over the garden and planted hundreds of azaleas to determine which varieties would best survive in the Washington, D.C., region. Currently more than 750 varieties of azaleas grow here, representing choice native species and all the major hybrid groups, including the evergreen Glenn Dales, Kurumes, and Pericats and the deciduous Knap Hills and Ghents. Extensive plantings of hundreds of varieties of Satsuki azaleas from Japan extend the flowering season into June. There are also some fine tree specimens of dawn redwood, Japanese snowbell, stewartia, China fir, and umbrella pine. In spring, dogwoods, rhododendrons, daffodils, and tulips add to the brilliant array of azaleas. This is a single-season garden, although a major goal is to add more plants to extend the time of bloom.

McCRILLIS GARDENS (9 miles northwest of Washington, DC; 41 miles south of Baltimore) 6910 Greentree Road, Bethesda, MD 20817 **TEL:** (301) 365-5728 **OPEN:** Daily 10-dusk **TOTAL ACRES:** 5 **SPECIAL COLLECTIONS:** Shade garden, azaleas, rhododendrons, exotic shrubs and trees   ZONE 7 **H** P PA T

In addition to formal gardens and dramatic spring displays of azaleas and flowering trees, Brookside Gardens offers beauty and tranquility.

WILLIAM PACA GARDEN
ANNAPOLIS

A formal pleasure garden suitable for an aristocrat of the 18th century complements the beautiful Georgian town house designed by William Paca, a signer of
the Declaration of Independence and a Revolutionary War governor. Paca's
gracious house and garden were strongly influenced by his visits to England.
Described as the most elegant garden in Annapolis, his garden was buried
under a hotel and bus terminal until the 1960s, when the preservation organization Historic Annapolis, Inc., and the state of Maryland purchased the house
and property. The intricate reconstruction process ended in 1977.

At the back of the house spreads an open, handsome, and precise garden,
made all the more visible for the lack of mature trees. This formal terraced garden,
enclosed by stone and brick walls, is meticulously outlined in dominant evergreen rectangles and bisected by paths of pebble and brick. High hedges of red
cedar and wax myrtle enclose five elegant terraces designed around horticultural
themes. The terrace closest to the house features a rose parterre of boxwood and
antique roses. Other flower parterres with old-fashioned favorites are centered
around a southern magnolia tree underplanted with English daisies. The second
level holds green "rooms" of boxwood and holly, some in topiary form. Only
trees, shrubs, and flowers known in Paca's lifetime are planted here. The terraces
end in an informal area of wildflowers and native shrubs interspersed with
English garden flourishes such as a striking, white, Chinese Chippendale bridge
arching over a small pond and a two-story pavilion that offers views of the entire
garden. Throughout, potted plants and flower accents change with the season.

WILLIAM PACA GARDEN (30 miles southeast of Baltimore) 186 Prince George Street, Annapolis, MD
21401 TEL: (410) 263-5553 OPEN: Mon.-Sat. 10-4, Sun. 12-4, March through Dec., except Thanksgiving
and Christmas; Fri., Sat., Mon. 10-4, Sun. 12-4, Jan. through Feb. TOTAL ACRES: 2 SPECIAL COLLECTIONS:
Historic design, parterre gardens, topiary, roses   ZONE 7 F G HO T WS

LONDON TOWN PUBLIK HOUSE
EDGEWATER

The Publik House, a popular inn during colonial times in the tobacco and ferry-
crossing port of London Town, eventually served as an almshouse for several
generations. Restoration of this historic landmark began in 1970, and today it is
a museum surrounded by 12 acres of attractive gardens and woodlands along
the banks of the South River. Hilly and winding trails connect naturalistic garden
areas containing rhododendrons, azaleas, camellias, and tree peonies. The Spring
Garden holds more than 20,000 daffodils, primroses, magnolias, and later
perennials. In turn, the Winter Garden displays trees noted for their ornamental
barks, berries, and colorful foliage. At trail's end, a boardwalk wanders through
a salt marsh, offering a view below of knolls planted with native and exotic
species. An additional ten acres have been acquired to extend the garden and
wooded areas.

LONDON TOWN PUBLIK HOUSE (30 miles east of Washington, DC) 839 Londontown Road, Edgewater,
MD 21037 TEL: (410) 222-1919 OPEN: Daily 10-4, March through Nov.; Sat.-Sun. 10-4 Dec. through Feb.
TOTAL ACRES: 22 SPECIAL COLLECTIONS: Spring bulbs, azaleas, peonies, irises
                                        ZONE 7 F H HO P PA T V WS

At the William Paca Garden, terraces lead to this stylish summer ho
a refreshing retreat and viewing pavi

UNITED STATES NATIONAL ARBORETUM
WASHINGTON, D.C.

Established by an act of Congress in 1927 as a research and educational center specializing in trees and shrubs, this U.S. Department of Agriculture facility only really began fulfilling its purpose following World War II. Today this important arboretum spreads its horticultural bounty over 444 acres in the northeast section of Washington, D.C. The facility's first major planting project began in 1946 with a collection of azaleas on Mount Hamilton, the highest point of the park. The arboretum opened to the public soon after, and more than 30 other fascinating and important plant collections and gardens have been added since. The result is a national collection of natural treasures.

The original grouping of 400 azaleas has expanded to an incomparable collection of some 70,000 plants with more than 1,900 cultivars and species. Two main displays are especially notable during the spring season in what is called Azalea Valley. The original Glenn Dale varieties, large-flowered Japanese hybrids, bloom on Mount Hamilton's upper slope while on the lower slope the Ghent and Mollis hybrids thrive. Additional native and exotic species combine each spring to set the arboretum ablaze with a stunning array of reds, pinks, whites, and deep purples. Dogwoods crown this panoply of color with their delicate white petals.

The 2.5-acre Japanese garden and viewing pavilion provide a suitable setting for the 53 bonsai specimens and viewing stones given by the Japanese to mark the United States Bicentennial. Designed by Masao Knoshita, a Japanese-American, the garden begins with a dark, mystic grove of Japanese cedars under-

planted with wildflowers and ferns. A sunny garden follows, leading to a formal walled area where stone and water are balanced against Japanese red maples, flowering cherries, and crape myrtles, following traditional Japanese design.

At the end of the garden path, different pavilions house the National Bonsai and Penjing Museum, the world's only museum devoted to the art and science of bonsai and penjing. Some notable examples in the Japanese pavilion are the great Japanese red pine, a 201-year-old specimen formerly in the collection of the Imperial Japanese household; a 376-year-old Japanese white pine; a 271-year-old Sargent juniper; and a 121-year-old Higo camellia. The more recent Johy Y. Naka Pavilion showcases 56 bonsai grown and pruned in the United States.

Fountains and Corinthian columns saved during the Capitol's restoration form the centerpiece of a classical garden at the National Arboretum.

Brilliant red azaleas are part of the thousands of multicolored azaleas that can be seen in springtime on the hillsides and in the woodlands of the National Arboretum.

An adjoining center holds the penjing collection, displaying the Chinese precursor of the bonsai art form and exhibiting the alternative technique for dwarfing plants with some 30 rare examples. Not only are the plant specimens unusual, ranging in age from 36 to 220 years old, but the dwarf Chinese elm, Chinese paupers tea, small leaf banyan, and others are shown in exceptional antique Chinese porcelains.

Among the arboretum's other important gardens is the dramatic 2.5-acre National Herb Garden, divided into three main parts. A formal knot garden is laid out with dwarf evergreens in an intricate pattern resembling knots in the 16th-century English garden tradition. A historic rose garden holds more than 200 types of old roses, also referred to as heritage or antique roses. The collection also includes later hybrid tea roses such as 'La France', introduced in 1867, along with a selection of hybrid perpetual roses popular in Victorian times. The third section is devoted to herbs used in colonial households and by Native Americans.

William T. Gotelli, a New Jersey building contractor who made a hobby of gathering dwarf conifer specimens while on his worldwide travels, donated his distinctive collection in 1962, and it is now one of the arboretum's most significant collections. The Gotelli Dwarf Conifer Collection includes some 1,500 specimens representing fir, cedar, juniper, spruce, yew, hemlock, and others that grow at abnormal rates for their species. These popular conifers are displayed on a five-acre hillside allowing them to be seen from all sides, the better to display their form, color, texture, and branching patterns.

Another important area, the New American Garden, reflects recent advances in awareness of native plants and developments in garden design. Lavish use of grasses and plants in massive drifts are reminiscent of prairie landscapes, and are carefully selected for color, year-round interest, and ease of maintenance. Wolfgang Ohme and James von Sweden, well-known exponents of the natural garden movement, designed this garden using ordinary as well as unusual grasses in surprising and random juxtaposition with other native plants and traditional garden flowers. Naturalized perennials from asters to yuccas add seasonal color.

In the southeast quadrant of the arboretum, Fern Valley offers a magical natural woodland area planted with ferns, wildflowers, and native shrubs and trees. The half-mile trail through the valley features plants that grow in microclimates designated as northern forest, Piedmont, southern lowlands, southern mountains, prairie, and meadow. Perennials thrive in the arboretum's northeast corner, including a comprehensive display of daylilies and select peonies. Here, too, bloom more than 160 award-winning bearded irises along with Siberian irises in a wide variety of colors.

Although the National Arboretum tends toward naturalistic plantings and quiet areas for strolling, one area aims for a striking effect: the National Capitol Columns display located near the main ellipse meadow. A sculpture garden on

In April, crabapples and spring bulbs display their delicate colors along Hickey Hill Road, in the arboretum's southeast corner.

a truly grand scale, this landmark contains 22 of the 30-foot-high Corinthian columns designed by Benjamin Latrobe for the Capitol building. Removed from their original site in the late 1950s, the columns were re-erected here in an acropolis-like setting. Additional elements include a reflecting pool, water stair, and fountain, all according to a design by noted landscape architect Russell Page, created shortly before his death in 1985.

The National Arboretum is a rewarding place to visit throughout the year, offering indoor collections and evergreens in winter, followed in spring by the blooms of camellias and the explosion of azaleas, rhododendrons, dogwoods, magnolias, and crabapples, as well as many formal garden areas of annuals and perennials. Recognized as an important research center, the arboretum also possesses one of the best international herbariums, with a broad representation of over a half million dried specimens of plants cultivated around the world.

UNITED STATES NATIONAL ARBORETUM (2.3 miles northeast of the U.S. Capitol) 3501 New York Avenue, N.E., Washington, DC 20002 **TEL:** (202) 245-2726 **OPEN:** Mon.-Fri. 8-5, Sat.-Sun. 10-5, except Christmas **TOTAL ACRES:** 444 **SPECIAL COLLECTIONS:** Bonsai and penjing, azaleas, herbs, roses, daylilies, aquatic plants, ornamental grasses, dwarf conifers, hollies, exotic and native shrubs and trees

ZONE 7 A C G **H** L P PA T V WS

On a hillside site of about five acres, the Gotelli Dwarf Conifer Collection, one of the finest in the world, presents a fascinating selection of shapes and textures.

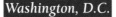
DUMBARTON OAKS
WASHINGTON, D.C.

In 1920, when diplomat Robert Woods Bliss and his wife, Mildred Barnes Bliss, returned to Washington, D.C., from war-ravaged Europe, they eagerly sought a restful country retreat. Their efforts resulted in a garden distinguished by its combination of exuberant architectural details and exquisitely restrained plantings. The Blisses found a suitable property in Georgetown, a large farm on 54 hilly acres above Rock Creek, originally called Rock of Dumbarton and later named The Oaks. They combined these names into Dumbarton Oaks, hired an architect to restore the 1801 federal-style brick mansion, and turned their attention to the grounds. In landscape designer Beatrix Farrand, Mildred Bliss found someone who shared both her admiration of European gardens and her vision of private landscaped grounds as a place for both comfortable entertaining and simple, everyday pleasures. The professional relationship and friendship of these two women would last for 40 years.

Farrand's first challenge was the sloping area to the east and north of the mansion, where she would create a series of terraces and theme gardens. Before a shovelful of earth was turned, however, Farrand carefully studied the lay of the land, in her words "listening to the light and wind and grade." She then drafted numerous sketches and engineering drawings to show her clients alternative ways to achieve the terracing. The final design choice was felicitous; today, these terraces and associated gardens seem like natural expressions of nature itself.

There are many planted areas to experience. In spring the intimate Star Garden, immediately to the east of the mansion, presents a beautiful display of white azaleas—alba Indicas, an unusual plant grown in Japan for centuries. For contrast, the nearby Green Garden provides a large, formal outdoor entertainment space behind the glass-roofed orangery. Attached to the east side of the mansion, its design comes from a North European forerunner of the conservatory and greenhouse. A dramatic, huge black oak overhangs the lawn, one of the original trees planted here in the 18th century. The muted colors, fitting to the combination of grass, trees, and ivy, is typical of Farrand, who favored a discreet and subtly modulated palette. The only other touches of color come from purple wisteria, white azalea, and wood hyacinth. Here and there are handsome marble tables and seats, potted lemon trees, and garlanded trophies formed by British stone carver Frederick Coles.

The balustrade along the front of the Green Garden overlooks a swimming pool and the Pebble Garden. Stone steps descend and divide, curving around a marvelous stone basin festooned with reliefs of bulrushes and sculptured foliage. The adjacent Pebble Garden's intricate mosaic of small stones depict a sheaf of wheat, part of the Bliss family coat of arms, and best appreciated from above. The mosaic, executed by Vincent de Bennedetto, is part of a central fountain that spills onto the stones, revealing their vivid, varying tones. A curving path leads to the Beech Terrace, named for an enormous American beech tree. To the east, steps lead to Urn Terrace, one of the estate's many garden jewels. Around the central accent—a carved stone urn, copied from the 18th-century French terra cotta original now displayed indoors—swirl pebble mosaics and beds of English ivy.

The east steps lead to the formal Rose Garden, a favorite of both Farrand and Bliss. The garden, geometric in design, was planned and executed in the naturalistic manner of 17th- and 18th-century English gardens. Plantings are both straightforward and dramatic, with the sober faces of specimen English and

April, vaulted ceilings of pink cherry blossoms along Prunus Walk offer a prelude he naturalistic areas and formal "garden rooms" at Dumbarton Oaks.

Cascades of forsythia and flowering cherry trees herald the beginning of spring in this garden, resplendent in all seasons.

American boxwoods providing complementary backgrounds to roses in summer and stand-alone grace notes in winter. This planting plan has been much simplified from Farrand's original design, except for the west bed, where roses, wisteria, clematis, and winter jasmine climb up the west wall.

Still to the east, the broad flight of steps leads to the final two terraces. The first, Fountain Terrace, is an Italianate presentation of twin fountains set in a smooth lawn. Unlike Farrand's other tableaux, flowers here are a substantial and central design element, with beds aglow with tulips in the spring, and in summer a riot of snapdragons, summer foxgloves, pinks, dahlias, and an unusual border of night-scented nicotiana. In fall, chrysanthemums take their turn. A retaining wall of quiet creepers is a background to this brilliant display. To the north, a charming wrought-iron gate leads to the last of the terrace areas, Arbor Terrace. Farrand's original design called for herb plantings within an intimate "secret garden"—today white azaleas and multicolor oleander abound with a place of rest provided by a cedar arbor

At Dumbarton Oaks, a tool shed with a Portuguese tile roof overlooks the cutting garden. Abundant sprays of flowers bloom here in summer and autumn.

with seats and a handsome wall fountain. Returning to Fountain Terrace, the east steps lead to Melisande's Allée, a meadowlike area that in season blooms in colorful delight. Stately silver maples surround the lawn area. At the allée's south end beckons the quietly spectacular Lover's Lane Pool and its associated amphitheater, a stage-like area with three-tiered seating opposite. A stately maple, classic stone columns, and a bordering grove of bamboo enhance the serenity.

The classical Terrior column and other decorative stone sculptures and plants hold the color of winter when it snows.

Dumbarton Oaks's synthesis of simple, approachable, and individual garden components within a lavish, complex, and inventive design is a tribute to its designer. As Beatrix Farrand's greatest work, it will offer enduring lessons to gardeners for generations to come.

DUMBARTON OAKS 1703 32nd Street, N.W., Washington, DC 20007 **TEL:** (202) 339-6401 **OPEN:** Daily 2-6, April through Oct.; daily 2-5 Nov. through March; except holidays **TOTAL ACRES:** 16 **SPECIAL COLLEC- TIONS:** Estate garden, terrace gardens, pebble garden, orangery   **ZONE 7** **F** **G** **H** **HO** **L** **T** **WS**

In fall, chrysanthemums adorn the seasonal borders of the Fountain Terrace. Mature trees with their autumnal foliage frame the formal walled garden.

The Japanese-style garden at Hillwood features a waterfall cascading down a hill into quiet pools decorated with the traditional arched bridge, shrubs, stones, and snow lantern.

HILLWOOD MUSEUM AND GARDENS
WASHINGTON, D.C.

Marjorie Meriwether Post, one of the wealthiest women in the world, lived at Hillwood until her death in 1973. Today her grand mansion is an outstanding museum of art and antique treasures set within 25 acres of woodlands and land-scaped gardens. Post considered her 12-acre garden overlooking Rock Creek Park an extension of her residence's luxurious interior, and the various pleasure gardens reflect her international interests. Outside the mansion's French drawing room is a French parterre garden decorated with 18th-century statues and fountains. A small, formal rose garden leads to an English-style Friendship Walk where in spring mounds of azaleas bloom in shades of red, pink, white, and lavender, all accented by magnolias and dogwoods. The Japanese-style garden offers interesting ornaments and a waterfall cascading into tranquil pools. Post favored rare and beautiful orchids and collected more than 2,000 plants. A newly restored green-house displays orchids from her collection, as well as new acquisitions.

HILLWOOD MUSEUM AND GARDENS 4155 Linnean Avenue, N.W., Washington, D.C. 20008 **TEL:** (202) 686-8500 **OPEN:** Tues.-Sat. 9-5, March through Jan. *By reservation only*; Renovations scheduled, call ahead **TOTAL ACRES:** 25 **SPECIAL COLLECTIONS:** Estate garden, French and English gardens, Japanese garden, orchids, azaleas

ZONE 7 C **F** G **P** R **T** V **WS**

KENILWORTH AQUATIC GARDENS
WASHINGTON, D.C.

A mosaic of hardy and tropical waterlilies, lotuses, and native flora float on this 12-acre island, the only national park devoted exclusively to aquatic plants. Across from the National Arboretum, Kenilworth is bordered by 44 acres of tidal marsh on the east bank of the Anacostia River. This unusual garden began as the hobby of Walter B. Shaw, a Civil War veteran. Along with his daughter, he expanded it into the largest commercial nursery of aquatic plants in the country. In the 1920s, thousands visited this fascinating collection of aquatic exotics: lotuses from the Orient, blue lilies of the Nile, and South American specimens such as the dramatic six-foot platters of *Victoria amazonica*. The Department of the Interior rescued the gardens from destruction and in 1938 they reopened as part of the National Park Service.

Hardy lilies with their smooth-edged pads bloom in June and July while the more tender tropical lilies are stored in greenhouses until May, then planted in their containers in the ponds. Large and sometimes fragrant, they are distinguished by their rippled edges and bloom in July and August. In summer come the lotus blossoms, including the pink-tinged East Indian variety believed to be from the oldest viable seeds ever found. In addition, many native bog plants and marsh wildlife thrive among the lily ponds.

KENILWORTH AQUATIC GARDENS Anacostia Avenue and Douglas Street, N.E., Washington, DC 20020 TEL: (202) 426-6905 OPEN: Daily 7-4 TOTAL ACRES: 12 SPECIAL COLLECTIONS: Waterlilies, native bog plants

ZONE 7 A G **H** P T **V** WS

TUDOR PLACE
WASHINGTON, D.C.

Martha Parke Custis Peter purchased the land for Tudor Place with an inheritance from her grandparents, Martha and George Washington. Since 1805, six generations of the Peter family have lived in this lovely federal estate, high on a hill overlooking the Potomac River. Opened to the public in 1988, it is today a National Historic Landmark. The garden still retains a gracious layout of sweeping lawns, parterres, and woodlands within 5.5 acres. The south lawn is decorated with specimen trees, some dating from the 19th century, and in spring flowers with dogwood, redbud, and plum trees along with beds of daffodils. Late spring and summer sees the more formal north garden filled with color from old-fashioned perennials and rose bushes arranged within an intricate flower knot of English boxwood hedges. Old garden roses include damasks, moss roses, and some beds of the ever-blooming China rose 'Old Blush', possibly planted by Martha Peter herself. The entrance's remarkably dense circle of boxwood is nearly two centuries old. Also of interest is the former bowling green, now a green-and-white garden with a lily pond. Conifers, southern magnolias, hollies, and old flowering shrubs surround Tudor Place, offering a setting of southern tranquility in the nation's capital.

TUDOR PLACE 1644 31st Street, N.W., Washington, DC 20007 TEL: (202) 965-0400 OPEN: Mon.-Sat. 10-4, Sun. 12-4, April through May and Sept. through Oct.; Mon.-Sat. 10-4, other months TOTAL ACRES: 5.5 SPECIAL COLLECTIONS: Historic garden, parterres, boxwood, old-fashioned flowers, roses

ZONE 7 **F** G HO PA **T**

UNITED STATES BOTANIC GARDEN
WASHINGTON, D.C.

Among the institutional grandeur of Washington's mall sits one of the oldest botanic gardens in America, the United States Botanic Garden. Chartered in 1820 at the behest of George Washington, the garden had to wait until 1925 for funds to be appropriated for the present facilities. The handsome conservatory houses a permanent display of tropical, subtropical, and desert plants under 29,000 square feet of glass. Major collections include palms, bromeliads, cactuses, ferns, and a sizable collection of orchids.

Four spectacular flower and plant shows are organized every year: an Easter show featuring masses of spring bulbs; an outdoor summer terrace display highlighted by hundreds of flowering and foliage plants in hanging baskets; a fall show of chrysanthemums; and a poinsettia show during the Christmas holidays. Across Independence Avenue, the Botanic Garden Park features a notable collection of diverse summer-blooming annuals and perennials centered around the Bartholdi Fountain, designed by the sculptor of the Statue of Liberty. Each garden demonstrates plants and design principles suitable for the urban or suburban dweller.

The conservatory has been in continuous operation since its construction in 1933. In 1997 it closed for an estimated three years to undergo extensive renovations and construction of the new National Garden on three adjacent acres. Plans include an environmental learning center, a rose garden, and a water garden dedicated to the First Ladies of the United States.

■ UNITED STATES BOTANIC GARDEN First Street and Maryland Avenue, S.W., Washington, DC 20024 TEL: (202) 225-8333 OPEN: Daily 9-5 TOTAL ACRES: 5.25 SPECIAL COLLECTIONS: Flowering trees, dwarf conifers, holly, herbs, grasses, bonsai ZONE 7 C G H PA R T WS

FRANCISCAN MONASTERY GARDENS
WASHINGTON, D.C.

A surprising sanctuary of religious shrines and lush gardens amid the bustling political capital of the United States, the Franciscan Monastery contains replicas of the major shrines and chapels in the Holy Lands set within luxuriant floral surroundings. Stepping beyond its massive portals feels like crossing the threshold into early Christianity. The imposing main church with its Rosary Portico and cloister opened in 1899 while the gardens debuted in 1920. Here impressive rose parterres of more than a thousand plants face an array of evergreens repeating the shape of the columns and rounded arches of the cloister. In another small garden, white birches form a centerpiece for bedded annuals and clipped hedges.

Down the hill and into the woods, the lower gardens offer larger landscaped areas with seasonal flowers massed near entrances to shrines, grottoes, and around stations of the cross. Throughout the 15 acres open to the public, thousands of daffodils and tulips bloom in spring, followed by azaleas, rhododendrons, and a great variety of lilies, perennials, and annuals. Dogwoods, Japanese maples, magnolias, and weeping willows also decorate this spiritual retreat.

■ FRANCISCAN MONASTERY GARDENS 1400 Quincy Street, N.E., Washington, DC 20017 TEL: (202) 526-6800 OPEN: Daily 9-5, Sun. 10-5 TOTAL ACRES: 15 SPECIAL COLLECTIONS: Spring bulbs, roses, azaleas, rhododendrons, lilies, shrines ZONE 7 G H P T V

Bishop's Garden, Washington National Cathedral
Washington, D.C.

Below the towering spires and flying buttresses of Washington National Cathedral lies the serene Bishop's Garden, where plants common in monasteries of the 14th century grow alongside plants relevant to American history. The cathedral close, designed by the firm of Olmsted Brothers, was completed in 1928. For the next eight years Mrs. Florence Bratenahl, wife of the first dean of the cathedral, served as the cathedral's landscape designer and contributed to the design and the planting schemes of the gardens. Stately atlas cedars from Jerusalem flank the garden's Norman Court entrance. Stone walls enclose garden areas with such themes as herbs from Charlemagne's plant list and boxwood from the gardens of Presidents Washington, Jefferson, and Madison. Fragrant roses, annuals, and perennial borders are edged with curbstones from the streets of historic Alexandria, Virginia. Throughout, sculptures and stone artifacts from medieval and contemporary times embellish this garden for the ages.

Bishop's Garden, Washington National Cathedral Massachusetts and Wisconsin Avenues, N.W., Washington, DC 20016 **Tel:** (202) 537-2937 **Open:** Always open **Total acres:** 3 **Special collections:** Medieval gardens, historic plants, herbs, roses   **ZONE 7** **G** **T** **WS**

A 15th-century stone bas relief depicting saints and martyrs is framed by white peonies in the upper perennial border at the Bishop's Garden.

At Middleton Place in South Carolina, the spreading limbs of live oaks offer a backdrop of antiquity to this antebellum plantation garden.

Virginia

Mount Vernon Estate and Gardens
MOUNT VERNON

"My agricultural pursuits and rural amusements…have been the most pleasant occupation of my life, and the most congenial to my temper," George Washington once confessed to a friend. Throughout a lifetime of wars, revolutions, and political turmoil, the "rural amusements" of the nation's first President were played out at Mount Vernon, his handsome Virginia plantation overlooking the Potomac and the distant Maryland shore. With a surveyor's eye, a mathematician's sense of proportion and space, and a farmer's familiarity with the land, he carried out an ambitious landscaping plan despite months and even years of absence. He often resorted to directing the work by letter.

Today, thanks to extensive archaeological research and the tireless work of the Mount Vernon Ladies Association, who own and maintain this historic national treasure, Mount Vernon's gardens can be seen much as they were in their creator's time. In a sense, to walk around the grounds is to experience the man himself, for while Washington's gardens and pleasure grounds are formal, disciplined, and impressive, they somehow remain humble in spirit.

Mount Vernon's property, part of a larger parcel farmed by a succession of ancestral Washingtons since 1674, came into George Washington's possession in 1754 following the death of his older half-brother. At the time the tidewater plantation consisted of a somewhat smaller and more modest main house

Old-fashioned flowers, such as these foxgloves, remind visitors that this is a garden steeped in history as well as beauty. Washington nurtured plants from all over the world here.

and associated grounds, situated on a rise 250 feet above the Potomac River and surrounded by some 2,000 acres of fields and woodlands (the land holdings eventually grew to five contiguous farms and 8,000 acres). Washington's responsibilities as a professional soldier kept him from taking up residence immediately, but five years later, following the enlargement of the main house and Washington's marriage to Martha Custis, he resigned his colonel's commission and moved his new family to Mount Vernon. At the time he told a friend that he anticipated "more happiness in retirement than I ever experienced amidst a wide and bustling World." By all accounts, his early years at the plantation fulfilled those hopes.

Although Washington was a progressive farmer, intent on raising large-scale field crops, and aided by a workforce of some 200 employees and slaves, Mount Vernon's landscaping was of abiding concern. "I do not hesitate to confess," he wrote his manager, "that reclaiming, and laying the grounds down handsomely to grass, and in woods thinned or in clumps…is among my first objects and

Double arched walkways flank the front of the house. These provide a point of order and symmetry that contrasts with the rolling hills and wooded areas sloping down to the Potomac River.

wishes." Washington envisioned a scheme to satisfy his old-fashioned love of order and symmetry, while incorporating some "modern" details. For examples of the former he had only to recall many fine old-colony plantations—Belvoir, Gunston Hall, Williamsburg. From these traditional models he took Mount Vernon's balanced and formal design, adding a large bowling green before the west front with acre-sized geometric gardens on each side. For new ideas he sent off to England for a number of gardening books, including Batty Langley's *New Principles of Gardening,* the most influential voice of the new English Romantic school. From Langley he apparently borrowed serpentine walks, groves or trees planted in "natural seeming groups and thickly," wilderness areas, and the "ha-ha," a continuous walled moat separating the landscaped areas and lawns from working fields, making it possible to enjoy unbroken vistas without straying livestock.

Except for a few early tree plantings, actual work on the estate grounds was delayed until 1785, when Washington resigned his Revolutionary War general's commission and retired to private life for the second time. He rode almost daily through his woodlands, selecting promising young trees and shrubs, tagging poplars, locusts, sassafras, dogwoods, maples, flowering crabapples, and hundreds of other specimens for transplantation to their appointed locations. Writing friends and acquaintances for novel plant materials, he asked one for "scions of Aspin [sic] tree," another for horse chestnuts, and a third for choice linden trees. He recruited a nephew to bring back mahogany seeds from the West Indies, and another relative to send seeds of South Carolina's greater magnolia. And he put men to work sculpturing the earth, on one occasion creating a pair

of mounds at the foot of the bowling green to serve as pedestals for a newly introduced species of Chinese weeping willow, which had come to him by way of Madeira. He saw to every detail of their planting, from pruning and staking to positioning them according to their potential for mature height and width. Some of these arboreal works survive to this day, including two paired tulip poplars along the winding walks on either side of the green, and some original pines, transported in three wagonloads from the nearby Dogue Farm for transplanting in the so-called wilderness.

The lower garden, begun perhaps as early as 1760, was the first of the formal gardens to be planned and put to use. Walled with brick and located on south-sloping land, its exposure naturally lent itself to producing early ripening fruits and fast-maturing vegetables. The beds were divided into large squares on two terraced levels, with additional cold frames on the lower terrace, espaliered fruit trees against the south-facing brick, and a small seed house and necessary (outhouse) for storage of plant materials and tools. Originally rectangular in shape, it was extended to a curving shield shape in 1785. Today's garden, recreated in the 1930s, follows these basic guidelines. Mount Vernon's gardener-interpreters are not always able to grow authentic 18th-century varieties of all that is discussed in Washington's diaries and correspondence, but they do consistently follow old-time cultivation practices. One example is a pair of dipping cisterns, one on each level of the kitchen garden, which expose well water to the sun, the better to soften it. The notion at the time was that soft water made plants more vigorous.

Washington laid out the upper garden to the north of the house in a mirror image of the kitchen garden. Although kitchen crops may have predominated in the earliest years, the area was and continues to be chiefly planted in annual and perennial flowers. As no detailed records survive of Washington's favored flowering species, Mount Vernon's restorers have used plant lists from comparable Virginia gardens and the notes of some of Washington's visitors to re-create the gardens on view today. The resulting neat, brick-edged beds are "laid out in squares and boxed with great precision," as one guest recalled. Filled with more than a hundred colonial favorites, including blue flax, bouncing bet, cornflowers, fritillaria, heliotrope, larkspur, love-lies-bleeding, snow-in-summer, sweet alyssum, and verbena, in several instances the beds are centered by a fruit tree, another of Langley's recommendations. To divide the enclosures Washington planted walls of boxwood, evidently using specimens provided by his old friend Light-Horse Harry Lee of Stratford Hall.

Adjoining the upper garden, Washington built a greenhouse; though the original burned in 1835, it has been carefully reproduced. Featuring seven tall, south-facing windows to indulge his interest in raising plants alien to Virginia's climate, it was ready in 1786 when he wrote Mrs. Margaret Carroll, whose Maryland hothouse he had earlier admired, asking for suitable cuttings. She responded with five boxes and twenty small pots of plants. Like the original, today's greenhouse contains tubs of citrus, sponge tree, oleander, jasmine, aloe, and palmetto during the winter months; they are moved outside in warm weather.

MOUNT VERNON ESTATE AND GARDENS (20 miles south of Washington, DC) South end of George Washington Memorial Parkway, Mount Vernon, VA 22121 **TEL:** (703) 780-2000 **OPEN:** Daily 8-5, April through Aug.; daily 9-5 March through Sept.; daily 9-4, Nov. through Feb. **TOTAL ACRES:** 6 **SPECIAL COLLECTIONS:** Garden design and plants representing George Washington's layout

ZONE 7 A C F G HO P R T V WS

...nies, foxgloves, and irises were beloved flowers in Washington's day, as evidenced by ...ers written by visitors to Mount Vernon during the late 18th century.

River Farms
Alexandria

Now the home of the American Horticultural Society, River Farms was once owned by George Washington, who purchased the original 1,800 acres in 1760. Although he never lived here, Washington spent a great deal of time riding over the property and used it for planting rye, wheat, and corn. Known by various names under different owners, 50 acres of the original land tract were purchased by the American Horticultural Society in 1973 and renamed River Farm. The house, restored and refurnished, now serves as offices for the society. Determined to make River Farms "a home for American horticulture," the society designed the landscape to include different gardens used to display and test the horticultural value of various plants. Many areas are sponsored by national plant organizations, including societies specializing in ivy, marigolds, cactuses and succulents, dahlias, irises, daylilies, lilies, and chrysanthemums. In addition, the grounds include a wildflower meadow, woodland walk, rose garden, water garden, and dwarf fruit tree orchard. It is fitting that this land first owned by George Washington, himself an avid horticulturist, is now home to an organization dedicated to spreading knowledge and enthusiasm of gardening throughout the country.

River Farms (20 miles south of Washington, DC) American Horticultural Society 7931 E. Boulevard Drive, Alexandria, VA 22308 **Tel:** (703) 768-5700 **Open:** Mon-Fri. 8:30-5, except holidays **Total acres:** 50 **Special collections:** Display gardens representing many flower societies, major All-American Rose Selection display   **ZONE 7** G H HO P T V WS

Gunston Hall
Lorton

Gunston Hall was the home of George Mason, author of the Virginia Declaration of Rights and framer of the United States Constitution. Mason began building his house in 1755 on the 5,000-acre plantation he inherited from his father. Sited on a bluff, the house provided a good view of the Potomac River. Today, the house and 550 of the original acres have been designated a national historic landmark administered by the National Society of the Colonial Dames of America.

The formal gardens were restored by the Garden Club of Virginia in 1950 under the direction of Alden Hopkins, landscape architect for Colonial Williamsburg. These served as a place for quiet reflection for George Mason, where, his son John wrote, he would often "walk for a considerable time wrapped in meditation...." One of the landscape's most interesting features, the 200-foot-long boxwood allée, is thought to have been planted by Mason two-and-a-half centuries ago. Boxwood also outlines the four formal parterres, two with central topiaries and two carpeted by grass and featuring rectangular flower beds.

Gunston Hall is currently undergoing extensive renovation based on archeological and archival research, to make the grounds as historically accurate as possible. While the lower gardens will continue to be maintained as an example of Colonial Revival gardens, the upper garden is being reinterpreted as a landscape even more precisely authentic to the times and lifestyle of George Mason.

Gunston Hall (20 miles south of Washington, DC) Va. 242, Lorton, VA 22079 **Tel:** (703) 550-9220 **Open:** Daily 9:30-5, except Christmas **Total acres:** 550 **Special collections:** Historic design, boxwood hedges, flower parterres   **ZONE 7** F G HO P T V WS

OATLANDS PLANTATION
LEESBURG

The gardens at Oatlands today reflect the tastes of three different people living in three different times. The plantation was first built around 1800 by George Carter, great-grandson of Robert "King" Carter, who at one time was reputed to own a third of Virginia. Carter cut terraces into the steep hillside leading down from the house, bringing closer the sweeping vistas of wide open fields and the far-off Blue Ridge. The terracing also provided a flat and protected area in which to grow fruits, flowers, and vegetables. In 1810 he built what is now one of the oldest greenhouses on the East Coast. When purchased by Mr. and Mrs. William C. Eustis a century later, the gardens were in a state of ruin. The Eustises restored much of the ground's original beauty, replanting many of the boxwood hedges; creating parterres; and adding a bowling green, a rose garden, and a reflecting pool. However, when the National Trust for Historic Preservation received the property in 1982, the gardens were once again in disrepair. Alfredo Siani, a former airline executive with a love of gardening, was hired to restore, re-create, and renew their grandeur. When he first took the job, Siani reported crawling on his hands and knees to get through some of the garden paths, but his undaunted efforts in both gardening and research are paying off, and the garden is slowly reviving.

OATLANDS PLANTATION (35 miles northwest of Washington DC) 200850 Oatlands Plantation Lane (US 15), Leesburg, VA 20175 **TEL:** (703) 777-3174 **OPEN:** Mon.-Sat. 10-4:30, Sun. 1-4:30, April to mid-Dec., except Thanksgiving **TOTAL ACRES:** Gardens 4.5, estate 260 **SPECIAL COLLECTIONS:** Herbaceous borders, peonies, boxwood parterres, roses, specimen trees   **ZONE 7** **F** G **H** HO P PA T WS

Shrubs and garlands of roses pay tribute to the original grandeur of Oatlands' gardens, begun in the early 19th century.

Monticello
Charlottesville

In 1809, approaching the end of his second term as President of the United States, Thomas Jefferson wrote, "I begin already to be much occupied in preparation for my departure to those scenes of rural retirement after which my soul is panting." His destination: his beloved Monticello. Here he developed and perfected his many contributions to American gardening, of which he felt, "No occupation is so delightful to me as the culture of the earth, and no culture comparable to that of the garden...though an old man, I am but a young gardener." After Jefferson's death on July 4, 1826, much of his landscape and gardening work fell into ruin and eventually disappeared. In 1939 the Garden Club of Virginia began a restoration with scholarly research, patient archaeological studies, and hard work. In 1987 the Thomas Jefferson Center for Historic Plants opened here, devoted to the collection, preservation, and distribution of Early American plant varieties.

Jefferson began building Monticello—Italian for "little mountain"—in 1768, when he was just 25 years old. Situated on part of his father's estate in the Blue Ridge mountains, Jefferson's property grew to 5,000 acres. He developed it largely

as a self-sufficient plantation, moving from tobacco to wheat as the principal crop, while engaging in lifelong cultivation experiments with such crops as corn, potatoes, and fruits.

With the foresight of a landscape designer, Jefferson planted many shade and flowering trees around Monticello, his notes revealing a clear sense of how they would relate to the house when they matured. Already an accomplished gardener, Jefferson wrote his own garden book, a collection of gardening wisdom

Jefferson's landscape design included not only flower beds but also an "ornamental forest," where trees were pruned to give the appearance of an open woodland.

begun at age 23 and added to for the next 57 years. Eventually published in 1944, it reveals the eclectic range of his gardening pursuits: Arikara bean and Mandan corn, gifts of Lewis and Clark; 36 varieties of European grapes in his vineyards, many collected by Jefferson himself; rice from the South Seas, a gift of Capt. William Bligh; and such flowering trees as the mimosa and golden-rain, both introduced from China.

Although there is no formal record of Jefferson's gardening accomplishments at Monticello before his retirement—an event-filled time—he did travel widely to see the great gardens of the Continent during his years as ambassador to France, from 1784 to 1789. Accompanied by his old friend and ambassador to England, John Adams, he also visited many English gardens, commenting, "The gardening in that country is the article in which it surpasses all the earth." He regularly sent plant specimens home to friends, in return soliciting American varieties for introduction to European gardens. This exchange was a matter of profound importance to him: "The greatest service which can be rendered any country is to add a useful plant to its culture…one service of this kind rendered to a nation is worth more than all the victories of all the most splendid pages of their history, and becomes a source of exalted pleasure to those who have been instrumental in it."

As his years of public service came to an end, Jefferson gave serious attention to Monticello's grounds and gardens. The trees he planted as a young man were now tall enough to provide shade from the summer sun. In the English manner, he trimmed their lower branches to create open groves with parklike vistas, underplanting them with such shrubs as pyrocanthus, evergreen privet, and kalmia. Jefferson had his own favorites among the trees, some for their rarity—the then recently introduced copper beech, ginkgo, and mimosa—and others for their uniquely handsome presence. Of the trees planted in his lifetime, at least five are still alive: two tulip poplars, a sugar maple, a European larch, and a red cedar.

The famous portico of Monticello faces the Roundabout, designed by Jefferson as an informal winding walkway with ribbon borders of flowers outlining a great expanse of lawn. Oval flower beds add color alongside the walk, today planted to reflect his original choices: showy bulbs in April, followed by biennials and peren-

nials in May. From summer to fall bloom such annuals as zinnias and heliotrope. One bed holds *Jeffersonia diphylla,* or twinleaf, a spring woodland flower named in his honor by botanist Benjamin Barton.

Also re-created, the vegetable terrace is a laboratory and kitchen garden where Jefferson experimented with 250 varieties of more than 70 different species of vegetables. A garden pavilion set in the middle of this plateau served as his retreat, where he could overlook his trial bed of diverse crops. Remembering Jefferson's role

The winding flower walk on Monticello's west lawn blooms with larkspur, sweet William, and other late-spring flowers. A European larch dating from Jefferson's era is in the background.

as an inventor, it is easy to understand his intense interest in strange and exotic plants and in developing improvements in agricultural methods.

Today 40 acres are cultivated at Monticello with the flowers, fruits, and vegetables loved and planted by Jefferson. A few wild varieties are included, along with some modern cultivars resembling earlier varieties. This is true to the spirit of Jefferson, whose curiosity and passion for the works of nature is best expressed by his own confession, "There is not a sprig of grass that shoots uninteresting to me."

Monticello Thomas Jefferson Memorial Foundation (122 miles southwest of Washington, DC) P.O. Va. 53, Charlottesville, VA 22902 **Tel:** (804) 984-9822 **Open:** Daily 9-4:30 Nov. through Feb.; 8-5 March through Oct., except Christmas **Total acres:** 40 **Special collections:** Historic plant collections of flowers, fruits, and vegetables ZONE 7 C F G H HO P PA R T V WS

AGECROFT HALL
RICHMOND

Agecroft Hall was originally built more than 500 years ago in the Irwell River Valley in England. Through the years, the house fell into disrepair and, in 1925, was purchased by Thomas Williams, a wealthy American financier. Williams had the building shipped to Virginia and rebuilt, not as it had been in England, but as a charming and comfortable early 20th-century house. Situated on 23 acres overlooking the James River, the house did not lose its past, however, and opened to the public in 1969 as a museum to interpret life in an English manor house during the 16th and 17th centuries. The gardens were originally designed by Charles Gillette to include typical British landscape design elements such as brick walls, stone walkways, and boxwood hedges. The sunken garden immediately behind the house was patterned after the Pond Garden at Hampton Court Palace in England. A brick wall surrounds the garden, echoed by a perimeter planting border filled with softly colored flowers. Within a frame of English ivy and gravel paths gleams a central pool. Crape myrtle trees, planted in a long allée parallel to the sunken garden, offer brilliant pink blooms in summer. The Tradescant Garden honors the early plant explorer, John Tradescant, who is credited with introducing many native Virginia plants into the horticultural trade, including spiderwort, widow's tears, passionflower, and cardinal flower.

AGECROFT HALL (115 miles south of Washington, DC) 4305 Sulgrave Road, Richmond, VA 23221 **TEL:** (804) 353-4241 **OPEN:** Tues.-Sat. 10-4, Sun. 12:30-4, except holidays **TOTAL ACRES:** Gardens 2, grounds 23 **SPECIAL COLLECTIONS:** Elizabethan herb garden, formal flower gardens **ZONE 7 F G H HO P WS**

MAYMONT
RICHMOND

In 1886, Maj. and Mrs. James Dooley purchased a hundred-acre farm along the banks of the James River. Their estate, Maymont, was to become a showplace for the entire region in an age when landscaping on a majestic scale was considered an essential part of a grand American home. Although the mansion was finished in 1893, it took 30 years to complete the gardens. The Dooleys traveled the world, gathering ideas and inspiration. The result is obvious at Maymont, which features an Italian garden, a Japanese garden, a European grotto garden, and an arboretum. Although many of the trees and shrubs planted by the Dooleys nearly a century ago have matured and grown, the gardens still look very much the same as during their tenure. High bluffs, interesting rock formations, streams, and deep ravines provide a vibrant natural backdrop for the many formally planted areas. The Italian Garden, completed in 1910, includes terraces, parterres, clipped evergreens, fountains, statuary, and a Renaissance-style pergola. In the Japanese garden, a 45-foot waterfall creates a dramatic backdrop for carefully clipped trees and shrubs, pools, raked sand beds, and interesting stones. The arboretum still holds many trees the Dooleys planted a century ago, including golden larch, Persian ironwood, and white enkianthus.

MAYMONT (115 miles south of Washington, DC) 1700 Hampton Street, Richmond, VA 23220 **TEL:** (804) 358-7166 **OPEN:** Daily 10-5, Nov. through March; daily 10-7, April through Oct. **TOTAL ACRES:** 100 **SPECIAL COLLECTIONS:** Daylilies, herbs, rhododendron, Japanese stroll garden, English courtyard garden, Italian-style garden **ZONE 7 G H HO P T WS**

Tulip-lined walls and long brick walkways contribute to the air of formality that characterizes this Virginia House garden. The Waddells collected statuary and other garden art during their many trips abroad.

VIRGINIA HOUSE
RICHMOND

In 1917, international diplomat Alexander Waddell and his wife, Virginia, began creating an estate along the banks of the James River. Considered a part of the American country place movement, the buildings and grounds of Virginia House, as the Waddell's home was called, were not completed until 1940.

The grounds include pools, canals, and statuary. The landscape was designed by Charles Gillette, an interpreter of distinctively southern gardens. Although Gillette included both English and Mediterranean design elements at Virginia House, the gardens are definitely southern in style, featuring such regional favorites as southern magnolias and dogwoods. The most formally planted areas are found close to the house, where terraced gardens are filled with bedding plants. Beyond this lie open fields and mature woodlands which, with a good view of the James River, help create a magnificent vista. In spring, the garden offers displays of tulips, English wallflower, forget-me-nots, and pansies planted against a backdrop of dogwood and redbud trees. Summer brings ox-eye daisies and poppies blooming profusely in the wildflower meadow, while fall perennials such as asters and bush clover offer autumn color. The Waddells collected outstanding statuary and garden art for their gardens during their travels. It was Mrs. Waddell, though, who perhaps loved the garden best. In writing of their home, Alexander referred to the garden as the "Pleasances," noting they were created by his wife, "born of her sensitive comprehension and her love of leaf and tree and bud and flower."

VIRGINIA HOUSE (115 miles south of Washington, DC) 4301 Sulgrave Road, Richmond, VA 23221 **TEL:** (804) 353-4251 **OPEN:** Mon.-Sat. 10-4, Sun. 12:30-5, except holidays **TOTAL ACRES:** 8 **SPECIAL COLLECTIONS:** Spring bulbs, summer annuals, roses, azaleas, water garden   ZONE 7 **F** G **H** HO P PA WS

The gardens at the Governor's Palace beautifully illustrate the formal gardens so popular with the early colonists. Here boxwood is clipped and pruned to create columns and parterres.

Colonial Williamsburg
Williamsburg

For three-quarters of a century before the founding of the United States, the town of Williamsburg was capital of the Crown Colony of Virginia. Though small (originally 283 acres), the town was of marked elegance, having been designed from the outset to express the power and dignity of the crown. Its success was largely the work of Francis Nicholson, Royal Governor from 1698 to 1705, who persuaded the General Assembly to provide money for the Governor's Palace and Capitol building. And it was Nicholson who laid out the grid pattern of parallel and perpendicular streets, setting regulations as to how individual buildings would be sited. With the exceptions of the Capitol and William and Mary College, which were to be three-quarters of a mile apart at opposite ends of a "noble street mathematically streight [sic]," and of the palace, which was generously provided with acreage, individual buildings were typically to be contained on half-acre lots. Within each lot, it was stipulated that householders should erect a dwelling at least 30 feet wide by 20 feet deep, at least 10 feet high at the roofline, and set back 6 feet from the street. All residents were expected to have a fenced garden and an orchard, not only for their own food needs, but to beautify the community as a whole. The plan achieved its ambitious ends, bringing forth many fine houses and scores of handsome and elaborate gardens. It is these gardens, restored much as they were two centuries ago, that make a trip to Colonial Williamsburg as rewarding for the gardening enthusiast as for the historian.

The reconstruction of the gardens is part of a truly astonishing effort of historical research, going back to 1780 when Virginia's government abandoned

Loyalist Williamsburg to move the Capitol to the more centrally located Richmond. With all its important functions taken away, Williamsburg's collection of fine old structures and gardens fell into neglect, and a century and a half later no traces of the dignity and grandeur of the place remained. Then in 1926 a local minister, the Reverend Dr. W.A.R. Goodwin, prevailed on John D. Rockefeller, Jr., to underwrite the restoration of the central historical portion of Williamsburg to its original 18th-century condition. Today, Colonial Williamsburg shares its re-created glory with well over a million visitors a year, and an important element of their enjoyment comes from its many gardens.

The horticultural-historians of Colonial Williamsburg have rigorously pursued authenticity. Though very few specific clues exist as to how individual gardens looked, a great deal is known about the kinds of gardens the transplanted English admired, and these models have been followed. Virtually all are in the formal Dutch-English style adapted to the climate and soil of Virginia, reflecting the taste of William of Orange, for whom Williamsburg is named, and of Queen Anne who succeeded William and Mary. As gardens in urban England began to embrace a more natural style, the settlers of Virginia were in no mood to romanticize the all-too-abundant wilderness that lay just beyond the town's limits. They wanted a style that bespoke control over nature, and they found it in the tidy topiary, trim parterres, and brilliant flower beds of King William's Hampton Court.

Colonial Williamsburg's garden restorers meticulously used plant materials appropriate to the original gardens, some 500 different species of flowers, shrubs, and trees known to have grown here prior to the

While symmetry and formality were preferred at Williamsburg, it was difficult to keep the wilderness out of the small kitchen gardens.

Revolution. Most are native to this continent; others were brought over by English colonists; and a few came from Europe and the Orient via England, through a vast international trade network that spread plant materials and altered gardening all over the civilized world. Also in the interest of historical accuracy, the restorers have tried to use "unimproved," nonhybridized varieties of plant materials, though some heritage plants have been bred out of existence over the years.

Of the 180 acres in Colonial Williamsburg's historic district, over 90 are lawns and gardens. The most impressive lawn stretches more than two blocks before the Governor's Palace. Catalpa trees, spaced a hundred feet apart, line both sides, descendants of those admired by Thomas Jefferson two centuries ago. A native American tree, identifiable by its heart-shaped leaves and bunches of white flowers, this highly ornamental, fast-growing and dense shade tree was introduced to English and American gardeners by Mark Catesby, an English naturalist collecting in the Carolinas about the time Williamsburg was laid out.

More than 25 gardens are open daily to the public; another 75 can be seen by appointment. In all they range from small formal gardens attached to the houses of ordinary colonial Williamsburg citizens, to larger and more elaborate gardens associated with the dwellings of the gentry, and the imposing formal gardens surrounding the Governor's Palace. Credit for these latter gardens goes chiefly to Alexander Spotswood, Nicholson's successor in the Governor's seat between the years 1710 and 1722. Though the palace succumbed to fire and the gardens were mowed under after the war, horticultural historians found a partial guide in the so-called "Bodleian Plate," an engraved view circa 1740 showing the building's facades, complete with depictions of the layout of the ten-acre Ballroom Garden at the back of the palace. Archaeological digging further revealed the original paths, bed locations, and shards of urns and lead finials used as decorative accents.

The re-created Ballroom Garden is a a noble attempt at recalling the fine estates of late 17th-century England. Surrounded by a rose-colored brick wall and shut in behind elaborate wrought-iron gates, the garden is classically geometric. Its design is bilateral, with eight diamond-shaped parterres of edging box and six topiary yaupon hollies on either side of the center line. Within the parterres a robust mix of periwinkles provides this garden's only hint of a color other than green, mingling with the English ivy. The arrangement and form of the dozen topiary yaupon, clipped to a cylindrical shape and about 15 feet high, are references to the Twelve Apostle groupings found in formal English gardens of an earlier generation. At a level below the Ballroom Garden, a smaller garden displays long beds of brilliant red tulips in April. Tulips, cultivated by the Dutch with a fervor unmatched for any other flower, were still exotics in many parts of the Colonies, but already a favorite flower in Williamsburg. The colorful displays are set off by boxwood topiary and an allée of American beech, pleached into arbor-like tunnels to create areas of shade and privacy. Also of note are an exceptionally fine maze garden of American holly, modeled on one of yew at Hampton Court; a mount created to provide a lookout (and hide an icehouse); and a canal.

The gardens of private citizens are also of interest, as those of George Wythe show. Wythe, Thomas Jefferson's law teacher and himself a signer of the Declaration of Independence, built his home on two half-acre lots, allocating much of the additional space to plantings. The front formal garden is in the form of a long bowling green, deeply carpeted in grass and bordered by box and topiary. Fruit and kitchen gardens line a side of the property, as well as an herb garden with box hedges and topiary at each corner. Behind the house to the west, a pleached arbor of American hornbeam provides a restful retreat. Similar formal arrangements, though on a smaller scale, can be found in dozens of other Williamsburg gardens, together presenting the most extensive display of the Dutch-English gardening style to be seen today. And how wonderfully everything grows! It is easy to understand why Williamsburg resident John Custis, father of Martha Washington's first husband, wrote a London friend in 1725, "I have a pretty little garden in which I take more satisfaction than in anything in this world."

COLONIAL WILLIAMSBURG (42 miles northwest of Norfolk) Colonial Parkway, Williamsburg, VA 23187 TEL: (757) 229-1000 or (800) HIS-TORY OPEN: Daily 9-5:30 TOTAL ACRES: Garden 90, estate 180 SPECIAL COLLECTIONS: One of the finest colonial revival gardens in the U.S., formal parterres, cottage gardens, historic plants, spring bulbs, annuals, crape myrtles ZONE 7 A F G H HO P PA R T V WS

Norfolk Botanical Garden
Norfolk

In 1938, 200 men and women from the Works Progress Administration cleared dense vegetation from around Lake Whitehurst and then planted 4,000 azaleas. The resulting large display of spring-blooming shrubs proved spectacular, but it was only the beginning of what today comprises a collection of diverse gardens able to please the most discriminating horticulturist. Twenty theme gardens each offer a distinct contribution, focusing on a particular type of plant, such as roses, herbs, and holly, or a type of garden, such as Japanese, fragrance, hummingbird, or butterfly. The Healing Garden, for example, displays both common and rare plants that have been used medicinally. The All-America Display Garden shows flowers and vegetables considered the cream of the crop. A Renaissance Garden created in the style of a 16th-century Italian landscape includes three terraced lawns and statuary representing each of the four seasons. A nearby garden holds more than 200 different varieties of perennials as well as woody ornamentals and annuals. A network of trails, paths, and canals makes this the country's only botanical garden that can be explored by foot, train, or boat. In combining the beauty of a natural setting with the planning of formal gardens, Norfolk Botanical Gardens achieves its goal of promoting horticulture and environmental awareness.

Norfolk Botanical Garden (42 miles southeast of Williamsburg) Airport Road, off Azalea Garden Road, Norfolk, VA 23518 **Tel:** (804) 441-5830 **Open:** Daily 8:30-dusk **Total acres:** 175 **Special collections:** Azaleas, camellias, rhododendrons, roses, annuals, perennials, butterfly-hummingbird garden

ZONE 7 A F G H P PA R T V WS

In spring, a cloud of pale pink and white dogwoods provides a delicate backdrop for the more intense hues of bright pink azaleas that step up a gentle grassy slope at Norfolk.

Kentucky

ASHLAND
LEXINGTON

Nestled in the bluegrass country of Kentucky is Ashland, the former home of Kentucky congressman, statesman, and speaker of the house, Henry Clay, and his wife, Lucretia, both of whom loved their gardens. In the height of their glory in the mid-1800s, the gardens here were grand and glorious, encompassing over 600 acres and including formal areas, a greenhouse, and orchards. Today's small, formal garden is the work of the Garden Club of Lexington, which in 1950 chose a design popular during the mid-19th century, with long walkways and geometric planting beds surrounded by a brick wall.

The present garden, situated close to the original farm manager's house, measures only 180-by-105 feet. But it is reminiscent in mood to the Clays's original estate, including plants beloved in that period along with ivy-draped brick walls and clipped boxwood. Low-growing hedges border much of the garden, offering boundary lines and a backdrop for the flowers. In summer, parallel borders are flush with the bright colors from daylilies, astilbes, geraniums, dahlias, and ferns, changing to the amber and golden colors of autumn. Along with roses, a small, but outstanding peony collection complete the personal style of this garden. Enjoy a stroll; it is easy to imagine Henry and Lucretia, arm in arm, beside you.

ASHLAND (74 miles east of Louisville) 120 Sycamore Road, Lexington, KY 40502 **TEL:** (606) 266-8581 **OPEN:** Daily dawn-dusk **TOTAL ACRES:** 20 **SPECIAL COLLECTIONS:** Historic house, boxwood, old-fashioned flowers   **ZONE 6** **F** **G** **H** **HO** **P** **R** **T** **V** **WS**

LEXINGTON CEMETERY
LEXINGTON

In the mid-19th century, many people in the United States began migrating to the cities. Rural cemeteries, with their wide-open spaces and carefully planted grounds, began to serve as public parks, offering a quiet haven in which families could spend a peaceful Sunday afternoon. Among the most important of these was Lexington Cemetery, established in 1849.

Within the cemetery's 170 parklike acres are two formal garden areas—a sunken garden and a three-acre flower garden. Both bring delight in each season, as thousands of bulbs bloom in spring, followed by summer annuals, and fall foliage. During winter months, evergreen trees and shrubs, considered the backbone of the gardens, are shown to best advantage. Lexington Cemetery showcases an unusually varied and exciting tree collection, including more than 200 different species. Among them are common favorites—dogwoods, weeping cherries, and southern magnolias—as well as some more unusual specimens, such as ginkgo and the magnolia known as the cucumber tree. The cemetery's mission has always been to "serve the living while honoring the dead," a goal accomplished in the successful combination of fine sculpture, stonework, and the quiet dignity of nature.

LEXINGTON CEMETERY (74 miles east of Louisville) 833 W. Main Street, Lexington, KY 40508 **TEL:** (606) 255-5522 **OPEN:** Daily 8-5 **TOTAL ACRES:** Garden 3, grounds 170 **SPECIAL COLLECTIONS:** Flowering trees
                                                                                                     ZONE 6 **P**

The colors of autumn line the gravel pathways at Ashland. Six brick parterres create the framework for a profusion of annuals and perennials that offer different colors and textures each season.

Bernheim Arboretum and Research Forest
Clermont

Bernheim Arboretum and Research Forest is the fruition of a young German immigrant's dream. Isaac Bernheim wanted to create a nature sanctuary that would serve as a refuge for birds and animals and a place of peaceful meditation for people. Today the combination of heavily wooded areas, meticulously maintained gardens, and wide-open grassy meadows fulfill Bernheim's vision. The arboretum's grounds, which opened in 1929, have changed dramatically over the years; time and resources have transformed the poor, worn-out farmland into open fields lush with grasses and wildflowers, and rich, deep forests underplanted with ferns and flowering shrubs.

Of the 14,000 acres owned by the Bernheim Foundation, 2,000 are open to the public, the remainder kept as a research forest for Kentucky's colleges and universities. Within the large public area spread 20 miles of hiking paths, Lake Nevin, a Nature Center building, and the 250-acre arboretum itself, which holds over 1,800 labeled plants. Collections of particular interest include the holly collection, considered one of the largest in the United States, and groupings of nut trees, crabapples, and ginkgoes.

Bernheim Arboretum and Research Forest (30 miles south of Louisville) Ky. 245, Clermont, KY **Tel.:** (502) 955-8512 **Open:** Mon.-Sat. 9-5, Sun. 12-4 **Total acres:** 270 **Special collections:** Arboretum, hollies, crabapples, ginkgoes
ZONE 6 P PA T WS

CHEEKWOOD
NASHVILLE

In the early 1900s, Joel Cheek made a fortune with a special blend of coffee that he named after a local hotel in downtown Nashville: the Maxwell House. He and his wife, Mabel, who were both very interested in Georgian architecture, enjoyed the fruits of his success by traveling throughout Europe, collecting ideas for creating their own estate. In 1928 they bought a hundred acres of land eight miles southwest of Nashville, and began to create their Tennessee estate, called Cheekwood (Mabel's maiden name was Wood). They then hired well-known architect Bryant Fleming to design the house and gardens. So beautifully did Fleming blend these two elements that the question still remains: Does the house set off the gardens or do the gardens complement the house?

In order to best take advantage of the cool winds, the house was built on top of a hill. But much of the hillside was composed of limestone, making planting difficult—but not impossible. The resulting gardens tumble down the hillside and are beautiful from any viewpoint, either looking down from the house, or up from the base of the incline. Particularly outstanding is the boxwood collection.

This was Joel Cheek's favorite plant, and he scoured the countryside looking for large, mature specimens to purchase from families in surrounding areas.

In the 1950s, the couple's descendants donated the house and 55 acres of land to a nonprofit organization in Nashville with the stipulation that it be maintained as a cultural center for the region.

Today, many different community groups have combined forces to develop Cheekwood into a first-class public garden. For example, the Herb Society of Nashville created a formal herb garden here, and in 1968 Nashville resident Cora Howe donated the Howe Garden, an exciting native plant garden that includes a wide diversity of indigenous plants as well as a historic stone

Pools, fountains, and streams tumble down the hillside in front of the mansion at Cheekwood. Strategic use of stones, statuary, and plants makes each of these a secret garden.

The vibrant hues of coreopsis and larkspur create a bright spot in the garden. Cheekwood's perennials and wildflowers unveil colorful blossoms from spring through fall.

wall and toolshed. In 1985, the Howe Garden was the recipient of a trillium collection, now considered the largest in the southeast region of the United States.

Also of interest, the Burr Garden includes a fine iris collection as well as a multitude of roses, vines, and fragrant plants. In spring, the nearby Hardison Daffodil Garden displays both heirloom varieties and the newest cultivars and hybrids of this cheerful flower. For Cheekwood's Japanese Tea Garden, a dry streambed was constructed, with pebbles giving the illusion of water in a stream. Also featured in this traditional garden are a bamboo gate and a collection of dwarf conifers.

Offering visitors a different horticultural experience, and making the gardens a pleasure throughout the year, are the Cloud Forest Greenhouse, home to species native to a Central American cloud forest, and the orchid greenhouse. To best enjoy the outside gardens, though, spring is the time to visit Cheekwood, when azaleas and dogwoods transform the woodlands and hundreds of colorful blooming bulbs bring the more formal areas to life.

Cheekwood is the happy result of a love and passion for gardening of original owners, and the determination and dreams of a civic organization that desired a public garden for its city. The result is a joyous blending of people and plants, past and present.

CHEEKWOOD (208 miles east of Memphis) 1200 Forrest Park Drive, Nashville, TN 37205-4242 **TEL:** (615) 353-2148 **OPEN:** Mon.-Sat. 9-5, Sun. 11-5, except holidays **TOTAL ACRES:** 55 **SPECIAL COLLECTIONS:** Boxwoods, dogwoods, orchids, trilliums, herbs   **ZONE 7** C **F** G **H** HO P PA **R** T WS

THE HERMITAGE
HERMITAGE

When Andrew and Rachel Jackson moved to the wilderness of Tennessee in 1804, they set out to create an estate that would be both beautiful and appropriately impressive, as suited to his growing reputation as a national politician. The result—the Hermitage—included over a thousand acres in its glory. Heavily influenced by the homes of Virginia politicians whom he visited, Jackson hired English gardener William Frost to design similar gardens at the Hermitage.

The estate of the seventh President of the United States has been maintained by the Ladies' Hermitage Association since 1889, and today covers 625 acres. The one-acre formal garden, called Rachel's Garden, still adheres to the original English design. Four large squares of grass are bordered with perennials, annuals, and herbs, intersected with pebble walks. Where the walks cross at the garden's center lie geometric planting beds bordered with beveled handmade bricks and filled with seasonal bedding plants. A visitor to the Hermitage in the early 19th century wrote that he had never seen anyone more fond of flowers than Rachel Jackson. Her passion has inspired generations of gardeners to maintain her gardens in the same spirit of love in which they were planted so long ago.

THE HERMITAGE: HOME OF ANDREW JACKSON (12 miles east of Nashville) 4580 Rachel's Lane, Hermitage, TN 37076 TEL: (615) 889-2941 OPEN: Daily 9-5, except third week of Jan., Thanksgiving, and Christmas TOTAL ACRES: Garden 1, grounds 625 SPECIAL COLLECTIONS: Old-fashioned flowers, magnolia and hickory trees from Andrew Jackson's era   ZONE 7 F G H HO P PA R T WS

DIXON GALLERY AND GARDENS
MEMPHIS

Dixon Gallery and Gardens offers an oasis of shade and botanical splendor just minutes away from downtown Memphis. Originally the home of Margaret and Hugo Dixon, the grounds still exude the charm of their elaborate estate garden, planted in the 1940s. The Dixons, both of whom loved nature and gardens, actively participated in the design of the garden, hiring Hope Crutchfield to create an overall plan for the grounds.

Crutchfield's design was based on an English-park theme, with long vistas and a collection of small garden rooms. The grounds, which cover 17 acres, were landscaped on two main axes, one with the house at the south end and an outstanding sculpture, called "Europa and the Bull," at the north end. The other axis runs east-west, and was known to the Dixons as the Venus allée after the statue of Venus by Wheeler Williams, which Hugo Dixon commissioned in 1963. Close to the residence stands the camellia house, a slat building containing an outstanding camellia collection, and a cutting garden, where flowers and greens are grown for arrangements in the house.

Dixon Gardens is particularly beautiful in spring when its multitude of azaleas and plantings of woodland wildflowers are in bloom. With its combination of formal "garden rooms" and naturalized areas, Dixon offers visitors visual pleasures and a quiet haven from the city bustle in any season.

DIXON GALLERY AND GARDENS (208 miles west of Nashville) 4339 Park Avenue, Memphis, TN 38117 TEL: (901) 761-2409 OPEN: Tues.-Sat. 10-5, Sun. 1-5, except holidays TOTAL ACRES: 17 SPECIAL COLLECTIONS: Camellias, cutting garden, English parklike landscape   ZONE 7 C F G H HO P T WS

OPRYLAND USA
NASHVILLE

In this entertainment resort complex, three indoor gardens, or "interiorscapes," cover seven acres with a dramatic selection of tropical and subtropical trees and plants. Although this massive collection is primarily from Florida and is displayed in a commercial context, its variety and design results in an unusual, contemporary conservatory. One garden displays under glass some 10,000 tropical plants representing more than 215 species set among waterfalls, rocky coves, and terraces surrounded by clusters of flowers. Another area, the Cascades, emphasizes water underneath what is considered one of the largest glass roofs in the world. Here, three waterfalls ranging from 23 to 35 feet in height tumble from the top of a 40-foot-high simulated mountain into a large lake, all surrounded by more than 8,200 tropical ornamental plants. The third garden under glass, Delta, is more of an emporium with a river running through it, its design reflecting a southern scene of palms, mahogany trees, Spanish moss, camellias, and magnolias.

OPRYLAND USA 2800 Opryland Drive, Nashville, TN 37214 **TEL:** (615) 889-1000 **OPEN:** Always open
TOTAL ACRES: 7 **SPECIAL COLLECTIONS:** Tropical and subtropical trees and plants   C G H P R

Although she loved bright colors in much of the landscape, Margaret Dixon was said to have liked white flowers close to the house, such as the impatiens planted in this courtyard garden.

ELIZABETHAN GARDENS
MANTEO

In 1587, 108 men, women, and children set sail from England, eventually arriving on what was to be known as Roanoke Island, off the coast of North Carolina. Their goal was to establish the first English-speaking colony in the New World. Sadly, their mission was never accomplished, and the entire colony disappeared without a trace, a mystery that remains in the annals of American history. Although the colony was never established, the spirit of these brave settlers has been beautifully commemorated in the creation of the Elizabethan Gardens adjacent to the Fort Raleigh National Historic Site. The idea of Elizabethan Gardens originated with the North Carolina Garden Club in 1950. Members sought to establish a garden reminiscent of a 16th-century English pleasure garden, the kind of garden that the first colonists would have been familiar with in their homeland.

The original plans were modest. But when the garden club received a collection of priceless European antique garden statuary from the honorable John Hay Whitney, ambassador to England in the 1950s, the project's scope expanded to create gardens worthy of such a gift. The collection included an ancient Italian fountain and pool with balustrade, porphyry marble wellhead, sundial, fonts, stone steps, and benches dating from the 15th century.

Today, the gardens, which were designed by two well-known architects, Richard Webel and M. Umberto Innocenti, cover ten acres along the shores of

In early summer, bright pink blossoms from crape myrtle trees create a colorful frame for the antique statuary, pool, and balustrade of the Sunken Gardens.

Roanoke Sound. Present in this landscape are many of the elements popularized by English landscape designers in the late 16th century, including a mount, sunken gardens, formal herb gardens, a thatched gazebo, sweeping lawns, and marble fountains.

The Gate House, patterned after a 16th-century orangery, sets the stage for the garden beyond. Just east of this reception area lies Shakespeare's Herb Garden, displaying medicinal, fragrant, and culinary herbs mentioned in Shakespeare's writing. Paths lead to the nearby Queen's Rose Garden where rose lovers from all over the world can enjoy many different varieties of the genus, including grandiflora, floribunda, shrub, and climbing and hybrid tea roses. Recent additions include the 'Sir Walter Raleigh' and 'Virginia Dare' cultivars.

The ground's most stunning feature, the Sunken Garden, offers geometric planting beds framed with clipped

Many lush and colorful plants, such as these red hibiscus, blue salvia, and yellow cannas, can be easily grown during the summer months in the Elizabethan Gardens, located along the North Carolina coast.

boxwood. Pink crape myrtle trees encircle the Whitney fountain. Within each planting bed, flowers are changed several times a year to showcase seasonal color. Brick paths dissect this garden, which is surrounded by a double hedge of 11 foot yaupon hollies.

Adjacent rolls the Great Lawn, where broad expanses of cut green grass allow a view of the surrounding masses of azaleas, camellias, and rhododendrons. The garden's formal areas are edged by more naturalized regions, where native wildflowers, ferns, and shrubs abound. Wild orchids (including a stand of pink lady's-slippers), bloodroot, and foam flowers are only a few of the many species that carpet the forest floor in spring. Here, too, are found twin oaks, estimated to be more than 300 years old. Native trees include oaks, yaupon holly, myrtle, pine, cypress, wild olive, sassafras, and dogwood.

Paths leading from the sunken gardens to the Overlook Terrace and on to the Water Gate and gazebo are lined with a variety of plants, including a rare sea holly, century plants, and yuccas. The Water Gate marks the place where the early colonists were thought to have first come ashore. Inspired by the past, the Elizabethan Gardens gracefully combine beautiful plants, priceless statuary, and a love of gardening in a 16th-century pleasure garden.

ELIZABETHAN GARDENS (190 miles northeast of Raleigh, adjacent to Fort Raleigh, Roanoke Island) 1411 Highway 64/264, Manteo, NC 27954 **TEL:** (919) 473-3234 **OPEN:** Daily 9-5, until 8 in summer **TOTAL ACRES:** 10 **SPECIAL COLLECTIONS:** Camellias, azaleas, hydrangeas, roses, crape myrtles, native plants

ZONE 7 **F** **G** **H** **P** **T** **V** **WS**

TRYON PALACE GARDENS
NEW BERN

Soon after William Tryon became North Carolina's Royal Governor in 1767, he took on the construction of a permanent seat of government at New Bern, a thriving town at the confluence of the Neuse and Trent Rivers. To ensure the work went smoothly and that the results were suitably grand, Tryon brought with him British architect John Hawks and professional landscape gardener Claude Joseph Sauthier. According to contemporary reports, the collaboration produced one of the most elegant English-style residences in colonial America. Unfortunately, Tryon's original "palace" was short-lived—political turmoil and fire all but destroyed house and grounds by 1798. Resurrected through the extraordinary efforts of New Bern's citizens and painstaking historical reconstruction, Tryon's palace and his gardens live again, providing visitors with a unique view of "pure English taste" as it was understood in the colonies circa 1770.

Since most of the original records for Tryon's palace, including plant lists and garden layouts, were lost, much of the ground's reconstruction is understandably speculative. However, knowing that Hawks and Sauthier were under instructions to work in a traditional manner, landscape architect Morley Jeffers Williams and his associates have sought additional guidance from the plans and actual gardens of contemporary British estates of comparable size and wealth. The majority of the trees, plants, and flowers selected for the restored gardens are known to have been used in the United States by 1771, either as natives or as European imports, of which there were already a substantial westward flow.

Modern Tryon Palace offers 14 acres of lush lawns, formal parterres, private gardens, kitchen gardens, and a wilderness walk. Visitors approach along an avenue of Darlington oaks, named for Dr. William Darlington, the late 18th-century American physician and botanist who extensively catalogued native American flora. At the avenue's end, twin brick guardhouses mark the entrance to the grounds. Within the gates, a circular cobbled driveway surrounding an impeccable greensward leads to the palace itself, a graceful Georgian-style brick building, three-stories high in the center, with colonnaded arcades connecting to smaller east and west wings. In the style of the day, the public side of the palace is severe and rather plain, with the best and most colorful parts of the gardens hidden from view in private areas behind the buildings.

At the exit of the west colonnade, a brick walk leads past hawthorn bushes and plantings of ivy, oxalis, and other flowering plants to the first of the "fancy" gardens, the wall-enclosed Green Garden. Designed to be seen most effectively from an upstairs window, this garden is distinguished by its handsome scrollwork of dwarf yaupon holly surrounded by white gravel. At its four corners stand living sculptures, four cherry laurel trees sheared to identical height and shape. Triangular beds of periwinkle edged with lavender cotton, a charming

A serpentine brick walk winds through a scroll garden of annuals and evergreen hedges.

In Tryon Palace's Green Garden, dwarf yaupon holly, periwinkle, and ivy create carpets of green in varying shades and textures.

limestone statue, and, in July, crape myrtle, also offer visual delight.

Beyond the Green Garden lies another enclosed garden, the dazzling Maude Moore Latham Memorial Garden, named after Tryon Palace's principal modern benefactor. The most ornate of the restored gardens, its intricate pattern of undulating S-curves recall those popularized in 18th-century England by artist William Hogarth. His influential treatise on aesthetics declared the S-curve "the line of beauty," discernible in everything from the shape of a woman's figure to the "winding walks and serpentine rivers" of the English landscape. Colorful beds of annuals are contained within scrollwork hedges of dwarf yaupon holly meticulously trimmed every few weeks during the height of the growing season. The changing flower displays include 30,000 tulips underplanted with pansies in spring; marigolds, geraniums, salvias, begonias, verbena, and white alyssum bedded in summer; and a brilliance of chrysanthemums in royal reds and golds blooming through fall and into early winter. Sinuous paths of rosy red brick add color as they wind among the separate beds, where Italian marble statuary allude to the seasons. Oleander, bay, cassine holly, and an unusual species of boxwood (*Buxus harlandii*), identifiable by its notched, willowy leaves and billowy form, provide a year-round evergreen background.

To the south are two parallel allées—garden walkways flanked with shrubbery or trees so dense as to form visual walls. The first, Hawks' Allée, honors the palace's original architect, John Hawks, with tall, clipped holly trees, flowering shrubs, and lilies-of-the-valley. The second, Pleached Allée, is named for the two rows of yaupon holly pleached or plaited along an overhead support to create a leafy bower framing a view of the Trent River.

Beyond, the wilderness walk offers the first clues of the naturalistic revolution in garden design poised to sweep the colonies. The walk circles the south lawn, leading toward the river and back again to the palace. Open expanses of lawn bordered by selected trees and shrubs simulate a more natural landscape, though hardly a wilderness, except perhaps to an 18th-century gentleman accustomed to past formalism.

The wilderness walk also leads to the oblong Kellenberger Garden, dedicated to Mr. and Mrs. John A. Kellenberger, son-in-law and daughter of Maude Moore Latham. This privy garden, enclosed within high brick walls, relies as much on color as its broderie design. A walkway bisects the garden, with four inside-curved beds framed in sweet alyssum on the west; four rectangular beds bordered by germander on the east. Both sets of beds center on their own small fountains rising above a changing tapestry of bulbs and summer annuals, including old-fashioned varieties of begonia, portulaca, marigold, ageratum, celosia, and zinnia. Along the walls redwood trellises support ivy and jasmine.

Alongside the palace's east wing is the kitchen garden, in colonial times the major source of provisions for the family's table. Great care was given to plan such gardens for maximum productivity and visual appeal, with beds of vegetables mixed with the occasional flowers, the latter used for strewing as well as household cuttings. Herbs, for culinary and medicinal uses, often edged beds. Two dipping wells remind the visitor that 200 years ago all household water traveled in buckets. Also of note are a stand of leaf tobacco, once grown for household use, and a variety of corn cultivated by local Native Americans for thousands of years.

Other service areas adjoining the kitchen garden include poultry yards, a dovecote, and a Work Garden where cold frames, hot beds, and a lath-walled shade house raise plants both for Tryon Palace's gardens and for sale. Particularly notable are the 18th-century types of gourds cultivated here, grown chiefly to be cured and made into all sorts of dippers, bowls, and covered containers.

Three small 18th- to early 19th-century residences—the Stanley, Stevenson, and Jones Houses—are also part of the Tryon Palace complex; each offers its own charming garden on a smaller scale.

TRYON PALACE GARDENS (90 miles north of Wilmington) 610 Pollock Street, New Bern, NC 28563 **TEL:** (919) 514-4900 **OPEN:** Mon.-Sat. 9-4, Sun. 1-4, except holidays; until 7 in summer **TOTAL ACRES:** 14 **SPECIAL COLLECTIONS:** Colonial revival garden design; parterre gardens; historic plants and vegetables

ZONE 8 F G H HO P T V WS

ORTON PLANTATION GARDENS
WINNABOW

Amid lagoons and lakes along the banks of the Cape Fear River stands Orton Plantation, a classic antebellum plantation house and garden. Raided by Lord Cornwall in 1776 and used as a hospital during the Civil War, it was once one of the most prosperous rice plantations in the Cape Fear area. Today the rice fields are sanctuaries for wildlife, but the elegant Greek Revival mansion remains with its history and gardens.

The gardens seen today began in 1910 when James and Luola Sprunt constructed terraces and planted camellias, azaleas, banana shrubs, and rhododendrons. During the 1930s their son, James, enlarged the garden to the present size of about 20 acres and introduced a greater variety of ornamental shrubs. With the advice of landscape architect Robert S. Sturtevant of Groton, Massachusetts, James Sprunt laid out formal and natural gardens, taking advantage of the impressive oaks, pleasant walkways, and water views. Under the shade of live oaks dripping in Spanish moss and sometimes festooned with wisteria and Cherokee roses, spread azaleas, camellias, and flowering fruit trees in spectacular spring colors. Oleander, crape myrtle, and hydrangeas follow in summer. Below the terraces and overlooking a lagoon that was once a rice field, a scroll garden with dark evergreen hedges encloses beds of sun-loving annuals.

ORTON PLANTATION GARDENS (18 miles south of Wilmington) 9149 Orton Road S.E., Winnabow, NC 28479 **TEL:** (910) 371-6851 **OPEN:** Daily 8-6, March through Nov. **TOTAL ACRES:** 20 **SPECIAL COLLECTIONS:** Azaleas, camellias, gardenias, crape myrtles, live oak trees   **ZONE 8 A F G H P PA WS**

Hundreds of azaleas blaze in spring at Orton Plantation, where gnarled live oak trees, woodland paths, and lagoons complete a picture of southern charm.

Sarah P. Duke Gardens
Durham

What began with a passion for irises and as a recreation area for students on the Duke University campus in Durham, North Carolina, has become one of the most visited gardens in the state. The Sarah P. Duke Gardens, named for a relative of the university's founder, opened in 1934 in a wooded valley at the suggestion of Frederick M. Hanes, the university's medical department chairman and an iris connoisseur. Not surprisingly, it was filled with his favorite flower. Two years later, the current garden began to take shape. Its centerpiece—a dramatic series of flagstone terraces cut into the sloping site—was the work of noted landscape designer Ellen Shipman. Today the terrace beds host an abundance of seasonal plantings punctuated with conifers and such flowering trees as dogwood, redbud, crabapple, and ornamental cherry. Crowning the terraces, an octagonal pavilion is overrun with the languid lavender panicles of Chinese wisteria in April. Below the terrace steps spreads a naturalistic pool flush with goldfish and waterlilies.

Paths lead away from the terraces, across 55 acres of spectacular gardens holding more than 2,000 plant species. Included are displays of tulips, daffodils, and peonies in spring; daylilies and popular annuals such as petunias in summer; and some 7,000 chrysanthemums in fall. Even winter is of interest, with holly and other evergreen shrubs, such fruit-bearing specimens as firethorn, and deciduous trees with colorful bark or attractive silhouettes.

As bright and graceful as a southern belle's gown, this wisteria-covered pavilion beckons visitors to its shady interior.

Principal features include the Azalea Court, where some of the 300 plants bloom well into June, and a walled rose garden with 300 shrubs. This so-called Rose Circle is reached via a graceful allée of lindens, limbed up to create an arcade. Befitting a site nestled against the Carolina pinelands is the H.L. Blomquist Garden of Native Plants, home to more than 650 species representing indigenous flora of the Southeast arranged in varying microclimates that mimic their natural habitats. The plantings are complemented by a waterfall and a spring-fed pond planted with mosses and such carnivorous specimens as Venus flytrap and pitcher plants, which thrive in boggy conditions. A slate-roofed pavilion supports an often-overlooked native: the lilac-flowered American wisteria. Another pond lies in the Asiatic Arboretum, a 20-acre site begun in 1989 and inhabited by a collection of species native to the East, such as various bamboos, rhododendrons, maples, and forsythias—many raised from seeds sent by Asian botanic gardens.

SARAH P. DUKE GARDENS (24 miles northwest of Raleigh) Duke University and Academy Roads (west side of Duke University), Durham, NC 27402 TEL: (919) 684-3698 OPEN: Daily dawn-dusk TOTAL ACRES: 75 SPECIAL COLLECTIONS: Terrace gardens, roses, irises, ferns, native plants   ZONE 7 **H** P WS

In spring, pink dogwoods complement the brighter hues of tulips and pansies, in of the many terraces below the central pavilion at the Sarah P. Duke Gard

J.C. RAULSTON ARBORETUM
AT NORTH CAROLINA STATE UNIVERSITY
RALEIGH

Dr. J.C. Raulston, professor of ornamental horticulture and director of the arboretum at North Carolina State University, was a self-described "plant evangelist." He started with a mission in 1978—to convince landscape designers, home gardeners, and the nursery business that there was more to gardening than azaleas, geraniums, and pachysandra. With drive and enthusiasm, he took a flat piece of land two miles from downtown Raleigh and turned it into one of the most exciting horticultural institutions in the country.

Here, more than 5,000 species from around the world have been planted within an aesthetically designed landscaped. The gardens include a white garden filled with flowers, variegated and silver foliage, and a Victorian gazebo set against a dark background of hollies and conifers. Elsewhere lie an intimate Japanese-style Zen garden, a French parterre garden, a water garden, and small specialty gardens for wildflowers, vegetables, and reading. Within a lath house grow some 1,500 species of shade-loving plants, allowing gardeners to see how plants rarely seen in the Piedmont, such as rhododendrons, heaths, and heathers, can thrive if properly planted.

Perhaps the most outstanding garden in Raulston's arboretum is the 300-foot-long perennial border, one of the largest and most varied in America. Here, the selection of plants and color scheme follow those of Gertrude Jekyll, the British doyenne of the perennial border. A marvel of diversity, color, and texture from the months of May to November, this is a garden not to miss.

In addition, the arboretum contains the world's largest collection of redbud trees; a rare species of Japanese crape myrtle gathered in Japan for its extra hardiness and attractive red, flaking bark; an important collection of juniper ground covers with more than 50 cultivars; and dwarf loblolly pines.

Each year, the arboretum distributes to the nursery trade close to 200,000 cuttings, complete with background information on their culture and commercial value—all to encourage the use of a wider variety of plants. Dr. Raulston, an innovator and leader in the gardening world, was especially admired for what he accomplished at this arboretum in such a short time. In promoting the rare and unusual as well as the known and popular, along with creative landscaping techniques, he established a strong legacy that will live on. When he died in 1997, the university's arboretum was renamed in his honor.

J.C. RAULSTON ARBORETUM AT NORTH CAROLINA STATE UNIVERSITY (24 miles southeast of Durham) 4301 Beryl Road, Raleigh, NC 27606 **TEL:** (919) 515-3132 **OPEN:** Daily dawn-dusk **TOTAL ACRES:** 8 **SPECIAL COLLECTIONS:** Perennial borders, redbuds, juniper ground covers, native plants, rare shrubs and trees from around the world   **ZONE 7** **F** **H** **L** **P** **T** **V** **WS**

BILTMORE ESTATE
ASHEVILLE

When George Washington Vanderbilt reached manhood in the 1880s he found his temperament didn't suit entering the glamorous life of Newport and New York. He wanted a serious vocation to fill his days. Biltmore, the 125,000-acre estate he created in the backwoods of North Carolina's Blue Ridge, filled this void. This, the grandest private residence ever built in the United States, gave

Vanderbilt a forum to explore and develop important innovations in gardening, forestry, and agriculture. Nearly a century later his gardens and grounds remain among the most beautifully integrated displays of horticultural talent and imagination anywhere on this continent. Reduced to a more manageable 8,000 acres and open to the public year-round, today the estate is under the supervision and ownership of George Vanderbilt's grandsons.

Vanderbilt first encountered Biltmore's site in 1885 when visiting nearby Asheville, a popular health resort during the Gilded Age. At age 23 he determined to have the valley for himself and immediately began buying land, eventually laying claim to 5,800-foot Mount Pisgah, Looking Glass Rock, and over 200 square miles of hills, valleys, streams, and lakes. He then turned to a family friend, beaux arts architect Richard Morris Hunt, to design a house in the grand tradition of the French châteaux of the Loire. Hunt in turn recommended the reigning master of naturalistic landscaping in America, Frederick Law Olmsted, to plan the surrounding gardens and parks. Work began in 1890, with the vast 250-room house—itself covering an amazing four acres—completed in 1895, the grounds a few years later.

Although Olmsted came to Biltmore expecting to create a parkland such as New York's Central Park or Boston's Back Bay Fens, two of the public schemes for which he is still celebrated, he soon determined a new approach was needed. "My advice," the landscape designer counseled, "would be to make a small park into which to look from your house; make a small pleasure ground and gardens; farm your river bottoms chiefly to keep and fatten livestock and with a view to

As colorful as a patchwork quilt, spring-blooming flowers adorn the English garden in front of the Biltmore greenhouse. It is still used to supply the grounds with a vast number of bedding plants.

manure; and to make the rest a forest, improving the existing woods and planting the old fields." Vanderbilt, who did not seem to realize that even his wealth was finite, bought the ambitious scheme in its entirety, although not all was executed.

In all there are 75 acres of formal gardens. A vast 3.5-acre grassy esplanade fronts the house, bordered to the north and south by double rows of mature tulip trees. Immediately to the south stands Library Terrace, its latticework covered with old wisteria and trumpet creeper vines, presided over by statuary. Below and to the east lies the Italian Garden, dominated by three spring-fed and exceptionally beautiful formal pools, laid out along a long, narrow axis. The pool closest to the house contains the sacred lotus of Egypt; the next, concentric rings of ornamental grasses in the raised center, with aquatic plants on the margins; the third features flowering waterlilies. The tangles of ivy clinging to the stone retaining wall dividing the Italian Garden from the higher bowling green was apparently started from cuttings collected on a visit to Sir Walter Scott's Kenilworth Castle in England. Parallel to the stone wall on its lower side, a shrub garden shows Olmsted's masterful accommodation to naturally irregular

terrain. Known as "The Ramble," its winding gravel paths lead through a park of specimen Chinese holly, Japanese cut-leaf maple, purple beech, native azaleas and dogwoods, and other favorites.

The adjoining square-shaped Walled Garden, designed with a nod to Elizabethan English tradition, is a glorious four-acre celebration of flowering annuals, perennials, and bulbs sheltered within stone walls that ensure privacy and protection from the elements. Along

Although formal gardens are found close to the house, Olmsted designed more naturalized landscapes on the vast estate.

these walls, wide floral borders come alive in February with the bright, dainty yellow rosettes of winter aconites. In March come purple hyacinths and sunny daffodils, followed in turn by peonies, irises, daylilies, phlox, bleeding heart, and loosestrife. Toward the garden's center, on both sides of a central grape arbor, is a series of symmetrical pattern beds planted in mirror image. Beginning in April, some 50,000 fall-planted tulips and Dutch irises bloom here, followed in mid-May by a second display of marigolds, dahlias, cannas, zinnias, and salvias, and in September with a climax of showy chrysanthemums. Flowering trees are featured too, with espaliered fruit trees silhouetted on walls and weeping cherries and double dogwoods used as freestanding accents. Some 80 varieties of roses assembled in a collection numbering more than 2,500 plants fill this garden's lower south side. Many are old-fashioned favorites but, as a designated All-America Rose Selections Display Garden, Biltmore shows some of the best new hybrids.

At the far end of the Walled Garden, completing the enclosure, stand the conservatory and adjoining greenhouses. Rebuilt in 1957 according to Hunt's original 1890 specifications, these brick, stucco, and glass buildings function much as they did in Vanderbilt's time. In the 40-foot-high central gallery such large and dramatic exotics as palm and banana trees soak in sun and warmth between stints in the mansion's Palm Court. Smaller cactuses, orchids, and other tropical plants rest in adjacent climate-controlled rooms. Along with the 20,000 bedding annuals grown here, the greenhouses provide Biltmore House with a constant supply of cut flowers as well as many plant materials sold at the Biltmore Nurseries, an important adjunct to the estate's self-support.

Biltmore's formal gardens and buildings find their contrast in the estate's 20-acre Azalea Glen, located south of the conservatory in a woodland cul-de-sac that originally served as a pinetum. Here Olmsted envisioned a fine collection of spruce, fir, cedar, hemlock, and bald cypress—just one part of a vast arboretum intended as the backbone of a larger project—to regenerate the overcut and unmanaged forests within Vanderbilt's lands. He wrote to Vanderbilt: "That would be a suitable and dignified business for you to engage in: it would, in the long run, be probably a fair investment of capital and it would be of great value to the country to have a thoroughly well-organized and systematically conducted attempt in forestry made on a large scale." Escalating costs resulted in the pinetum being the only part of the arboretum completed. It holds many remarkable specimen trees, including *Franklinia,* a native American species rather like the magnolia in appearance. The extraordinary botanists and plant collectors John Bartram and his son, William, discovered this tree in the wilds of coastal Georgia in 1765. Naming it for Benjamin Franklin, they cultivated the species and distributed its seeds far and wide. Another rare species on view is the torreya, also called stinking cedar or nutmeg yew, a relative of the yews collected in the Florida panhandle. Now on the endangered list in its natural habitat because of a naturally occurring tree blight, Biltmore's torreyas are the only known healthy specimens remaining. Also deserving attention is the dawn redwood, a descendant of seeds distributed to Biltmore by the National Arboretum in the 1950s following the redwood's discovery in China in the previous decade. Until then, this tree was known only in fossilized form and was believed to be extinct.

The Azalea Garden was the passion of Olmsted's designated horticulturist-in-residence, Chauncey Beadle, who came to Biltmore in 1890 and went on to develop what is widely judged to be the largest and most complete collection of native American azaleas in the world. Beadle also collected Asiatic and American azalea hybrids, and beginning in 1940 planted out the best of his discoveries in this grove. Lovely any time of year, this garden is extraordinary in May.

Olmsted's forestry recommendations fared better than the arboretum, as Vanderbilt perceived a direct means of earning income to offset his huge costs. He first hired American conservationist Gifford Pinchot (later the first director of the U.S. Forest Service and founder of the influential Yale School of Forestry), and then Dr. D.A. Schenck (who opened the Biltmore School of Forestry), to supervise the work. He gave them more money and a larger work force for forestry management and experimentation than was available at the time to the entire U.S. Department of Agriculture. From Biltmore's hundred-acre nursery they sold more than two million young trees per year, while selectively cutting and reforesting thousands of acres of second-growth forest.

BILTMORE ESTATE (226 miles west of Durham) 1 North Park Square, Asheville, NC 28801 TEL: (704) 274-6333 or (800) 543-2961 OPEN: Daily 9-5, except Thanksgiving and Christmas TOTAL ACRES: Landscaped 75, estate 8,000 SPECIAL COLLECTIONS: Walled English garden, Italian pool garden, roses, azaleas, rhododendrons, hollies ZONE 7 A C F G H HO P R T V WS

MIDDLETON PLACE
PINESVILLE

Carved out of the wilderness of South Carolina tidewater country, the 65 acres of man-made terraces, lakes, groves, and flower beds that make up the grounds of Middleton Place are the earliest landscaped gardens in America. Dating from 1741 and the creation of a notable southern family of gentlemen-statesmen, Middleton Place was conceived on a scale of grandeur that would not be attempted again for generations.

Henry Middleton, the man responsible for the estate's overall design, received the property as part of his wife's dowry. He managed vast plantations of rice and became one of the most influential political figures of his day, eventually rising to become president of the First Continental Congress. By combining the classic formal style in vogue in Europe with local considerations of site, terrain, climate, and agricultural economy, Middleton's resulting design was very much an American original.

Middleton Place is situated along the western shore of the broad and serene Ashley River, the principal highway in the 1700s for commerce with the busy, sophisticated port of Charleston, 20 miles downstream. Unusual in this part of the South Carolina lowlands, the property possesses a 35-foot-high elevation with broad vistas. It was here, on a bluff where the river takes a sharp bend, that Middleton determined to site his house and main gardens. With the help of a professional English gardener whose name has been lost to history, and an army of some one hundred slaves, the landscaping began.

Middleton's overall plan, a superb exercise in 18th-century garden geometry, adapted the natural contours of the land. In the French tradition the principal landscaped elements are arranged around a main axis, here running east-west

Henry Middleton, a pioneer in using exotic plants, was one of the first to plant camellias and aza-leas. Today, his azalea collection numbers more than 35,000.

Records indicate that it took Henry Middleton more than ten years to terrace and landscape his estate's grounds. Two sets of lakes, which represent butterfly wings, have become the garden's trademark.

from the plantation's entry gates, through the mansion's central hall, down a series of sculptured terraces, between a pair of "butterfly" lakes, to the rice fields and the river landing beyond. This axis, in turn, becomes one leg of a very large, precisely drawn right triangle within whose framework the property's octagonal sunken garden, rectangular parterres, Sundial Garden, and Reflection Pool, are oriented to the northwest.

The lakes particularly capture the imagination. Two matched artificial lakes—shaped in an English picturesque style to resemble a pair of butterfly wings—were hand dug by Middleton's army of workers out of the soft, stoneless flood-plain as part of an intricate system of irrigation for the nearby rice fields. A grassy bridge separating the lakes, the "body" of the butterfly, provides an avenue to the river. The excavated earth was sculptured into descending, undulating, symmetrical terraces, an American variation on the French *rampe douce*. The Rice Mill Pond on the lakes' southern boundary, created by damming the mouth of a natural creek, supplies water for the lakes as well as irrigation for the rice fields.

Northeast of the main axis, formal gardens present pure geometry. Symmetrical beds of boxwood and crape myrtle are separated by a checkerboard of parallel and perpendicular paths and allées in the tradition of Le Nôtre. The allées, now matured into dense green walls, lead to surprising vistas of distant river and rice marshes, or of nearby formal gardens and pools. Approaching from the house, the visitor first encounters the sunken octagonal garden, where gentlemen once played lawn bowls while ladies looked on from the shade of the sweet olive trees. Farther along, pie-shaped segments in the Sundial Garden repeat the design of the larger garden triangle. To its side lie two so-called Secret Gardens, tightly enclosed and intended for private conversation or peaceful solitude. Below the second of these stretches the Magnolia Walk, named for the line of magnolia trees whose immense, cupped ivory flowers, presented above leathery green leaves, waft their fragrance in May and June. Treelike crape myrtle shrubs bordering the parterre unfold their crinkled, watermelon-pink flowers throughout the summer.

Specimens of what are believed to be the first *Camellia japonica* to grow in America stand at the four corners of the formal parterre, brought to Middleton in 1786 by noted French botanist Andre Michaux. Sent to America by the French government to acquire new plant materials for Louis XVI's gardens, Michaux most likely brought the camellias along to give his American hosts in trade. Three of Michaux's gift camellias still bloom profusely, their trunks grown to tree size over two centuries, with one reaching 25 feet into the air. Hundreds of other, newer varieties of camellias also grow on the estate, beginning their bloom in November and reaching a flowering peak in February and March.

As the camellias wane, the first of the plantation's azaleas begin their annual spectacular show, with many native species growing abundantly around a pool on the formal garden's northern boundary. Some 35,000 plants dazzle the eye on the hillsides above the Rice Mill Pond, but one of the hybrid Indica azaleas is of particular interest. Identifiable by its dusty rose, trumpet-shaped blooms, this exotic shrub most likely came from Middleton's neighbor, the Reverend John Grimke Drayton, who in 1840 was the first gardener to introduce this plant from Asia by way of England.

Not to be missed on a tour of the formal gardens is the Middleton Oak, said to be a thousand years old. Standing more than 90 feet tall, with a massive trunk measuring 30 feet around, this monarch spreads its network of branches 145 feet in all directions. It is found on the east side of the gardens, overlooking the rice fields.

Descendant Williams Middleton sided with the Southern cause before the Civil War, and was active in the secession movement, supplying the South with laborers and materials in the defense of Charleston and Fort Sumter. In 1865 Sherman's army ransacked and burned the 300-foot-long house, leaving its main and north-flanking wings an empty shell. Two decades later the region was hit by an earthquake in 1886, which toppled the gutted parts of the house, emptied both butterfly lakes, and destroyed the plantation's elaborate system of waterworks. Happily, the Middleton family managed to hold on to the property through the years and beginning in 1916, under the aegis of descendant J.J. Pringle Smith and his wife, began the enormous task of restoring Middleton to its former glory.

Today, the gardens look much as they did in antebellum days, and the estate makes an effort to re-create the flavor of plantation life, with farm yards, stables, sugarcane works, and a blacksmith shop. Designated a National Historic Landmark, Middleton Place won the coveted Bulkley Medal in 1941, which was bestowed by the Garden Club of America "in commemoration of 200 years of enduring beauty."

MIDDLETON PLACE (14 miles north of Charleston) Ashley River Road, Pinesville, SC 29414 **TEL:** (803) 556-6020 **OPEN:** Daily 9-5 **TOTAL ACRES:** 65 **SPECIAL COLLECTIONS:** Oldest landscaped garden in U.S., azaleas, camellias, crape myrtles, magnolias, live oaks ZONE 8 F G H HO P PA R T V WS

A sense of serenity surrounds Middleton Place, which has known both the affluence of the antebellum South and the ravages of the Civil War

The knobby knees of the southern cypress trees give a wild and untamed look to this bog, which also supports such traditional spring-blooming plants as daffodils and rain lilies.

Magnolia Plantation
Charleston

Ablaze with the countless millions of dazzling azalea blossoms that open each spring beneath stands of ancient live oaks and strands of Spanish moss, this is the quintessential southern plantation garden. It also ranks as one of the oldest; the formal brick-bordered parterre installed to enhance the original manor house in the 1680s still lies preserved at the garden's center. This historic garden's heart, now housing boxwood-lined beds of seasonal ornamentals, is today surrounded by 50 acres of diverse plantings that display bold sweeps of color year-round.

Set along the Ashley River some ten miles from Charleston, the property that comprises Magnolia Plantation has been carefully tended by ten generations of the distinguished Drayton family, including the Reverend John Grimke Drayton. This Episcopal minister expanded the existing gardens in the then fashionable, naturalistic English style, installed lakes and paths, and opened his property to the public in 1870. By 1900 the gardens were being hailed as an attraction on par with Niagara Falls and the Grand Canyon. Mr. Drayton also became an important horticulturist, introducing the dainty Indica azalea into cultivation in the United States in 1848. He was also among the first to plant the common camellia outdoors. Today, some 250 varieties of Indica azaleas and more than 900 varieties of common and sasanqua camellias inhabit the gardens.

Magnolia Plantation's allure lies in the soft, seemingly unstudied style of the plantings, which sprawl across rolling fields and cling to woodland slopes as if designed by nature. Here, untamed meadows of daffodils ramble around the feet of dogwoods, and tangles of wisteria clamber over loblolly pines. Soaring

While Magnolia Plantation's gardens offer 12 months of color, spring brings the greatest delights, with abundant blooms from such southern favorites as azaleas and dogwood trees.

sycamore and longleaf pine trees mingle with Japanese cherries and wild plums, while velvety saucers of gardenias and hibiscus blend with little trumpets of yellow jessamine and honeysuckle. The romantic mood is heightened where the gardens skirt the four lakes—pools so still and dark that they mirror the magnolias, palmettos, Cherokee roses, and daylilies rising along their banks. More otherworldly still are brooding bald cypress trees, their knobby "knees" breaking the placid water surface.

The gardens also encompass formally landscaped areas, including a maze wrought from seven-foot-tall hedges of holly and camellia; a topiary garden with animals sculptured in fig vines; an 18th-century-style herb garden; and a bed of 60 specimens, from aloe to wormwood, which are mentioned in the Bible. Another man-made feature is a 7,000-square-foot greenhouse sheltering ginger, jasmine, and other tropical plants that grow on Barbados, the New World ancestral home of the Drayton family.

Since 1975 the entire 500-acre site has been managed as a wildlife refuge, where peacocks and foxes are as welcome as tulips and tea olives. A 125-acre former rice field—abundant with waterlilies, zephyr lilies, lotuses, pitcher plants, and native grasses—attracts hundreds of bird species. And the adjoining Audubon Swamp Garden, an eerie and enchanting 60-acre cypress and tupelo swamp, is ringed with shrubs, palmettos, ferns, wildflowers, and bog specimens. It serves as home to a host of wildlife such as herons, egrets, osprey, otters, and yes, alligators.

Magnolia Plantation (10 miles north of Charleston) S.C. 61, Charleston, SC 29414 **Tel:** (803) 571-1266 **Open:** Daily 8-5:30, March through Oct.; call for times Nov. through Feb. **Total acres:** Garden 50, grounds 500 **Special collections:** Oldest public garden in U.S., plantation style, azaleas, camellias, tropical plants, topiary, swamp garden   **ZONE 8** A   C   F   G   H HO P PA   T   V WS

Heyward-Washington House Garden
Charleston

One of the most important houses in Charleston's charming historic district is the Heyward-Washington house, a typical southern gentleman's home where Thomas Heyward, a signer of the Declaration of Independence, lived. This is also where George Washington stayed in 1791 for more than a week. Old World charm has been re-created at the rear of this house, with a period garden that exemplifies the geometric design of an 18th-century Charleston garden.

Within a long rectangle of brick walls and paths lies a circle of heirloom plantings that include Cherokee roses, dianthus, stock, phlox, pansies, and others. Based upon extensive research, only plants introduced into cultivation prior to Washington's visit were used. An herb garden just off the separate kitchen building contains the plants necessary for cooking and healing, some planted in the form of a traditional intertwined knot design. Many old-fashioned plants were gathered for the Heyward-Washington re-creation from nearby gardens. These are visible via a stroll along the historic streets.

HEYWARD-WASHINGTON HOUSE GARDEN 87 Church Street, Charleston, SC 29401 TEL: (803) 722-2996 OPEN: Daily 9-5, except holidays TOTAL ACRES: Less than 1 SPECIAL COLLECTIONS: Historic design and plants; heirloom plants and herbs   ZONE 8 F H HO P T

Cypress Gardens
Moncks Corner

Cypress Gardens, a 162-acre forest filled with Spanish moss-covered cypress trees growing out of the water, becomes an aquatic wonderland in early spring. Once part of a prosperous rice plantation, the swamp was used to flood the surrounding inland rice fields of this antebellum estate. It fell into disrepair after the Civil War, and in 1909, Benjamin R. Kittredge, a successful business-man, purchased the swamp and began to transform it. He planted thousands of azaleas, camellias, dogwoods, magnolias, and bulbs, including the native Atamasco lily bulb, and Mrs. Kittredge's favorite—the winter-blooming daphne.

The effect of masses of ornamental shrubs was enhanced by planting at the swamp's edge—in this way the reflection in the dark water doubled the brilliant colors. A tannic acid in the water gives it an unusually intense reflective quality. This showcase garden was opened to the public in 1932. In March and April, spectacular red, orange, pink, and white azaleas bloom along with Chinese wisteria vines and many other flowers. Striking among this display are the knees of the cypress trees, rounded spikes around the base of the trees that keep them balanced in the swampy ground. The colorful swamp can be explored on more than two miles of winding footpaths, in places alongside the original dikes of the rice fields. A more exciting way to travel is via flat-bottom boat, available for rental on the premises. Other times of the year, although not as spectacular, are also interesting. Winter offers the bloom of sasanqua camellias and more than 200 varieties of japonica, sweet olive, daphnes, and scented varieties of narcissus, along with alligators, birds, and other wildlife.

CYPRESS GARDENS (24 miles north of Charleston) 3030 Cypress Gardens Road, Moncks Corner, SC 29461 TEL: (803) 553-0515 OPEN: Daily 9-5 TOTAL ACRES: 162 SPECIAL COLLECTIONS: Azaleas, camellias, wisteria, bulbs, native Atamasco lilies, swamp garden   ZONE 8 F G P R T V WS

Brookgreen Gardens
Murrells Inlet

The magical union of nature and art is magnificently displayed at Brookgreen Gardens. Originally developed in the 1930s for the home of Anna and Archer Huntington, the gardens are located on the grounds of an abandoned antebellum rice plantation. Careful attention was given to preserving the 200-year-old live oaks found on the site, and today they serve as a centerpiece for the garden.

During the Depression, when artists were struggling to support themselves, Archer Huntington became a patron for many American sculptors, providing both financial and moral support. As a result of his patronage, Brookgreen grew into a showcase for many pieces of outstanding American sculpture. Today the collection contains more than 500 pieces of all shapes, sizes, and styles. The sculpture is displayed at Brookgreen Gardens amid plants carefully selected to highlight and enhance the art. Particularly outstanding is the collection of dogwood trees that bloom white and pink in spring. Formal garden rooms provide the backdrop for many classic pieces, including Anna Huntington's magnificent "Diana and the Hunt." The marsh area, part of the surrounding preserve, showcases the more contemporary pieces in a natural setting.

Considered the first public sculpture garden in the United States, Brookgreen includes a 50-acre wildlife sanctuary. It continues to grow and evolve, both as an outdoor sculpture gallery and as an important public botanical garden that today hosts more than 2,000 varieties of native and naturalized plants.

Brookgreen Gardens (81 miles north of Charleston) US 17 south, between Murrells Inlet and Pawley's Island, SC 29576 **Tel:** (803) 237-4218 **Open:** Daily 9:30-4:45, except Christmas **Total acres:** 300 **Special collections:** American representational sculpture, azaleas, live oak allée, magnolias, native plants   ZONE 8 F G H HO P PA R T V WS

Plants are carefully chosen for their size, color, and texture to create a visually exciting counterpoint to Brookgreen Garden's dramatic sculptures.

CALLAWAY GARDENS
PINE MOUNTAIN

Fiery red and fragile, the plumleaf azalea blooms briefly in summer, but only in one area of the world. This rare shrub is indigenous to the southwest corner of Georgia and the adjoining corner of Alabama, within a 100-mile radius of Blue Springs. Cason Callaway often picnicked at Blue Springs, 70 miles south of Atlanta, and it was here one summer day in 1930 that he discovered this almost extinct wild azalea. A man of action and means, Callaway decided to protect this endangered species, as well as to build a summer retreat here on Pine Mountain at the end of the Appalachian range.

Nearby at Warm Springs, his friend President Franklin Roosevelt summered at the "little White House." At Callaway Gardens, thousands of acres were transformed into one of the great azalea gardens of the South. It also became a distinguished recreational resort. Fred Galle, a noted azalea specialist, was persuaded to leave the University of Ohio and become the Director of Horticulture. For the next thirty years, Galle designed and expanded the garden; close to 20,000 plants and trees were planted each year. Dams were constructed and 13 man-made lakes were created throughout the wilderness areas. Special collections of magnolias, crabapples, dogwoods, mountain laurels, oakleaf hydrangeas, and sourwoods were planted along scenic trails that wind over ten miles amid lakes and forests of oaks, maples, and loblolly pines. The hollies constitute one of the largest collections in the country with some 400 varieties of American, English, and Japanese plants.

Today thousands of plumleaf azaleas survive, no longer endangered, along with 14 other species of native azaleas that were planted. Only 16 native azalea species are known in North America and Callaway Gardens is an important showcase for these delicate flowers. Sometimes called the "bush honeysuckle,"

These delicate azalea blooms are among the thousands that appear each spring at Callaway Gardens in southwest Georgia. Many different varieties are on display.

these natives are deciduous. The first blooms begin in early March with the white and pink Piedmont and lemon-scented Florida azalea and end in July with the pinkish-red plumleaf flower.

Some of the northern hybrid azaleas do not grow in this climate. Here the showstoppers are cultivated hybrids of azaleas and rhododendrons from Asiatic evergreen species. Galle planted more than 700 varieties and close to 300,000 plants. In spring, a spectacular array of color overwhelms the woodlands. Banks of evergreen Glen Dales, Satsukis, and Kurumes carpet the forest floor and line five miles of lakeside paths.

A focal point designed by Galle is the Azalea Bowl, 3.5 acres filled with resplendent purple, pink, mauve, red, white, and yellow azaleas. Wildflowers, rhododendrons, and mountain laurels also add their color in spring. In 1985 the John A. Sibley Horticultural Center

At Callaway Gardens, thousands of azaleas bloom in shades ranging from bright red, to pink, purple, orange, and white. Thirteen lakes help reflect the beauty of flowers and shrubs.

was added. This innovative conservatory has a design that is both dramatic and subtle. Fiberglass domes float above different display levels while trellis-styled columns of burnished steel support the structures. At the center of this five-acre complex there is a lavish floral gallery with ramps winding around the displays of spring bulbs, summer tropicals, fall chrysanthemums, and amaryllis and poinsettias in winter. Other galleries include a rock wall garden filled with azaleas, ferns, and camellias; a 20-foot high waterwall; and a fern grotto. Outdoors are seasonal topiary displays.

Cason Callaway's interest in farming led to the creation of a vegetable garden, one of his last projects before he died in 1961. On a seven-acre field over 400 varieties of fruits, vegetables, and herbs grow in attractive demonstration gardens to educate visitors and to provide food for the resort's restaurants. The garden is also used as the set for *The Victory Garden South* television program. The latest addition to the garden resort is the Day Butterfly Center, patterned after similar ones in Great Britain. A stunning glass, octagonal conservatory encloses a tropical butterfly garden. One thousand butterflies from 50 species fill the room of dense tropical foliage with "flowers of the air." Amid plants from South America, Malaysia, and Taiwan, an Ecuadorian owl butterfly may feed near hummingbirds.

CALLAWAY GARDENS (77 miles southwest of Atlanta) Ga. 78, Pine Mountain, GA 31822 **TEL:** (706) 663-2281 or (800) CALLAWAY **OPEN:** Daily dawn-dusk **TOTAL ACRES:** 14,000 (resort complex) **SPECIAL COLLECTIONS:** Azaleas, hollies, rhododendrons, native plants, set for *The Victory Garden South*, butterfly conservatory   **ZONE 8** A C F G H HO P PA R T V WS

Atlanta Botanical Garden
Atlanta

Located on 30 acres at the northern end of Piedmont Park, the Atlanta Botanical Garden features an All-America Rose Selections Garden as well as specialty gardens of perennials, herbs, wildflowers, vegetables, and Japanese flora. An interesting rock garden shows how southern plants can be used in a setting usually associated with high-altitude plants. An oasis in the middle of busy Atlanta, the gardens were designed as demonstration theme gardens for homeowners but offer ideas and pleasure for all garden enthusiasts.

The garden was conceived in the 1970s and realized many of its plans in the 1980s, culminating with the Dorothy Chapman Fuqua Conservatory, the centerpiece of the garden that opened in 1989. Under a glass canopy thrive more than 6,000 plant species from tropical and desert climatic zones around the world. Priority is given to plants that are rare or endangered. The rotunda has a 14-foot waterfall over volcanic lava and surrounded by unusual palms, ferns, and hundreds of species orchids that grow in the wild. Free-flying birds and the recent addition of poison-arrow frogs from the rain forests of South America add to the wonder of this indoor experience. Almost extinct, these so-called jewels of the forest are being bred in captivity.

The garden is a leader in the study and recovery of carnivorous plants. Behind the conservatory awaits a bog with a display of Venus flytrap, pitcher plants, sundews, and many others. At the opposite end of the planted gardens, a five-acre Upper Woodland showcases a fragrant camellia collection along with a selection of southeastern native plants and a glade of delicate ferns.

Atlanta Botanical Garden 1345 Piedmont Avenue, Atlanta, GA 30309 **Tel:** (404) 876-5859 **Open:** Tues.-Sun. 9-6 **Total acres:** 30 **Special collections:** Urban-theme gardens, orchids, conservatory, carnivorous plant bog, roses, rock garden, tropical and desert plants

ZONE 8 C F G H L P R T V WS

Founders Memorial Garden
Athens

The first garden club in America, the Ladies Garden Club of Athens began in 1891; today there are almost 10,000 garden clubs across the country. The historic headquarters and a two-acre garden commemorating the founding now rests on the campus of the University of Georgia.

The small but charming garden includes a colonial boxwood garden enclosed by a white-picket fence. A terrace behind the fence overlooks an expanse of lawn with annuals and perennial borders edged in a serpentine of red brick and, at the opposite end, a round pool framed by a screen of bamboo. The garden is also a study center and includes collections of the flora of Georgia and the Piedmont. Besides mature oaks the garden features the spring blooms of dogwoods, redbuds, azaleas, and rhododendrons. In addition, seasonal color includes a winter display of camellias.

Founders Memorial Garden (75 miles northeast of Atlanta) University of Georgia, 325 S. Lumpkin Street, Athens, GA 30602 **Tel:** (706) 542-0842 **Open:** Daily dawn-dusk, except holidays **Total acres:** 2 **Special collections:** Colonial boxwood garden, Piedmont flora

ZONE 7 H P

Barnsley Gardens
Adairsville

Unlike most wealthy, antebellum southerners, Godfrey Barnsley never actually grew cotton. Instead he worked as a broker, buying and selling this king of plants all over the world. Barnsley was also an avid horticulturist, and wherever his ships sailed, he would instruct the captains to bring back exotic plants. These he placed on his massive Georgia estate, which at one time swelled over 10,000 acres. Barnsley hired New York landscape designer Andrew Jackson Downing to design his gardens. Today the Barnsley Gardens still display many features considered Downing trademarks, including rockeries, an oval boxwood parterre, fern glades, and an English-style woodland garden. Although only portions of the mansion remain, they have been sown with a profusion of plants that climb and tumble, making the ruin gardens among the most beautiful on the estate.

Sixteen acres have been planted to convey a sense of the period and place when Barnsley was active (up to 1873). In addition to great quantities of foliage accurate to that era, the gardens have become a showplace for many heirloom plants grown in the South before the Civil War, including such unusual specimens as the green rose and the old-fashioned reseeding petunia. Today Barnsley Gardens also includes a fine collection of lilacs, a plant rarely grown in the South. Careful records are being kept to determine which cultivars perform best in this region, making the gardens both a monument to the past and a garden for the future.

Barnsley Gardens (60 miles north of Atlanta) 597 Barnsley Gardens Road, Adairsville, GA 30103 **Tel:** (770) 773-7480 **Open:** Sat.-Sun. 11-dusk, March through Nov. **Total acres:** 16 **Special collections:** Old-fashioned flowers, woodland garden, lilacs, roses, Andrew Jackson Downing design

ZONE 7 **F** G P PA **T** WS

Massee Lane Gardens
Fort Valley

Massee Lane Gardens, the headquarters of the American Camellia Society, began when David Strother decided to plant a few camellias after a devastating storm in 1936 destroyed his peach crop. A network of other camellia enthusiasts exchanged plants and eventually Strother developed an important collection, which he donated to the American Camellia Society in 1965, along with farm acreage and funding for a new site. Today there are more than a thousand varieties here, including *Camellia japonica,* the species famous for the size and beauty of its flowers; *C. sasanqua,* with smaller blooms; *C. sinensis,* known as tea plant; and *C. reticulata,* grown in the greenhouse because of its lower cold tolerance. When winter comes to the South and few flowers are in bloom, camellias star in colorful arrays of pink, red, and white. Flowers begin blooming in November and peak in February or March. There are some smaller gardens of roses, daylilies, herbs, perennials, and an enclosed Japanese-style garden. In addition, the adjacent Taylor Stevens Gallery houses one of the largest collections of porcelain birds and other figures by Edward Marshall Boehm.

Massee Lane Gardens (108 miles southeast of Atlanta) 1 Massee Lane, Fort Valley, GA 31030 **Tel:** (912) 967-2358 **Open:** Daily 9-4 April through Nov.; Mon.-Sat. 9-5, Sun. 1-5 Dec. through March **Total acres:** 10 **Special collections:** Headquarters of the American Camellia Society

ZONE 8 A C **F** G **H** HO P **T** WS

Florida

Vizcaya
Miami

The finest interpretation of a Renaissance garden to be seen in the United States is at Villa Vizcaya, dubbed a Mediterranean Xanadu on Miami's Biscayne Bay. Owned and operated by Dade County, Florida, the fabulous house and grounds were inspired by the villas and hill gardens of 16th- and 17th-century Italy and modified with élan to suit the subtropical climate, terrain, and exuberant plant life of Florida. Villa Vizcaya was originally conceived as the winter retreat of James Deering, heir to the International Harvester fortune. In 1914, when he hatched his ambitious plan, Deering was a 53-year-old Chicago-based bachelor

A graceful mosaic of greenery, stone, and water, Vizcaya was completed in 1916. Its Old World charm and elegance belies its youthful history.

with cultivated tastes and a fragile constitution brought on by pernicious anemia. At the suggestion of his doctor, Deering investigated a warmer climate in which to spend the coldest months of the year—he decided on Miami, Florida, well before it became a popular resort.

Deering purchased 180 acres along swampy Biscayne Bay, and set his crews to clearing and draining the site and building a railroad spur to the property. Along with Paul Chalfin, a Harvard-educated painter and curator at the Boston Museum of Fine Arts, he went off to southern Europe to survey the best architectural and garden designs the Continent had to offer. Chalfin's job was simple—to make virtually anything Deering saw and coveted a part of the future villa. With no asking price too great, they set to purchasing and shipping home a vast treasure of furnishings and architectural fragments. Their game plan was to collect and reassemble the parts in such a way that when Vizcaya was complete it would appear as though it had grown old gracefully on Biscayne Bay for several hundred years. To an extraordinary degree they succeeded. What Chalfin could not buy for his patron he sketched and remembered, to be re-created with modern materials in Miami. At some point Chalfin was joined in this extraordinary effort by beaux arts architect F. Burrall Hoffman and Diego Suarez, an Italian-educated, Columbian-born landscape architect. A thousand artisans, many brought over from Italy, were put to work in the enterprise. Construction and landscaping went on for nearly five years, with Chalfin as the guiding genius.

Tucked amid Vizcaya's ten acres of formal grounds and sweeping vistas are private nooks and small "garden rooms." A fern grotto, baroque garden house, and lagoon garden are highlights.

Since Deering wished to save the native hammock trees growing thickly on the natural limestone ridge above the tidal shoreline, the only suitable site for the house and grounds was on the marshy margins of the bay itself. To create the necessary foundations and raise the grounds above sea level, costly pilings and other massive engineering works were carried out. In addition to the 70-room Villa Vizcaya, designed in a palace-fortress style around a central courtyard, the plans also called for some 10 acres of formal gardens, a scattering of pavilions, grottos, lakes, canals, an elaborate waterfront, and an Italian baroque farm village where staff for the household and the adjoining farmlands could live and work.

On Christmas, 1916, Deering's winter getaway opened for its first season. Splendid as the architectural works are, the landscaping and formal gardens have always been Vizcaya's real glory. In keeping with the style of the mansion, Suarez's magical green landscape echoed many Italian gardens. Where the originals naturally relied on Mediterranean species and were usually terraced and hilly, Suarez came up with a number of ingenious solutions and substitutions to contend with the flatter and more humid Florida coast. For example, for boxwood he substituted the so-called Australian pine (also known as horsetail beefwood and she-oak), which is not pine at all but takes well to shearing and thrives on the Florida coast. For shade trees, he used native evergreen oak, known locally as live oak. Likewise, to fill expanses of flat ground he created parterres, using Australian jasmine to form the close-cropped patterns traditionally planted in boxwood.

The estate has a happy relationship with Biscayne Bay's waterfront. The mansion's main eastern facade is close to the shore, overlooking a 300-foot-long, curving seawall that literally embraces the bay. Some 50 feet off the seawall, but within its sheltering arms rises the extravagant creation known as the Great Stone Barge. Functioning effectively as a breakwater, the 176-foot-long barge is more importantly a fantasy island, richly embellished with elaborate sculptures depicting mythic sea creatures carved by Alexander Calder.

As is traditional with Renaissance gardens, the formal gardens at Vizcaya are seen to best advantage from above, on the mansion's terraces. In particular, the main gardens reveal themselves as an architectural extension of the south terrace, a vast fan-shaped outdoor wing of the house itself. Suarez chose the area off the south terrace to do his most elaborate work, including an extensive lagoon and dozens of small tree-covered islands, informal areas that are no longer part of the property. The main gardens, arranged on a cross axis, cover ten acres and include the traditional furnishings of an Italian garden—extensive water displays, sculptured grass beds, classical statuary, decorative balustrades and staircases, topiary-style trees and shrubs, and carpetlike parterres of low-clipped hedges. All is arranged in a pleasing contrast of form and texture, much as one would decorate a formal interior. Also authentic to Renaissance style is the near absence of flowers; though bright bougainvillea and begonias enliven the garden in summer, the principal horticultural effect Suarez sought and achieved is one of cool greens.

The paths from the south terrace to the mount are straight and symmetrical, drawn along either side of a central pool, itself framed by allées of rectangularly clipped live oaks. They terminate in a superb water stairway, from either side of which lead paths to either a cool grotto within the mount or its tree-shaded top— for views of the gardens, villa, and the Bay of Biscayne beyond. The mount is also the site of the summerhouse where guests often arrived by gondola, for which a Venetian-style landing, complete with striped mooring poles, was provided.

Several lesser gardens complement the main garden. Behind the mount, on the west side, the Sensory Garden features aromatic herbs. On the mount's east side is the much larger Fountain Garden, named for the 17th-century Italian pedestal fountain at its center and displaying subtropical trees and shrubs, including Surinam cherry, Macarthur palm, and two native Floridian trees, black ironwood and pigeon plum. East lies the Maze Garden, with hedges of native coco plum, and the Theater Garden, a miniature evocation of the ancient outdoor theaters of Greece and Rome. Here turf seats beckon an imaginary audience before an elevated stage with wings of trimmed hedges and a cast of classical statuary. Tucked in the northeast corner of the complex (and actually enclosed within the walls of the south terrace), the Secret Garden offers grottoes dripping with water and a green and very private interior.

The glory days of Villa Vizcaya lasted less than a decade. When the work on the gardens was completed in 1923, Deering's health began to deteriorate rapidly, and he died two years later. Within a few months Vizcaya was further punished by a major hurricane, when winds and salt water devastated the gardens. Though Deering's heirs, with the help of Chalfin, nursed the property back to life, it was seldom used for several decades. In 1952 Deering family descendants transferred the house and gardens to Dade County and it is once again a showplace. Vizcaya's farm village has also been rejoined to the estate and is in the process of being restored.

Vizcaya Biscayne Bay, 3251 S. Miami Avenue, Miami FL 33131 **Tel:** (305) 250-9133 **Open:** Daily 9:30-5, except Christmas **Total acres:** 10 **Special collections:** Italian Renaissance design, fountains, grottoes

ZONE 10 H HO P R T WS

*Best seen from above, the formal gardens include such intricate de
as clipped evergreen, antique statuary, and stone w*

Fairchild Tropical Garden
Miami

Fairchild Tropical Garden changed the face of this part of southern Florida in 1938, turning what one contemporary account called a "rocky tree-dotted, weed-choked nothing" into a luxuriant paradise of palms and ferns, cycads and bromeliads. In the decades since, it has become the largest botanical garden specializing in tropical flora in the continental United States.

Fairchild was the idea of Robert H. Montgomery, an attorney so devoted to raising tropical exotics that his hobby soon outgrew his Florida estate. Working with David Fairchild, one of the world's preeminent plant hunters and botanists,

Montgomery selected a sloping 83-acre site on Biscayne Bay in south Miami and enlisted the landscape architect William Lyman Phillips (who was also involved with Bok Tower) to effect the transformation. Phillips's ingenious design has remained largely unchanged and continues to delight visitors with the drama of contrasting scale: broad, tranquil vistas that disappear into dense, informal pockets of plantings so accessible that they invite touch, smell, and close examination.

Velvety expanses of lawn and 11 lakes are surrounded by more than 6,000 plants, many of which are endangered in their native habitats. Outstanding among them is the collection of some 2,800 palms representing 900 species, from stately royal palms, to crimson-stemmed lipstick palms, to bulbous bottle palms. The Bailey Palm Glade is one of the garden's most stunning features, where the graceful fronds of Chinese fan palms and compact clusters of miniature date palms ring a placid pool.

Equally important at Fairchild Tropical Gardens are the cycads: primitive, palmlike, evergreen trees that bear seed cones resembling those of a conifer. Although cycads are rapidly disappearing from the wild, the gardens raises most of the 200 species known.

Year-round color and fragrance are contributed by more than 700 species of flowering plants, including frangipani, ylang-ylang, hibiscus, and

Tropical treasures such as the variegated acrinum lily (top) thrive next to a small fish pond while elsewhere, new varieties of old favorites are on display, such as this hibiscus, 'Tequila Sunrise' (bottom).

Fairchild's palm collection, which includes the fishtail palm shown above, is a safe haven for the genes of many species that are threatened or endangered in their native habitats.

bougainvillea. The garden also holds such rarities as the floss silk tree—whose downy flowers measure four inches across—and the cannonball tree, whose prodigious blooms blanket its trunk and give way to ball-shaped fruits.

Fairchild Tropical Garden is also home to a simulated rain forest, where the splash of a waterfall provides soothing background music. The lofty tree canopy shades a floor of feathery ferns and conceals such treasures as bromeliads and orchids, many of which are epiphytic and grow high among the branches. Those species of orchid that cannot tolerate Florida's occasionally erratic temperatures are sheltered in the 16,000-square-foot Windows to the Tropics conservatory, along with equally tender beauties such as anthuriums, heliconiums, and tropical waterlilies. In contrast to these lush specimens are the century plants, prickly pear cactuses, African aloes, and other dryland natives found in the sandy soil of the arid rock garden.

Visitors who wish to take in the entire garden at a glance can climb to the scenic overlook. Rising 18 feet above sea level—one of the highest elevations in the area—this embankment is encircled by flowering trees and affords a panorama of the gentle terrain as it stretches across the lakes to the outlying Everglades, mangrove preserve, and clusters of native plants known as hammocks.

Fairchild Tropical Garden (10 miles south of downtown Miami) 10901 Old Cutler Road, Miami, FL 33156 **Tel:** (305) 667-1651 **Open:** Daily 9:30-4:30, except Christmas **Total acres:** 83 **Special collections:** Largest tropical botanical garden in continental U.S., palms, cycads, tropical trees, orchids, flowering vines

ZONE 10 C **F** G **H** P P PA **R** T **V** WS

FOUR ARTS GARDEN
PALM BEACH

Nestled behind the Society of the Four Arts Library in downtown Palm Beach awaits a charming garden. First created by members of the Palm Beach Garden Club in 1938 as a demonstration garden, the grounds included seven different theme gardens: a Moonlight Garden, Chinese Garden, Jungle Garden, Spanish Garden, Tropical Fruit Garden, Rose Garden, and British Colonial Garden. Several years ago, most of the gardens were re-landscaped to blend their boundaries, though essential elements of each are still evident. The Chinese Garden remains enclosed by high white walls and contains a small pool, moss-covered stones, antique statuary, and Oriental plants. Adjacent is the Moonlight Garden, designed in a crescent shape and planted with white flowers, many of which bloom and are most fragrant during evening hours. From here, a stone path leads into the Jungle Garden, home to many common houseplants of tropical origin, such as begonias, prayer plants, palms, and bromeliads.

The Four Arts Garden provide proof that many conventional landscape plants native to more temperate zones can also be grown in the south Florida environment. It also serves as a showcase of unusual native and tropical plants. This combination of traditional and tropical plants makes this garden interesting.

FOUR ARTS GARDEN (75 miles north of Miami) Four Arts Plaza, Royal Palm Way, Palm Beach, FL 33480 **TEL:** (561) 655-7226 **OPEN:** Mon.-Sat. 10-5, Sun. 2-5 **TOTAL ACRES:** 1 **SPECIAL COLLECTIONS:** Demonstration gardens, Chinese garden   **ZONE 9**   A   C   F   G   H   HO   L   P   PA   R   T   V   WS

This small pool and fountain, part of the Spanish Garden at Four Arts, offers ideas to local gardeners who want to include traditional landscape elements within their Florida gardens.

Bok Tower Gardens
Lake Wales

Edward Bok, a Dutch immigrant who made his fortune as a publisher and author, once said, "Make the world a bit better or more beautiful because you have lived in it." Bok Tower Gardens, built in the 1920s, are proof he took his own advice.

Bok first began purchasing land for the gardens in 1922. In hiring Frederick Law Olmsted, Jr., to create a design, his only instructions were to create a garden that would "touch the soul with beauty and quiet." Located at an elevation of 295 feet, Florida's highest, the gardens today are indeed both serene and beautiful. Central to them is the historic bell tower that houses a carillon of 57 bronze bells. The garden's 128 acres include wide, graceful paths winding through wooded areas planted with hundreds of azaleas, camellias, and magnolias. An impressive collection of palms includes the native fan palm, Everglades palm, needle palm, Queen palm, and cabbage palm. The North Walk is lined with giant crinum lilies, cycads, and coontie (now a threatened species in Florida). This path leads to the Window by the Pond, a nature observatory where visitors can sit undetected and watch birds, fish, and small mammals in and around the pond. Naturalist John Burroughs perhaps best captured the essence of Bok Tower Gardens when he wrote, "I come here to find myself. It is so easy to get lost in the world."

Bok Tower Gardens (55 miles south of Orlando) 1151 Tower Boulevard, Lake Wales, FL 33853 **Tel:** (941) 676-1408 **Open:** Daily 8-5 **Total acres:** 128 **Special collections:** Azaleas, camellias, palms

ZONE 9 F G H HO P PA R T V WS

Harry P. Leu Gardens
Orlando

Close to downtown Orlando on the shores of Lake Rowena lies Leu Gardens, the former home of Harry P. Leu and his wife, Mary Jane. A Florida native, Leu had long enjoyed a successful business career when he bought the property in 1936. He and his wife spent the next 25 years developing the gardens on their property and, in 1961, donated the house and grounds to the city of Orlando.

Leu Gardens includes an impressive number of small theme gardens which, when taken together, create a cornucopia of horticultural delights. Its outstanding camellia collection includes more than 2,000 specimens and is reputed to be the largest in the Southeast. These are at their peak from October through March. The rose was Mrs. Leu's favorite flower and the rose garden, a traditional European-style garden, contains more than a thousand rose bushes. It is said to be the largest formal rose garden in the state. Not all the plant collections here focus on such traditional plants, however. A native plant garden displays many of Florida's indigenous plants of horticultural value. Adjacent to this, the Ravine Garden offers tropical plants such as bird of paradise, banana, ginger, tree ferns, palms, and flowering vines. Along with the Leu House Museum, an outstanding example of a restored 19th-century Florida home, the gardens give visitors a rare glimpse of old Florida, when folks strolled through the garden at a leisurely pace and actually stopped to smell the flowers.

Harry P. Leu Gardens (89 miles northeast of Tampa) 1920 N. Forest Avenue, Orlando, FL **Tel:** (407) 246-2620 **Open:** Daily 9-5, except Christmas **Total acres:** 50 **Special collections:** Camellias, roses, azaleas, native plants

ZONE 9 C F G H HO P T V WS

CYPRESS GARDENS
WINTER HAVEN

When Richard Pope first bought seemingly useless bog land and shared his plans to turn it into a public garden, locals called him "swami of the swamp," and doubted his good sense. Today, local folks are grateful for Pope's foresight and vision, for the swampland is now a botanical treasure, annually drawing thousands of visitors from all over the world.

Founded in 1936, Cypress Gardens was considered Florida's first theme park, and earned Pope a new nickname, "father of Florida tourism." Covering 200 acres, the gardens contain lakes edged with ancient cypress trees and many different formally planted gardens. While water-ski shows and hostesses in antebellum gowns have helped put Cypress Gardens on the map, the floral displays remain the true drawing card. Today the botanical collection features more than 8,000 varieties of plants and flowers from 90 different countries. The displays are designed to educate as well as delight, and each plant is labeled with both common and botanical names and its native country. A botanical walking tour brochure that describes many of the plants in depth is available.

Many separate theme gardens are included under the umbrella of Cypress Gardens. In a further effort to educate, the Plantation Garden displays flowers and vegetables designed to help regional gardeners know how and what to plant in their own gardens. Also within this area are a butterfly garden, an herb and scent garden, and a vegetable and fruit garden. Hundreds of butterflies from many tropical regions reside in the adjacent, Victorian-style glass house. In 1997 the Biblical Garden opened, featuring more than 25 species of plants mentioned in the Bible. Five new animal habitats have been added to the zoo, which houses such unusual species as

Evoking the feel of a tropical rain forest, waterfalls create a backdrop for some of the 8,000 varieties of plants at Cypress Gardens.

wallabies, coatimundi, tamarins, and capybaras. The Birdwalk also opened in 1997, a free-flight aviary that is home to such species as lories and lorikeets.

Although floral displays provide interest throughout the year, four different annual flower festivals are of particular note. The spring event showcases 25 huge topiaries, including an 18-foot Easter bunny and a 50-foot-long inchworm. In summer, the Victorian Garden Party show depicts a 19th-century riverside town populated with 80 life-size topiary figures planted with creeping fig vine. Fall offers more than 2.5 million chrysanthemum blooms, while winter celebrates the poinsettia with more than 40,000 plants in such unusual arrangements as a 16-foot mountain range and waterfall. Pope was rumored to have designed his flamboyant, exuberant gardens through the viewfinder of a camera, the results concurrent with his philosophy—"If it ain't fun, the heck with it!"

CYPRESS GARDENS (56 miles south of Orlando) 2641 S. Lake Summit Drive, Winter Haven, FL 33884 **TEL:** (941) 324-2111 **OPEN:** Daily 9-5:30, later depending on season **TOTAL ACRES:** 200 **SPECIAL COLLECTIONS:** Orchids, epiphytic plants, cycads, butterfly conservatory, biblical garden, topiary

ZONE 9 C F G H HO P PA R T V WS

Cypress Gardens this century plant (opposite) contrasts sharply with the soft pet of grass and delicate bedding plants found just beyond.

Marie Selby Botanical Gardens
Sarasota

On a small spit of land sandwiched between sparkling Sarasota Bay and Hudson Bayou lies the only garden in the world dedicated to epiphytes, a most remarkable type of plant. Spread over 11 acres of shorefront, the gardens specialize in "air plants"—particular types of orchids, ferns, and other specimens that grow not in soil but in trees—and that seemingly live on air.

This unique garden opened in 1975 on the former estate of a longtime Sarasota resident and nature-lover who bequeathed her property to the public. With land at a premium, a vertical garden was not only a prudent use of space, but also offered these endangered tropical natives, which are disappearing with the destruction of the rain forest, a safe new home.

The Marie Selby Botanical Gardens shelter more than 14,000 plants, many of them collected by the garden's experts on some one hundred expeditions into the wilds of Costa Rica, Brazil, and Borneo. There are an amazing 5,000 orchids alone—from well-known dendrobiums and cattleyas to such rarities as the pumpkin-scented *Epidendrum ilense* from Ecuador and the fragrant vanilla orchid from Central America. Most of these are displayed throughout the 6,000-square-foot Tropical Display House, where they dangle overhead, peeking around posts, and winding along a 10-foot-tall volcanic rock wall in junglelike profusion. Second in prominence to the orchids are the bromeliads, such as *Aechmea Chantinii*, of which Selby maintains more than 3,000. These plants are joined by other exotics from all corners of the globe and in all colors of the rainbow, including scarlet torch ginger from Indonesia, golden-orange heliconias from Ecuador, and yellow-green pitcher plants from Borneo.

Beyond the greenhouse doors are plants suited to Florida's subtropical climate, including a stand of towering Oldham bamboo; a grove of banyan, otherwordly trees related to the fig; and an array of date, saw palmetto, fishtail, and other palms. Adding exotic color are the voluptuous blooms of the hibiscus garden—some of which reach ten inches in diameter—and a koi pool of tropical waterlilies that float serenely beneath a gentle waterfall. As if the flowers did not provide enough color, there is also a butterfly garden bursting with passionflower, lantana, and salvia, whose bright, nectar-rich blooms attract monarchs, fritillaries, and other creatures. Also indicative of Selby's commitment to conservation is its collection of cycads—strange, palmlike specimens known to have existed 200 million years ago and now considered rare. Visitors can enjoy a stroll through the Baywalk Sanctuary, where paths wander among a swamp of mangroves and other wetland denizens that protect the shoreline and provide an animal habitat.

Another group of plants fascinating not only for their appearance but also for their function is found in the Tropical Food Garden. Here, malabar spinach from Sri Lanka twines alongside the so-called vegetable sponge from Africa. Edible when young, it is more commonly known as a source of bath sponges. Other tropical edibles include pineapples and papayas, bananas and black sapote, and cerimoya and cassava.

Marie Selby Botanical Gardens (58 miles south of Tampa) 811 S. Palm Avenue, Sarasota, FL 34236-7726 **Tel:** (941) 366-5731 **Open:** Daily 10-5, except Christmas **Total acres:** 11 **Special collections:** World's largest collection of African violets, epiphytes, orchids, bromeliads, tropical foods

ZONE 9 C **F** G **H** HO P PA **R** T **V** WS

Alfred B. Maclay State Gardens
Tallahassee

Alfred B. Maclay was a wealthy financier from New York who, like many others, fell in love with northern Florida while on vacation. Impressed with the beauty of the southern woods, he and his wife moved to the Tallahassee area in 1923 and began creating the garden of their dreams. Because he loved camellias and azaleas and because the family was not in residence during the summer months, Maclay designed his gardens to be at peak bloom in winter and early spring.

Today, the property includes the garden's 28 landscaped acres, a large lake, and picnic and recreation facilities. While the grounds are always attractive, Maclay's influence is most apparent from January through April when more than 150 varieties of camellias and more than 50 varieties of azaleas transform the grounds into a fairyland of color and fragrance. The gardens also protect many threatened and endangered plants. Maclay, who collected native species to inter-plant among his beloved camellias and azaleas, included plants considered rare even in the 1940s, including Chapman's rhododendron and stinking cedar.

■ **Alfred B. Maclay State Gardens** 3540 Thomasville Road, Tallahassee, FL 32308 **Tel:** (904) 487-4115 **Open:** Daily 9-5 **Total acres:** Garden 28, park 1,200 **Special collections:** Camellias, azaleas, rare native plants

ZONE 9 F H HO P PA T WS

Designed to be in peak bloom from February to April, the spring displays of the Maclay Gardens vary from woods full of azaleas to planting beds bursting with pansies.

Alabama

Bellingrath Gardens
Theodore

A technicolor drama unfolds every month on the banks of the bayou south of Mobile. More than a hundred thousand flowers planted each season make this extravagant floral display unlike any other in the country. Spring begins with a profusion of over 100,000 bulbs, followed by 200,000 azaleas, summer annuals, and a crescendo of chrysanthemums. The year ends with a blazing flourish, the garden aflame with red poinsettias.

It all began in the early 1920s when Walter Bellingrath decided he needed a retreat from the stress of making millions in the bottling and marketing of Coca-Cola—he was the man responsible for making this a "summer drink" and for creating the six-pack. Here in Alabama, Mr. Bell, as he was called, established Bell Camp, a rustic fishing camp to enjoy with his buddies. In the meantime his wife, Bessie, started collecting azaleas and camellias, planting hundreds, then thousands, around the lodge.

After a grand tour of Europe in 1927, the couple decided to transform their home and garden into something grander. Although he hired George Rogers, a fashionable Mobile architect, to enact his garden vision, Mr. Bell applied his

In autumn, white and gold chrysanthemums cover the terrace of a Japanese teahouse at Bellingrath Gardens.

business acumen to the creation of the garden. Viewing his personal pleasure garden as a marketing opportunity, he opened his garden to the public for a fee in 1933, actively promoting its beauty through advertisements. The response was so staggering that the sheriff's department was called out for traffic control. Today it claims to attract millions of visitors annually.

There are 65 landscaped acres on the 905-acre estate, with individual garden areas joined by bridges, ponds, and flagstone walkways. In spring, more than 250,000 azalea shrubs bloom and flowering bulbs carpet the earth. Flower-edged trails lead to the first garden, in an unexpected Oriental-American style. This area is dominated by an arched half-moon bridge painted red which is transformed into an arc of chrysanthemums in autumn. Flamingoes and swans can be spotted from the traditional Japanese teahouses and torii gates. Stepping stones and red rails guide visitors to a Chinese pagoda. The main path leads to Mirror Lake, a five-acre centerpiece surrounded by willows, live oaks, banks of azaleas, and later, pinwheels and ribbons of changing seasonal color. An observation platform offers a splendid vista of flowers, bayou, and birds.

The mansion, a museum of antiques collected by the Bellingraths, features terraces and courtyards carpeted with flowers. Fountains and sculptures fill any empty spaces. Adjacent to the house is a gallery of porcelain birds. The estate also holds a small conservatory with tropical plants. Though rimmed with colorful blossoms, the Great Lawn on the southern side of the mansion provides a

At Bellingrath, thousands of annuals and perennials start in the greenhouse, to be planted with stunning effect in all seasons.

respite from the abundance of flowers. The last garden before the exit presents a lovely acre of roses, in bloom for almost nine months in this welcoming climate.

Bellingrath is famous for its chrysanthemums, possibly the largest outdoor collection in the world. In autumn, when most mums are seen indoors in conservatories, an extravaganza takes place in all areas of the garden. They are everywhere—from cascading mums, a Bellingrath specialty, to mum standards, towering topiaries, bedding plants, and hanging baskets. The great diversity of this plant is shown to best advantage each November when the display of some 60,000 chrysanthemums understandably draws the most visitors.

The numbers at Bellingrath are indeed staggering: 2,500 roses, 4,000 camellias, 10,000 waterlilies, 90,000 bulbs, 200,000 azaleas, and thousands of mums. An inventory of the varieties reads like a horticultural encyclopedia. The activity behind the scenes at Bellingrath is as impressive as the pyrotechnic display outdoors. With the exception of azaleas, camellias, and some other flowering trees and shrubs, all the plants are planted and uprooted for each season. The 40,000 square feet of greenhouses are where the real gardening takes place. Seeds and cuttings are always in process for the next blooming period with as many as 300,000 containers at various stages of growth.

BELLINGRATH GARDENS (20 miles south of Mobile) 12401 Bellingrath Gardens Road, Theodore, AL 36582 **TEL:** (334) 973-2217 **OPEN:** Daily dawn-dusk **TOTAL ACRES:** 65 **SPECIAL COLLECTIONS:** Japanese garden, azaleas, annuals, chrysanthemums, roses, spring bulbs, camellias

ZONE 8 · A · C · F · G · H · HO · P · PA · R · T · V · WS

Birmingham Botanical Gardens
Birmingham

Established in 1962 by the city of Birmingham, this botanical garden is today a diversified complex. Paths lined with crape myrtle lead past a floral clock to a sparkling conservatory that shelters many types of tropical and desert plants. Winter brings camellias and orchids, displayed in adjacent buildings. The formal rose garden's 150 varieties of hybrids are specifically selected for Birmingham gardens. A pergola marks the entrance to the Ireland Old-Fashioned Rose Garden, featuring 50 types of roses from around the world and concentrating on varieties in existence prior to the introduction of hybrid teas in 1867. A distinguished Japanese-style garden, one of the botanical garden's most popular sites, opened in 1968. Here are the traditional symbols of a torii gate, the Dragon's Head Stone, the Falls of the Seven Virtues, as well as bonsai, a Zen garden, and a 16th-century-style teahouse, built for the New York World's Fair and given as a gift by the Japanese government. Also of interest is the Fern Glade and the nearby rock quarry, where wildflowers native to Alabama grow. Other areas display irises, daylilies, rhododendrons, and demonstration gardens.

■ **Birmingham Botanical Gardens** (262 miles north of Mobile) 2612 Lane Park Road, Birmingham, AL 35223 **Tel:** (205) 879-1227 **Open:** Daily dawn-dusk **Total acres:** 67 **Special collections:** Orchids, camellias, ferns, Japanese garden, roses, *Southern Living* demonstration garden

ZONE 7 C G **H** L P **R** T V **WS**

Jasmine Hill Gardens
Montgomery

Tucked into the Appalachian foothills north of Montgomery beckons a little bit of Greece—a garden with the tranquil lines of a Mediterranean courtyard and a sculpture collection drawn from the ancient world. Jasmine Hill was the dream of Benjamin and Mary Fitzpatrick, who picnicked on a hillside beside an antebellum cottage here in 1920. They were so taken with the site's natural beauty that they eventually bought the property, turning the cottage into an estate and the overgrown grounds into 20 acres of gardens. Fascinated with classical art, the couple traveled some 20 times to the Mediterranean, over the decades commissioning replicas of nearly 40 noteworthy artworks. These were shipped to rural Alabama and sprinkled throughout the gardens, which opened to the public in 1974.

The garden's centerpiece, arrayed around a lily pool, is the re-created ruin of the Temple of Hera in Olympia, Greece. Above another pool, as if poised for flight, stands the "Nike of Samothrace," her winged figure reflected in the water and echoed by the airy heads of the sacred lotus. The "Venus de Milo" awaits beneath a Japanese cherry tree, its delicate white blooms shimmering against her marble form. The cool contours of the statuary are offset by richly colorful plantings: irises, azaleas, and wisteria in spring; gardenias, hydrangeas, and crape myrtle in summer; chrysanthemums in fall; and camellias and jasmine in winter. Along a walkway is another colorful touch: a 200-foot-long wrought-iron fence whose floral and natural motifs are painted in bright primary tones.

■ **Jasmine Hill Gardens** (94 miles south of Birmingham) 3001 Jasmine Hill Road, Montgomery, AL 36096 **Tel:** (334) 567-6463 **Open:** Tues.-Sun. 9-5, except holidays **Total acres:** 20 **Special collections:** Azaleas, camellias, cherry trees, sculpture

ZONE 8 **F** G **H** P **PA** T **WS**

NATCHEZ MANSIONS
NATCHEZ

The multitude of mansions in Natchez are noted for their antebellum architecture, antiques, and—in springtime—brilliant gardens filled with bulbs, dogwoods, mounds of azaleas, and live oak trees with their drapery of Spanish moss. In spring and fall many private houses are opened to the public during Pilgrimage Week, sponsored by the Natchez Pilgrimage Tours.

Montaigne, an Italian-style-style villa built by a Confederate general, has an abundance of azaleas surrounded by century-old oaks and over 350 varieties of camellias. Other private mansions with lovely gardens are Elms Court, D'Evereux, and Cherokee. Some can be seen year-round. Stanton Hall, a prototypical southern mansion, built in 1857 and today a house museum, has a landscaped courtyard ablaze with color in spring. Now an inn, Monmouth Plantation, the home of an early Mississippi governor, still retains its expansive lawns and lovely formal gardens. Roses, camellias, bedded annuals, fountains, statuary, and an impressive vine-covered pergola decorate its garden.

NATCHEZ MANSIONS For information on seasonal tours contact Natchez Pilgrimage Tours, Stanton Hall, 401 Hight Street, Natchez, MS **TEL:** (601) 442-6282 or (800) 647-6742 **OPEN:** Daily 9-4:30, except during Pilgrimage week **SPECIAL COLLECTIONS:** Azaleas, camellias   **ZONE 8 F H HO P T WS**

Before the Civil War, Nachez boasted of a "millionaire on every hill," most of whom built magnificent southern mansions and landscapes, such as Stanton Hall, shown above.

AFTON VILLA
ST. FRANCISVILLE

An arcade of live oaks, with a haze of Spanish moss dripping languidly from their limbs and dangling over a riot of azalea blooms, provides a haunting introduction to a romantic garden among the ruins. Rather than a historic re-creation, this garden is a poignant evocation of a grandeur long past.

Afton Villa was once the most imposing estate in West Feliciana Parish—the 1849 plantation residence of a demanding mistress, Susan Barrow. She lavished 8 years on creating the 40-room Gothic Revival mansion, as well as elaborate gardens that stretched over 20 acres. Working with a landscape architect, probably from France, Barrow installed seven massive terraces that swept down to a ravine, replete with a greenhouse to supply the household with fresh flowers and fruits—even pineapples. The gardens gradually deteriorated after the Civil War, and it was not until 1915 that a new owner, digging on the property, discovered a set of stone steps. The remnants of the gardens were unearthed and the landscape restored according to its original 19th-century plan. An old, red-flowered azalea, traditionally called the Pride of Afton, was still standing and was propagated to produce thousands of the azaleas that dot the property today. Subsequent owners in the 1940s also restored the mansion, which was destroyed by fire in 1963.

The 250-acre property again lay in ruins until 1972, when Morrell and Genevieve Trimble, civic-minded Louisianans dedicated to preserving their state's heritage, once again reclaimed the gardens. They were inspired by the work of Vita Sackville-West, who in the 1930s created a landscape around the derelict ruins of the Elizabethan-era Sissinghurst Castle in Kent, England. Her work prompted the Trimbles to use existing elements—such as brick terraces and walls and the brick, stone, and stucco structure of the mansion—as the foundation and inspiration for 10 acres of manicured

Although the original mansion burned in the 1960s, the manicured grounds, profusion of flowers, and touches such as this peacock, make Afton Villa feel like the home of a friend.

planting beds, enhanced by 30 more acres of rambling parkland.

They were also guided by Dr. Neil Odenwald, director of the School of Landscape Architecture at Louisiana State University in nearby Baton Rouge. The result is a spirited array of color, texture, and form superimposed on the

Susan and David Barrow began work on Afton's gardens in 1849, but did not complete them until 1857. Their tree-lined drive still offers a sense of southern charm and hospitality.

melancholy remnants of an opulent antebellum estate.

Snaking along for a half mile, the entry drive comes alive in early spring with mound after mound of flamboyant red, pink, coral, rose, purple, and lavender azaleas flowering at the base of a double row of more than 250 oaks. This avenue of blooms ends in a graveled court marked by four classical stone statues —Diana, Apollo, Hospitality, and Abundance—which the Trembles imported from Vincenza, Italy. The sculptures, shaded by a sprawling live oak and surrounded by regimented rows of 'Oxford Yellow' and 'Ivory Floradale' tulips, tower above the fringe-like blades of mondo grass. Tiny white buttons of bridal wreath spirea blossoms foam from pots at their feet.

Beyond the figures lie the remains of the villa, its craggy walls of crumbling brick ringing naturalistic drifts in season of tulips, daffodils, irises, salvias, impatiens, cleome, foxglove, and delphinium. The walls themselves, patterned with spidery shadows cast by gnarled redbud and live oak branches, are pocked with little tufts of English wallflowers, sedums, and wild ferns. They are also overrun by cascades of creamy 'Henryi' clematis, yellow Carolina jessamine, and purple wisteria. Masses of violets, ajuga, blue phlox, and veronica scramble over forlorn piles of rubble and poke up from cracks in the terrace.

Steps lead to the first terrace, a formal parterre where tidy boxwood hedges enclose seasonal displays of sparkling white and yellow tulips and daylilies. Providing color are pockets of pink camellias, blue hydrangeas, white 'Iceberg' roses, and red azaleas. The original Pride of Afton, with its vivid, translucent, red blooms, still grows here as well.

The remaining five terraces form a sort of grand staircase leading to the ravine. Three flights of stone steps descend the gradual slope, linking the broad expanses of brick where resident peacocks often strut. The terraces host symmetrical boxwood-lined beds filled with begonias, marigolds, pansies, and calla lilies and are punctuated by Italian marble statuary, pots of plumbago, and Versailles boxes holding cherry laurel standards.

Brick walks also weave among examples of flowering specimens that might have been used in the 19th-century garden, such as dogwood, camellia, mock orange, and althaea. At the end of the terraces lies an intricate maze of the evergreen banana shrub and sweet olive.

On a more intimate scale is the so-called Music Room, where four marble cherubs, each playing an instrument, perform for an audience of white tulips—including 'Thalia', 'Mount Hood', and 'White Lion'—in spring, and delicate white-mottled caladiums in summer. A cluster of white-flowering cherries and a stone path flows into a sea of daffodils; more than 80,000 bulbs of 'Carlton', 'Silver Chimes', 'Delibes', and 'Yellow Sun', among others, have naturalized and blanketed the vast ravine. These are complemented by azaleas and numerous species indigenous to the area, including the dainty silverbell tree, bigleaf

The ruins of the old plantation house now serve as a courtyard garden. Stone steps hold cascades of trailing ivy while flowers bursting with exuberant color bloom in every nook and cranny.

magnolia (known locally as cowcumber), and the exceptionally fragrant winter honeysuckle. The parkland provides a visual pause from the architectural feel of the intensely planted gardens. Here, lush lawn meanders into stands of venerable live oaks, cedars cloaked in wisteria, wild azaleas, and tulip trees. There is also a pond, reached after crossing three bridges and climbing a hill. Installed in the late 1970s to bring the soothing presence of water to the gardens, it is framed with oaks and azaleas, including the white-blooming 'Fielder's White' and 'Mrs. Gerbing' cultivars.

Perhaps the most soulful site amid these gardens of ghostly beauty is the cemetery, where the original owner of the property lies buried. Here stand grave markers for Bartholomew Barrow, and his son, David, the prosperous cotton planter whose wife, Susan, commanded construction of the mansion. It is enclosed simply and serenely with hedges of sweet olive and camellia.

AFTON VILLA (37 miles north of Baton Rouge) US 61, 4 miles north of St. Francisville, LA 70775 **TEL:** (504) 635-6773 **OPEN:** Daily 9-4:30, March through June and Oct. through Nov. **TOTAL ACRES:** 40 **SPECIAL COLLECTIONS:** Live oak avenue, azaleas, daffodils, magnolias, parterres, annuals, perennials

ZONE 8 A F H P PA T WS

Live oak trees dripping with Spanish moss guard one of the classic Italian stone statues. The garden has benefited from a succession of owners who have resurrected its beauty.

Rosedown Plantation
St. Francisville

"My gardens are in perfect order," Martha Turnbull penned in her garden diary on February 1, 1848. As owner of the incomparable Rosedown Plantation, Martha had reason to be proud of her antebellum gardens. The original formal gardens at Rosedown comprised 28 acres surrounding the mansion. As was typical with many southern plantations, the gardens combined formal French style with the more naturalistic English landscape design. Sadly, the diary entries became less cheerful as the Civil War took a terrible toll on the region, and the gardens. After the war Turnbull descendants made every effort to maintain the gardens, but resources were scarce and it was not until the plantation was bought by Catherine Underwood in 1956 that the grounds were restored to their original glory.

Although the gardens were overgrown, the original design was still quite evident. Many of the trees and shrubs that Turnbull planted during the first half of the 19th century are still alive today, making Rosedown one of the nation's most important collections of historic plants. Its most recognizable feature is the live oak avenue leading to the house, composed of trees that are now nearly 200 years old. Walking beneath their moss-hung boughs, it is easy to drift back in time.

Rosedown Plantation (35 miles north of Baton Rouge) 12501 State Highway 10, St. Francisville, LA 70775 **Tel:** (504) 635-3332 **Open:** Daily 9-5, March through Oct.; daily 10-4, Nov. through Feb., except Christmas **Total acres:** 28 **Special collections:** Live oaks, hydrangeas, camellias, azaleas, roses, parterre gardens   ZONE 8 F G HO P PA T WS

Hodges Garden
Many

In the 1940s, early conservationists A.J. Hodges and his wife, Nona Trigg Hodges, recognized the need to reforest and help restore much of the land in eastern Louisiana, which had been stripped of vegetation by lumber companies. So Hodges bought a 4,700-acre tract of land once called the most barren land in Louisiana, and turned it into an experimental arboretum.

The abandoned stone quarry found on this land was transformed into a formal garden, and today Hodges Garden includes 70 landscaped acres planted to take advantage of the unusual rock formations. Careful selection of plant material has stretched the growing season to span the calendar, treating visitors to blooms throughout the year. One highlight is a petrified tree thought to be thousands of years old. Spring blooms come from tulips, roses, bulbs, pansies, anemones, columbine, and such flowering trees as dogwood and magnolia. In summer arrive hydrangeas, waterlilies, butterfly bushes, and more. Chrysanthemums, a second rose display, and autumn foliage offer color in fall, while winter honeysuckle, camellias, and a Christmas lights festival draw visitors during the colder months. The conservatory and greenhouses host such exotic tropical plants as palms, orchids, bromeliads, and bougainvilleas. Appropriately called a garden in a forest, Hodges offers a network of nearby hiking trails and ten miles of paved roads.

Hodges Garden (75 miles south of Shreveport and 15 miles south of Many) US 171, Many, LA 71449 **Tel:** (318) 586-3523 **Open:** Daily dawn-dusk, except Christmas and New Year's Day **Total acres:** 70 **Special collections:** Formal gardens, roses, herb garden, rock garden   ZONE 8 C F G H P PA R T WS

Once the site of a quarry, Hodges Garden incorporates unusual stonework in its design. Here flowers and ferns grow between rocks as water cascades over stone steps into the pool below.

AMERICAN ROSE CENTER
SHREVEPORT

Forty-two acres of roses are enough to make even the most exacting rose lover beam with pleasure. This is what is offered at the American Rose Society headquarters in Shreveport, where 20,000 rose bushes delight visitors. The gardens began in 1972 when the society (formed in 1899) moved from Columbus, Ohio, to Louisiana to take advantage of the longer growing season. Located on a 118-acre tract of sunlit planting beds complemented by piney woods that offer welcome shade, the center is composed of 60 individual gardens, with more than 450 different varieties, including floribundas, hybrid teas, grandifloras, and miniatures. Theme gardens, donated by rosarians or rose societies, are all family-size, allowing homeowners to take away ideas and information for growing roses in their own backyards. Central to the gardens, the Windsounds Tower is surrounded by All-America Rose Selections winners, past and present.

The American Rose Society is dedicated to helping Americans grow their national flower. Its display garden in Shreveport is a living celebration of a nation's love affair with the rose.

AMERICAN ROSE CENTER (249 miles northwest of Baton Rouge) 8877 Jefferson-Paige Road, Shreveport, LA 71119 TEL: (318) 938-5402 OPEN: Daily 9-5, April through Oct. TOTAL ACRES: 118 SPECIAL COLLECTIONS: Major collection of roses, camellias, azaleas, flowering trees

ZONE 8 **F G H P PA T**

Live Oak Gardens (Rip Van Winkle Gardens)
New Iberia

Located on Jefferson Island, one of five "islands" (actually salt domes) rising out of the south Louisiana marshland, Live Oaks Gardens are considered an English garden in a tropical setting. The island was the winter retreat of the 19th-century actor Joe Jefferson, best known for his portrayal of Rip Van Winkle and the site is also known as the Rip Van Winkle Gardens. Jefferson's charming, comfortable house built of heart cypress has been restored and now serves as a museum for the gardens. The J.L. Bayless family purchased the property in 1917. Bayless gives the camellia credit for sparking his interest in gardening, writing "I was highly impressed to find these lovely green bushes with red flowers in the dead of winter." This inspiration prompted both a large collection of camellias and the magnificent gardens that surround the house, which were designed to gracefully blend traditional plants, such as camellias, roses, azaleas, and crape myrtles, with plants native to this semitropical region of Louisiana. Among the stunning live oaks that give the garden its name are specimens dating back 300 years. Their gnarled, weathered beauty is complemented by a variety of blooming trees and shrubs, including oleanders, magnolias, gardenias, and hibiscus. In winter, camellias take center stage, followed by blooms from thousands of early spring bulbs. A small Japanese tea garden provides interest year-round.

Live Oak Gardens/Rip Van Winkle Gardens (172 miles west of New Orleans) 5505 Rip Van Winkle Road, New Iberia, LA 70560 **Tel:** (318) 365-3332 **Open:** Daily 9-5 **Total acres:** 25 **Special collections:** Live oak trees, azaleas, camellias, hibiscus   ZONE 9 F G H HO P R T V WS

Jungle Gardens
Avery Island

Avery Island and its 200-acre Jungle Gardens is home to a variety of plants and animals including black bears and raccoons. But to most Americans, it is best known for its acres of red peppers, the base of the McIlhenny Company's Tabasco sauce. Just after the Civil War, Edmund McIlhenny used pepper plants growing on Avery Island to make a spicy sauce so unique it was patented. Today's visitors are treated to much more than rows of red peppers. McIlhenny's son, Edward A. McIlhenny, an enthusiastic and knowledgeable naturalist, traveled the world looking for new plants and observing wildlife. He is credited with introducing hundreds of new varieties of plants into the horticultural trade. McIlhenny planted many exotic plants in his own garden on Avery Island, including Chinese timber bamboo, lotus and papyrus from the upper Nile, and irises from Siberia. Many of the garden's plants are more traditional, however, such as the thousands of azaleas and irises that are at their peak of bloom from late February to late April. The large and impressive camellia collection is best seen from November to March. One of the most spectacular sights on Avery Island is the estimated 20,000 snowy egrets that migrate annually from South America. Edward McIlhenny helped save this bird from extinction in the late 19th century.

Jungle Gardens (120 miles west of New Orleans) Avery Island, LA 70613 **Tel:** (318) 369-6243 **Open:** Daily 9-5, except holidays **Total acres:** 200 **Special collections:** Azaleas, camellias, irises
ZONE 9 F P PA T V

NEW ORLEANS GARDEN DISTRICT
NEW ORLEANS

Unlike the private courtyard gardens of the French Quarter, the Garden District displays the *richesse* of the new Americans who settled here after the Louisiana Purchase in 1803. They filled their Greek Revival houses with rococo antiques and their gardens with statues, fountains, pavilions, and flowers. By 1850, this was the address to have for social prestige in New Orleans, and still is today. Bordered by St. Charles Avenue, Magazine Street, and Louisiana and Jackson Avenues, the district's houses are mostly private, their classical porticoes and cast-iron balconies forming the framework for many of the remaining gardens. Here, carefully clipped hedges, geometric borders, and garden furniture are set in formal arrangements, complementing the magnolias, gardenias, crape myrtles, camellias, oleanders, night-blooming jasmines, and other southern blossoms that can be seen in different seasons. Roses are also popular, including a Confederate rose, that begins the day as a white flower, turn pink in the afternoon, and red by sunset. A tour of this urban neighborhood provides an interesting garden experience. Spring is the best season to visit for flowers.

NEW ORLEANS GARDEN DISTRICT For information on seasonal blooms contact: Convention and Visitors Bureau, 1520 Sugar Bowl Drive, New Orleans, LA 70179 **TEL:** (504) 566-5011 or (800) 672-6124

ZONE 9 A **H** HO P **T** V

Flaunting the charms of the Old South, bright pink azaleas create a gracious entrance to this grand colonial revival mansion, one of many on St. Charles Avenue in the New Orleans Garden District.

LONGUE VUE GARDENS
NEW ORLEANS

This gracious urban estate on the outskirts of New Orleans reflects the historic traditions of the city and the wealth of its builders. French, Spanish, and English settlers have left their imprint in the courtyards of the French Quarter and the suburban gardens of the city's Garden District. But Edith and Edgar Stern built on a grander scale. Between 1939 and 1942 the Sterns constructed a Greek Revival mansion in the English country-house style and surrounded it with gardens. Eight acres were divided into six picturesque "garden rooms" around a large formal garden with fountains reminiscent of the Alhambra and Generalife Gardens in Granada, Spain.

Mrs. Stern, daughter of the founder of Sears, Roebuck and Company, decided to commission Ellen Biddle Shipman, a popular landscape architect who had designed many other famous country estates, to apply her talents to Longue Vue. Shipman laid out the basic design of a formal garden with unusual plantings. Interestingly, William and Henry Platt designed the Stern's house; it was their father, landscape designer Charles Platt, who supported Ellen Shipman in her early career. Later, in 1966, William Platt redesigned the garden, adding its major distinction, the water gardens.

A romantic avenue of arched oaks, typical of southern mansions, leads to the forecourt of the main house. The focal point of the garden is on the south side of the mansion where a terrace off the grand dining room overlooks a vista of the formal gardens. Adjacent, the Portico Garden is decorated with sweet olive trees, pleached gardenias, and a delicate crape myrtle, still in the original Shipman design of a formal English garden. Rose standards, floribundas, and camellias fill four geometrically clipped boxwood parterres.

The main event, the Spanish Court in the center of the expansive green lawn framed by a curved loggia, is designed as a rectangular reflecting pool. Within, ten pairs of jets release water in graceful arches across the pool. A channel connects it to a round pool set in a patio of herringbone-patterned bricks. Pots of flowers change with the seasons and colorful ixoras, tulips, hibiscus, begonias, and lilies fill the *jardinières* set against a background wall of varied shrubs and trees. In spring, curls of wisteria cover the colonnade, with southern pines, magnolias, and oleanders beyond.

On either side of the Spanish Court stand six smaller areas of boxwood enclosures decorated with colorful accents of potted flowers and splashing fountains. Some of the fountains are of particular interest, as they are copies of Alhambra designs by William Platt. In all, 23 antique and contemporary fountains grace the garden. In addition, polished pebbles in black and tan are arranged in designs copied from streets in Barcelona, completing the Spanish motif. The effect is soothing and cooling in this southern climate of hot and humid summers. Other smaller gardens include a yellow garden filled with golden-colored annuals and perennials, a wildflower garden offering a variety of native blooms, and a Pan Garden. The latter, a cozy corner, features a statue dedicated to Ellen Biddle Shipman. The garden at Longue Vue opened to the public in 1968.

LONGUE VUE GARDENS 7 Bamboo Road, New Orleans, LA 70124 **TEL:** (504) 488-5488 **OPEN:** Mon.-Sat. 10-4:30, Sun. 1-5, except holidays **TOTAL ACRES:** 8 **SPECIAL FEATURES:** Spanish and English garden design, parterres, fountains   **ZONE 9** **F** **G** **H** **HO** **P** **T** **WS**

The fountain in the Spanish Court at Longue Vue, with ten pairs of water arches, the focal point of the garden, which also features a semicircular loggia

CHAPTER 4

GREAT LAKES AND PLAINS

■

Ohio

Indiana

Illinois

Michigan

Wisconsin

Minnesota

Iowa

Missouri

Kansas

Nebraska

South Dakota

North Dakota

Lilies, climbing roses, dusty miller, and sedums line brick walkways in the English Walled Garden at the Chicago Botanic Garden.

215

KINGWOOD CENTER
MANSFIELD

Flowers are found in every nook and cranny of the grand estate now known as the Kingwood Center. The former home of Charles Kelley King, president of the Ohio Brass Company, the French Provincial-style house is set off by a sweeping front lawn interspersed with curved beds full of plants showing off the colors of the season. In spring, these beds are filled with 55,000 tulips, creating an exuberance of blooms not to be missed. Forty thousand summer annuals replace the bulbs as the weather warms, presenting a sometimes surprising combination of colors and textures. In autumn, ornamental grasses and fall-blooming annuals flower beneath colorful deciduous trees, all cloaked in the rich hues of the season. In addition, peacocks with brilliant tails strut across the shady lawns, and an astonishing diversity of waterfowl (over a hundred are permanent residents) swim on the duck pond.

Behind the mansion, deciduous trees underplanted with low-growing annuals line both sides of a long grassy allée. At the allée's far end, a fountain marks the estate's eastern boundary. At the entry to the allée closest to the mansion grows a formal herb garden surrounded by a brick terrace. Its center presents a colorful knot garden, with low-growing hedges planted to look as if they have been interwoven. On either side, planting beds mirror one another in design, but contain different kinds of herbs, offering both the rhythm of repetition and the excitement of variety. Culinary, medicinal, and fragrant herbs are on display.

A knot garden adjacent to Kingwood Hall forms one end of an allée lined with flower borders that change with the season.

The perennial garden adjacent to the allée doubles as both a colorful display and an educational garden. Here visitors enjoy the beauty of the plants and learn which perform well in midwestern gardens. Color groupings also play an important part in this garden's overall design. The layout is similar to that of an English country garden, with brick pathways and geometrically shaped planting beds, a design that complements the formal architectural style of Kingwood Hall. When viewed as a whole, the effect is of patches of blending and contrasting colors.

The most recent garden at Kingwood Center, the Terrace Garden, was built on two different levels and provides almost two acres of delight for all the senses. Varying color and texture may be expected in many gardens, but here sound and movement are also given prime consideration. Movement is provided by the many birds and butterflies attracted to the garden's plants. Many ornamental grasses have also been included, and the wind rippling through their long stems creates yet another dance of graceful motion. To delight the ear, water swirls in pools

The Pink Garden at Kingwood Center displays such formal landscape elements as brick walks and white statuary against a backdrop of woods and grassy lawns.

and fountains, birds add their chirping and singing, and wind chimes contribute their musical tones as they swing gently in the breeze.

The Terrace Garden, designed by Paul Roszak, includes trees, shrubs, perennials, and annuals in both formal and informal areas. The formal sections feature long walkways lined with serviceberry that in spring creates a white fragrant cloud through which visitors stroll. These are best viewed from either the pond area by the original stable and carriage house or from Kingwood Hall, which allows for an overall view. At the central axis of these long walks stands a fountain surrounded by myrtle, spring tulips, and summer annuals. As the garden has grown and matured, trees and shrubs have created intimate "garden rooms" inviting visitors to find a quiet spot to sit and contemplate.

Kingwood Center's benefactor, Charles Kelley King, specified in his will that the center be used for the enjoyment of the people of Mansfield, and that it should become a center for horticultural education. Happily, his wishes have come to fruition. Plant collections have always been important at Kingwood Center, both for their aesthetic value and for their research potential. Through its visual displays of plants and flowers and its educational offerings, the center serves as a hub for all those who wish to learn about gardens and gardening.

KINGWOOD CENTER (80 miles southwest of Cleveland) 900 Park Avenue West, Mansfield, OH 44906
TEL: (419) 522-0211 **OPEN:** Daily 8-dusk, April through Oct.; 8-5 Nov. through March, except Christmas
TOTAL ACRES: 47 **SPECIAL COLLECTIONS:** Estate garden, bulbs, annuals, herbs   **ZONE 5** G H HO P

Stan Hywet Hall and Gardens
Akron

The magnificent Stan Hywet Hall and Gardens offers a glimpse of Tudor England in Central Ohio. Complete with sweeping lawns, large flower gardens, a formal walled garden, and stately mansion, this former home of F.A. Seiberling, co-founder of the Goodyear Tire and Rubber Company, encompasses 70 acres. The Seiberlings, who had six children, wanted to create a place where they could both enjoy their family and entertain weekend guests. The solution was this country estate, reminiscent of the stately homes they had visited in England.

After much searching, the Seiberlings bought 3,000 acres of land near Akron, Ohio. An old quarry that had been on the property at one time provided inspiration for the estate's name, Stan Hywet, which comes from the Middle English words for stone quarry. The property's breathtaking views of the countryside became the focal point for both the grounds and the house, dictating, for example, the Great Hall's orientation to the west to take advantage of the stunning view of the wooded hills and ravines beyond.

Today, thanks to an enthusiastic board of trustees and a dedicated staff, the house and grounds once again appear much as they did when the Seiberlings were in residence. Formal gardens surround the house, while more naturalized areas may be discovered at distant spots. Most of the property was designed by the landscape architect Warren Manning, best known for his role in helping to design New York's Central Park. However, the estate's small, walled, English garden is the work of Ellen Biddle Shipman, whose plan specified the more than 1,500 flowers and bulbs that continue to bloom here each year. This garden became a favorite spot for Gertrude Seiberling—she often came to enjoy a moment of peace and quiet. Appropriately, the perennial beds are filled with many of Mrs. Seiberling's favorite flowers, including hollyhocks, phlox, roses, and blue sage. A reflection pool, fountain, and benches add to this garden's charm. Stan Hywet's other formal areas include a rose garden and a Japanese garden, where stone steps lead visitors into a ravine. Here, in a peaceful, shady nook, are found stone lanterns, clipped evergreens, and bamboo. Shadows created by the finely etched leaves make a lacy pattern on another scenic pathway, the Birch Allée, which extends from the manor house. A stroll beneath the arching branches is especially spectacular in autumn when the leaves turn a brilliant gold. At the end of this 550-foot-long allée, stone teahouses frame wonderful views of the Cuyahoga Valley.

On the east side of the Birch Allée blooms a cutting garden. During the growing season, blossoms from such plants as sunflowers, zinnias, eucalyptus, peonies, and various flowering bulbs such as tulips and lilies as well as snapdragons and coneflowers are cut for use in the magnificent floral arrangements that grace the interior of the house. Before Stan Hywet Hall rolls the Great Lawn, a massive expanse of grass reminiscent of the lawns of English estates. An adjacent long allée of London plane trees is underplanted with rhododendrons and azaleas, particularly beautiful in spring and early summer. Stan Hywet, a rich horticultural treasure, stands as a living tribute to a family's generosity.

.**Stan Hywet Hall and Gardens** (40 miles south of Cleveland) 714 North Portage Path, Akron, OH 44303 **Tel:** (330) 836- 5533 **Open:** Daily 9-6, except holidays **Total acres:** 70 **Special collections:** English garden designed by Ellen B. Shipman, landscape by Warren Manning

ZONE 5 C F G H HO P PA R T WS

arched trunks and golden autumn leaves of silver birch trees create
allée leading to stone teahouses at Stan Hywet Gardens.

CLEVELAND BOTANICAL GARDEN
CLEVELAND

Located in the city's downtown district, Cleveland Botanical Garden has long been an oasis of green—and yellow, pink, red, orange, and every other flowering hue. First established in 1933 as the Garden Center of Greater Cleveland, the name was changed in 1994 to better describe the educational opportunities and horticultural displays the gardens offer. A combination of formal gardens, open grassy areas, and woodland walks provides downtown Cleveland with a "pocket wilderness" and the opportunity to find nature only a few steps from urban life.

Central to the gardens is a well-known herb garden originally planted by the Western Reserve Herb Society. This is a formal garden, where geometric planting beds surround a knot garden of such small plants as santolina, germander, dwarf boxwood, lavender, and thyme, painstakingly arranged to present the appearance of having been woven together. The rose garden features both old-fashioned and modern varieties that reach full glory in early summer. Close by, in front of the main building, are lily pools, a reading garden, and a formally landscaped terrace. Adjacent, a steep ravine has been beautifully planted as a Japanese garden where carefully placed boulders, rocks, and clipped shrubbery create the illusion of a stream tumbling down a mountainside. At the base of the hillside is a Japanese teahouse surrounded by a traditional Japanese garden. Also of interest, the Wildflower Garden holds many of Ohio's native plants, both delicate and hardy.

CLEVELAND BOTANICAL GARDEN 11030 East Boulevard, Cleveland, OH 44106 TEL: (216) 721-1600 OPEN: Mon.-Sat. 9-5, Sun. 12-5 TOTAL ACRES: 7.5 SPECIAL COLLECTIONS: Herb garden, rose garden, Japanese garden   ZONE 5 G P PA T WS

FELLOWS RIVERSIDE GARDENS
YOUNGSTOWN

A broad expanse of lawn, a Victorian gazebo, and thousands of blossoms greet visitors to Fellows Riverside Gardens, a stunning flower garden located close to Youngstown, Ohio, within 2,500-acre Mill Creek Metropolitan Park. Although the park was established in 1891, the gardens were not created until 1958, the legacy of a Youngstown garden enthusiast, Elizabeth A. Fellows, who left both the land and money to build and maintain them. The gardens comprise formal and informal areas, designed both to delight visitors with enticing floral displays and teach about the plants that grow well in this climate. Hundreds of large, mature trees, including magnolias, crabapples, and a cornucopia of conifers, create a rich backdrop for a profusion of bulbs celebrating the coming of spring, as well as bedding plants that bloom all summer. Fellows's favorite flower was the rose, and the terrace and pavilion are surrounded by them in every hue. A carpet of low-growing annuals rises in front of rows of tall, stately dahlias, offsetting their huge pink, yellow, white, and orange blossoms. Visitors can follow the flagstone path leading through the herb garden, and explore the rock garden, where dwarf conifers and other low-lying plants are artistically displayed alongside stones and boulders.

FELLOWS RIVERSIDE GARDENS (75 miles east of Cleveland) Mill Creek Park, 123 McKinley Avenue, Youngstown, OH 44509 TEL: (330) 740-7116 OPEN: Daily dawn-dusk TOTAL ACRES: 11 SPECIAL COLLECTIONS: Formal gardens, bulbs, annuals, specimen trees   ZONE 5 G H L P PA T V WS

A millstone path flanked by tall herbs valued for their medic values beckons visitors at the Cleveland Botanical Gar

Holden Arboretum
Kirtland

Dedicated to the education of visitors and the wise stewardship of the land, Holden Arboretum offers an interesting place to experience trees of all kinds. Here trees are beautifully displayed in many different settings—in a forest, at the water's edge, and as a backdrop for more formal garden areas. Among the many collections of specific groups of shrubs and trees are lilacs, crabapples, and rhododendrons used in a natural setting. The Rhododendron Garden is particularly lovely in late spring and covers nearly 40 acres with vibrant and unusual specimens. Visitors are encouraged to peruse the gardens, identify their favorites, and then determine which varieties will do best in their own gardens. In addition, the arboretum has long been involved in maple sugar research, and the sugar maple tree receives special attention. In early spring, throngs of visitors can see maple syrup being made the old-fashioned way.

Holden Arboretum's emphasis on native plants translates delightfully into woodlands, bogs, prairies, dry creek beds, sand barrens, and rocky cliffs, all planted with the wildflowers, ferns, and native shrubs suitable to each ecosystem. In addition, 20 miles of hiking trails wander through many of these natural areas. Although most of the arboretum is planted informally, its main display garden presents a formal landscape best viewed in spring and summer. However, the true glory of Holden Arboretum shines through in autumn, when thousands of trees gracing the grounds turn fiery shades of gold and orange.

Holden Arboretum (30 miles east of Cleveland) 9500 Sperry Road, Kirtland, OH 44094 Tel: (216) 946-4400 Open: 10-5 Tues.-Sun., except holidays Total acres: 3,100 Special collections: Rhododendrons, lilacs, sugar maples, specimen trees   ZONE 5 A F G H L P PA V WS

Inniswood Botanical Garden
Westerville

Inniswood Botanical Garden represents the legacy of two sisters, Grace and Mary Innis, who loved nature and gardening and wanted to share their passion with others. During the last years of her life, Grace (who died in 1982) worked with the Ohio Metro Park System, developing a master plan for the elaborate gardens as a tribute to a beloved sister and a gift to the people of Ohio. Through her generosity, nearly 200,000 people each year enjoy these gardens. Inniswood's extensive network of nature trails and series of gardens still reflect Grace Innis's artistic creativity. Although not formally trained as a horticulturist, she was an enthusiastic plant breeder with a special interest in peonies, hostas, daylilies, and daffodils. Many of the hybrids and cultivars she developed were named for her, including a peony, 'Her Grace'; the hosta 'Inniswood', and the narcissus 'Inniswood' and 'Innisberg'. Gardens such as the woodland wildflower garden and the rock garden were built to re-create their natural ecosystem. Perhaps the most outstanding garden area here is the herb garden, with four vine-covered pergolas and a Victorian gazebo. Thriving within this setting are many theme gardens such as the Thyme Garden, Knot Garden, and Bee Garden.

Inniswood Botanical Garden (18 miles north of Columbus) 940 S. Hempstead Road, Westerville, OH 43081 Tel: (614) 895-6216 Open: Daily 7-dusk Total acres: 92 Special collections: Peonies, hostas, rock garden, herb garden, theme gardens   ZONE 5 H HO L P T WS

DAWES ARBORETUM
NEWARK

One would be well rewarded by a visit to Dawes Arboretum at any time of year, but it is in the fall, when the leaves turn their splendid orange and red, that this arboretum presents its most spectacular displays. Dawes Arboretum was founded by Beman and Bertie Dawes simply because they loved trees and wished to share their passion with as many people as possible. By 1929 they had acquired almost 300 acres of farmland near Newark, which they immediately began planting as a public arboretum. In addition to the trees, they added gardens and, in 1932, planted a huge shrub border that spelled out their name, DAWES. The word ARBORETUM, also spelled out in shrubbery, was added a decade later. The total length of the lettering stretches more than a third of a mile.

The arboretum has become an unquestioned success, with more than 2,000 species of woody plants attractively planted throughout the 1,149 acres that now make up the grounds. Although emphasis remains focussed on the tree collections, the gardens here are worthy of attention. At the Visitor Center, for example, a bonsai collection displays carefully pruned miniature trees. In addition, a Japanese Garden, Shade Garden, and Tall-Grass Prairie are also found within the arboretum grounds, easily accessible via the four-mile Auto Trail.

DAWES ARBORETUM (30 miles east of Columbus) 7770 Jacksontown Road, S.E., Newark, OH 43056 **TEL:** (740) 323-2355 **OPEN:** Daily, except holidays **TOTAL ACRES:** 1,149 **SPECIAL COLLECTIONS:** Crabapples, holly, azaleas, Japanese garden, bonsai   **ZONE 5** A G P PA T V WS

Autumn is an exciting time to visit Dawes Arboretum, home to more than 500 tree varieties, including bald cypress and lacebark pine as well as unusual maples and crabapples .

Indiana

Eli Lilly Garden at the Indianapolis Museum of Art
Indianapolis

Whereas Robert Indiana's well-known statue, "Love," on the grounds of the Indianapolis Museum of Art may give visitors their first smile, the abundance of flowers and trees found nearby match the aesthetic delights found inside. Formal gardens, fern-clothed ravines, and sweeping expanses of lush lawn all serve to beckon visitors into the welcoming landscape of this outstanding art museum. This was the original home of Hugh McK. Landon, an official for the Indianapolis Water Company. In 1908 he built a 22-room, 18th-century, French-style mansion on a piece of property overlooking a canal, and then began developing the grounds. He hired Percival Gallagher of the Olmsted Brothers landscape architectural firm in Brookline, Massachusetts, to help design the gardens, and together they spent the next seven years turning the grounds into a showplace.

In 1932 the estate was purchased by Mr. and Mrs. J.K. Lilly, Jr., a couple who made their fortune in the pharmaceutical industry. The estate was eventually donated by their heirs to the Art Association of Indianapolis. Those who wander the grounds, now encompassing 152 acres and a large lake, may have the sensation of being a privileged guest.

Close to the Lilly Pavilion of Decorative Arts awaits the Formal Garden, one of the most outstanding of all the garden areas. This manicured garden includes vine-covered trellises, planting beds filled with colorful seasonal annuals, and shade-loving plants blooming at the feet of magnificent, mature trees. In the spring season, a host of foxgloves unfold spires of pink, white, and mauve, while roses scent the air and sweet William and Deptford Pink flowers tumble among the rocks.

Close by the entrance of the museum building, the Plaza Garden's plantings of perennials and annuals showcase the fountains and sculpture to best advantage. Next visitors can explore the aptly named Garden For Everyone, designed to be enjoyed in many different ways. Beds are raised, allowing easy access to wheelchair-bound guests and those unable to move about easily. Many richly scented and textured plants are included in the plantings here, encouraging visitors to make this an interactive experience by touching and smelling the plants and delighting all their senses.

Through the years much of the Olmsted Brothers's original plan for the landscape at this site became overgrown, but restoration has recently begun. Among the most interesting of these rejuvenated areas is the ravine garden, holding many different varieties of ferns, shrubs, and native wildflowers. In all, the stunning presentation of plantings on the grounds surrounding the museum provides a graceful reminder that a garden can often provide the best example of the union of art and nature.

Eli Lilly Garden at the Indianapolis Museum of Art 1200 W. 38th Street, Indianapolis, IN 46208 **Tel:** (317) 923-1331 **Open:** Daily dawn-dusk **Total acres:** Garden 26, grounds 152 **Special collections:** Estate garden, ravine garden, sensory garden, perennials, daffodils

ZONE 5 A C G H HO L P R T V WS

The Eli Lilly Garden transforms into a rainbow of color in late spring as foxglove, climbing roses, salvia, and pansies burst into bloom. Carpets of grass create a frame of green for the flowers.

Oakhurst Gardens
Muncie

Mature oak trees in this Victorian garden gave the name to the house that George and Frances Ball built in 1895 in a wooded area atop the bluffs overlooking the White River. Frances and her daughter Elizabeth developed the original gardens on this property, which was restored and opened to the public one hundred years later. They began with a small cutting garden, adding an English border garden and eventually expanding into a quaint cottage garden. When Elizabeth returned from Vassar College with a degree in botany, they developed a kitchen and a rock garden, and collected native wildflowers for the woodlands surrounding their house. Today, colorful pebble mosaics decorate paths through these woods, known for their seasonal beauty. A graceful willow tree decorates the English lawn garden planted with traditional bulbs, annuals, and perennials. Today, a small rock garden, herb garden, and lily pond reflect the ideas of this mother and daughter. Though Oakhurst Gardens is in the middle of Muncie, it still retains a natural country setting. It also serves as a base for environmental studies within the Minnetrista Cultural Center created by later members of the family.

Oakhurst Gardens (65 miles northeast of Indianapolis) 600 W. Minnetrista Boulevard, Muncie, IN 47303 Tel: (765) 282-4848 Open: Tues., Sat. 10-5, Sun. 1-5, March through Dec., except holidays; Jan. through Feb. by appointment only Total acres: 5.3 Special collections: Cottage-style garden plantings, native wildflowers

ZONE 6 G P T WS

Irwin Home and Garden
Columbus

In 1864, Joseph I. Irwin built a modest house at Fifth and Mechanic Street (now Lafayette) that was eventually developed into a stately home with an equally grand landscape. Joseph's grandchildren, J. Irwin and his sister, Clementine, were both born in this house. J. Irwin Miller, who became an internationally known industrialist, instigated the greatest changes to the house and grounds. In 1910, he hired Massachusetts architect Henry A. Phillips to enlarge the house and plant the gardens, which were completed in 1911.

Phillips patterned the garden after an estate garden located on the outskirts of Pompeii, Italy. The center section of the garden was excavated to a low level and the excess soil was used to make a small hill to provide a bit of privacy to the garden. At the top of this hill stands a Roman garden house.

The gardens are composed of nine different areas, stretching from the garden house at the west to the east terrace adjacent to the house, where two open pergolas allow magnificent views of the grounds. On the raised eastern terrace, another historic motif decorates the roof beam of the covered area. An appropriate quote from Scottish poet Robert Burns reads: "An' when fatigued wi' close employment a blink o' rest's a sweet enjoyment." In keeping with the Italian garden style, greenery plays a big part throughout this garden, and sweeping lawns and ivy-covered beds offer a backdrop of green. Two long, matching beds on the upper terrace are planted in perennials chosen for pattern and seasonal color. Other locations and planters are filled with annuals, offering a variety of hues during different seasons. In spring, the brilliance comes from pansies and flowering bulbs while begonias and petunias shine in summer. In fall, sedum and chrysanthemums add autumnal shades. Annuals are grown from seed in the 7,500-square-foot greenhouse on the grounds.

Four statues representing ancient Greek scholars—Socrates, Plato, Aristotle, and Diogenes—await on the upper terrace, overlooking the lawn. Clipped hedges of Japanese yew and boxwood delineate the walkways and steps leading to the sunken garden's central pool. And at the far end of the sunken garden, steps lead upward to a long cascading fountain and the garden house beyond. Parallel to the garden house spreads a 30-by-80-foot herb garden. This area was a special project of Clementine Miller Tangeman. Here more than a thousand plants representing a hundred species of culinary, medicinal, and fragrant herbs are planted.

On the north side of the Irwins' garden, a semicircular brick wall provides an interesting backdrop for a bronze Japanese statue of an elephant. Adjacent lies the Crane Statue Garden, featuring a large Florentine statue of this bird within a courtyard bordered by evergreen shrubs. Trees lining the slope leading to the garden house are large linden, while Bradford pear trees and Norway spruce embellish other areas in the garden. The Irwin house has been occupied by the Miller family since 1864. In a show of their generosity and love of the garden, they open the grounds to the public every weekend during the growing season to allow others to enjoy this magical place.

Irwin Home and Garden (48 miles south of Indianapolis) 608 Fifth Street, Columbus, IN 47201 **Tel:** (812) 376-3331 **Open:** Sat.-Sun. 8-4, April through Oct. **Total acres:** Less than 1 **Special collections:** Italian-style garden, fountains, English herb garden **ZONE 6** **P**

The garden at the Irwin estate includes the major elements of a for Italian garden—water, stone, and green

CHICAGO BOTANIC GARDEN
GLENCOE

The Midwest is a landscape of soft, horizontal vistas, and the Chicago Botanic Garden makes the best possible use of that sense of space. Nearly two dozen gardens entice visitors off main walkways, from the Dwarf Conifer Garden to the Aquatic Garden. But an overall sense of openness and oneness is what gives the Chicago Botanic Garden its peaceful, unrushed feel.

This integrity is achieved by the lagoons that link the gardens and provide fluid views: a hint of the quiet Japanese Garden, the energy of the Waterfall Garden, a fuzzy impression of reeds ahead. Water also provides a palette on which to mix the reflected glow of red maples in fall, or dabs of white water-lilies. Smith Fountain rises like Old Faithful, a plume of spray that spreads like a diaphanous skirt when the wind blows. And around Chicago the wind does blow! The garden's horizontal order is molded with berms and hillocks in order

Purple irises create a splash of color in the Japanese Garden, best viewed from across the lake. The garden was designed by Koichi Kawan.

to break the ruthless gusts. These subtle touches of landscaping also help to make each new area a surprise.

Chicago Botanic Garden, which opened in 1972 in the city's northwest suburbs, is reminiscent of the renowned garden islands of Suchow, China. Its 385 acres include 75 acres of waterways, 9 islands, and more than a million plants. A high point, literally, is the Waterfall Garden, where water cascades down boulders. Footbridges cross the 45-foot cascades, providing close-ups of buttery yellow marsh marigolds, turtlehead's fat pink flowers, and languid cut-leaf sumac, plus long views of the tree-framed lagoon beyond. The trees are part of Turnbull Woods, where pink spring beauties and other wildflowers light the ground. Turnbull Woods presents another fanfare in autumn with the yellows, reds, and golds of witch hazel, maple, and oak.

By May, the six "rooms" of the English Walled Garden are a feast of flowers, spilling from beds and pots: lady's mantle and fox-glove, daisies and speedwell, and hundreds of others. Above, the sloping meadows of the English Oak Meadow are braided with banks of black-eyed Susans, sunflowers, zinnias, and vivid purple verbena. Waud Circle Garden, which extends the season for annuals into the fall, displays thousands of flowers, including crimson dahlias and golden coleus, with yews and Hinoki cypress adding vertical structure.

The Japanese Garden is soothing, with its carefully pruned pines, cherry trees offering clouds of blossoms in spring, and redtwig dogwoods providing

Designed to teach as well as delight, the botanic garden's displays often include plants rarely seen in a home garden, such as seed heads from ornamental onions and blooming spiked thistle, shown above.

late fall color. A mix of hard and soft textures intrigues the visitor: foliage engulfs rock and rocks part foliage. In summertime, prodigious collections of lilies and daylilies are full of dazzling variety. Like ice-cream choices, it is hard to find a favorite among raspberry ruffles, lemon blooms, or double peach. Visitors will find the prairie, flowing along the banks of the meandering Skokie River, at its best in late summer, when its gold and bronze grasses are studded with purple ironweed, amethyst asters, and sun-polished goldenrod.

The Chicago Botanic Garden protects endangered plants among its 7,000 species and exhibits new varieties of viburnum, ash, penstemon, and others bred to withstand the city's harsh weather. Exhibit halls, classrooms, a library, and educational greenhouses round out the complex and serve to foster horticultural knowledge.

Other areas include a garden for the disabled, where plants are placed so those in wheelchairs can see them. In addition, bulbs, roses, herbs, vegetables, and rock garden plants all have their own displays. Fountains and statuary abound, including a whimsical sculpture of Carl Linnaeus, inventor of the taxonomic system, surrounded by hide-and-seek creatures. And the landmark carillon rises over all.

CHICAGO BOTANIC GARDEN (28 miles north of Chicago) 1000 Lake Cook Road, Glencoe, IL 60022 **TEL:** (847) 835-5440 **OPEN:** Daily 8-dusk, except Christmas **TOTAL ACRES:** 385 **SPECIAL COLLECTIONS:** English walled garden, Japanese garden, prairie garden, aquatic garden, dwarf conifers

ZONE 5 C F G H P PA R T V WS

Chicago Park District Gardens
Chicago

Chicago's parks are so woven into the fabric of the city that the evocative gardens sometimes become mere backdrops for other events: jazz festivals in Grant Park, slow-pitch softball in Humboldt Park, and trips to the Lincoln Park Zoo. Yet the gardens are artful, some even designed to reflect the Midwest's wind-blown grace. Jens Jensen, the progenitor of the Prairie School of landscape design, was instrumental in designing Chicago's 500-plus parks. Encompassing about 7,000 acres scattered across Chicago, some are simple city parks, others floral delights.

Directly south of the Museum of Science and Industry along Lake Michigan, **Jackson Park** blends lagoons, recreation, and gardens. Wandering the winding paths of its Japanese Garden, visitors can glimpse the museum's dome through the trees as they note an island, arched bridge, pools, and subtle stonework. Frederick Law Olmsted, father of American landscape architecture, helped design Jackson Park's flower beds—a four-season visual feast. In winter, circular beds faced with sweeps of stone are anchored by trees whose bare limbs assume balletic forms. Spring bursts with crabapple blossoms, then peonies. Summer into fall the beds are ablaze with annuals and perennials. In the shade, white wands of cimicifuga mingle with ferns, pink obedient plant, and low mounds of white-and-green pulmonaria. Viburnums and hydrangeas add shrub accents.

Across from Oak Street Beach, the **Rosenbaum Perennial Garden** adds a colorful new canvas to the city's floral art. Among sun-splashed lawns, framed by awnings of trees, the garden's perennials undulate with casual elegance. Great drifts of white coneflowers, black-eyed Susans, daylilies, and others dance in Lake Michigan breezes.

At the south end of **Lincoln Park,** Lincoln Gardens centers on the plaza and monument to Lincoln. It is pretty homage, with broad beds of bulbs blooming in spring and followed by an array of flowers, from tall white sprays of 'Snowbank' boltonia and meadow rue's pink mist to ground-hugging bronze ajuga and shiny wild ginger. Blue bellflowers, cranesbill geraniums, lavender, and other cool-hued flowers contrast with hot rose champion, 'Goblin' gaillardia, and more. Fountain grass, spires of miscanthus, and spiky porcupine grass provide focal points.

Although its plants have changed with the times, **Grandmother's Garden,** outside the Lincoln Park Zoo, has remained in the same spot since the 1890s. An informal contrast to the nearby conservatory, this garden is awash with color in long beds that curve through green lawns in flowing figure eights, each bed a different mix of flowers. Clumps of red-hot poker, 'Black Knight' butterfly bush, and 'Galahad' delphinium create drama in one bed while blue forget-me-nots and shooting stars flutter among bleeding hearts and coral bells in another. Annuals include 'Apricot Brandy' cockscomb and scented nicotiana.

Garfield Park Conservatory, among the largest indoor gardens in the world, may be one of the nation's best-kept secrets. More than four acres of Jensen-designed habitats display ferns, cactuses, and tropical palms, each in its natural setting. Outside, formal fountains, flower beds, and a quiet lagoon tune down stress levels.

Chicago Park District Gardens: **Jackson Park** 6401 S. Stony Island Avenue; **Lincoln Park** 1600 N. Dearborn Street; **Grandmother's Garden** Stockton Drive and Lincoln Park West; **Garfield Park Conservatory** 300 N. Central Park Boulevard **Tel:** Department of Public Information (312) 742-7529; Garfield Park (312) 746-5100 **ZONE 5** A C **H** P PA **T**

A living tribute to the Bard of Avon, the small Shakespeare Garden on the campus of Northwestern University displays many plants and flowers found in Shakespeare's works. Here roses and phlox, pansies and peonies weave a poem of delight.

Shakespeare Garden
Evanston

The Shakespeare Garden on the campus of Northwestern University in Evanston, Illinois, fulfills William Shakespeare's description of a garden: "…flowers purple, blue, and white: Like sapphire, pearl and rich embroidery." Here, students come to recite the sonnets of the Bard, and garden lovers come to fill their eyes with pastel hues of Elizabethan flowers.

It all began when the Garden Club of Evanston decided to participate in the celebration of the 1916 Shakespeare Tercentenary by building a Shakespeare Garden. They called on the services of master landscape architect Jens Jensen, best known for his designs of large Chicago parks and informal prairie-type plantings. He complied with their wishes, and designed this charming little garden planted with flowers mentioned in Shakespeare's plays and sonnets. This is the smallest and one of the most formal of Jensen's gardens. The play of sun and shadow, an important element in all his designs, can be found here, where dappled shade and streaks of sun become as important as the leaves and petals. A double row of hawthorn trees surrounds and frames the 70-by-100-foot garden. Over the years, the garden has grown and matured, and today stone paths are lined with bee balm, roses, violets, and foxglove, and herbs such as thyme and rue.

Shakespeare Garden (12 miles north of Chicago) Northwestern University, Sheridan and Garrett Roads, Evanston, IL 60201 **Tel:** For tours only (847) 869-2657 **Open:** Daily dawn-dusk **Total acres:** 1 **Special collections:** Flowers from Shakespeare's writings, Jens Jensen design   **ZONE 5** A H P T

Baha'i House of Worship
Wilmette

When members of the Baha'i faith in Wilmette, Illinois, decided to build a house of worship in the early 1900s, their plans included a white building with intricate scrollwork, and a series of avenue gardens. The number nine, a symbol of unity in the Baha'i faith (a religious movement that originated in 19th-century Iran), became an important element in the design. Indeed, planners stipulated that there should be nine gardens, each containing both unifying and diversifying elements to represent the variety and unity of humanity.

The nine gardens, which were not created until 1952, radiate from the central building, each with a boundary of clipped yew and Chinese junipers. In front of the evergreen borders, collections of colorful bedding plants give each individual garden a distinct personality. Some beds comprise a casual collection of many different flowers, while others present a strict geometric formality. In spring, tulips and other flowering bulbs bloom in great profusion, creating a sea of color. As spring fades into summer, irises and poppies unfurl themselves, while such bedding plants as petunias and begonias put on a show until frost robs them of their rainbow hues. The long gardens at the Baha'i House of Worship add a sense of symmetry and balance to the ornate scrollwork found in the building. Long rows of clipped hedges and broad paths of manicured grass allow the gardens to provide a perfect place for quiet meditation.

Baha'i House of Worship (15 miles north of Chicago) 600 Sheridan Road, Wilmette, IL 60091 **Tel:** (847) 853-2300 **Open:** Daily 10-10, May through Aug.; daily 10-5, Sept. through April **Total acres:** 7 **Special collections:** Formal gardens, Chinese juniper trees   **ZONE 5** **G** **H** **HO** **P** **T**

In summer, the purplish spikes of blazing stars, also known as gayfeathers, complement the silhouette of Chinese junipers at the Baha'i House of Worship.

Washington Park Botanical Garden
Springfield

Washington Park Botanical Garden began in 1902 with a small greenhouse meant to grow a few bedding plants. Over time, it has become one of the region's most interesting horticultural attractions. The park, now listed as a National Historic Site, was designed by landscape architect O.C. Simonds, who is well known for many of his midwestern landscape designs, including Michigan's Cranbrook House and Gardens and the Morton Arboretum.

In response to local interest, the park district constructed a conservatory and horticultural center in 1972. Today the 50-foot-wide Conservatory Dome holds many exotic tropical plants native to warm regions throughout the world. Orchids, palms, and bromeliads are only some of the plantings grown here. The conservatory also presents changing seasonal displays that celebrate spring, Christmas, orchids, bonsai, and chrysanthemums. Outdoor displays also play an important role. Particularly exciting is the Rose Garden, where more than 3,500 plants bloom in waves of color. In the Shade Garden, hostas, ferns, impatiens, begonias, and caladiums thrive in a sun-dappled setting. Other gardens of interest are the Monocot Garden, with its impressive iris collection, the Daylily Garden, and a new rock garden.

Washington Park Botanical Garden (100 miles northeast of St. Louis, MO) 1740 West Fayette Avenue, Springfield, IL 62704 **Open:** Daily dawn-dusk, except Christmas **Total acres:** 20 **Special collections:** Roses, irises, daylilies, shade plants, rock garden   **ZONE 5** A C G H L P PA T

Lincoln Memorial Garden
Springfield

This native woodland garden along Lake Springfield's southern shore was designed in 1936 by Jens Jensen. Famous for his naturalistic designs, Jensen's basic plan consisted of a series of interconnected nature trails bordered by arrangements of native plants. He sought to create a sense of the midwestern landscape that President Abraham Lincoln would have known from his time in Springfield. Like spokes of a wheel, the trails lead to eight circular areas where curved benches of stone are positioned to foster friendly gatherings. Each strategically placed bench is inscribed with one of Lincoln's inspirational sayings.

Groves of oak and hickory, open meadows of sun-loving prairie species, and groupings of small flowering trees and shrubs form the borders between meadows and woods. In springtime, dogwoods, redbuds, and crabapples bloom along with carpets of woodland wildflowers such as trillium, bloodroot, and bluebells. One of the state's many endangered species is found in the garden— the silverbell tree, known for its delicate flowers. Summer is the time for prairie grasses and flowers such as purple coneflower, liatris, and prairie rose. Fall follows with asters, goldenrod, and the yellow and scarlet hues of the trees. In winter, maple syrup production is a popular demonstration project. The garden is a project of the Garden Clubs of Illinois.

Lincoln Memorial Garden (11 miles from downtown Springfield) 2301 E. Lake Drive, Springfield, IL 62707 **Tel:** (217) 529-1111 **Open:** Tues.-Sun. dawn-dusk, Feb. through Dec., except holidays **Total acres:** 77 **Special collections:** Wildflowers, flowering trees, Jens Jensen design   **ZONE 5** G P T WS

Morton Arboretum
Lisle

In the late 1800s, Joy Morton founded the Morton Salt Company; in 1922, he established the Morton Arboretum. One was his business, the other his pleasure. Dr. Charles Sprague Sargent, an early director of Boston's Arnold Arboretum, told Joy, "You realize, I hope, that you will be remembered for the arboretum long after the salt business is forgotten." Today the Morton Arboretum is one of the finest in the world. Starting with Morton's estate in Lisle, west of Chicago, the arboretum has grown to 1,700 acres of woodlands, prairies, ponds, and gardens representing more than 3,600 species. Because of its enormous size, areas have been grouped around 13 trails, all of which can be reached by roads. Like most arboretums, this one is organized by groups: maples here, oaks there, azaleas and rhododendrons not far from the viburnums. Morton also presents entire plant "cultures" in sections devoted to Europe, the Appalachians, Illinois, and other regions. Intriguing plants from Russia and northeast Asia include magnolia vine, kiwis, paperbark maple with exquisite exfoliating cinnamon bark, spireas with noteworthy foliage, and an Oriental cousin of the vining Dutchman's pipe.

Morton Arboretum shows off spectacular collections, including one of the country's premier restored tall-grass prairies, the Schulenberg Prairie. This area provides a glimpse of the vast grasslands that once stretched over the Midwest, but were mostly all plowed under. Since prairie grasses grow in clumps, the spaces between are filled with flowers. Accordingly, in spring this prairie is lit by feathery heads of the purple-pink pasque flower, followed by tall, elegant spires of white baptisia. Here, too, rattlesnake-master unfolds intricate green geometry and prairie dock rises high with yellow daisies and huge elephant-ear leaves. Pink prairie rose suffuses the air with sweet scent and dropseed, that most gorgeous of grasses, swirls patterns of fine blades against the ground. Later, purple coneflower and blue lead plant poke through switch grass and towering stalks of big bluestem.

At the other end of the spectrum, the arboretum's hedges present calm, orderly views. Centered on four white columns, they form the oldest public hedge demonstration garden in the United States. These precisely cut low green walls show what gardeners can do with common hedge choices as well as with unusual selections such as hemlock, white pine, and shingle oak. Nearby spreads the arboretum's spring glory: its crabapple collection, smothered with shades of pink, white, and red. On the other side of the arboretum lies another example of what spring can bring: thousands of daffodils tracing patterns in green glades punctuated by trees. Close by lies the aptly named Joy Path, Morton's favorite walk. The trail winds from Thornhill Education Center past perennial beds devoted to fragrance and color, continuing on toward the quiet scenery of Lake Marmo, framed by pines. While the maple woods turn fiery in fall, the cool pines remain dignified all year. Arboretums were originally established to delight and educate, and Sterling Morton Library remains as valuable a resource as the trees. Like zoos, arboretums are aware of the need to preserve. In conjunction with the Chicago Botanic Garden, the Morton Arboretum is working to preserve such endangered plants as forked aster and eastern prairie fringed orchid, as well as habitats enchanting to gardeners and bird-watchers alike.

Morton Arboretum (25 miles west of Chicago) 4100 Ill. 53, Lisle, IL 60532 **Tel:** (630) 719-2400 **Open:** Daily 7-dusk **Total acres:** 1,700 **Special collections:** Native woodlands, tall-grass prairie, diversity of trees, crabapples

ZONE 5 F G H L P PA R T V WS

e Morton Arboretum is home to many exciting collections of trees, as well as h flowering shrubs as this stand of pink rhododendron (opposite).

Cantigny
Wheaton

Ten acres of formally landscaped gardens grace the grounds of the former home of Robert McCormick, onetime editor and publisher of the *Chicago Tribune*. McCormick, who inherited the land and a small house from his grandfather, was the commanding officer of the First Division during World War I. He subsequently named the estate Cantigny after a small town in France, site of the first American victory of the war.

In the early 1930s Robert and his wife, Amy, decided to make Cantigny a showplace, hiring an architect to completely renovate the house. They then began to work on the gardens, and the grounds have been continually improved in size and scope since. In 1967 Franz Lipp, a noted landscape architect, designed 21 different gardens and plant collections to be incorporated into the estate and today visitors stroll through a series of manicured lawns connecting these spots of delight.

The scope of the gardens at Cantigny is staggering, and each area is worthy of a visit in itself. Those faced with the delightful challenge of touring the entire ten acres of gardens have a choice. Visitors who have come to learn should bring pencil and paper to note the multitude of ideas that will arise while touring the inspiring displays. For those who are here simply to enjoy the fragrance and beauty of the flowers, the only tools needed are the senses, poised to experience a spectacular show.

Masses of bedding plants can be found in several of the gardens where, in summer, vibrant colors shimmer in the Illinois sun. In the Bur Oak Garden, layers of flowers have been planted to create a living rainbow of colors. Marigolds alternate with purple impatiens, pink petunias, and multicolored snapdragons while flowering vines cover elaborate lattice frames within this garden. Redbrick paths weave in and out of the flowers, allowing visitors to become a part of the landscape itself. Although this garden is spectacular in summer, it is even more so in spring, when thousands of tulips herald the season. In autumn, baskets of chrysanthemums adorn posts lining the walks.

The Fountain Garden is also in its glory in spring, when flowering trees and shrubs fairly burst with blossoms. Not all the gardens here are so vibrantly colored. The Green Garden, for example, is best viewed in winter, when competition from other gardens is greatly reduced. Here visitors marvel at the many shades of green found so abundantly in the plant world. Also of interest are the Scalloped Gardens, found on either side of the lawn east of the Visitor Center. These are thoughtfully planted with such shade-loving plants as begonias, impatiens, and caladiums.

Popular with those who have their own gardens, the Idea Garden presents common and unusual plants used in a variety of ways. For example, a wire chaise lounge form planted with grass creates—what else?—a lawn chair. This garden is divided into four areas, displaying herbs, vegetables, planted containers, and in the fourth quadrant, a children's garden. The latter's innovative gardening and topiary figures make it a favorite for all ages.

Cantigny (30 miles west of Chicago) 1 South, 151 Winfield Road, Wheaton, IL 60187 Tel: (630) 668-5161 Open: Tues.-Sun. 9-dusk, March through Dec.; Fri.-Sun. 9-dusk, Feb.; except holidays Total Acres: 10 Special Collections: Estate garden, spring bulbs, summer annuals, topiary

ZONE 5 F G H HO P PA R T V WS

ention to detail, typified by this mosaic walk, is seen throughout Cantigny. Thousands of
ding plants, such as salvias, petunias, and verbenas (opposite), are massed annually.

CRANBROOK HOUSE AND GARDENS
BLOOMFIELD HILLS

In January 1904, work began on a project in Bloomfield Hills, Michigan, that would eventually transform a corner of old worn-out farmland into a place of such beauty as to draw visitors from all over the globe. Cranbrook was the home, estate, and dream of the publisher of the *Detroit Evening News,* George Booth, and his wife, Ellen, both of whom were intimately involved with the American arts and crafts movement. The Booths's dream was to make Cranbrook an educational community in which horticulture, art, and craft would be an integral part of both home and work life. Although their proposed school of landscape design was never established, they did develop the grounds around the family home into ambitious gardens.

The estate's design reflects the work of several landscape architects, although the greatest influence came from O.C. Simonds, who worked at the estate for 13 years, beginning in 1910. Simonds, a follower of Jens Jensen, labored hard to ensure that the gardens and architecture fit the natural contours of the land. The result is a feeling of grace and balance between the grounds and the modern architecture of the buildings.

The grounds immediately surrounding the house were designed as formal Italian gardens. Intricate stonework, statuary, and long swaths of green lawn all contribute to the overall impact. At the east side of the mansion lies a formal, symmetrical herb garden. Planted and maintained by the Michigan branch of the Herb Society of America, it includes herbs used for cooking, medicine, and crafts.

Round heads of alliums contrast with the spiked swords of irises in the perennial beds of Cranbrook's terrace garden, which was fashioned in a formal Italian design.

Beyond the Sunken Garden's high fieldstone walls, planting beds are filled to bursting with seasonal color. Visitors can walk past the formal gardens to the landscape beyond, where many additional informal areas also offer lovely views. More than a hundred different species of trees grow at the estate,

Triangles and squares filled with useful herbs lie within low-growing hedges of small clipped boxwood, all providing an air of formality in keeping with the Cranbrook gardens.

presenting quite a spectacle as their leaves turn brilliant colors in autumn. In April and May, a stroll along the path leading to the Kingswood Lake boathouse becomes a trip through a flower fairyland, amid ground covered with small spring-blooming bulbs.

Past the boathouse awaits the recently restored Oriental Garden, one of the estate's original gardens. In addition, many wooded areas are planted with such shade-tolerant shrubs as rhododendron, azalea, and viburnum. Other areas of interest include a bog garden, where irises and other water-loving plants thrive, and the Greek Theater, surrounded by flowering shrubs. One of Cranbrook's most pleasing gardens, Ellen's Garden, is planted in Ellen Booth's favorite colors, pink and purple. The original lily pool, at one time full of exotic waterlilies, is now called the Reflection Pool and serves to mirror the colorful annuals and perennials that surround it. Here, too, is found a peony collection, a real treat for visitors in spring.

Today Cranbrook holds the distinction of being one of the largest public gardens in North America to be completely planted and maintained by volunteers. In keeping with the Booths's passion for community, it remains a mecca for those who love to work and learn together.

CRANBROOK HOUSE AND GARDENS (22 miles northwest of Detroit) 380 Lone Pine Road, Box 801, Bloomfield Hills, MI 48303 **TEL:** (248) 645-3149 **OPEN:** Daily 10-5, May through Oct. **TOTAL ACRES:** 40 **SPECIAL COLLECTIONS:** Italian-style garden, spring bulbs, sunken garden, herbs

ZONE 6 A F G H HO P T WS

Anna Scripps Whitcomb Conservatory
Detroit

One of Detroit's more popular getaway spots is Belle Isle, home to the Belle Isle Zoo, the aquarium, and the beautiful Anna Scripps Whitcomb Conservatory. In 1883 Frederick Law Olmsted, designer of New York City's Central Park, developed a master plan for the grounds of Belle Isle with his characteristic grace. Its center-piece, the original conservatory, was built in 1904 and has long been a source of pride for Detroit's citizens. Designed by Albert Kahn and patterned after Thomas Jefferson's Monticello, it was completely rebuilt beginning in 1949 and dedicated to Detroit philanthropist Anna Scripps Whitcomb in 1955.

More than a million people have visited the conservatory, which now includes several different display rooms. In the Palm House, large trees, such as great palms that measure up to 60 feet in height and weigh as much as 8,000 pounds, bring a touch of the tropics to the Midwest. Many of the palm trees now grow-ing in the conservatory are native to Florida, though species indigenous to Africa and Asia are also present.

The Tropical Room is home to an outstanding orchid collection, one of the largest in the country. In and among the orchids thrive brilliantly colored vines and tropical flowers such as bougainvillea, allamanda, stephanotis, and hibiscus. In addition, tropical fruit trees such as breadfruit, papaya, pomegranate, lemon, and orange not only bloom, but bear fruit in this indoor garden.

Nearby, the Cactus Room provides quite a contrast, with such desert plants as aloe, agave, and yucca, as well as many different species of cactus. Although

The bronze "Children's Temperance Fountain" is nestled among orchids and framed by the leaves of a heliconia in the Anna Scripps Whitcomb Conservatory in Detroit.

this collection includes species from many different arid regions, the majority of the plants exhibited are native to the deserts of the American Southwest. The aptly named Fernery showcases a splendid diversity of ferns, from diminutive spleenworts to huge Australian tree ferns.

Arguably, the most spectacular displays may be found in the Show House, where the exhibits change several times a year. The six major floral shows staged here are the Winter Show, featuring cyclamen and primrose; Easter, with lilies, spring bulbs, and azaleas; Mother's Day, when amaryllis takes center stage; Summer, with fuchsias, gloxinias, caladiums, and coleus; the Chrysanthemum Show, which displays this plant's amazing diversity of color and flower; and the Christmas Show, when thousands of pink, white, and red poinsettias herald the season.

While the plants in the conservatory can be enjoyed year-round, the formal gardens outside also provide a source of pleasure. Here, the careful selection of plant material allows an abundance of color and beauty from March to October. In April and May, azaleas and other rhododendrons create a colorful backdrop to the spring-blooming bulbs. Late spring and early summer bring tulips, poppies, delphinium, and phlox in a riot of color, and in June, old-fashioned garden roses reach their peak.

ANNA SCRIPPS WHITCOMB CONSERVATORY Belle Isle, Detroit, MI 48207 **TEL:** (313) 852-4065 **OPEN:** Daily 10-5 **TOTAL ACRES:** 5 **SPECIAL COLLECTIONS:** Tropical plants, desert plants, orchids, old-fashioned roses
ZONE 6 C F H P PA T WS

MATTHAEI BOTANICAL GARDENS
ANN ARBOR

From the long, dangling fingers of the giant staghorn fern to the lilac-lined pathways surrounding the formal herb garden, the Matthaei Botanical Gardens offer diversity, beauty, and excitement. Opened in 1907 under the auspices of the University of Michigan, the gardens encompass 350 acres, including a 17,000-square-foot conservatory that is home to more than 1,500 species of plants noted for their beauty or economic value. Three different display houses— Tropical, Warm Temperate, and Arid—showcase an astonishing variety of plants.

Outside are such areas of interest as the Gateway Garden, which features ornamental plants developed from wild species indigenous to the New World. The Herb Knot Garden presents herbs used in cooking, medicine, fragrance, and crafts, all within a formal European design. Plants and ferns native to Michigan and the Great Lakes area are the focus of the Woodland Wildflower Garden. Surrounded by a maple and yew hedge, the Rose and Perennial Garden's formal English design is filled with more than 120 different varieties and cultivars. While these formal garden areas are certainly beautiful, the more natural areas also possess special charm. Of particular note are the reconstructed wetlands, planted with reeds and sedges, and the Prairie Plantings, complete with showy wildflowers and native prairie grasses. Not content to rest on its laurels, the Matthaei has three new attractions in the planning stage—an Ethnobotany Trail, a collection of native Michigan trees, and a bonsai display.

MATTHAEI BOTANICAL GARDENS (42 miles west of Detroit) University of Michigan, 1800 N. Dixboro Road, Ann Arbor, MI 48105 **TEL:** (313) 998-7061 **OPEN:** Daily 8-dusk, except holidays **TOTAL ACRES:** 350 **SPECIAL COLLECTIONS:** Herb garden, roses, perennials, wildflowers, tropical plants
ZONE 6 C F G H HO P T WS

The display gardens at Michigan State University include many unusual combinations of plants. They are used to educate students about how to grow and landscape with perennials and annuals. Many of the plants are new to the horticultural trade.

Horticultural Demonstration Gardens
East Lansing

A college is, by definition, a place of learning. But not all learning takes place in the classroom. At Michigan State University in East Lansing, a school with a rich heritage of famous botanists and important horticultural research, the campus itself provides many opportunities for furthering knowledge of plants, people, and gardening. World-renowned horticulturists, such as Liberty Hyde Bailey and William James Beal, have been closely associated with this university, originally known as Michigan State College of Agriculture. Today, the school continues its tradition of horticultural excellence by creating and maintaining gardens. Although the entire campus is beautifully landscaped, three areas have been set aside as gardens, each representing unique interpretations of the magical blend of plants and people.

The first, the **Horticultural Demonstration Garden,** was developed primarily for educational purposes. Its goal was to determine which annuals, perennials, and roses best grew in this area, and to give horticulture and landscape design students an outdoor laboratory for field work. An added benefit of these educational endeavors, of course, is the beauty and fragrance the gardens provide throughout the growing season. Made up of five distinctly different gardens—

the Annual Trial Garden, the Foyer Garden, the Rose Garden, the Perennial Garden, and the Idea Garden—this area at the southern end of campus has become one of the most scenic spots in all of the large state of Michigan, where students and visitors alike come to learn from and enjoy the tremendous number of flowers.

Serving as a giant entrance hall, the Foyer Garden is decorated with trellises and flowering vines, offering a perfect vantage point from which to view the surrounding gardens. By midsummer, the Annual Trial Garden, in which more than a thousand new cultivars are tested each year, is a mass of glorious color, while the nearby Perennial Garden is filled with both old-fashioned and soon-to-be favorites. The plants in the latter garden have been chosen for their beauty, ease of care, and ability to offer interest and color throughout much of the growing season. Several family-size plots comprise the Idea Garden, filled with a variety of plants used in innovative and interesting ways and offering a rich harvest of creative ideas.

The university's next garden area, the **W. J. Beal Botanical Garden**, was first created by William J. Beal in 1873, as an outdoor laboratory for his botany students. Beal planted 140 species of native and naturalized grasses and wildflowers on a small plot of land near the Red Cedar River on campus, thus giving his students an easily accessible place in which to study plants in the field. Beal's original weed patches, as they were affectionately called, have today grown to include more than 5,000 different kinds of plants. Like a living textbook, they are carefully labeled and grouped into four main areas: plant families, useful plants (including those used in medicine, food, as fiber), forest communities (where trees and understory plants are planted together as they are found in nature), and landscape plants (which include plants of ornamental value).

The final garden area, the **4-H Children's Garden**, offers a surprise at every corner and fun planted in every bed. One of the most popular sites on campus, this treat for all ages was designed in part by children at the MSU Laboratory School. From the swinging gate to Alice in Wonderland's evergreen maze, the garden offers an interactive experience. Plants grown here were chosen for their names (such as trumpet vine and 'Piccolo' cosmos, grown close to the Dance Chimes), for education (geraniums, black-eyed peas, hibiscus, and okra, for example, are all native to Africa and planted in the African-American garden), and for fun (such as the alphabet garden, which goes from asters to zinnias). One of this garden's goals is to help children make the connection between the many commercial products for which plants are the primary source and the plants themselves. For example, cotton such as that used to make T-shirts and blue jeans grows in the Cloth and Color Garden, while the Cereal Bowl Garden sprouts wheat, corn, and oats.

Southeast of East Lansing, **Hidden Lakes Arboretum** provides a home to thousands of labeled trees and shrubs on 670 acres. The arboretum, also owned by Michigan State University, offers students and visitors the opportunity to hike amid several miles of mature trees, visit indoor gardens featuring such plants as bamboo, sugarcane, and tapioca, or wander the outdoor gardens, specializing in plant collections such as azaleas, lilacs, and magnolias.

HORTICULTURAL DEMONSTRATION GARDENS (88 miles west of Detroit) Michigan State University, Wilson and Bogue Streets, East Lansing, MI 48824 **TEL:** (517) 355-0348 **OPEN:** Daily dawn-dusk **TOTAL ACRES:** 7.5 **SPECIAL COLLECTIONS:** Roses, annuals, perennials, wildflowers, children's garden

ZONE 5 C **F** G **H** HO P PA R T WS

Dow Gardens
Midland

As water spills and tumbles over huge white boulders, and the rich growth of conifers sways in the breeze, visitors to Dow Gardens might think they are deep in the heart of a wilderness rather than only a few steps away from Main Street, Midland. Originally the home of Herbert Dow, founder of Dow Chemical Company, and his wife, Grace, the estate today is living testimony not only of Dow's tremendous love of plants, but also of his sense of humor, energy, and creativity, as evidenced in a landscape of red lacquered bridges, berms called "the bumps," and other imaginative features.

Herbert Dow began the gardens in 1900 with the help of Elzie Cote, his chief gardener. Together they dug, planted, and transformed woods and fields into the stunning landscaped garden that now covers 112 acres. Among their achievements is a man-made lake, half a mile long, with a shore that gently twists and curves to give the impression that it has been there forever. In addition, red bridges span the stream, offering views of the surrounding landscape.

The continually changing displays at Dow Gardens include both natural, informal settings and formal areas such as the rose and herb gardens. Today, rhododendrons and crabapple trees both receive special attention here, as researchers try to determine which cultivars and varieties perform best in this climate and are most resistant to pests and disease.

Dow Gardens (128 miles northwest of Detroit) West Street at Andrews and Eastman Avenues, Midland, MI 48640 **Tel:** (517) 631-2677 **Open:** Daily 10-dusk, except holidays **Total acres:** 112 **Special collections:** Estate garden, rhododendrons, crabapples, roses **ZONE 5** C F G H HO P T WS

Grand Hotel
Mackinac Island

Touted as the world's largest summer hotel, the Grand Hotel on Mackinac Island has long been an attraction. And since the early 1980s, when the hotel made a commitment to improve the grounds and landscaping, it has become an intriguing horticultural destination as well. The hotel grounds include natural wooded areas, landscaped sections, and many gardens. The overall design dates from the Victorian era, and includes such plants prized by turn-of-the-century gardeners as old-fashioned roses, cosmos, hollyhocks, and heliotrope. Each year more than 110,000 annual plants are sown—and the effect is understandably stunning. An especially pleasant place to take in the view is from a rocking chair on the hotel's long, white porch, on which bloom thousands of red geraniums, a Grand Hotel trademark. Guests are greeted with a profusion of flowers and encouraged to visit the gardens for pleasure, relaxation, and meditation. It is possible to walk to many garden areas from the hotel, including the Rose Walk, the formal Tea Garden, and the Wedding Garden. No automobiles are allowed on the island. As the landscape here has grown and matured, newer gardens have been added, including a recently installed wildflower hillside garden in front of the porch, and the meditative Labyrinth Garden, patterned after one found at Chartres Cathedral, in France.

Grand Hotel (300 miles north of Detroit) Mackinac Island, MI 49757 **Tel:** (906) 847-3331 **Open:** Daily dawn-dusk, May through Oct. **Total acres:** 150 **Special collections:** Victorian flower bed, topiary, labyrinth garden **ZONE 5** F G H HO PA R T V WS

Two bridges span the small stream created by Dow's youngest son, Alden. An architect who studied with Frank Lloyd Wright, he considered water an essential element of the landscape.

MITCHELL PARK CONSERVATORY
MILWAUKEE

During their long winter of cloudy days and freezing temperatures, sun-starved citizens of Milwaukee are drawn to Mitchell Park Conservatory like bees to flowers. When the original conservatory was constructed at the very end of the 19th century, the surrounding 60 acres were developed into a park that included outdoor gardens such as the sunken garden, built in 1904. In 1955 the old conservatory was deemed no longer functional and replaced by three glass-domed buildings, each representing a different ecosystem. The Show Dome, perhaps the most popular today, is transformed five times a year to display different garden themes, based on ethnic, holiday, or seasonal displays. Through the magic of show horticulture, this dome may at any one time be a Polynesian tropical garden, a Smoky Mountain spring woodland, or anything in between.

The Arid Dome offers an example of conservatory horticulture at its best. Here, the conservatory staff demonstrates its impressive knowledge regarding the exact

At Mitchell Park, the Arid Dome houses a world class collection of cactuses, palms, and succulents.

cultural conditions needed to grow the variety of plants exhibited, as well as the ability to provide these conditions. On display are the different ecosystems found within arid regions, including an oasis planted with palms and pampas grass, and an arroyo, a deep gully created by sudden torrential rain, planted with cactuses and succulents. Plants from many different desert regions are also represented, including the Sonoran Desert of the American Southwest and northern Mexico, and the deserts of South America, southern Africa, the Canary Islands, and Madagascar.

The warm and humid Tropical Dome provides the perfect solution to the winter blues. Within, more than a thousand species of plants thrive, collected from tropical regions all over the world. Water tumbles over impressive rock structures, creating a constant mist to accompany the sounds of a waterfall and allowing for an instant imaginative trip to regions far away. In addition, impossibly intricate orchids dangle gracefully from trees or peek out from under lush, big-leaved shrubs. Many of the plants found in this dome represent species of great economic value, such as coffee, rubber, mahogany, and chocolate, as well as the favorite food plants banana, orange, and papaya. While the domes provide refuge from winter weather, the adjacent outdoor sunken garden is enormously popular during spring and summer months. Here, at the height of season, grow popular bedding plants as well as an impressive display of beautiful blooming waterlilies.

MITCHELL PARK CONSERVATORY 524 S. Layton Boulevard, Milwaukee, WI 53215 TEL: (414) 649-9830 OPEN: Daily 9-5 TOTAL ACRES: 60 SPECIAL COLLECTIONS: Desert plants, tropical plants, orchids, sunken garden   ZONE 5 C F G H HO P PA V WS

In addition to attractive outdoor displays, Mitchell Park Conservatory offers three distinctly different indoor landscapes—the Show Dome, the Arid Dome, and the Tropical Dome.

Boerner Botanical Gardens
Hales Corners

The view just outside the Garden House at Boerner Botanical Gardens is stunning. While the distant vista encompasses seemingly endless miles of trees and grassy fields, intricately designed and immaculately maintained formal gardens bloom close at hand, all combining to convey the feel of a grand European estate. This is exactly what Alfred Boerner had in mind in 1932, when assigned the task of creating a botanical garden at Whitnall Park. A landscape architect working for the county, he dreamed of creating a corner of Europe at this park near Milwaukee. Today the result of Boerner's work shines in the L-shaped collection of formal gardens surrounding the small stone house used as a Garden Center. Separate areas are delineated, such as the Rose Garden composed of 350 different kinds of roses, and the Perennial Garden, planted with almost 10,000 plants. Horticultural collections include herbs, shrubs, daylilies, crabapples, and many other types of plants, grown not simply for the beauty of their display, but also to determine which cultivars and species perform best in this climate. The botanical garden now bears Boerner's name, a tribute to his vision made reality.

Boerner Botanical Gardens (12 miles southwest of Milwaukee) Whitnall Park, 5879 S. 92nd Street, Hales Corners, WI 53130 **Tel:** (414) 425-1131 **Open:** Daily 8-dusk, April through Oct. **Total acres:** Garden 40, arboretum 1,000 **Special collections:** Tulips, peonies, roses, herb garden, crabapples

ZONE 5 G H P P PA T WS

Olbrich Botanical Gardens
Madison

Although a visit to Olbrich Botanical Gardens is a treat any time of year, it is perhaps in the middle of the cold Wisconsin winter that visitors best appreciate the warmth, sunshine, and abundant greenery of the 10,000-foot conservatory. Its rich history began in 1916, when Michael Olbrich started purchasing land along the shore of Lake Monona with the intent of creating a public garden for the people of Madison. Decades later, this vision has resulted in the 14-acre garden that bears his name. Outdoors, ten specialty gardens are connected by a network of pathways. The newest area, the Sunken Garden, is framed by a shrub hedge and features an 80-foot-long reflecting pool. The Rock Garden is planted with alpine plants and dwarf conifers on a dry, mountainlike slope. Other garden areas focus on particular plant collections, such as wildflowers, herbs, hostas, dahlias, irises, roses, and shade plants.

The Bolz Conservatory shelters more than 750 tropical plants as well as a bamboo arbor, large palm trees, and a waterfall that tumbles into a bubbling stream. Several species of birds, including canaries, waxbills, and diamond doves, make their homes here as well.

Olbrich Botanical Gardens (77 miles southwest of Milwaukee) 3330 Atwood Avenue, Madison, WI 53704 **Tel:** (608) 246-4550 **Open:** Daily 8-8, June through Aug.; daily 8-4, Sept. through May; except holidays **Total acres:** 14 **Special collections:** Wildflowers, herbs, roses, irises, rock garden, sunken garden, tropical plants   **ZONE 5** C F G H P PA V WS

Paine Art Center and Arboretum
Oshkosh

If you've ever wanted to skip down a primrose path, the Paine Art Center and Arboretum is the place to do it. The Primrose Path, found in a carefully planted woodland garden, is only one of several pleasing landscaped areas in this arboretum, first established by lumber magnate Nathan Paine in 1930.

Paine envisioned an estate surrounded by a landscape that would include not only gardens built to suit the formality of the house, but also more natural areas showcasing trees and shrubs native to Wisconsin. Today, the grounds of the arboretum successfully accomplish this goal. The sunken English Garden, with its low stone walls, fountain, and stone walkways, presents an almost exact replica of the Dutch Pond Garden found at Hampton Court, England. In turn, the Herb Garden's brick paths create geometrical beds planted with herbs used for medicine, fragrance, or ornamentation in the 18th century. In the Rose Garden, more than one hundred hardy rose bushes surround a fountain and reflection pool.

The newest addition to the arboretum, Mr. McGregor's Garden, was created for children and features plants mentioned in Beatrix Potter's fabled *Tales of Peter Rabbit*. Adjacent to the formal gardens, natural areas include a tree and shrub collection and a prairie-woodland garden. Paths of all types, from formal stone to woodland mulch, invite visitors to wander through the arboretum.

Paine Art Center and Arboretum (85 miles north of Milwaukee) 1410 Algoma Boulevard, Oshkosh, WI 54901 **Tel:** (920) 235-6903 **Open:** Tues.-Sun. 10-4, except holidays **Total acres:** 9.2 **Special collections:** Formal gardens, roses, herbs, children's garden   **ZONE 4** F G H HO P PA R T WS

ed iris leaves offer sharp contrast to the colorful mounds of coreopsis, coneflower, bee
n, and yarrow found in this perennial bed at Boerner Botanical Gardens (opposite).

Minnesota Landscape Arboretum
Chanhassen

Swaths of prairie, formal geometric beds filled with seasonal color, herb gardens, and acres of trees composed in unquestionably beautiful woods—all are found on the grounds of this treasure, the Minnesota Landscape Arboretum. As one of the country's northernmost botanical gardens, it is important both as a display garden and for the research conducted here. The arboretum also serves as a clearing house for information on northern climate gardening.

The grounds of the arboretum opened in 1958 and cover 939 acres, including many different types of landscapes. Among the most important features are the Home Demonstration Gardens, created in 1985. Divided into nine different sites, this area offers living proof that productive and visually pleasing landscapes can be created anywhere, even on a small scale. Within the Garden For Small Spaces, diminutive plants grown in containers and small beds show that limited space should not be a deterrent to beautiful gardening. Other home demonstration gardens showcase fruits, vegetables, native plants, herbs, and cut flowers.

Summer's center stage belongs to the annual beds, bursting at the seams with colors of every hue. Flowers create striking displays which, much to the delight of the repeat visitor, reflect a different creative theme each year. As an example, the year the topic was argyle socks, beds were planted in clever diamond shapes. In other years flower beds have resembled patchwork quilts or Matisse paintings. As might be expected, the Perennial Garden's long-lived plants have been chosen for their ability to withstand harsh midwestern winters as well as their offerings of color and interest throughout much of the growing season. In addition, new species and cultivars are tested for their horticultural value each year.

Used both by individual families and the public school system, the Learning Center teaches children about plants, touching on botany, natural science, and gardening. The Prairie Area serves as a living tribute to the thousands of acres of natural prairie that once flourished in Minnesota. Today wildflowers and grasses grow together in this naturalized area.

The Three Mile Drive winds through the arboretum, allowing visitors to view many different kinds of horticultural collections, including outstanding flowering crabapples, azaleas, hedges, weeping trees, and lilacs. Of particular interest is the Hosta Collection, recognized by the American Hosta Society as a National Display Garden. For those who enjoy traditional gardens, the modern rose garden, herb garden, and rock garden offer a different horticultural experience.

The arboretum staff is dedicated to offering visitors an educational experience as well as an aesthetic one, and many classes and workshops are given throughout the year. An extensive labeling system also helps visitors identify various plants. And for those who see and want, the Andersen Horticultural Library's computerized index of cultivated plants allows gardeners to find a commercial source for more than 47,000 different plants.

Minnesota Landscape Arboretum (21 miles southwest of Minneapolis) 3675 Arboretum Drive, Chanhassen, MN 55317 **Tel:** (612) 443-2460 **Open:** Daily 8-dusk, except holidays **Total acres:** 939 **Special collections:** Demonstration gardens, hosta glade, wildflowers, Japanese garden, perennials, annuals, prairie plants   ZONE 4   C   F   G   H   L   P   PA   R   T   V   WS

Tall spires of yellow cockscomb dominate this planting bed, vivid proof that the Minnesota Landscape Arboretum spotlights much more than trees.

LYNDALE PARK GARDENS
MINNEAPOLIS

Located in Lyndale Park on the shore of Lake Harriet is Minneapolis's **Rose Garden**, the second oldest in the nation. It was built by Theodore Wirth, the designer of the first municipal rose garden in Hartford, Connecticut. Sixty-two rose beds flourish on two acres, showcasing hybrid tea, grandiflora, floribunda, miniature roses, and an All-America Rose Selections Test Garden. Across the road from the rose garden is a rock garden that has gone through several stages—from an original design described as the Devil's Lapful, later leveled by a tornado, to today's diversified selection of dwarf conifers and hardy alpines on three acres.

Three miles away is the **Eloise Butler Wildflower Garden and Bird Sanctuary**, established in 1907 by a group of botany teachers. Here trails wind through 14 acres of varied landscape. Visitors may stroll through woodland, swamp, upland, and prairie habitats. Those touring the gardens from May through July may also view various rare and endangered wildflowers native to this region.

LYNDALE PARK GARDENS: ROSE GARDEN E. Lake Harriet Parkway and Roseway Road **ELOISE BUTLER WILDFLOWER GARDEN AND BIRD SANCTUARY** 1 Theodore Wirth Parkway, Minneapolis, MN 55209 **TEL:** (612) 370-4900 **OPEN:** Daily dawn-dusk; Butler closed Nov. through March **TOTAL ACRES:** Park 63 **SPECIAL COLLECTIONS:** Roses, rock garden, wildflowers   ZONE 4 | A | **H** | P | PA | T | V

COMO PARK CONSERVATORY
ST. PAUL

Citizens and visitors of St. Paul, Minnesota, can enjoy a tropical day, any day, at the conservatory that graces this city. With arched domes of glass protecting a multitude of tropical plants from the harsh Midwest climate, the Como Park Conservatory is a dream put into action by Park Superintendent Frederick Nussbaumer. He saw it become reality when the conservatory, built for $58,000, opened to the public in 1915. Although at the time the building was state-of-the-art, by 1980 major renovations costing 12 million dollars were necessary.

Today, the conservatory includes a Palm Dome housing palm species from all over the world interplanted with other tropical plants such as orchids and bromeliads. The Fern Room's various species are planted alongside a rock wall from which water drips into a pool, giving the appearance of a grotto. In addition, the conservatory's talented staff creates five different floral display shows in the Sunken Garden that span the calendar from spring through winter. Just north of the conservatory lies the Ordway Japanese Garden, designed in the Sansui style to show a mountain-and-water landscape. The Viewing Stone overlooks the entire garden, encompassing a waterfall, teahouse, and traditional zigzag bridge.

COMO PARK CONSERVATORY (10 miles east of Minneapolis) 1325 Aida Place, St. Paul, MN 55103 TEL: (612) 487-8240 OPEN: Daily 10-4, Oct. through March; daily 10-6, April through Sept. TOTAL ACRES: 450 SPECIAL COLLECTIONS: Palms, ferns, Japanese garden, bonsai

ZONE 4 F G P PA T V WS

NOERENBERG GARDENS
ORONO

In this unexpectedly beautiful garden, green swaths of grass decorated with graceful beds of colorful flowers spill down toward the shore of Minnetonka, one of Minnesota's lovely lakes. In the late 19th century, this lake served as a focus for the summer houses of some of the country's most wealthy citizens, including Frederick Noerenberg, who went on to establish a full-time residence here. Unfortunately, due to the terms of his will, his magnificent Queen Anne-style mansion was torn down after the death of his last heir. Luckily, the 73 acres of gardens that were Noerenberg's pride and joy are as stunning today as they were when the family was in residence. With unusual combinations of colors and textures, plantings of annuals and perennials blend and complement one another to present a vista of horticultural excitement. Many plants in which Noerenberg took great pride—lavender, peonies, monkshood, and Solomon's seal among them—still grow in the gardens today. Mixed in are native plants, including several species of penstemons, ornamental grasses, ornamental vegetables, herbs, and new cultivars of popular bedding plants. The Noerenbergs' influence remains unmistakable. The grape arbor, although rebuilt twice, still holds the grapevines they planted. And the original boathouse continues to welcome visitors to the lakeshore, a suitable entryway to the grandeur of these gardens.

NOERENBERG GARDENS (15 miles northwest of Minneapolis) 2840 North Shore Drive, Orono, MN 55391 TEL: (612) 559-6700 OPEN: Daily 8-dusk, May through Sept. TOTAL ACRES: 73 SPECIAL COLLECTIONS: Annuals, perennials, wildflowers, native plants

ZONE 4 F H P PA T

The Noerenberg boathouse on the shore of Lake Minnetonka provi‹ stunning backdrop for flowers, native grasses, and a sweeping l

Iowa

DES MOINES BOTANICAL GARDEN
DES MOINES

Exotic and native plants are featured at the Des Moines Botanical Garden, which opened in 1979 on 14 acres along the east bank of the Des Moines River. The conservatory's towering geodesic dome, 150 feet in diameter and 80 feet high, shelters more than a thousand species and varieties of fascinating plants from around the world.

Specialized collections include cactuses and succulents, such as teddy-bear cactus, century plants, elephant's foot, and carrion flower; a bonsai display that is considered one of the ten best in the country, including shrubs and trees over one hundred years old; and more than 200 species and varieties of orchids shown in a long sequence of different blooms. A large balcony offers views of the flora below.

Seasonal changes are beautifully represented with elaborate floral exhibitions. These form an enjoyable progression, from the traditional spring bulbs and Easter lilies to summer with its begonias and caladiums. Autumn is marked by lavish displays of chrysanthemums, while winter is celebrated with a spectacular array of poinsettias. Outdoors along the river walk, visitors enjoy collections of phlox, coral bells, astilbe, daylilies, hostas, and thousands of annuals as they bloom in different seasons. In addition, a cottage garden planted with traditional perennials, a welcoming butterfly garden, and an interesting herb garden add to the diversity.

DES MOINES BOTANICAL GARDEN 909 E. River Drive, Des Moines, IA 50316 **TEL:** (515) 242-2934 **OPEN:** Mon.-Thurs. 10-6, Fri. 10-9, Sat.-Sun. 10-5, except holidays **TOTAL ACRES:** 14 **SPECIAL COLLECTIONS:** Desert plants, bonsai, orchids, cottage garden, herbs   **ZONE 5** C **F** G **H** P **R** T **WS**

A dramatic steel sculpture, "Spectral Liberation" by Christiane Martens, complements the geodesic dome of the conservatory, which houses more than a thousand exotic plants.

This cast-iron deer is an old friend to longtime visitors to Brucemore. Enclosing the garden is an ornamental white fence, added in the 1950s, that nicely frames the perennial border.

BRUCEMORE
CEDAR RAPIDS

A formal garden originated on this 26-acre Victorian estate with its first owner, Caroline Sinclair, who lived here from 1886 to 1906. The second owner, Mrs. George Douglas resided here until 1937. She expanded the garden, possibly influenced by Gertrude Jekyll, the acclaimed British horticulturist. Although the current garden contains some plants dating from Mrs. Douglas's time, it is not a restoration of the original but rather seeks to capture the ambience of a Victorian garden. The 21-room Queen Anne-style mansion with its one-acre garden is a property of the National Trust for Historic Preservation.

In spring, sumptuous peonies frame the more than 400 roses occupying the two center beds—polyanthas from the early garden, as well as grandifloras, floribundas, and hybrid tea roses. June brings irises, delphiniums, and Asiatic and trumpet lilies in the gardens. In summer, phlox and daylilies line the ornamental white fence enclosing the garden. Within, cosmos, cleome, and others bloom in an old-fashioned summer array. When the weather cools, butterflies group around asters, while a last group of roses, accompanied by salvias, bloom before winter sets in.

BRUCEMORE (124 miles northwest of Des Moines) 2160 Linden Drive S.E., Cedar Rapids, IA 52403 **TEL:** (319) 362-7375 **OPEN:** 8-4:30 Mon.-Sat., June through Oct. **TOTAL ACRES:** 1 **SPECIAL COLLECTIONS:** Peonies, roses, lilies, annuals

ZONE 5 **G** **H** **HO** **P** **WS**

Missouri Botanical Garden
St. Louis

The Missouri Botanical Garden opened in 1859 as one of the first public gardens in the United States. It remains one of the finest. Its impetus was the vision of Englishman Henry Shaw, who immigrated to the then-frontier town of St. Louis and established a successful hardware store. Shaw shaped his idea of a nonpareil garden with the expertise of the great naturalists of that era: Asa Gray, George Engelmann, and Thomas Nuttall. The Missouri Botanical Garden began on the prairies outside St. Louis, but eventually the city surrounded it. Today, its 79 acres include nearly two dozen gardens anchored at the edges by buildings, beginning with the entrance to the gardens, Ridgway Center.

With an arched canopy and sunburst of windows, and an auditorium, floral display hall, garden shop, and galleries, Ridgway Center hints at the magnitude of the gardens beyond. It opens onto Spoehrer Plaza with its classic fountain. Nearby lies Linnean House, the oldest display greenhouse west of the Mississippi. Nandinas, impatiens, begonias, star jasmine, and, especially camellias, form the core of the collection housed within.

Outside, lily pads float within pools set like shimmering jewels amid perennial beds. Here, court gardens cap the perennial beds with intimate grace. One, the Cohen Court Garden, glows with a yellow theme, including yellow pansies and coreopsis, tall orange-yellow ligularia, and golden hosta. A few steps down the path, hostas spill over the edges of the subdued, tree-shaded Hosta Walk. Towering blue-green umbrellas of *Hosta* 'Frances Williams' and daintier forms mix with lace-leaved bleeding hearts, spotted pulmonaria, coral bells, and fuzzy wands of astilbe. From sun-dappled shade, the path passes the Flora Gate into the bright light of the Goodman Iris Garden, a color carnival in May. Iris was the Greek goddess of the rainbow and these beds appropriately glow in a rainbow of colors.

South of Linnean House, the Gladney Rose Garden offers formal order: an old-fashioned white wooden fence encircling rows of roses whose beds echo the circular theme. Peach, pink, blushing white, sultry red—the huge blooms are at their peak in early June. Just beyond are bulb gardens in shifting drifts of crocuses and daffodils, tulips, hyacinths, and huge round heads of flowering onion that bloom in colorful succession. The arching arms of pink-flowering crabapples and garnet redbuds provide structure for the mix of bulbs and perennials.

Repeating the rose garden's circular theme, the round pool of the Milles Sculpture Garden floats with Victoria lily pads the size of coffee tables. Rising from the pool are tall columns topped by angels trumpeting the presence of the garden's most spectacular building: the Climatron. The most stylish of Buckminster Fuller-inspired geodesic domes, the Climatron rises like a Land of Oz dream. Within lies part of the garden's renowned orchid collection plus an extravagant world of tropical plants. Garish banana plants vie with coffee trees and bougainvillea, African gardenias, and Arabian jasmines alongside waterfalls and pools. The Climatron gives only a sample of the tropical species the garden protects. The Missouri Botanical Garden has become a leader in identifying and preserving plants from the world's tropical rain forests, and its Center for Plant Conservation coordinates the efforts of 25 botanic gardens and arboretum nationwide.

The Climatron, filled with more than 1,400 species of plants from tropical regions throughout the world, is reflected in the lily ponds at Missouri Botanical Garden.

The adjacent Shoenberg Temperate House gathers plants from the world's "Mediterranean" zones, including California, Australia, and Mediterranean countries. A highlight is the walled Moorish Garden, one of the first types of formal gardens. Within Temperate House live rose-toned oleander, yellow broom, amethyst beautyberries, biblical plants such as pomegranates and olives, rosettes of wild buckwheats, plus carnivorous plants. Outside, the path curves past the Heckman Rock Garden and dwarf conifers into the Azalea Bowl. In late spring, the azaleas, magnolias, and rhododendrons create an Impressionist painting of soft pinks and peach, ruby, and the palest ivory.

Paths to the southwest of the Climatron converge at the Kemper Center. Sometimes it is enough to fill one's eyes with beauty and one's spirit with calm in a botanic garden. But sometimes botanic gardens spark ideas. The William T. Kemper Center for Home Gardening is a gardener's paradise of catalogs, courses, and horticulture. Touring the eight acres filled with 15 sampler gardens can fill a day. Tucked next door to a shade garden, a butterfly garden arches with buddleias and other butterfly-tempting plants. Farther along, a bird garden is filled with buckthorn and red flowers sought by hummingbirds. Topiary and a child-size maze intrigue youngsters in the children's garden, while parents soak up scents in the adjacent fragrance garden. Other samplers include a prairie garden, fruits and vegetables suitable for the Midwest, and a city garden focusing on compact species and container gardening.

Past the boxwoods, the Chinese Garden, a Henry Moore sculpture, and a rose test garden, the English Woodland Garden fulfills a tired visitor's desire for

Missouri Botanical Garden's Japanese garden was designed in 1977 by Koichi Kawana, who warned that simplicity should not be confused with plainness. Today, this graceful blend of lakes,

quiet, careless, natural woods. Tall oaks and maples provide color in autumn. Spring sees a canopy of dogwoods, serviceberries, viburnums, and magnolias arch above beds of bluebells laced with Dutchman's breeches, columbine, trillium, hellebores, violas, and hundreds of other wildflowers.

Behind the 120,000-volume library lies the garden's historic district. Here visitors can find Henry Shaw's home, an herb garden, and a Victorian garden. It's hard to resist the maze, a botanic puzzle whose paths twist and turn between yew hedges.

Seiwa-En, the "garden of pure, clear harmony and peace," spreads over the botanical garden's farthest corner. The largest Japanese garden in North America, Seiwa-En's 14 acres center on a lake. As in all Japanese gardens, the sculptured views represent larger landscapes of mountains, earth, and sky, as well as a serene, meditative environment. Footbridges arch over water filled with koi, carp whose color and form are as flowerlike as the lotus and waterlilies they float past. Japanese maples, flowering cherries, and rhododendron glow with color against gray tree trunks and a white pine backdrop. Gravel gardens are raked to resem-

islands, and lagoons is one of the largest traditional Japanese garden in North America. Manicured specimens of Kurome azaleas complement the stones and raked sand.

ble waves moving across the sea or wind across grasses. In addition, peonies and chrysanthemums—meaningful in Oriental art—provide artistic presence in Seiwa-En. A teahouse stands serenely apart on its own island.

In 1926, as a hedge against increasing pollution, Shaw purchased land 35 miles southwest of St. Louis, intending to relocate his botanical garden. Pollution waned and the garden stayed put, but the **Shaw Arboretum** now fills 2,500 acres of the Gray Summit site on Mo. 100. Conifers of the world, their dark green beauty brightened by thousands of spring-flowering bulbs, are a highlight. The rest of the Shaw Arboretum is mainly a natural mix of Missouri landscapes, from oak-hickory woods and wildflowers to marshes rich with reeds and blue-flowered pickerel weed.

MISSOURI BOTANICAL GARDEN 4344 Shaw Boulevard, St. Louis, MO 63110 **TEL:** (314) 577-5100 **OPEN:** Daily 9-8, Memorial Day to Labor Day; daily 9-5, Labor Day to Memorial Day **TOTAL ACRES:** 79 **SPECIAL COLLECTIONS:** Japanese garden, Climatron conservatory, demonstration gardens, aquatic gardens, tropical plants, azaleas, irises, hostas, maze   **ZONE 6** C F G H HO L P R T V WS

THE JEWEL BOX
ST. LOUIS

Tiers of glass rectangles rise to form a sparkling tower called the Jewel Box, a conservatory located on 17 acres within the center of Forest Park, one of the largest urban parks in the country. The design of this conservatory is an elegant combination of international modernism, with its goal of functional design and its art deco styling, which softens the edges of squares and rectangles. With its lapped-glass detailing and verticality of the design, this modern Gothic-like structure attracted thousands of visitors when it was built in 1936. A major, multimillion-dollar renovation is underway, to be completed early in the year 2000.

Although its exterior is unusual, the conservatory's interior exhibitions follow the traditional pattern of showcasing giant palms and other tropical trees, with aerial walkways from which to view changing floral displays. Five seasonal shows are presented each year: Christmas, with traditional poinsettias; a New Year's show, with azaleas, roses, bougainvillea, and amaryllis; an Easter show of lilies, palms, and hydrangeas; a Mother's Day display of fuchsias, marigolds, ageratum, and salvias; and a summer show featuring coleus, asparagus, caladiums, dracaenas, and others.

Outside the gardens, walkways lined with masses of roses, annuals, and perennials weave between large lily pools. Forest Park, site of the 1904 World's Fair, has within its two square miles many important cultural, recreational, and horticultural attractions. These include fine specimen trees and the formal gardens that complement the prominent Round Fountain.

THE JEWEL BOX Forest Park, 1501 Oakland Avenue, St. Louis, MO 63122 **TEL:** (314) 531-0080 **OPEN:** Daily 9-5 **TOTAL ACRES:** 17 **SPECIAL COLLECTIONS:** Conservatory design, tropical plants, annuals

ZONE 6 A C F H P PA T

CHANCE GARDENS
CENTRALIA

What started in 1935 as a retirement hobby for inventor-industrialist A. Bishop Chance soon became a showplace garden. When Chance died in 1949, his heirs created a foundation to ensure its continued existence.

Surprisingly small, the garden is less than an acre in size. But since it is filled with an abundance of seasonal splendor it seems much larger. Visitors enter the garden through a Japanese-style torii gate, leading to raised beds edged in stone and planted with masses of traditional flowers, both annuals and perennials. The garden's calendar begins in spring with mixed tulips, followed by summer's sun-loving flowers and closing with a dazzling mixture of mounds of different colors and varieties of chrysanthemums.

Across a low, pine-topped berm, a miniature rock-strewn area features a brook fed by a stream cascading down a rocky slope. Adjoining the gardens stands Chance's Victorian home, now a museum. Both house and garden are on the National Register of Historic Places.

CHANCE GARDENS (140 miles west of St. Louis) 319 Sneed Street, Centralia, MO 65240 **TEL:** (573) 682-5513 **OPEN:** Daily dawn-dusk, April through Oct. **TOTAL ACRES:** Less than 1 **SPECIAL COLLECTIONS:** Spring bulbs, summer annuals, perennials

ZONE 5 HO P

POWELL GARDENS
KINGSVILLE

Powell Gardens is the fruition of the dreams of George Powell, a Missouri farm boy who became a highly successful banker and trucking magnate. In 1988, the family foundation decided to turn the family farm into a public botanical garden. In spite of its short history, Powell Gardens has quickly grown into an inspiring horticultural treasure. This is in part due to good plans, an exquisite natural area, and an enthusiastic, dedicated staff. Its four main areas include an international vegetable garden and a perennial garden with more than 500 varieties of plants organized by theme; one area displays plants attractive to butterflies, another shows sun-loving plants, and another features flowers suitable for shade. The two-acre rock and waterfall garden, dubbed the "enchanted woods," offers thickets of native trees, more than 900 azaleas, and shade-loving plants such as hostas and ferns amid a flowing stream and tumbling waterfall. Also of interest is the large wildflower meadow that also features native grasses.

POWELL GARDENS (30 miles southeast of Kansas City) 1609 N.W. US Highway 50, Kingsville, MO 64061 TEL: (816) 697-2600 OPEN: Daily 9-dusk, April through Oct.; daily 9-5, Nov. through March; except holidays TOTAL ACRES: 835 SPECIAL COLLECTIONS: Rock and water garden, perennials, wildflowers

ZONE 6 **F G H P PA WS**

A convention of bright tulips greets the spring in the Rock and Waterfall Garden at Powell Gardens. Although young and still growing, the gardens have made their mark in the Midwest.

Kansas

Botanica, The Wichita Gardens
Wichita

Botanica, the Wichita Gardens, defies both a young history and limited size to offer visitors a valuable horticultural experience. In 1982, the city of Wichita joined forces with the Wichita Area Garden Council to establish this center. Its purpose is to provide a pleasant garden setting and a place for horticultural education. The resulting 9.5-acre Botanica beautifully fulfills its original goals by offering pleasing vistas and opportunities to learn about plants and gardens. The Entry Garden, where flowering plants are changed seasonally, immediately welcomes with a wave of color. Flowering vines such as clematis and morning glory beckon visitors down the concourse and into the garden.

The Shakespeare Garden showcases plants and flowers that William Shakespeare wrote about or which were popular during his lifetime. Nearby, the Butterfly Garden lures both native and migratory butterflies with a variety of nectar-rich flowers. A teaching garden displays a variety of plants that are well-suited to this Kansas climate, as well as different design techniques and garden "hardscapes" that can be incorporated into the home garden.

Additional theme gardens include a series of water ponds, a wildflower meadow, and a woodland area. Plant collection gardens encompass roses, peonies, junipers, and pines.

Botanica, The Wichita Gardens 701 Amidon, Wichita, KS 67203 Tel: (316) 264-0448 Open: Mon.-Sat. 9-5, Sun. and holidays, 1-5, Tues. 9-8, June through Sept.; Mon.-Fri. 9-5, Jan. through March; except holidays Total acres: 9.5 Special collections: Theme gardens, butterfly garden, Shakespeare garden   ZONE 6 F G L T WS

One of Botanica's newest gardens, the Beverly R. Blue Teaching Garden provides a space for discussions about which plants grow best in Kansas, and a showcase for various garden designs.

Nebraska

Sunken Gardens
Lincoln

From an abandoned neighborhood dump came a striking botanical garden and out of the Great Depression came the work force which made it possible. In the winter of 1930, City Commissioner E.M. Bair was able to give temporary jobs to more than 200 men. Their assigned project was to construct a garden out of a 1.5-acre creek basin, with sheer cliffs on all sides. Fill dirt, truckloads of rock, and the ensuing terraces made the lot manageable, and eventually the sunken gardens emerged.

The garden's focal point is its water displays, including a cascading waterfall and two reflection pools in which grow several varieties of waterlilies, including some rare species. Many perennial beds grace this bowl-shaped garden, including colorful Asiatic lilies, delphinium, coreopsis, columbine, hibiscus, and purple coneflower, as well as flowers of more subtle shades such as sedum, coral bells, and lady's mantle. It is the display of annual flowers, reputed to be the largest in the region, that draws visitors by the thousands. Each year sees the planting of 50,000 annual flowers in this small garden. It takes city crews five days to put in the small seedlings, which quickly grow and transform the garden into a carnival of color. Old favorites such as ageratum, impatiens, begonias, caladiums, marigolds, and salvia grow side by side with more exotic flowers, such as cannas and bananas, which are treated as annuals in the midwestern climate.

Sunken Gardens 2740 A Street, Lincoln, NE 68502 **Tel:** (402) 441-7847 **Open:** Daily dawn-midnight, May through Oct. **Total acres:** 1.5 **Special collections:** Pools, aquatic plants, perennials, annuals

ZONE 5 H P PA T WS

An abandoned creek bed and neighborhood dump was transformed into the magnificent Sunken Gardens in Lincoln, Nebraska. Colorful koi swim among waterlilies in the large reflection pools.

McCrory Gardens
BROOKINGS

Since 1984, award-winning McCrory Gardens, named in honor of a former director, has been adding to its ornamental gardens and its arboretum, dedicated to researching species that can be grown in the northern plains. The major display gardens offer ideas for landscaping home gardens, with exhibits of junipers, shrubs, turf, and annual and perennial flowers. The gardens currently showcase some 15,000 annual flowers, part of McCrory's All-America Display Garden, as well as a growing collection of perennials for this prairie climate. Daisies and pasque flowers in different colors are among the favorites. Hugh quarry stones were used to form the walls of the striking rock garden, providing outcroppings for plants to grow in a naturalistic-looking manner. Here displays focus on herbaceous plants native to the Rocky Mountains and Black Hills. such as rosy paintbrush, mariposa, cranesbill, harebell, and others. Planted in 24 formal raised beds in a brick courtyard surrounded by ponderosa pine trees are roses in more than 1,000 different varieties and colors. The Centennial Prairie Garden has plants from four native communities—tall-grass and shortgrass prairies, and the woodland and montane prairies of the Black Hills. Here visitors can inspect such wildflowers as pasques, liatris, and coreopsis. Also of note are the sensory garden, children's maze garden, cottage garden, and herb garden.

McCRORY GARDENS South Dakota State University, Brookings, SD 57007 TEL: (605) 688-5136 OPEN: Daily dawn-dusk TOTAL ACRES: Garden 20, arboretum 45 SPECIAL COLLECTIONS: Prairie plants, rock garden, annuals, roses, maze   ZONE 4 A H P T

In summer the annual display and trial gardens feature beds of flowers arranged in circles and arcs of rainbow colors at the McCrory Gardens.

North Dakota

INTERNATIONAL PEACE GARDEN
DUNSEITH

Straddling the border between Manitoba, Canada, and North Dakota—almost in the geographic center of North America—lies the International Peace Garden, dedicated to the long-standing amicable relations between the United States and Canada. The garden was established in 1932 at the urging of Dr. Henry Moore, a Canadian horticulturist who wanted to praise peace through the beauty of plants. Indeed, much of the glory in this particular garden stems from the natural wilderness of the Turtle Mountain area, including two crystalline glacier lakes. Hiking trails and two 3.5-mile driving loops, one on each side of the border, wind through this pristine preserve of woodlands and prairies, a habitat for a diverse range of wildlife and waterfowl.

Paths wander through display gardens and an arboretum showcasing the hardy trees and shrubs able to withstand this region's severe climate. A walking tour also takes in a floral clock whose 12-foot-diameter face is rendered in a bright array of contrasting bedding annuals. More than 200,000 annuals—such as marigolds, geraniums, and salvias—are also planted throughout the gardens. They are complemented in summer by hundreds of Asiatic lilies and cannas. There is also a sunken garden, a perennial plot, and a wildflower area. A carillon bell tower chimes every quarter hour and can be heard throughout the gardens.

INTERNATIONAL PEACE GARDEN N. Dak. 1, Dunseith, ND 58329 **TEL:** (701) 263-4390 **OPEN:** Always open
TOTAL ACRES: 2,369 **SPECIAL COLLECTIONS:** Floral clock, annuals, perennials, wildflowers, arboretum
ZONE 4 A F G H L P PA R T V WS

Dramatic displays of annuals at the International Peace Garden provide an impressive approach to the Peace Tower, whose four columns represent the corners of the world coming together.

CHAPTER 5

SOUTHWEST AND THE ROCKIES

Texas

Oklahoma

New Mexico

Arizona

Colorado

Utah

The Southwest's oldest arboretum and botanical garden, Arizona's Boyce Thompson Arboretum spotlights plants from the earth's varied deserts and drylands.

Texas

DALLAS ARBORETUM AND BOTANICAL GARDEN
DALLAS

In the 1930s, the leading citizens of Dallas decided their city deserved and needed a public garden in which to celebrate the wealth of plants that grew so well in their corner of Texas. Early in that decade, philanthropist Everette Lee DeGolyer began searching for a site suitable for an arboretum, but it was nearly 50 years before his dreams became a reality—ironically, on land that he once owned. The Dallas Arboretum and Botanical Society formed in 1977; three years later the City of Dallas purchased the DeGolyer Estate, and later the adjacent Camp Estate, to form the 66-acre grounds for the botanical garden.

The site, located on the eastern shore of White Rock Lake, seven miles east of downtown Dallas, provided an ideal setting for the development of what was to become one of the most popular attractions in the entire Southwest. Almost 33 acres are maintained as formal gardens, planted for year-round color and interest. When spring comes to the Jonsson Color Garden, some 150,000 bulbs burst into bloom, complementing one of the largest public azalea collection in the country, with an estimated 20,000 multicolored bushes of more than 2,000 varieties.

Many separate formal gardens are found on the grounds. Surrounding the DeGolyer House, built in 1940 in the Spanish colonial revival style, are 4.5 acres of gardens: a magnificent magnolia allée, a wisteria-covered pergola, a rose garden, and a sunken garden designed as an English perennial cottage garden. A quarter-mile linear garden called the Hunt Paseo de Flores, links the DeGolyer gardens to another section, the Camp Estate. This area provides the setting for the large mansion that serves as the arboretum's headquarters. Here, the Lay Ornamental Garden showcases native Texas plants in their glory against a backdrop of waterfalls. Nearby are the Hidden Garden, a limestone fern grotto, and a collection of bronze animal sculptures donated by Dallas businessman Trammell Crow.

The newest, and perhaps most unusual, area is A Woman's Garden, dedicated in 1997. Located adjacent to the DeGolyer House, it was designed by Morgan Wheelock with a deep respect for nature and a belief that intimate contact with the natural world results in a richer human experience. A Woman's Garden is made up of a series of "garden rooms" in which plantings and "hardscapes" have been carefully chosen to illustrate the combination of strength and softness that makes up the character of women. For example, soft, rich lawns are edged with slate and marble chip walks, and graceful, drooping racemes of white wisteria are trained as single stem standards along an allée.

Within A Woman's Garden complex, the Pensive Poetry Garden offers visitors a quiet, sweet-scented haven in which to read or meditate. Some of the more interesting plantings here include a Persian parrotia, desert willow, redbud, American smoke tree, and golden rain tree, all of which provide interesting foliage, texture, or flowers throughout the year. A traditional knot garden and fragrant roses are also included in this small, intimate area, while a long, formal path leads to the Loggia Lawn and the Reflective Basin. An

An extravaganza of tulips and pansies mark the arrival of spring at the Dallas Arboretum. The arboretum hugs the eastern shore of White Rock Lake, seen peeking through the background.

18-foot-tall sculpture, "The Trumpeters," created by William Frances Duffy, is visible from the main terrace level. Both art and music are important elements of A Woman's Garden. The "Infiniti III Wind Harp," designed by Ross Barrable, is an elliptical framework mounted on a pedestal and containing a series of metal strings. Wind blowing across the lake, causes the strings to vibrate, creating soft, lovely music.

Two important sculptures on loan from the Dallas Museum of Art will eventually become permanent additions to the garden. The first, "Playdays," is a bronze sculpture created in 1925 by Harriet Frishmuth, a student of Auguste Rodin. It depicts a young girl with four frogs at her feet spraying water into a pool, and will be permanently situated in the Pecan Parterre Garden. The other, "Young Faun," was designed by Brenda Putnam. This small satyrlike figure, shown as if he were scampering up a hill, tail fluffed by the wind, will be placed near the Pulpit Garden.

Since its beginning, the mission of the arboretum has been to promote art and the enjoyment and knowledge of horticulture, as well as provide a suitable site for research. With the opening of A Woman's Garden, the arboretum illustrates a renewed dedication to fulfilling its original goals.

■ **DALLAS ARBORETUM AND BOTANICAL GARDEN** (7 miles east of downtown Dallas) 8525 Garland Road, Dallas, TX 75218 **TEL:** (214) 327-8263 or (214) 327-4901 **OPEN:** Daily 10-6, March through Oct.; daily 10-5, Nov. through Feb. **TOTAL ACRES:** 66 **SPECIAL COLLECTIONS:** Azaleas, magnolias, native plants, woman's garden, perennials, hardy ferns ZONE 8 F G H HO P PA T WS

DALLAS HORTICULTURE CENTER
DALLAS

The Dallas Horticulture Center, founded in 1941 as a garden for the Texas centennial, today combines intriguing display gardens with a commitment to helping conserve the environment. It also offers extensive urban horticulture programs, including classes and workshops that help educate the public. The beauty of its 7.5 acres of gardens alone is quite effective in inspiring people to care about their environment.

One of the most important collections here, the Texas Native Plants Collection, includes wildflowers and woody plants native to the horticulturally rich Edwards Plateau and Texas Hill Country. In addition, formal gardens at the center include an antique rose garden bordered by old-fashioned perennials; the Physic Garden, where medicinal and culinary plants are grown; the Shakespeare Garden; an iris garden with more than 300 iris cultivars; and a butterfly garden filled with plants to attract caterpillars and butterflies. The Earthkeepers Garden and the Xeriscape Garden are designed to demonstrate environmentally sound gardening practices, while the Grand Allée presents a glorious promenade bordered with Savannah hollies, surrounded by azaleas, and ending in a 50-foot geyser. Inside the conservatory thrives a rare collection of plants native to Africa, including unusual species of flowering aloes and euphorbias and a magnificent specimen of the traveler's palm.

■ **DALLAS HORTICULTURE CENTER** (2 miles from downtown Dallas) 3601 Martin Luther King Boulevard, Fair Park, Dallas, TX 75315 **TEL:** (214) 428-7476 **OPEN:** Always open **TOTAL ACRES:** 7.5 **SPECIAL COLLECTIONS:** Native plants, antique roses, irises, butterfly garden   **ZONE 8** A C H L P PA T V WS

FORT WORTH BOTANIC GARDEN
FORT WORTH

Although the Great Depression of the 1930s spelled disaster for many gardens, it became the saving grace of the Fort Worth Botanic Garden. For it was federal funds allotted for public works that built the garden. When completed in 1935, it was one of the largest in the country. Building on the interest in roses paramount in Fort Worth during the 1930s, the park commissioners who supervised the garden developed an extensive rose display that today remains one of the garden's most exciting collections. In addition to the more traditional rose displays, there is also a miniature rose garden and the Republic of Texas Rose Garden, which includes old rose varieties grown between the years 1836 and 1845.

In 1973 a Japanese garden was created on the grounds, at the site of an old gravel pit. Designed by Kingsley Wu, its 7.5 acres include five pools, a pavilion, and a teahouse. The Fort Worth Botanic Garden also hosts a 10,000-square-foot conservatory and collections of cactuses, daylilies, irises, and chrysanthemums, among others. While the colorful displays are beautiful, much of the garden's focus remains educational. By displaying plants, both native and exotic, which perform well in the Fort Worth area, the garden helps area residents learn which plants will be successful on their own property.

■ **FORT WORTH BOTANIC GARDEN** (34 miles west of Dallas) 3220 Botanic Garden Boulevard, Fort Worth, TX 76107 **TEL:** (817) 871-7689 or (817) 871-7686 **OPEN:** Daily 8-11 **TOTAL ACRES:** 109 **SPECIAL COLLECTIONS:** Roses, Japanese garden, daylilies, irises   **ZONE 7** F C G H P R T WS

TYLER ROSE GARDENS
TYLER

Although many people think Texas is all about cactus and sagebrush, the East Texas town of Tyler will change those thoughts. Since the 1920s, Tyler has been a center of rose cultivation for the entire country. One out of every five rose bushes sold in the United States today is grown in Tyler.

To best display the flower that put Tyler on the map, the town developed the Municipal Rose Garden in 1952. Two thousand or more bushes are planted each year, keeping the 14-acre garden filled to the brim with healthy, roses of every sort and variety, representing both old-fashioned heritage roses as well as the newest cultivars available.

Tyler is an All-America Rose Selections Test Garden site, one of only 24 in the country. In addition, the Municipal Rose Garden includes a one-acre Heritage and Sensory Garden, planted with roses dating back to 1867. The Rose Festival is an important part of the Tyler calendar. For four days in mid-October, the town focuses entirely on roses. Festivities include a Queen's Tea—a city-wide garden party open to the public. The roses are pruned in September in preparation for the festival, making this a month not to visit the garden. In addition, the garden is sometimes closed when gardeners spray the plants for pests and diseases; visitors are advised to call ahead.

Although roses are this garden's most important offering, companion plants and flowers that bloom off-season are also represented. Particularly attractive are the Vance Burks Memorial Camellia Garden and a daylily collection. With its extensive floral displays full of beauty and fragrance, the garden is a fitting tribute to America's favorite flower.

TYLER ROSE GARDENS (100 miles east of Dallas) 420 Rose Park Drive, Tyler, TX 75754 TEL: (903) 531-1213 OPEN: Mon.-Fri. 8-5 TOTAL ACRES: 14 SPECIAL COLLECTIONS: Roses, daylilies, camellias

ZONE 8   A   G   H   P   PA   T   V   WS

One highlight of the Fort Worth Botanic Garden is a Japanese meditation garden (below), complete with waterfalls, pools of koi, a pagoda, lanterns, and an authentic teahouse.

LADY BIRD JOHNSON WILDFLOWER CENTER
AUSTIN

In 1983, former First Lady Lady Bird Johnson and a group of civic-minded citizens joined together to establish a national wildflower research center. Housed for 12 years in a modest facility near Austin, the center moved in April 1995 to a 42-acre site designed to demonstrate, in living color, the practicality and beauty of growing native plants throughout the country and, specifically, in Texas. One of the center's primary purposes is disseminating information about growing wildflowers—defined as native flowering trees, shrubs, grasses, and herbaceous plants—for each region of the United States. Naturally, the center's display gardens in Austin celebrate the wealth and wonder of native plants of Texas. They are best seen in April, at the height of bluebonnet season.

The gardens were designed by the well-known landscape architect Darrell Morrison, whose goal was to develop a landscape beautiful to look at. Maintained with sound ecological principles, they demonstrate the beauty of the native Texas landscape. Almost all plants used in the landscape here are native to within the area.

The center seeks to preserve native wildflowers, such as the bluebonnets and Indian paintbrushes seen above.

The grounds have been divided into many different garden and natural areas. The entrance walk connecting the parking lot to the buildings is planted as a restored wildflower meadow. At the entrance gate a water garden represents a pond ecosystem with bog plants and deep-water plants and organisms.

The majority of the buildings are set around an inner courtyard planted to demonstrate landscape uses of native plants. The result, sure to delight visitors, includes tall canopy trees offering much needed shade and a natural-looking "courtyard spring." A popular building at the center, the Little House, and its adjacent children's garden invite kids to learn fun, fascinating facts and folklore of plants and wildlife.

Perhaps one of the most important areas at the wildflower research center is the Home Comparison Gardens. Here, two plots of the same size and shape have been planted according to the same basic design: a central oval surrounded by wide planting borders. In the first garden, traditional landscape plants have been used—St. Augustine lawn grass and non-native trees, shrubs, and bedding annuals. The second garden exhibits native buffalo grass as turf, surrounded by ornamental native plants. Careful records are maintained, comparing the costs, time, and labor involved in keeping each garden looking good throughout the year—information vital to homeowners interested in using native plants. Other display areas include plants utilized for purposes as varied as attracting hummingbirds to dyeing cloth.

■ LADY BIRD JOHNSON WILDFLOWER CENTER 4801 LaCrosse Avenue, Austin, TX 78739 TEL: (512) 292-4200 OPEN: Tues.-Sun. 9-5:30 TOTAL ACRES: 42 SPECIAL COLLECTIONS: Native wildflowers, children's garden

ZONE 8 F G H L P PA R T V WS

The iris lily pond area at the Mercer Arboretum features more than 250 varieties of Louisiana irises. This arboretum is also noted for its extensive ginger collection.

Mercer Arboretum and Botanic Garden
Humble

Thelma Mercer was a woman who loved to share plants. As she and her husband, Charles, developed their 14 acres north of Houston into a graceful landscape, Thelma dreamed of making it into a garden that would captivate visitors for years to come. When the Mercers sold their land to Harris County in 1974 they stipulated that the land be used as a public park with an emphasis on display gardens and horticultural education. Today, the myriad gardens that comprise Mercer Arboretum and Botanic Gardens display many different gardening themes. Hundreds of plants representing different ecosystems cover 262 acres traversed by some five miles of walking trails and paths.

The garden areas range from a dryland garden, showcasing many of the plants native to western Texas, to the daylily collection, which includes more than 700 different varieties, to the tropical garden, where tender plants are carefully nurtured. The result is a stunning "rain forest" in a horticultural zone that is only considered subtropical. One of the most exciting plantings, the ginger collection includes not only sweet-scented butterfly gingers but also such unusual species as pine cone gingers, with their characteristic bright-red flowering cones.

Mercer Arboretum and Botanic Garden successfully blends plants from diverse ecosystems into garden displays that are both aesthetically pleasing and educational as well—thus fulfilling the wishes of the garden's first creator, Thelma Mercer.

Mercer Arboretum and Botanic Garden (25 miles north of Houston) 22306 Aldine-Westfield Road, Humble, TX 77338 **Tel:** (281) 443-8731 **Open:** Daily 8-5 Nov. through March; daily 8-7, April through Oct. **Total acres:** 262 **Special collections:** Native plants, daylilies, tropical garden, ginger, irises

ZONE 8 G **H** P PA T WS

Bayou Bend Collection and Gardens
Houston

Now called the jewel of Houston, Bayou Bend was the home of Miss Ima Hogg, daughter of former Texas Governor James S. Hogg. The inspiration for creating the gardens came to Miss Ima—as she was known to almost everyone—in 1927 following a visit to Middleton Plantation in South Carolina, where she enjoyed stunning displays of azaleas. Decades later, multitudes of colorful azaleas are found at Bayou Bend.

The house and first gardens at Bayou Bend, located at the bend of the Buffalo Bayou in Houston, were constructed in 1927. An avid collector, Miss Ima assembled a priceless assortment of antique American art and furnishings, housing them in her two-story pink stucco house. She then turned her attentions to the grounds, developing a series of eight separate, formal garden areas on 14 acres surrounding the estate—with azaleas playing a leading role. Miss Ima worked with nationally known landscape architects, including Ellen Shipman, but also relied heavily on Texan talent, primarily landscape designers Ruth London, C.C. (Pat) Fleming, and Gregory Catlow. The first landscaped areas included the East Garden where a variety of azaleas, planted in tiered beds bordered by evergreen privet, were complemented by boxwoods clipped into a scroll design.

The Clio Garden was also established in the early years of Bayou Bend. It was named for a statue of Clio, muse of history, which Miss Ima commissioned from a sculpture studio in Florence. Here, too, she purchased statues of Diana, the huntress, and Euterpe, muse of poetry and music. Diana now stands in the central garden, with the muses occupying two smaller gardens on either side. In addition to the statues, these gardens offer clipped boxwood hedges that create a multitude of geometric beds filled with dwarf azaleas and seasonal bedding plants. Perhaps the best known area is the butterfly-shaped garden, designed by Miss Ima with the help of the *Encyclopedia Britannica*. Clipped boxwood, rare camellias, and dwarf Karume azaleas compose the wings of the butterfly, while elaborate brickwork forms the body and antennae.

Also of interest are three other gardens: the Carla Garden, created after Hurricane Carla ravaged Houston in 1962 and left huge open spaces in the woodland area; the Topiary Garden, where an American eagle, squirrel, rabbit, deer, and a turkey have been created out of clipped hedges; and the White Garden, featuring white-blooming azaleas, bulbs, gardenias, antique roses, and hydrangeas. Although the formal gardens are the focal points of the estate, many natural areas contribute to its overall beauty. Wooded areas were carefully thinned and unusual woody species, such as Oriental pink magnolias and Mexican plums, were added. The driveway, created in the form of an English park drive, was left as natural looking as possible.

Since 1961 Bayou Bend's gardens have been supervised by the River Oaks Garden Club, whose enthusiastic members strive to retain its past glory while carrying forward the goals and dreams of Miss Ima. The site itself is administered by the Museum of Fine Arts in Houston.

Bayou Bend Collection and Gardens Museum of Fine Arts, 1 Westcott Street, Houston TX 77007 **Tel:** (713) 639-7750 **Open:** Tues.-Sat. 10-5, Sun. 1-5, Jan. through Feb., April through July, and Sept. through Nov.; call for hours in Dec., March, and August **Total acres:** 14 **Special collections:** Estate garden, azaleas, boxwood, topiary   **ZONE 9** F G H HO P T WS

The Diana Garden at Bayou Bend, a marble statue of the goddess stands ...ch over the formal pool and the garden, filled with azaleas.

SAN ANTONIO BOTANICAL GARDENS
SAN ANTONIO

Within a series of garden areas, the San Antonio Botanical Gardens celebrate the exotic as well as the natural, the formal as well as the informal. First opened in May 1980, the 33-acre public garden has grown and matured greatly.

A tour best begins at the Sullivan Carriage House, a turn-of-the-century historic building given to the gardens in 1987. Just beyond await the formal gardens, including the traditional Rose Garden, where both antique roses and new cultivars are planted; the Old-Fashioned Garden, displaying a mixture of heritage annuals and perennials; and the Sacred Garden, featuring plants mentioned in the Bible or which grew in biblical times. In this area flourish such ancient plants as oleander, pomegranate, myrtle, and fig. In the Herb Garden, culinary and medicinal plants used by early Texas settlers form an attractive display.

Of particular interest is the Garden for the Blind, which offers fragrant and highly textured plants chosen to delight all the senses. To help visitors orient themselves, a ceramic relief map of the garden is found at this garden's entrance and braille plaques identify the various plants.

A large Wisteria Arbor, resplendent in spring, shades visitors as they stroll from the formal areas to the Gazebo Overlook, which provides a beautiful view of the entire garden area. South of the overlook lies Kumamoto En, a Japanese garden designed by master artisans and gardeners from Japan. The stone walks, ponds, waterfalls, and bamboo fences found within this area of the San Antonio Botanical Gardens are all characteristic of a traditional Japanese garden. Here, too, a copper-roofed teahouse provides a quiet haven in which visitors can sit and meditate in conducive surroundings.

An unusual design feature of the conservatory at the San Antonio Botanical Gardens is its subterranean level created by three feet of a soil berm. All of the exhibition rooms are sunk below ground level, with glass pavilions rising 18 feet above the floor level.

The Conservatory Complex is comprised of earth-sheltered greenhouses that display tropical and desert plants. Covering about half an acre, this garden under glass is one of the most interesting in the Southwest. The Children's Garden, at the eastern edge of the complex, is the site of the highly successful children's program cosponsored by the Men's Garden Club of San Antonio and the Bexar County Master Gardeners. From seed to harvest, the plants grown in this garden are invariably loved into existence by the tiny hands that care for them.

Because the city of San Antonio is located at the juncture of three distinct growing regions—East Texas, the Hill Country and Edwards Plateau, and Southwest Texas—these gardens provide a natural place to display and demonstrate the landscape possibilities of the many native plants found within each region. Fifteen acres of the gardens are surrounded by a fieldstone wall and hold an extensive collection of native Texas plants, placed according to their indigenous region. Historical buildings have also been erected in each of the three native Texas display areas to complete the union of cultural history with the natural history of the state. The goals of the San Antonio Botanical Gardens have, since its inception, been to educate and inspire the public, and to provide an outdoor research facility for scientific purposes. These goals are met—and celebrated—daily at this impressive public garden.

SAN ANTONIO BOTANICAL GARDENS 555 Funston Place, San Antonio, TX 78209 **TEL:** (210) 207-3250 **OPEN:** Daily 9-6, except Christmas and New Year's Day **TOTAL ACRES:** 33 **SPECIAL COLLECTIONS:** Roses, old-fashioned flowers, Japanese garden, children's garden, native plants

ZONE 8 C F G H HO P R T WS

Moody Gardens
GALVESTON ISLAND

Galveston's Moody Gardens encompasses colorful display areas and the ten-story, glass Rain Forest Pyramid, showcasing specimens from some of the world's most exciting plant families. The 242-acre, nonprofit gardens are one family's response to a terrible accident. When Robert Moody's son suffered a severe head injury in a 1986 automobile accident, the best possible therapy proved to be rehabilitative horseback riding and horticulture therapy. Today, Moody Gardens offers individuals with disabilities a place to participate in gardening activities, for short visits or extended stays.

Outdoor plant displays focus on many of the vibrantly colored tropical and subtropical plants, such as hibiscus and crotons, which can be grown along the Texas Gulf Coast. But the real gem of the gardens is the Rain Forest Pyramid, which houses not only rain forest plants from South America, Africa, and Asia, but also wildlife native to these regions. The pyramid provides a fascinating place for observing nature, where giant Amazon fish and impossibly pink flamingos are only a glass pane away. The combination of colorful outdoor gardens and rain forest displays at Moody Gardens creates a delight for plant and flower lovers. It also stands as a living testament to the belief that one of nature's greatest gifts is the healing of body and soul.

MOODY GARDENS (45 miles south of Houston) 1 Hope Boulevard, Galveston Island, TX 77554 **TEL:** (409) 744-4673 or (800) 582-4673 **OPEN:** Sun.-Thurs. 10-6, Fri.-Sat 10-8, Sept. through May; daily 10-9, June through Aug. **TOTAL ACRES:** 242 **SPECIAL COLLECTIONS:** Tropical and subtropical plants

ZONE 9 C F G H P PA R T V WS

Oklahoma

Myriad Botanical Gardens
Oklahoma City

Although many urban areas boast a garden within their metropolis, the Myriad Botanical Gardens truly form the focal point of Oklahoma City. When the business community decided to revitalize the downtown area, it included plans for a garden inspired by Tivoli Gardens in Copenhagen, Denmark. The concept became reality, and the first phase of construction, including a lake, tunnels, and walkways, was completed in 1978. By 1988 sufficient funds had been raised and the stunning Crystal Bridge opened. The translucent, cylinder-shaped conservatory houses species indigenous to every continent except Antarctica. Within, plants are arranged into three major groups: the humid tropics, the dry tropics, and the Mediterranean or California zone.

Although plants are undoubtedly the garden's greatest draw, animals are not forgotten. Many small reptiles and amphibians, such as lizards and frogs, and several bird species, now call the Crystal Bridge home. The 17 acres of gardens surrounding the conservatory contain a 1.5-acre lake and are planted with ornamental plants either native to Oklahoma or ideally suited to the region's growing environment.

Now regarded as one of the Southwest's most exciting botanical attractions, Myriad Botanical Gardens draws visitors from all over the world. Its extensive educational program includes workshops for school children and a lecture series for adults, focussing on the understanding and appreciation of endangered tropical rain forest areas.

Myriad Botanical Gardens (109 miles southwest of Tulsa) 100 Myriad Gardens, Oklahoma City, OK 73102 **Tel:** (405) 297-3995 **Open:** Daily 9-6 **Total acres:** 17 **Special collections:** Tropical and subtropical plants   **ZONE 7** C **F** G P PA T WS

Hambrick Botanical Gardens
Oklahoma City

Although the National Cowboy Hall of Fame may seem to be an unlikely place for a horticultural treasure, the Hambrick Botanical Gardens, made possible through a generous donation by Hall of Fame trustee Freda Hambrick, has greatly enhanced the beauty of the hall's grounds. Landscape architect Bill Renner designed the gardens to both complement the hall's impressive architecture and to serve as a backdrop for a 33-foot-tall statue of Buffalo Bill surrounded by 17 fountains. Opened to the public in 1975, the gardens include many plants indigenous to western deserts. In addition to yucca, here thrive prickly pear cactus, which heralds spring with yellow blooms; silver century plants, which bloom only every hundred years; and grey santolina, known for its yellow ball-shaped flowers.

Flagstone paths lead past streams and waterfalls and through a forested area of Austrian pines to Persimmon Hill, named for the native fruit trees that grow in the area. Unusual specimens in this informal natural garden include a dwarf evergreen Hinoki cypress, only 14 inches tall even though it is more than 30 years old, and purple-leafed plum trees, offering burgundy foliage and fresh

Honor Heights Park peaks in spring, when more than 30,000 azaleas in 625 varieties burst into bloom. Muskogee has hosted an Azalea Festival every April for the past 30 years.

pink spring flowers. All together, the Hambrick gardens delight visitors coming to the Cowboy Hall of Fame and help to celebrate both the artistic and natural history of the region.

HAMBRICK BOTANICAL GARDENS (109 miles southwest of Tulsa) National Cowboy Hall of Fame and Western Heritage Center, 1700 N.E. 63rd Street, Oklahoma City, OK 73111 **TEL:** (405) 478-2250 **OPEN:** Daily 9-5, Sept. through May; daily 8:30-6, June through Aug. **TOTAL ACRES:** 2 **SPECIAL COLLECTIONS:** Desert plants   **ZONE 7** **F** **G** **H** **P** **R** **T** **WS**

HONOR HEIGHTS PARK
MUSKOGEE

Honor Heights Park offers 122 acres filled with nature trails, formal gardens, horticultural collections, and recreational facilities. First created in 1909, it was officially named in 1919 as a tribute World War I soldiers. This city park contains many areas of botanical interest, including a dogwood collection. Among the more than 20 dogwood species on display are Kousa and many different cultivars of flowering dogwood, best seen in spring when their pink and white blooms are at their peak.

The C. Clay Harrell Arboretum, dedicated in 1992, includes collections of crabapples, plums, pears, and cherries, as well as redbuds, maples, oaks, pines, and ashes. An extensive labeling system informs visitors about common and botanical names and the cultural needs of each kind of tree. In addition, the

Native Tree Collection presents many different species of trees and shrubs indigenous to Oklahoma, grouped together as they are found in nature.

Every season brings a new delight to Honor Heights Park, where a multitude of perennials and annuals line walks and waterways, filling the woods with fragrance and color. The impressive azalea collection encompasses more than 30,000 azaleas, representing 625 varieties. Each April, an azalea festival draws over 300,000 visitors to the park. Many return later in the spring, to enjoy the rose garden with its more than 30,000 shrubs.

HONOR HEIGHTS PARK (54 miles southeast of Tulsa) Agency Hill, N. 48th Street, Muskogee, OK 77401 **TEL:** (918) 684-6302 **OPEN:** Daily dawn-dusk **TOTAL ACRES:** 122 **SPECIAL COLLECTIONS:** Dogwoods, azaleas, flowering fruit trees, arboretum   **ZONE 8** **A** **H** **P** **PA** **T**

PHILBROOK MUSEUM OF ART
TULSA

In 1926, oil baron Waite Phillips and his wife, Genevieve, purchased 23 acres on which to build an Italian Renaissance Revival mansion. They hired architect Edward B. Delk and landscape architect Herbert Hare to create an estate in

which house and grounds would be gracefully balanced.

In 1939, the Phillips gave the estate to the city of Tulsa to be used as an art museum. The grounds include both formal areas, reflecting the Italian influence of the house, and informal swaths of broad sweeping lawns and wooded regions. Situated immediately behind the East Terrace, the formal garden was patterned after the garden at Villa Lante near Rome. Small clipped boxwood hedges form a crisscross pattern and a central water rill leads from the terrace to a small reflecting pool, banked by colorful shrubs, annuals, and perennials. The water serves to reflect a small temple, built on a mound, once the site of the Phillips' swimming pool and dressing room. To the east, a rock garden reminiscent of a European grotto garden follows the contours of the land, sloping down to Crow Creek, to pastures, an orchard, and a vegetable garden. Phillips's wish—that Philbrook

A small pond provides a reflective view of Philbrook's Italian Renaissance revival mansion.

"grow to be a symbol of a love of art and culture in the Southwest"—has come true.

PHILBROOK MUSEUM OF ART (109 miles northeast of Oklahoma City) 2727 S. Rockford Road, Tulsa, OK 74114 **TEL:** (918) 749-7941 **OPEN:** Tues.-Sat. 10-5, Thurs. until 8, Sun 11-5 **TOTAL ACRES:** 23 **SPECIAL COLLECTIONS:** Italian-style estate garden   **ZONE 7** **F** **G** **H** **HO** **P** **R** **T** **WS**

TULSA GARDEN CENTER
TULSA

Within the 45-acre Woodward Park, the Tulsa Garden Center occupies a building owned by many different people throughout the years. One, J. Arthur Hull, constructed a Victorian-style conservatory in 1924. Today, the conservatory has been carefully restored and now houses cactuses and succulents in one wing, and palms and tropical rain forest plants in another. One of the center's most spectacular gardens is the 4.5-acre Tulsa Rose Garden, dedicated in 1934 and situated on five terraces. The formality of this garden is enhanced by the junipers clipped into conical shapes and the reflecting pools found on each level. Here, some 9,000 shrubs represent more than 250 varieties of roses. Adjacent to this garden, the All-America Rose Selections Test Garden tests and displays roses from growers all over the country. Also of note, the Anne Hathaway Municipal Herb Garden, built in 1939, features many of the culinary herbs found in Hathaway's cottage garden in Stratford-upon-Avon, England.

The arboretum, originally planted in 1965, was renewed in 1997. Its 3.5 acres serve as a living tree museum to inspire and inform local gardeners as to the suitability of various ornamental trees for the Tulsa area. Throughout the years, the Tulsa Garden Center and Woodward Park have combined their efforts to bring delightful horticultural displays and useful information to the public.

TULSA GARDEN CENTER (109 miles northeast of Oklahoma City) Woodward Park, 2435 S. Peoria Avenue, Tulsa, OK 74114 **TEL:** (918) 746-5125 **OPEN:** Daily 6-11 **TOTAL ACRES:** 45 **SPECIAL COLLECTIONS:** Roses, herbs, arboretum   **ZONE 7** C G H HO L P PA T WS

OKLAHOMA BOTANICAL GARDEN AND ARBORETUM
STILLWATER

Originally created in 1935 as a living laboratory to assist in teaching and research at Oklahoma A & M College, the Oklahoma Botanical Garden and Arboretum has grown to encompass 75 acres of gardens, water ponds, and specialty home gardens. In addition, the *Oklahoma Gardening* television show maintains a studio garden here with 2.5 acres of vegetables, herbs, annuals, and perennials, as well as a fruit orchard, compost demonstration site, and greenhouse. Filming takes place every Tuesday, when the garden is closed to the public.

Each year, seven theme gardens are created, with such titles as an alphabet garden (with plants from asters to zinnias), a xeriscape garden, a demonstration of water-conserving landscaping, an orange garden, a medicinal herb garden, a hummingbird garden, and a "vegetables around the world" garden. New, permanent gardens include the Railway Garden that includes a train and miniature plant material, a rock garden, and a Japanese tea garden. The botanical garden also serves as headquarters for the statewide arboretum system, designed to provide educational opportunities for the general public as well as those in the turf and nursery industries. To that end, its wildscape demonstrates how homeowners can attract wildlife to their own backyards, and its turfgrass research center offers information about various grasses suitable for growing in Oklahoma.

OKLAHOMA BOTANICAL GARDEN AND ARBORETUM (65 miles west of Tulsa) 3425 West Virginia Avenue, Stillwater, OK 74074 **TEL:** (405) 744-6460 **OPEN:** Wed.-Mon. 8-5 **TOTAL ACRES:** 75 **SPECIAL COLLECTIONS:** Theme gardens, xeriscape, annuals, perennials, herbs, vegetables   **ZONE 7** A H P T WS

Rio Grande Botanical Garden
ALBUQUERQUE

The Rio Grande Botanical Garden is part of the Albuquerque Biological Park (known as Bio Park), a 170-acre complex that includes a zoo and aquarium. Situated along the banks of the Rio Grande River, it affords views of New Mexico's Sandia Mountains. The Botanic Garden, created in 1996, features exhibits that emphasize plants of the Southwest and the importance of water in dry climates. Phase one of the garden now encompasses 16 acres and will expand to include 52 acres. Highlights include an 11,000-square-foot conservatory designed as a pyramid, with two pavilions in tinted green glass. One pavilion displays desert plants from the Sonoran, and Chihuahuan, Deserts. Ocotillos with spikes of flame-colored flowers, barrel cactuses, chollas, and many others flourish here along with exotic plants from the Mediterranean in the adjacent pavilion.

Outdoors, there are small formal gardens and changing demonstration gardens. A Spanish-Moorish Court, the first of three planned walled gardens, has the ambience of a lush European courtyard and is decorated with a fountain, tiled benches, and an intricate floor design. The Jardin Redondo (the Round Garden), will have a lion fountain adapted from the famous fountain in the Alhambra in Granada, Spain. Water and pots filled with blooming flowers will fill out the garden. More than 600 rosebushes are slated to color the Ceremonial Rose Garden in spring and summer. Future projects include a butterfly garden, a children's fantasy garden, and native habitat gardens.

RIO GRANDE BOTANICAL GARDEN 2601 Central Avenue (next to Rio Grande River), Albuquerque, NM 87104 **TEL:** (505) 764-6200 **OPEN:** Daily 9-5; Sat.-Sun. until 6, June through Aug., except holidays **TOTAL ACRES:** 16 **SPECIAL COLLECTIONS:** Desert and Mediterranean plants   **ZONE 7** C **F** G **H** P **R V**

The Garden at El Zaguan (Bandelier Garden)
SANTA FE

On Canyon Road, a street lined with art galleries and adobe buildings typical of Santa Fe, a white picket fence signals a colorful surprise. Visible from the road, this small Victorian cottage garden offers passersby a lush display of vivid, old-fashioned flowers set against a dramatic vista of the Sangre de Cristo Mountains. Re-created in the early 1990s by the Historic Santa Fe Foundation, the Garden at El Zaguan began in the late 19th century when James Johnson, a successful Santa Fe trader, built a grand hacienda with a garden. Adolph Bandelier, an avid gardener and anthropologist who lived here from 1890 to 1891, also contributed to the design of the garden. At the same time, he was undertaking a major study of New Mexican Indian sites, and the nearby majestic Bandelier National Monument was named in his honor. This garden is called both Bandelier Garden and El Zaguan, Spanish for the breezeway at the house (a covered arched corridor), where a hanging swing glider offers visitors a restful viewing spot.

Today, Bandelier's plantings remain in this garden, where visitors can enjoy pink peony bushes that are more than a hundred years old, a large tamarisk tree,

Among the old-fashioned flowers that populate El Zaguan along Santa Fe's Canyon Road are blue delphinium and white baby's breath. They reach their crescendo in July.

and two large horse chestnut trees that flank the entrance to the garden. When restoration began in the early 1990s, two rectangular beds divided by crisscross paths were discovered and replanted with old-fashioned flowers as well as newer varieties—selections carefully chosen to recapture the spirit of the early garden. In the style of the influential English garden designer and colorist Gertrude Jekyll, warm, pastel colors are grouped together near the house. Pink roses, lavender, and peonies are framed by the deeper blues of delphinium, snapdragons, and lupines. In the middle beds, more delphinium, campanula, salvia, and scabiosa are accompanied by white daisies, lily-of-the-valley, ageratum, and lady's mantle billowing over the edges of the beds. Intense or "hot" colors of monarchs, heliopsis, and red-hot poker, and the sunny yellows of buttercups and calendulas are placed in different flower beds at the back of the garden. There are some old species of irises and such Santa Fe natives as the red-orange Austrian copper and yellow Sevilla roses. Decorative wrought-iron furniture painted in turquoise overlooks the kaleidoscopic array of color in this miniature oasis.

Many of the plants associated with more northern climates tolerate the heat of Santa Fe because of its high altitude and cool nights. The garden peaks in late June although year-round it is a restful, shady site where the casual charm of an English cottage garden meets the Southwest.

THE GARDEN AT EL ZAGUAN GARDEN (BANDELIER GARDEN) 545 Canyon Road, Santa Fe, NM 87501 **TEL:** (505) 983-2567 **OPEN:** Mon.-Sat. 9-5 **TOTAL ACRES:** Less than 1 **SPECIAL COLLECTIONS:** Victorian cottage garden flowers

ZONE 6 G P

Arizona

Desert Botanical Garden
Phoenix

In Phoenix, near the dry, glittering bed of the Salt River, Papago Park spreads a green belt of parkway, golf course, cultural attractions, a zoo, and a living monument to the tenacity and variety of desert life: the Desert Botanical Garden. Contradicting the notion that there's not much to see in a desert, the Desert Botanical Garden is the best place in the nation to see the broad range of plants that thrive in parched places, from the Americas to Africa, Asia, and Australia.

In a wild setting, desert plants give each other plenty of room and thus make the most efficient use of scarce water and nutrients. By fitting 4,000-plus species in its 145 acres, the Desert Botanical Garden allows a truly opulent look at the plants that assume a thousand-and-one strange and wonderful shapes in order to survive in sere places. Towering forests of saguaro cactuses crowd the trail, their arms oddly angled like mimes frozen in place. Here a desert wren perches on an arm budding from one cactus, while clusters of white flowers grow at the ends of another saguaro's arms. Glow-in-the-dark night bloomers, they beckon bats, birds, and other pollinators. In spring spidery, vase-shaped ocotillo cactuses are topped by tall wands of flame-red flowers attractive to humming-birds. The Desert Botanical Garden not only displays plants, it tells of the amazing ways in which these plants survive in severe conditions. For instance, to help retain moisture during summer's scorching heat, the ocotillo drops the green leaves clustering along its thin, spiny limbs, growing new leaves when the weather is more benign.

Desert plants often look as if they were devised on another world. But some are surprisingly familiar, such as the treelike palo verdes. On one of Phoenix's 100°F days, the best place in the garden is on a bench under the twisted limbs of the tallest palo verde tree, sipping prickly pear cactus iced tea. *Palo verde* means "green stick," after the tree's smooth green-glowing bark. In spring, the tree is covered by yellow flowers. The central Desert Discovery Trail shows off these and other desert classics, such as feathery mesquite trees, varieties of prickly pear cactus with fluorescent pink or yellow flowers, and a cactus whose linked limbs look like a puzzle gone wild: the jumping cholla. The cholla's spines will "jump" off the plant at the slightest touch, sometimes rooting in the ground to start a new plant.

Winding in a meandering circle, the main path passes the Cactus House, Succulent House, the auditorium and library, and three offshoot loops. One loop, devoted to the plants and people of the Sonoran Desert, exhibits the many ways in which southwestern peoples utilize the plants around them. Through five representative habitats, the trail leads from low desert and oasis past mesquite groves and dry grasslands to chaparral, while identifying plants and describing their uses. Stations scattered along the way show how to make a brush from yucca leaves, flour from mesquite beans, and other of life's necessities. Because of its high level of interpretation, the Desert Botanical Garden is one of the 12 botanical gardens accredited by the American Association of Museums.

Another loop, the Sonoran Desert Nature Trail, follows a steep grade past plants typical of the region: creosote, cactuses, and others. From the top of the trail, views take in Camelback Mountain, the Superstition Range, and the Phoenix Valley.

Spring is the time for color at the Desert Botanical Garden in Phoenix. In March, bluebells and brittlebush bloom in unison along paths that meander through the garden's 145 acres.

A third area off the main trail is the Center for Desert Living. Here exhibits include examples of desert landscaping, vegetable gardening, water conservation, and an energy-efficient house. In the Cactus House, species are grouped in eye-catching combinations: tall columnar cactuses with colonies of short, rounded cactuses nestled at their feet; queen of the night, whose brittle, withered-looking stems burst into bloom with huge, white, sweet-scented flowers; old man cactus whose round head is covered with a fuzz of white spines; golden barrel cactus, and many more, from dainty dwarfs to hulking giants. The Succulent House shows how Old World aloes and New World agaves came to similar conclusions about form and function. Both genera grow in similar, fleshy leaved rosettes—a terrific ecology lesson in convergent evolution by two groups of dramatically sculptural plants, represented here in all their glorious diversity. A surprising number of perennials color the desert—and the Desert Botanical Garden—each spring. Tall stalks of Mexican hat coneflowers are topped by velvety-red flowers. Desert lily's single stalk sways heavily with showy white lilies. Orange California poppies mingle with blue lupine. Among the many wildflowers, purple penstemon, red zauschneria, and copper-flowered devil's claws, whose odd black pods end in twisted talons, add bright spots of color to a dry landscape made three-dimensional by desert plants.

DESERT BOTANICAL GARDEN Papago Park, 1201 N. Galvin Parkway, Phoenix, AZ 85008 **TEL:** (602) 941-1225 or (602) 481-8139 **OPEN:** Daily 8-8, Oct. through April; daily 7-10, May through Sept. **TOTAL ACRES:** 145 **SPECIAL COLLECTIONS:** Desert plants   ZONE 9 **F** G **H** HO **L** P **R** WS

Boyce Thompson Arboretum
Superior

Col. William Boyce Thompson returned from a 1917 Red Cross mission to Russia during World War I and decided that plants were key to mankind's survival. As a mining magnate, he had the necessary means and 12 years later, he founded this arboretum, what he called "a beautiful and useful desert garden." Surrounded by the Tonto National Forest, the arboretum is divided into biogeographical areas. Trails wind around towering trees, through a canyon containing more than 50 species of eucalyptus, and by a man-made lake used for irrigation. The demonstration garden presents a series of water-efficient residential theme areas, while another area holds some 800 kinds of cactuses, including stately saguaros, paddle-shaped prickly pears, treelike chollas, and barrel cactuses. Mesquite, peanuts, beans, and palo verde grow in a legume garden. The arboretum holds a large display of Australian plants. Seasonal color varies with rainfall and temperature, with desert lupines, marigolds, and California poppies providing brilliant color after winter rains, followed by other wildflowers. Fall foliage can be intense with orange, rust, and gold, particularly from the pomegranate. The arboretum is also active in research and experimental cultivation and propagation of desert plants.

Boyce Thompson Arboretum (68 miles southeast of Phoenix) 37615 Ariz. 60, Superior, AZ 85273 **Tel:** (520) 689-2811 **Open:** Daily 8-5 **Total acres:** 323 **Special collections:** Desert plants, eucalyptus trees, Australian plants   **ZONE 8** A C F G H P PA T V WS

Red spires of blooming aloe reach for the sky while a saguaro stands guard at Boyce Thompson Arboretum, which holds miles of nature trails and a hidden canyon.

Arizona-Sonora Desert Museum
Tucson

The Arizona-Sonora Desert Museum is dedicated to the preservation of the desert environment. Part nature center, part museum, part zoo, and part botanical garden, it interprets the connections between all components of a natural community through living exhibits. The wonderfully designed botanical displays contain some 2,000 species of plants arranged in a variety of habitats: mountain, riparian, desert grassland, and desert garden. In the cactus garden alone, more than 200 species of cactuses and succulents flourish in a landscaped setting. The museum opened in 1952 as the result of the efforts of William Carr and Arthur Pack. Carr came from New York State, where he was involved in the American Museum of Natural History and in the development of Bear Mountain State Park. In Arizona, he crusaded for an outdoor museum and persuaded Arthur Pack, conservationist and editor of *Nature* magazine, to support his cause. The result of their work is today one of the outstanding natural outdoor museums in the country.

Arizona-Sonora Desert Museum (14 miles west of downtown Tucson) 2021 N. Kinney Road, Tucson, AZ 85743 **Tel:** (520) 883-2702 **Open:** Daily 7:30-6, March through Sept.; daily 8:30-5, Oct. through Feb. **Total acres:** 12 **Special collections:** Desert habitats and plants

ZONE 9 | F | G | H | HO | L | P | R | T | V | WS

Tohono Chul Park
Tucson

In 1966, Jean and Richard Wilson decided to create a short nature walk that would evoke the experience of the desert and an understanding of native plants. They began acquiring land, and ended up with 37 acres of loop trails, elaborate desert displays, and demonstration gardens. When the Wilsons dedicated the garden to the citizens of Arizona in 1985, additional land was donated, and Tohono Chul Park was formed. In the Tohono O'odham language, the name means "desert corner," and reflects this garden's unusual personal ambience and great variety.

Shaded trails bordered by lush, dramatic plants and trees of the desert wind around the different gardens. Three acres are devoted to some 400 species of plants from Arizona, New Mexico, and Texas. Exotic varieties from northern Mexico and other desert areas share the garden with the native saguaro-palo verde community of the great Sonoran Desert. The Demonstration Garden offers attractive, water-conserving fountains and a wide range of ideas for home and commercial landscaping. The Ethnobotanical Garden features a variety of historic crops grown by Native Americans in the Southwest as well as others introduced by explorers. The Hummingbird Garden's special plants attract the dainty birds, though other birds and wildlife can be seen throughout the park. The Children's Garden is designed with a look, touch, smell, and listen approach to plants to make the experience more tangible for the young. An exhibition gallery in an old, restored adobe building completes the charm of this Tucson oasis.

Tohono Chul Park 7366 N. Paseo del Norte, Tucson, AZ 85704 **Tel:** (520) 742-6455 **Open:** Daily 7-dusk **Total acres:** 48 **Special collections:** Xeriscape gardens, Native American garden, hummingbird garden

ZONE 9 | A | C | G | H | HO | L | P | PA | R | T | V | WS

Colorado

Denver Botanic Gardens
Denver

The Denver Botanic Gardens deliver more from its 23 acres than gardens twice its size. Situated in the heart of the city, it manages to display thousands of species with alchemical economy. Its rock garden is one of the finest in the nation and its xeric displays introduce a new constellation of plants. Across the street, at the Morrison Horticultural Center, classes and test gardens help make the gardens a learning center, one of only 12 botanic gardens to receive accreditation by the American Association of Museums.

From the city's beginnings, thanks to visionaries such as Mayor Robert Speer, Denver's dry plains were transformed into a city of parks and gardens. The Denver Botanic Gardens opened its gates in 1959. Just inside, in Boettcher Memorial Center, lecture halls, library, and indoor display gardens connect with the plexiglass dome of Boettcher Conservatory. There, a canopy of tropical trees shade cactuses, vines, and an understory that glows green in the low light.

Spread in front of the conservatory, the Water-Smart Garden's dozens of showy xeric species illustrate what can be done in a dry High Plains garden. Twisted, artistic Gambel oak, pine, and sumac form the backbone while silvery Russian sage and its mist of blue flowers create a screen, and burgundy gaillardia, yellow yarrow, and pink penstemon flaunt color. Other silver-leaved plants, such as nepeta, provide cool contrast with deep fuchsia four o'clocks and rambling poppy mallow known as wine cup for the color and shape of its flowers. Yuccas and cactuses add form and red sedum, pink ice plant, and orange butterfly weed contribute a range of hues.

The path bordering the Water-Smart Garden cleaves to an area shaded by flowering crabapples underplanted with carpets of blue veronica, clean-scented sweet woodruff, the fanlike foliage of lady's mantle, and autumn crocuses. Adjacent fountains and pools are graced by sculpture and waterlilies. Nearby, the iris garden—bearded and beardless, Siberian and spuria—is aflame in late spring with shades from velvet-black and grape to pinks and whites.

The walkway continues to a teahouse and a small but shapely Japanese garden. Here, native ponderosa pines have been molded by human design and the stream's edges are softened by yellow acorus and blue flag iris as the water flows into a duck- and koi-filled pond. Holly and mounding cotoneaster contribute to the tranquil, green theme. Another path leads from the conservatory through the Perennial Walk, bursting with coneflowers, lilies, red valerian, coreopsis, and hundreds of other species. The Perennial Walk is part of a larger collection known as the Romantic Gardens, which include fragrance, courtyard, and shade gardens.

Viburnums, maples, hawthorns, Kentucky coffee trees whose bare limbs become sculpture in winter, and many others show the range of trees and shrubs that can live in the West. Past the perennials, a pathway parts a trembling island of grasses and ravenna's plumed seed heads tower 12 feet over all. Here, too, are graceful maiden grass, airy red switch grass, narrow feather reed grass with its tall spray of tan seed heads, and nodding lanterns of quaking grass—a classy collection indeed.

The peony garden is a place to circle through a few times, so rich is it with tree peonies, singles, fat doubles, Japanese, and anemone peonies. Elsewhere, beds of lilacs in lavender, purple, and white bloom in spring. On sun-warmed banks,

The rock garden at the Denver Botanic Garden, seen here bursting with sun roses, peaks in June against a backdrop of city high rises.

mountain mahogany, apache plume, creeping kinnikinnik and its pink-belled relatives, and silver-leaved buffaloberry have a chance to show how attractive as well as tough western natives can be. Nearby, a bed protects endangered plants.

Waves of low grasses in the Plains Garden are punctuated by sunflowers, sand cherry, prairie clover, lavender blazing star, and blue-flowered lead plant. To keep the Plains Garden healthy, it is burned occasionally, and seeing the fresh green grasses sprout through charred black is always a splendid surprise.

In the southwest corner lies the jewel of Denver Botanic Gardens, its rock alpine garden—more than 4,000 species in ecosystems representing earth's alpine band. A fantasy of water-sculptured rock lines a stream bed and seems to tumble from high trails. Sedums and saxifrages from all over the world nestle among the boulders, quilting white limestone with color. Pink, ice-blue, and candy-striped creeping phlox sheet color across the Moraine Mound in spring. In fall, a slope of chrysanthemums becomes a shiny green curtain lit by white daisies. The dry steppes are tinted with red species tulips and dwarf blue iris from western Asia. In the lower meadows, pasque flowers and crocuses blend purple, pink, and other hues. Dwarf conifers and low-lying rhododendrons cluster along a high trail and rosettes of lewisia cling to scree, pink and peach flowers nodding in the wind. Week to week, the rock garden offers a full variety of delights.

■ **DENVER BOTANIC GARDENS** 909 York Street, Denver, CO 80206 **TEL:** (303) 331-4000 **OPEN:** Daily 9-5
TOTAL ACRES: 23 **SPECIAL COLLECTIONS:** Rock garden, xeriscape gardens, irises, peonies, perennials, ornamental grasses   **ZONE 5** C F G L P PA T WS

Denver Parks
DENVER

The dry prairies surrounding Denver support few trees, which makes the city's nationally known public parks all the more pleasant. In all, 250 parks take up 4,500 acres and hold nearly 600 flower beds. **City Park**'s 314 acres include dozens of flower beds set among broad lawns dotted with an elegant collection of trees. From the Natural History Museum a superb view of the Rockies is framed by rose gardens and Colorado blue spruce. **Washington Park**, with its walking paths, lakes, and mature trees, has graceful gardens of perennials and showy annual beds. Pale colors do not play well in Colorado's dazzling sunlight, so yellow coleus, deep purple basil and verbena, and red celosia are among the paint-box bright annual species. Downtown, **Civic Center Park**'s Greek open-air theater is ringed by beds bursting with colorful, aromatic blooms. **Cheesman Park**, which backs onto Denver Botanic Gardens, offers magnificent views and formal landscaping.Paths at **Sloan Lake Park** are also bordered with gardens.

■ **DENVER PARKS: CITY PARK** York and E. 17th Streets and Colorado Boulevard **WASHINGTON PARK** S. Downing Street and E. Louisiana Avenue **CIVIC CENTER PARK** York Street and E. 17th Avenue **CHEESMAN PARK** Franklin Street and E. 8th Avenue **SLOAN LAKE PARK** Sheridan Boulevard and W. 17th Avenue, Denver, CO 80206 **TEL:** (303) 964-2500 **OPEN:** Daily dawn-dusk **TOTAL ACRES:** Gardens 6, park 300 **SPECIAL COLLECTIONS:** Annuals, perennials, roses, sunken garden   **ZONE 5** A **H** P PA

Betty Ford Alpine Gardens
VAIL

North America's highest public gardens nestle in Colorado's Vail Valley, just off I-70 in the Rocky Mountains. Here the Betty Ford Alpine Gardens show what can be done with more than 2,000 species of shrubs and flowers at 8,200 feet. Although blooming starts later in the mountains, it lasts longer, and conifers and perennials flourish in Vail's bright days and cool nights. Founded in 1985, the gardens have been a special endeavor of former First Lady Betty Ford, whose family frequents Vail. Although the alpine garden covers little more than an acre, it does so intensively. Nearly two dozen varieties of dianthus spice the air with the scent of cloves. Penstemon blooms tall, short, and in many hues along with columbine and candytuft. Hundreds of others—some familiar, some not— spread low-lying color in summer. In the perennial garden, more than 1,500 species cluster on rocky mounds, linger near a pool, and crowd the paths. Potentilla, red-berried cotoneaster, and roses are among the numerous shrubs. Among the less-familiar flowers, creeping sun roses are covered with pink or yellow flowers, sweet-scented wallflowers bloom brassy yellow, and rose-colored monkey flowers sit pretty between a rock and a pool. The Alpine Gardens use its natural abundance of rock to contrast with the soft flow of greenery. In the Meditation Garden, lemon and woolly thyme weave together to create soothing ground patterns while a small stream spills into a pool. Daphne scents the air near benches and the whole is framed by Colorado blue spruce. The gardens also offers seed exchanges, classes, workshops, and hikes.

■ **BETTY FORD ALPINE GARDENS** (97 miles west of Denver) 183 Gore Creek Drive, Vail, CO 81657 **TEL:** (970) 476-0103 **OPEN:** Daily dawn-dusk, snowmelt to snowfall **TOTAL ACRES:** 1 **SPECIAL COLLECTIONS:** Alpine flowers and shrubs   **ZONE 4** G **H** HO P PA T WS

When the snow melts away in Vail, the Betty Ford Alpine Gardens take center stage. S here in late July, the gardens feature 500 different varieties of alpine and subalpine pla

Red Butte Garden and Arboretum
Salt Lake City

Surrounded by the picturesque panorama of the Wasatch Range at the mouth of the canyon it is named after, Red Butte Garden and Arboretum is a 160-acre botanical garden in progress. Since it opened to the public in 1985, 25 acres of gardens have been created to display the diverse flora of the Intermountain West with 60 more acres under development.

The first garden, the Four Seasons Garden, features year-round enjoyment and grand views. In spring, crabapples, cherries, magnolias, and flowering bulbs burst into bloom, followed in summer by perennials and annuals. In addition, the fruits and colors of trees and evergreen shrubs accompany the autumn and winter months.

A floral walk leads to the Terrace Gardens, which constitute three separate gardens for herbs, medicinal plants, and fragrance plants. Situated on steep slopes, the gardens are designed as a series of descending terraces, with walls of local red sandstone. Each garden is entered through a wisteria arbor that leads to overlooks of lower gardens. The Herb Garden occupies the upper terrace and features boxwood parterres filled with traditional culinary plants, as well as 18 different types of shrub roses. In the center of the complex, the Medicinal Garden, an informative, historical, and attractive garden, contains an important collection of plants because of its affiliation with medical and pharmacological research conducted by the University of Utah. Also of interest is the Fragrance Garden on the lowest terrace. This area is styled as a meadow of herbaceous plants and shrubs that are either aromatic or have the ability to release their fragrance when touched.

The floral walk continues to a Waterfall Display Garden, a refreshing cascade surrounded by daylilies, irises, and perennials. The cascade is the result of a dam on Red Butte Creek above, where a pool with aquatic plants and ornamental grasses forms the Water Pavilion Garden. At the end of the walk, there is wildflower meadow filled with color in summer and fall. Butterflies and hummingbirds may also be spotted here. And beyond lies a natural area, with four miles of trails leading through the rugged terrain to ridges and canyons, with vistas of the valley and Salt Lake City. New gardens in progress include a rose garden, a children's garden, and the Walk Through Utah Garden, which will have 15 acres of native flora.

The entire University of Utah campus—some 1,500 acres hosting more than 9,000 trees and shrubs—is regarded as an arboretum. One collection of special note within this landscape is the gathering of oak hybrids, the results of what is considered the most extensive hybridization project in the country. The university is planning to make 90 acres of natural areas with dramatic geological formations accessible to the public, an addition sure to captivate visitors for years to come.

RED BUTTE GARDEN AND ARBORETUM Research Park, 1300 Wakara Way, University of Utah, Salt Lake City, UT 84108 **TEL:** (801) 581-5322 **OPEN:** Daily 9-8, May through Sept.; Tues.-Sun. 10-5, Oct. through April **TOTAL ACRES:** Garden 25, grounds 160 **SPECIAL COLLECTIONS:** Herbs, daylilies, native plants, medicinal garden

ZONE 6 F G H P PA T V WS

The Red Butte Garden and Arboretum is nestled high on the foothills of the Wasatch Range, over-looking Salt Lake City. Along with majestic views, the gardens contain waterfalls and wooded paths.

GARDENS AT TEMPLE SQUARE
SALT LAKE CITY

The gardens at Temple Square, world headquarters of the Church of Jesus Christ of Latter-day Saints, cover ten acres with a massive collection of bulbs, annuals, and perennials designed to complement the temple and historic buildings. The gardens were designed to encourage peaceful contemplation. They create a sense of order with a pattern of formalized layouts—rows of trees, squares and circles of hedges, and lines of walkways and patios. Floral arrangements decorate all the nonwalking areas, and the flower gardens are completely replanted twice a year. A major part of Temple Square is actually a rooftop garden, with soil in places no more than 18 inches deep, with parking underneath. Throughout the garden, careful consideration is given to the sequence and duration of bloom. An early spring display, made possible by the heated facilities under the beds, begins with crocuses and dwarf irises, and ends with daffodils, tulips, pansies, and Iceland poppies. Summer brings the most intense blaze of color and elaborate floral combinations, a challenge in this high desert climate. Fall offers varied chrysanthemums, and Christmas caps the season in a drama of lights and music. Plants and trees related to the history of the temple are integrated into the garden, as well.

GARDENS AT TEMPLE SQUARE 15 East S. Temple Street, Salt Lake City, UT 84111 **TEL:** (801) 240-5916 **OPEN:** Daily 7-10 **TOTAL ACRES:** Gardens 10, grounds 20 **SPECIAL COLLECTIONS:** Spring bulbs, annuals

ZONE 6 G H HO P PA R T V WS

CHAPTER 6

THE PACIFIC

■

California

Oregon

Washington

Hawaii

Huge boulders shelter low-lying alpine plants at the Ohme Gardens in central Washington, where flagstone paths lead to breathtaking views of the Cascade Mountains.

Huntington Botanical Gardens
San Marino

Henry E. Huntington was a collector of real estate and business enterprises, of rare books and artwork, and, not least of all, of plants. The 150-acre garden that rings his former residence—a living, thriving library of 20,000 kinds of plants—attests not only to his nearly insatiable acquisitiveness, but also to his sophisticated eye. Partner in, then heir to, a railroading fortune founded on the fabled Southern Pacific Company, Huntington embarked in 1892 on a fateful trip to southern California. This visionary entrepreneur immediately recognized the area's unlimited and yet unexploited development potential and in 1898 established the efficient inter-urban railway system, the Pacific Electric Company, which would influence the growth of greater Los Angeles for decades thereafter.

He was drawn to the raw beauty of the San Gabriel Valley, where creased mounds of snow-capped mountains rise steeply above a broad plain. In 1903 Huntington purchased a foreclosed 600-acre ranch and increasingly turned his attention from commerce to culture. By the time of his death in 1927, he had accumulated more than four million books and manuscripts, thereby establishing one of the world's most important research libraries, and a trove of European and American fine and decorative arts. The collections are housed in his beaux arts mansion, which was constructed between 1909 and 1911, as well as in a library built in 1920, and a more recently completed gallery. The center opened to the public in 1928.

Huntington brought to his gardens the same organizational acumen he devoted to his public works projects, and the same standards of excellence with which

A parade of 18th-century statues keeps watch over Huntington's North Vista, which is surrounded by a camellia garden. The statues portray allegorical and mythological subjects.

he selected works of art. Seeking something more than a manicured estate garden, he insisted on gathering a significant botanical collection to further the art and science of horticulture.

Landscaping began in 1904. It was overseen—for 44 years—by William Hertrich, a German gardener who managed to cater to his employer's every whim while making major contributions to the design and development of the gardens. When Huntington demanded mature specimens for an instant "established" look, Hertrich traveled far and wide in

A stately saguaro stands at attention over an army of golden barrel cactuses in the 12-acre Desert Garden at Huntington Botanical Gardens. Night-blooming cereus spreads its arms in the background.

search of the perfect plants, shipping plants and materials back on a private railway spur. And when Hertrich suggested planting a dry slope with cactuses and succulents, Huntington quickly overcame his personal distaste of spiny plants—having had a painful encounter with one while in Arizona—and approved his gardener's plan.

Evidence of Huntington's primary passions are abundant throughout the grounds, which are arranged in 15 main areas. The lovely North Vista, a grass allée that draws the eye into the distant mountains, is lined with walls of camellias, azaleas, and palms. A baroque stone fountain serves as a focal point for this floral corridor, studded with 18th-century Italian statuary. The Shakespeare Garden, which is overseen by a statue of the Bard, spotlights many of the plants mentioned in his works, from crocus and columbine to pinks and poppies. The Rose Garden, a three-acre site with 4,000 plants, is encyclopedic, with 1,800 species and cultivars arranged chronologically to tell the 2,000-year history of this venerable flower. Examples of roses grown in ancient Greece through the latest types of English roses bloom in beds, arbors, and pergolas near an 18th-century French stone *tempietto*. The formal Herb Garden provides a primer on useful plants: Those that have served as medicines, foods, cosmetics, and dyes are gathered around an 18th-century wrought-iron wellhead from Germany.

The remaining gardens resemble nothing so much as galleries—exquisite works of botanical beauty arranged thematically, and aesthetically, within specialty landscapes. Established in 1905, the Palm Garden features more than 200 species of palms suited to the local climate, including date, jelly, fishtail, and fan

A marble chair fashioned in Florence and anchored by twin lions (above), among other statuary, beckons visitors to the Huntington Botanical Garden.

palms. The primary plant in the Australian Garden is the eucalyptus; 150 species of these aromatic trees and shrubs are joined by other specimens from the Southern Hemisphere such as acacias, bottlebrushes, and kangaroo paws, with their fuzzy, pawlike flowers.

The Subtropical Garden features plants from the Mediterranean, South Africa, South and Central America, and Southeast Asia. Along with jacarandas, cassias, and bauhinias is the bizarre ombú tree from Argentina, whose rumpled bark resembles elephant hide. Dense and dreamlike, the Jungle Garden teems with orchids, bromeliads, gingers, and ferns spreading around a waterfall. Tucked in a nearby bamboo grove is a series of pools stocked with lotus and waterlilies—the first landscaping project undertaken by Huntington.

One of the largest and most elaborate areas here is the Japanese Garden, commissioned by Huntington as a wedding gift for his second wife, Arabella. Accustomed to the comforts of East Coast living, the cosmopolitan Arabella was wary about the prospect of living in the Wild West, doubts her future husband tried to appease with this exotic pleasure garden. Amid apricots, cherries, wisteria, and magnolia, stands a Japanese country house furnished in the late 19th-century style of the Meiji period, along with pagodas and stone lanterns. Beneath an arching moon bridge shimmers a glassy pool of waterlilies, while a soothing Zen garden invites meditation with its "stream" of raked gravel.

Despite the diversity and vastness of the Huntington's riches, the jewel in its crown is unquestionably the Desert Garden—12 acres hosting more than 5,000 species of dryland natives, with an additional 3,000 specimens sheltered in a conservatory. The garden was never intended to replicate a desert; rather, it was Hertrich's particular genius to devise a naturalistic wonderland of these often bizarre plants, accenting their architectural shapes and pronounced textures. Everything from the gigantic treelike cactus *Cereus xanthocarpus*, one specimen of which weighs an estimated 15 tons, to the tiny knobs of Christmas-cheer sedum thrives amid 60 planting beds.

Above the main gardens lies the Huntington mausoleum, a domed marble monument in the classical style. It is set among lemon-scented eucalyptus, its smooth white trunks echoing the structure's columns and forging yet another elegant link between nature and the arts.

■ **HUNTINGTON BOTANICAL GARDENS** (12 miles northeast of Los Angeles) 1151 Oxford Road, San Marino, CA 91108 **TEL:** (818) 405-2141 **OPEN:** Tues.-Sun. 10:30-4:30, Memorial Day to Labor Day; Tues.-Fri. 12-4:30, Sat.-Sun. 10:30-4:30, Labor Day to Memorial Day, except holidays **TOTAL ACRES:** 150 **SPECIAL COLLECTIONS:** Estate garden, desert garden, palms, roses, Australian garden, Japanese garden

ZONE 9 F G H L P R T WS

In a kind of living encyclopedia, the Rose Garden at Huntington uses 1,800 chrono cally arranged species and cultivars to tell the history of America's favorite flo

Changing display gardens feature a striking mix of plant types shown in natural settings at Descanso Garden. Visitors will also find forests, streams, a lake, and a bird sanctuary.

Descanso Garden
La Canada Flintridge

In 1937, newspaper publisher E. Manchester Boddy purchased 160 acres of undeveloped woodland in the San Rafael foothills as the site for his new home. He christened the estate Rancho del Descanso, which translates from Spanish as "ranch of repose," a name that has become ever more fitting over time. Located just 15 miles from downtown Los Angeles, Boddy's former ranch has become a restful, spectacularly colorful refuge from urban sprawl.

Descanso Garden opened in 1953, on a firm foundation built by Boddy and selected horticultural associates. The media magnate was also a devoted amateur gardener who recognized that the verdant stands of California live oak blanketing his property provided the perfect conditions—filtered shade and acidic soil—for cultivating camellias. He recruited specialist J. Howard Asper, purchased 50,000 camellias from around the world, and eventually offered a stock of more than 600,000 plants at his nursery, even developing nearly 20 new varieties.

Still sheltered beneath gnarled oak limbs, some 60,000 camellias in 400 species and varieties—many developed at the gardens—form a forest of their own, some shrubs growing as tall as 20 feet. Within this 25-acre sylvan setting awaits a surprise: a Japanese garden that pays tribute to the Asian origin of many camellias. The tile-roofed teahouse, red Shinto bridge, and *minka,* or farmhouse, are surrounded by gardens featuring such traditional plants as azalea, cut-leaf maple, heavenly bamboo, and Japanese black pine, as well as pools filled with jewellike koi.

Boddy was also interested in roses. With the help of rosarian Dr. Walter E. Lammerts, the collection evolved into the International Rosarium, a five-acre attraction opened in 1994 to showcase more than 4,000 roses in an informal setting. With the San Rafael foothills as a backdrop, more than 20 themed garden vignettes—from an all-white garden to a Victorian garden replete with period gazebo—contain examples of species, heirloom, and modern roses. In addition, each section also contains companion plantings of flowering trees, shrubs, and perennials.

The camellia and rose collections are joined by irises—some 1,500 named varieties of the bearded type, many bred at Descanso—and a fragrant acre of lilacs. Because lilacs generally need a winter chilling for best performance, they are seldom raised successfully in mild climates. Here at Descanso some 50 varieties of lilac have been hybridized specifically for growth in southern California. In early spring, the garden's lavish displays of bulbs include about 12,000 tulips, followed by marigolds, impatiens, and dahlias.

As is fitting for a garden formed in an undisturbed habitat, Descanso also features a 7.5-acre planting of California natives in a natural chaparral area. The drought-tough specimens include manzanita, mesquite, mountain mahogany, California sage, and monkey flower. The nearby lake and bird sanctuary allows visitors to view up to 120 water and land bird species from a lakeshore shelter and observation station.

DESCANSO GARDEN (15 miles north of Los Angeles) 1418 Descanso Drive, La Canada Flintridge, CA 91012 **TEL:** (818) 952-4401 **OPEN:** Daily 9-4:30, except Christmas **TOTAL ACRES:** 160 **SPECIAL COLLECTIONS:** Estate garden, camellias, roses, irises, lilacs, Japanese garden   ZONE 9 **F** G **H** P **PA R** T **WS**

Many of the camellias that abound at Descanso Garden were developed on site. With some 400 varieties, a few soaring 20 feet high, the camellia collection is one of the largest in North America.

ARBORETUM OF LOS ANGELES COUNTY
ARCADIA

Like the region itself, the Arboretum of Los Angeles County is vibrant, vast, and diverse. On 127 acres once belonging to the Rancho Santa Anita, a private land grant of 13,319 acres deeded in 1839, the garden has plants from across the globe. The numbers are amazing: 36,000 specimens of more than 11,000 species, hybrids, and varieties, including 10,000 orchids alone. But the arboretum is, of course, more than a statistical standout. It is a repository of historic architecture, a sanctuary for wildlife, and a laboratory for preserving and propagating endangered plants.

The site was selected for a public garden in 1947 at the urging of Dr. Samuel Ayres, a member of a local horticultural organization who hoped to brighten southern California with the same sorts of exotic plants he had been gathering on his international travels. Others took up his cause, and the arboretum opened in 1955. It is arranged by geographical and other themes around a lagoon—actually a four-acre lake that formed in a fault. The resulting wetlands also make it an alluring destination for waterfowl.

Edging the lake is a tropical forest of cycads, palms, and ferns—many threatened in the wild—and a redwood grove. Across the water stands the arboretum's most recognizable landmark: a gingerbread-style Queen Anne cottage built between 1885 and 1886 by Elias "Lucky" Baldwin as a guest quarters. After buying the property in 1875, Baldwin spent part of his mining fortune on breeding racehorses and landscaping the then 8,500-acre ranch. A blue gum beside the cottage and ginkgoes near the 1879 carriage barn date from his residence, and some of the 200 peafowl wandering free are descendants of the three original pairs Baldwin imported from India.

Thanks to the area's gentle climate, a range of plants from mild zones thrive here, as evidenced by the impressive collections of Australian, African, South American, and Mediterranean natives, including 250 species of eucalyptus, 79 of ficus, and 70 of acacia. Other conditions in this San Gabriel Mountain valley have also inspired exhibits. The 200 drought-tolerant plants in the water conservation garden prove that an average annual rainfall of 18 inches is no barrier to a beautiful landscape, while twin greenhouses—one with filtered air, the other with unfiltered—demonstrate the toll pollution takes on plants. Two additional greenhouses shelter begonias, orchids, anthuriums, and other specimens too tender for occasional cold snaps.

A large section of the garden is devoted to naturalistic plantings near a rare virgin stand of mesa oaks. Here a waterfall dances over stacks of volcanic rock and flows into interconnected aquatic gardens of water hyacinths, irises, and waterlilies, while the Meadowbrook area offers an undulating idyll of spring bulbs and other plants flowering at the feet of birches, jacaranda, and paulownias—all surrounding a pond filled with Japanese carp.

More formal displays include a Victorian-style rose garden with many heirloom varieties introduced in the 1800s, a 1.2-acre herb garden, and a children's garden of scented, unusual, and easy-to-grow plants.

ARBORETUM OF LOS ANGELES COUNTY (23 miles east of Los Angeles) 301 N. Baldwin Avenue, Arcadia, CA 91007 **TEL:** (626) 821-3222 **OPEN:** Daily 9-5, except Christmas **TOTAL ACRES:** 127 **SPECIAL COLLECTIONS:** Tropical and subtropical plants, orchids, eucalyptus trees, aquatic garden, children's garden

ZONE 9 C F G H L P P PA R T WS

With the San Gabriel Mountains in the background, towering Mexican fan palms loom over the historic Queen Anne cottage at the Arboretum of Los Angeles County.

Ranchos Los Alamitos
Long Beach

The understated gardens at Ranchos Los Alamitos are rooted in the region's ranching tradition, reflecting the tastes of hard-working folk whose lives were tied to the land. Established in 1790, the onetime 300,000-acre ranch became home to the Bixby family in 1878. It was Susan Bixby who planted the now immense Moreton Bay fig trees framing the sprawling adobe house. She also buffered her hilltop home from the dusty ranchlands with a picket-fenced lawn and flower beds.

However, the gardens that have been preserved at this site, which opened in 1970, were created by Susan's daughter-in-law, Florence. Between 1906 and the 1940s, this determined, unpretentious woman encircled her home with a series of inviting outdoor "rooms" for relaxing and entertaining. Immediately surrounding the house are such spaces as the Secret Garden, an intimate courtyard with hibiscus and bougainvillea, and the South Garden, where blue-blossomed plumbago, periwinkle, and African lilies celebrate Susan's favorite color. Beyond the drive ringing the house lie gardens where Susan indulged her love of plants and that gradually screened views of encroaching urbanization. Shady walks are enclosed in allées of oleander, jacaranda, and pepper trees. A fragrant rose garden features some 200 specimens staged for waves of color, while a friendship garden is filled with flowers Florence received from friends. Demonstrating her interest in regional landscapes are a cactus garden, with many plants collected from the desert, and a secluded garden featuring native plants.

Ranchos Los Alamitos (24 miles south of Los Angeles) 6400 Bixby Hill Road, Long Beach, CA 90815 **Tel:** (562) 431-3541 **Open:** Wed-Sun 1-5 **Total acres:** 7.5 **Special collections:** Theme gardens, roses

ZONE 10 G H HO T WS

303

Rising from the Main Peristyle Garden, the building housing the J. Paul Getty Museum in Malibu re-creates the country retreat of a wealthy citizen of ancient Rome.

J. PAUL GETTY MUSEUM AND GARDEN
THE CENTRAL GARDEN AT THE GETTY CENTER
MALIBU AND LOS ANGELES

Two spectacularly different gardens enhance these cultural institutions, both part of a trust established by the preeminent oil tycoon and art collector. The **J. Paul Getty Museum,** which opened in 1974 to showcase Greek and Roman antiquities among other works, is modeled on a patrician's first-century A.D. villa discovered beneath the ashes of Mount Vesuvius, near Naples. Like the building itself, the five gardens speak of classical order and restraint, with symmetrical displays of such period Mediterranean plants as oleander, myrtle, roses, and violets. The Main Peristyle Garden serves as the museum's dramatic entrance. Immaculately clipped bay laurel standards and boxwood-hedged beds surround a pool enclosed in a colonnaded court, its walls adorned with trompe l'oeil garlands and other motifs adapted from ancient frescoes. Smaller gardens with similar designs and plantings flank the museum and occupy an inner court. An herb garden of specimens used for food, medicine, and ritual—from fennel to flax—re-creates a Roman kitchen garden beside an olive grove. Throughout the landscape stand bronze casts of sculptures from the original villa and replicas of period fountains.

In December 1997, a major event took place on a hilltop in the Brentwood section of Los Angeles—the opening of the new **Getty Center.** This important cultural complex incudes an art museum, a research library, and a garden. The modern buildings, designed by Richard Meier in the purist tradition, contrast dramatically with the different sensibility of Robert Irwin, the celebrated southern Californian artist chosen to design the garden. Stone pathways zigzag along rock-strewn streams that lead to a delicate waterfall. Below lies a large pool with a surprising centerpiece—an intricate maze of flowering azaleas arranged to seemingly float above the water. Other areas have installations of metal towers for bougainvillea bowers. Specialty gardens are in process, but while waiting for the garden to grow, there are always magnificent vistas framing the entire scene.

J. PAUL GETTY MUSEUM AND GARDEN (30 miles west of Los Angeles) 17985 Pacific Coast Highway, Malibu, CA 90265. *Closed for renovations* **TEL:** (310) 440-7300 **THE CENTRAL GARDEN AT THE GETTY CENTER** 1200 Getty Center Drive, Los Angeles, CA 90049 **TEL:** (310) 440-7300. *Fee and reservation for parking only* **OPEN:** Tues.-Wed. 11-7, Thurs.-Fri. 11-9, Sat.-Sun. 10-6, except holidays **TOTAL ACRES:** 80 **SPECIAL COLLECTIONS:** Robert Irwin garden design, maze, azaleas **ZONE 9** **F G P V WS**

Sherman Library and Gardens
Corona Del Mar

Set alongside the Pacific Coast Highway, the Sherman Library and Gardens is a secret pocket garden designed as an island of serenity in the sea of southern California bustle. A mere city block long, the garden presents a series of humanly scaled and meticulously tended outdoor rooms bursting with eye-catching color. The gardens grew from landscaping around the modest adobe office of Andrew Haskell, a local businessman who wanted to provide his community with a cultural center. Haskell was a longtime associate of Moses H. Sherman, a railway entrepreneur, and spent eight years turning the property into a public garden and library of regional history in his mentor's honor. It opened in 1966. Plantings range from dryland cactuses and succulents to tropical bromeliads and orchids—in more than 1,000 species. Tender specimens are housed in a conservatory, arrayed around a stone pool stocked with spangled koi. The outdoor gardens spread from an octagonal central court, which may blaze with marigolds in spring or poinsettias in winter. Tiled walks, many covered with arbors, weave around two shade gardens—cool oases of ferns and tuberous begonias—past the Tea Garden of fuchsias in hanging baskets and into the dazzling Rose Garden of some 45 climbers, floribundas, and hybrid teas. Finally, the Discovery Garden offers the visually impaired plants appealing to the senses of touch and smell.

SHERMAN LIBRARY AND GARDENS (46 miles south of Los Angeles) 2647 East Coast Highway, Corona del Mar, CA 92625 TEL: (714) 673-2261 OPEN: Daily 10:30-4, except holidays TOTAL ACRES: 2.2 SPECIAL COLLECTIONS: Desert plants, orchids, shade garden, roses   ZONE 9 C F G H L P R T WS

Balboa Park
San Diego

The cultural heart of the city, this 1,100-acre green space in downtown San Diego pulses with 14 museums, a world-class zoo, theaters, and other attractions. It is also one of America's most lushly landscaped urban parks, where groves of trees shade rolling lawns and masses of flowers sparkle in the perpetual sunshine.

Designated a public park in 1868, the once-arid tract turned green 24 years later, when horticulturist Kate O. Sessions began planting 100 trees per year for 10 years. Today it contains more than 14,000 trees, from diminutive cherries to gigantic eucalyptus. Two million plants transformed the park again in 1915, when it hosted the Panama-California Exposition. Remaining from this period is the 18,750-square-foot Botanical Building—then the largest lath structure in the world, which now houses 2,000 tropical plants. Also dating from the fair is a replica of the gardens at Alcazar Castle in Spain, with boxwood-lined beds of some 7,000 annuals, polychrome tile ornamentation, and sunken fountains. The remainder of the park features a desert garden of 1,300 drought-resistant specimens, a traditional Japanese dry landscape of sand and stone, and an impressive rose garden. Perhaps the most surprising "garden" in the park is at the San Diego Zoo, which features animal habitats and outstanding collections of orchids and gingers, as well as whimsical animal-shaped topiaries fashioned from olive trees.

BALBOA PARK (127 miles south of Los Angeles) 1549 El Prado, San Diego, CA 92101 TEL: (619) 239-0512 OPEN: Always open TOTAL ACRES: 1,100 SPECIAL COLLECTIONS: Roses, tropical plants, desert plants, topiary, Spanish garden, Japanese garden   ZONE 10 C HO P T V WS

GANNA WALSKA LOTUSLAND
SANTA BARBARA

The gardens at Lotusland are as eccentric, enchanting, and electric as their creator, opera diva Ganna Walska, who traded her extravagant costumes for gardening gloves and turned her Montecito estate into a stage set for her own theatrical brand of landscaping. After a star-crossed career and six storm-tossed marriages, the Polish-born Ganna Walska retired to California in 1941, purchasing a 37-acre property that had originally been developed as a nursery in the 1870s. Recasting herself as a "peasant gardener," Madame, as she was called, chose the lotus, a symbol of renewal, as the leitmotif for the garden that was to consume her for 43 years. It opened to the public in 1993.

If Walska's guiding image was the lotus, which today float like translucent goblets in the former swimming pool, her trademark became the exotic and dramatic plants that she collected in nearly unimaginable profusion, even excess. Separated into distinctive themed rooms, the garden comprises countless hundreds of bromeliads, ferns, succulents, and other tropical or semitropical specimens—from tiny Australian violets to stately Chilean wine palms.

A veritable forest of vertical and ball-shaped cactuses bristles along the entry to the simple stucco house. The door is guarded by a pair of fantastical weeping succulent trees whose snakelike tendrils writhe up, down, and sideways. Across the driveway thrive 130 species of aloe—spiky specimens with strappy, twisty leaves that are hardly worth growing individually, but en masse form a menacing jungle of whorling rosettes. They seem all the more bizarre juxtaposed against the pale turquoise, crescent-shaped pool lined with gaping abalone shells and refreshed by a three-tiered fountain fashioned from giant clamshells.

Visitors to Ganna Walska Lotusland are greeted by these exotic succulent trees (Euphorbia ingens), which guard the main house of the estate.

The remainder of the garden fans out beyond the house, where a terrace filled with geraniums and fuchsias creates a colorful exception to this otherwise subtly toned study in texture, form, and scale. Prominent among the diverse areas is the Blue Garden, which offers a muted array of hues from silver to deep blue-green rendered in blue fescue grass, Mexican blue palms, blue spruce, and blue atlas cedars. The walkways here are lined with broken chunks of aquamarine slag glass, which, glittering in the sun, are reminiscent of footlights.

Perhaps the highlight of Lotusland is the cycad collection, deemed one of the most outstanding in the world. With

The pool in the Aloe Garden at Lotusland is ringed by abalone shells; the giant clamshells on its far side were brought from the Tasman Sea and converted into fountains.

money being no object—even if Madame had to auction some of her famous flamboyant jewels to pay the bills—Walska accumulated more than 400 of these oddities known from prehistoric times. Sprinkling them across a lawn, she reserved three specimens of the rare *Encephalartos woodii* to be placed reverentially beside a reflecting pool.

As bold as her unconventionality and originality was Madame's sense of whimsy. An august amphitheater in a grove of crape myrtle has permanent patrons in a group of grotesque stone dwarfs, while a working 25-foot-diameter horticultural clock—the face depicted in multicolored, ground-hugging succulents—tells time for a menagerie of prancing topiary animals.

■ **GANNA WALSKA LOTUSLAND** (93 miles northwest of Los Angeles) 695 Ashley Road, Santa Barbara, CA 93108 **TEL:** (805) 969-3767 or (805) 969-9990 for reservations **OPEN:** Wed.-Sat. by reserved tour only, mid-Feb. to mid-Nov. **TOTAL ACRES:** 37 **SPECIAL COLLECTIONS:** Estate garden, tropical and desert plants, cycads, lotuses, blue garden

ZONE 10 F G P T WS

SANTA BARBARA BOTANIC GARDEN
SANTA BARBARA

Sprawling across a picturesque canyon skirting Mission Creek, the Santa Barbara Botanic Garden is a peerless 65-acre repository of California's native flora—from the agaves of its deserts to the madrone of its forests. It even hosts unique species of fuchsias and bush poppies indigenous to the islands in the Santa Barbara Channel.

The garden was proposed in 1926 by plant ecologist Dr. Frederic Clements, who favored displaying diverse specimens in naturally occurring communities. His concept has endured to this day, lending the gardens their naturalistic beauty; the landscape appears wild and unspoiled even though more than a thousand species have been planted since the garden's founding. Miles of trails hug hillsides overshadowed by the Santa Ynez mountains and overlooking the Pacific. They loop through meadows resplendent with wildflowers and grasses, arid outcroppings of cactus and mesquite, oak woodlands carpeted with ferns, and rugged arroyo and chaparral dense with evergreens. Sections are devoted to stands of important—and often endangered—California natives such as manzanita, redwood, and ceanothus, also known as California lilac, which is represented by some 70 species and varieties. An added bonus is the well-preserved sandstone Mission Dam, built from 1806 to 1807 by Chumash Indians at the request of the Santa Barbara Mission.

■ **SANTA BARBARA BOTANIC GARDEN** (2 miles from downtown Santa Barbara) 1212 Mission Canyon Road, Santa Barbara, CA 93105 **TEL:** (805) 682-4726 **OPEN:** Mon.-Fri. 9-5, Sat.-Sun. 9-6, March through Oct.; Mon.-Fri. 9-4, Sat.-Sun. 9-5, Nov. through Feb., except holidays **TOTAL ACRES:** 65 **SPECIAL COLLECTIONS:** Native plants and trees, fuchsias   ZONE 10 A F G L P PA T WS

HEARST CASTLE GARDENS
SAN SIMEON

Publishing magnate William Randolph Hearst remains a monumental figure in American history. Thus visitors think they are prepared for the lavishness of his 165-room, treasure-crammed "castle" perched high above the scalloped Pacific shoreline in the rugged ranchland surrounding the Santa Lucia Mountains. But still it comes as a surprise. Hearst called it *La Cuesta Encantada,* or the enchanted hill. Construction began in 1922 and was completed 25 years later, integrating 125 acres of meticulous gardens. Guided by architect Julia Morgan and floral designer Isabella Worn, Hearst looked to grand estates of southern Europe for inspiration and enhanced his extravagant villa with a dramatic, outsized interpretation of the Mediterranean landscape. Broad terraces cut into the steep hillside link the castle with three guest houses. Replete with ancient Roman artworks, the terraces hold glazed ceramic tiles, fountains, and such typical warm-weather plants as Italian stone pine, oleander, and myrtle. The formal, geometric style of the gardens is softened by extensive flower displays, from azaleas to camellias. Thousands of pansies, marigolds, begonias, and other bedding plants, bloom with more than a thousand rosebushes in some 80 varieties. Even the woodlands around the garden's fringes were an enormous undertaking, with more than 70,000 trees planted to help tie the gardens into the native California landscape.

■ **HEARST CASTLE GARDENS** (144 miles north of Santa Barbara) 750 Hearst Castle Road, San Simeon, CA 93452 **TEL:** (805) 927-2020 or (800) 444-4455 **OPEN:** Daily 8:20-3:20, except holidays **TOTAL ACRES:** 125 **SPECIAL COLLECTIONS:** Estate garden, roses, bedding plants   ZONE 9 F G HO P PA R T WS

Casa Grande, the main house at Hearst Castle, overlooks a courty brimming with lantana and roses and flanked by tangerine tr

Filoli
Woodside

The gardens at Filoli are quintessentially Californian: rooted in an earthquake, nurtured by the Gold Rush, and nourished by a sun-drenched climate that blurs the boundaries between indoors and out.

Cradled in a narrow, verdant valley of oak, redwood, and madrone, this 650-acre estate was built between 1915 and 1917 for William B. Bourn II, who compounded the fortune he gleaned from his Empire gold mine with success in utilities and wineries. Like many well-to-do San Franciscans, Bourn and his wife, Agnes, were so shaken by the shifting of the San Andreas Fault that leveled the city in 1906 that they moved to the sylvan countryside of the Santa Cruz Mountains, farther south on the peninsula. The property Bourn chose adjoined

Crystal Springs Lake, the reservoir for his water company, which supplied San Francisco. The name Filoli summarized his credo: "*fi*ght for a just cause, *lo*ve your fellow man, *li*ve a good life."

Bourn hired prominent California architect Willis Polk to design the mansion, a 43-room, redbrick residence adapted from the Georgian country houses Bourn admired in England and Ireland. Polk in turn enlisted Bruce Porter, a garden and interior designer, and Isabella Worn, whose floral arrangements were de rigueur in San Francisco society, to enhance the manor with formal gardens of a scale grand enough to rival the imposing natural landscape as well as the great estates of Europe.

Deep green germander and burgundy Japanese barberry intertwine with silvery santolina and blue-green lavender in Filoli's knot garden.

And impressive they were, spreading luxuriantly and leisurely across 16 acres. Yet, thanks to Polk's ingenious design, they appear as intimate as a rose arbor. The gardens were conceived architecturally as a succession of orderly outdoor "rooms," all enclosed within the structure of the forested foothills. Each space is walled by hedges or allées—of laurel, rose of Sharon, and copper beech, among others—and furnished with graceful, colorful plantings that lend a distinctive personality. Sprinkled throughout, unusual specimen trees, topiaries, and standards provide accents. When the William P. Roth family purchased the estate in 1937, they not only respectfully preserved this original scheme but enriched it by introducing hundreds of rhododendrons, magnolias, lilacs, peonies, and other plants. Filoli, remarkably intact and still immaculately groomed, opened to the public in 1975.

The gardens begin immediately off the mansion's rear facade, aligned along a 1,500-foot-long brick walkway that runs like a corridor through the open-air rooms. A pair of spacious terraces extends the indoor living space into a landscape of wisteria, clematis, and lantana that climb along the stone balustrades. Steps lead into the Sunken Garden, where two velvet patches of grass embrace a pool whose surface mirrors the surrounding mountains and dances from the soft spray of fountains. Echoing the reflecting pool is the former family swimming

e rays of the rising sun greet a Sunburst honey locust and the tranquil Sunken rden, where a double arcade of Irish yews surrounds the former swimming pool.

When Filoli's notable tulips are finished, flowering hawthorn and crabapple trees are in full bloom in the Upper Walled Garden, where boxwood hedges encase mounds of white violas.

pool, enclosed in a double arcade of Irish yews. All 210 of these sentinel-straight, upright evergreens at Filoli, and many of the hollies, were raised from slips grown on the Bourn estate in County Kerry, Ireland. In the distance, rising above a grove of gray-green olive trees sheared into goblet shapes, gleam the golden-yellow leaves of a Sunburst honey locust. Another magnificent specimen—a Camperdown elm, whose drooping, twisted branches reach to the ground—anchors the end of the nearby bowling green, which is lined on one side with a 200-foot-long row of interwoven sycamores.

The literal and figurative centerpiece remains the spacious Walled Garden, which itself contains several individual "rooms." At its center stands a sundial flanked by ranks of 14,000 tulips in spring, followed by dianthus, lobelia, and salvia in summer. A pavilion in the low brick wall overlooks a broad lawn and circular pool, in fall littered with a confetti of fanlike gingko leaves and brightened with beds of abundant sasanqua camellias. In one corner lies the tidy Dutch Garden, where tulips, then pastel impatiens are penned by knee-high boxwood hedges. In another is the Wedding Place—a set of turf steps whose masonry risers are overrun with creeping fig. The stairway, which is lined with potted petunias and overhung with branches of magnolia and weeping cherry, ascends to a 15th-century Venetian marble fountain.

To the other side of the sundial, the intricate Chartres Garden replicates in floral form the Jesse stained-glass window in the 12th-century French cathedral. Hedges of English holly represent the masonry between the upper and lower windows, while boxwood replaces the leading. Flowers, including violas and primroses, form colored panes. Beyond the garden walls lies the one area that defies the precise geometry of Porter's design and recalls the wilderness from which Filoli was wrested. The Woodland Garden, webbed with curving paths, is a wild tangle of azaleas, dogwoods, cyclamens, Japanese anemones, and other shade-lovers beneath a canopy of native coast live oaks. A wisteria-draped iron gate in the Walled Garden opens onto another allée of Irish yews, transforming the walkway into an enchanted tunnel and forming a sumptuous deep green backdrop for a riot of roses: ten beds aglow with the pinks, reds, peaches, and golds of some 500 shrubs. In the Knot Garden, strands of dark green germander, silvery santolina, blue-green lavender, and garnet red Japanese barberry seem to weave over and under one another in interlocking designs. These highly manicured gardens contrast with the field of daffodils cascading down a hillside opposite the yews, as well as with the rambling drifts of iris, lavender, artemisia, and delphinium in the perennial plots.

The parade of yews, and the gardens themselves, end at the aptly named High Place, a serene templelike semicircle of eight stone columns standing against a curtain of yews. The columns, clad in wisteria, supposedly served as ballast in ships that sailed to San Francisco during the Gold Rush. From here the vista stretches back across the gentle slope of the gardens and recedes into the treetops that overlook Bourn's crystal lake.

■ FILOLI (30 miles south of San Francisco) Canada Road, Woodside, CA 94062 **TEL:** (650) 364-2880 **OPEN:** Tues.-Thurs. by reservation only, Fri.-Sat. 10-2, mid-Feb. through Oct., except holidays **TOTAL ACRES:** Gardens 16, estate 650 **SPECIAL COLLECTIONS:** Estate garden, walled garden, camellias, theme gardens

ZONE 10 F G H HO P R T WS

SUNSET GARDENS
MENLO PARK

Like the magazine itself, the Sunset Gardens are an index to outdoor living in the American West, with planting areas corresponding to every major climate zone from the Arizona deserts to Washington's woodlands. *Sunset* magazine was founded in 1898 by the Southern Pacific Railroad to promote westward travel and has since become a popular lifestyle magazine. The 1.7-acre garden at corporate headquarters practices what the publication preaches: sensible, environmentally responsible landscaping within reach of regional gardeners.

The garden was designed in 1952 by Thomas Church, then a dean of contemporary landscape architecture and an advocate of gardens as outdoor "rooms" to extend indoor living space—a concept well suited to California's climate. Accordingly, the Sunset Gardens look much like a suburban backyard, with a sinuous six-foot-wide border of more than 300 trees, shrubs, ground covers, and flowers snaking around a bent grass lawn. At the hottest, sunniest end of the gardens grow dryland natives such as cactuses, yuccas, and matilija poppies. Coastal and central California is represented by camellias, Monterey pines, and incense cedars. In the northern California section are found examples of the state's famous redwoods, along with coast live oaks, hollies, and, of course, grapes. And the cool, shaded Pacific Northwest area boasts various woodland plants, including dogwoods, firs, and rhododendrons.

A 3,200-square-foot test garden displays plants and techniques under evaluation by the magazine's staff, and a butterfly garden features the brightly bloomed specimens, such as buddleia and salvia, that attract winged creatures.

■ SUNSET GARDENS (29 miles south of San Francisco) 80 Willow Road, Menlo Park, CA 94025 **TEL:** (415) 321-3600 **OPEN:** Mon.-Fri. 9-4:30, except holidays. **TOTAL ACRES:** 1.7 **SPECIAL COLLECTIONS:** Regional demonstration gardens, Thomas Church design

ZONE 10 H P T

GOLDEN GATE PARK
SAN FRANCISCO

San Francisco has never been shy about bending nature to its needs. Somehow, a grid of straight streets emerged on this peninsula of steep hills. And just as remarkably, one of America's largest and most beloved city parks—a 1,017-acre playground of field and forest, gardens and glades—arose from a wilderness of wind-whipped sand.

Golden Gate Park began in 1870 as a bold folly: a three-mile-long stretch of barren oceanfront called the Outside Lands since it lay beyond city development, was proposed for a park. The remote location was intended to draw residents out of urban congestion and into the healthful fresh air. Instead the unpromising spot drew jeers of disbelief—until a visionary engineer named William Hall stabilized the sand dunes with grasses and planted about 60,000 eucalyptus, pine, and cypress trees in five years, transforming perceived wasteland into prized park land.

Today the park features not only 680 acres of woods, but also 12 garden areas, 10 meadows, and 14 lakes along with a host of museums, recreation areas, statuary, and such quirky attractions as a bison paddock. The western half of the park, nearest the ocean, remains the less developed, as Hall had intended. At its edge, within earshot of the pounding Pacific, lies the eye-popping Queen Wilhelmina Tulip Garden, a formal layout of 40,000 tulips, daffodils, poppies,

The striking drum bridge in the Japanese Tea Garden is a smaller version of the steep, semicircular bridges in Japan that are designed to allow pleasure boats to pass beneath.

and primroses. The 1902 windmill standing guard over the plantings once pumped 20,000 gallons of water per hour for park irrigation.

In the park's eastern portion lie fragrant stands of redwoods and magnolias, as well as individual displays dedicated to roses, dahlias, fuchsias, and camellias. Tucked into the trees is the Shakespeare Garden—with plants, from aconite to yew, mentioned in the Bard's works. Here also stands the AIDS Memorial Grove, a peaceful hollow of dogwoods, pines, ferns, and poppies.

The park's most recognizable landmark is its Conservatory of Flowers, a magnificent glass palace dating from 1878 that was fashioned after a greenhouse at Kew Gardens in London. It contains such tropicals as palms, orchids, and tuberous begonias, as well as a lily pond. Nearly as venerable

The Conservatory of Flowers is fronted by beds filled with showy annuals at Golden Gate Park. Built in 1878, the conservatory houses tropical plants and a lily pond.

is the rustic Japanese teahouse, built for the California Midwinter International Exposition held in the park in 1894. It now anchors the oldest Japanese tea garden in America, a five-acre compound of tranquil ponds and streams amid flowering cherries, azaleas, Japanese pines and maples, bamboos, and camellias. Distinctive gates, bridges, and sculptures also distinguish this site, which contains a traditional Zen garden, a sunken garden, and a collection of dwarf conifers.

Perhaps the most appealing garden is the McLaren Rhododendron Dell, 20 acres of some 350 rhododendron species and hybrids. This garden was established in 1942 to honor John McLaren, a gardener from Scotland who loved rhododendrons and was also park superintendent from 1890 to 1943. Over these 53 years he introduced 170 rhododendron species and hybrids to the gardens, carrying on Hall's legacy and leaving one of his own: There are no KEEP OFF signs anywhere in the park.

GOLDEN GATE PARK Fell and Stanyan Streets, San Francisco, CA 94117 **TEL:** (415) 831-2700 **OPEN:** Always open **TOTAL ACRES:** 1,017 **SPECIAL COLLECTIONS:** Japanese garden, Shakespeare Garden, AIDS Memorial Grove, rhododendrons

ZONE 10 A C **G** **H** P **PA** T **WS**

STRYBING ARBORETUM AND BOTANICAL GARDENS
SAN FRANCISCO

The Strybing Arboretum is a jewel within a jewel: an exquisitely designed 70-acre enclave of 6,000 plant species nestled along the southern edge of Golden Gate Park. Opened in 1940, the arboretum drew its earliest plant collections from the park itself, concentrating on rhododendrons—including tender Vireya and Maddennii groups—and choice magnolias, such as the stunning, large-flowered Campbell magnolia. Over time, however, the arboretum began gathering specimens from areas across the globe with a climate similar to coastal California. Following a master plan developed in the 1960s by the distinguished landscape architect Robert Tetlow, the arboretum radiates from a lush central lawn and is organized by the geographic origins of the plantings. Some of the most engaging gardens feature specimens from close to home. The Redwood Trail winds through a stand of these noble indigenous trees, which tower over 100 species of such woodland companions as wild ginger and western azalea, while the 3.5-acre native garden glows with California poppies and Douglas irises amid manzanitas and buckeyes. From farther afield come the wiry-leaved grass tree of Australia, the voluptuous proteas of South Africa, the flame-flowered fire bush of Chile, and the fragrant bay laurel of the Mediterranean region.

Smaller gardens include a tapestry of dwarf conifers—from golden arborvitae to blue spruce—and a patchwork of aloes, agaves, puyas, and other succulents. For an unusual encounter, the moon-viewing garden offers a peaceful retreat from the wealth of plants: surrounding a small, placid reflecting pool is a Japanese stroll garden planted simply with dogwoods and camellias.

■ **STRYBING ARBORETUM AND BOTANICAL GARDENS** 9th Avenue and Lincoln Way, San Francisco, CA 94122 **TEL:** (415) 753-7089 or (415) 661-1316 **OPEN:** Mon.-Fri. 8-4:30, Sat.-Sun. and holidays 10-5 **TOTAL ACRES:** 70 **SPECIAL COLLECTIONS:** Rhododendrons, magnolias, redwoods, native plants, dwarf conifers

ZONE 10 G **H** L P **P** PA **R** T WS

RUTH BANCROFT GARDEN
WALNUT CREEK

Spiny and spiky, formidable and fantastical, the 2,000-odd species in the Ruth Bancroft Garden form a sort of oasis in the desert—an oasis of natives from dry-land habitats across the globe. Here, on four acres of a former walnut orchard, is a remarkable archive of aloes, agaves, euphorbias, echeverias, piñon pines, and palo verdes that rival any botanical collection.

The garden began modestly in the early 1970s, as lifelong plant enthusiast Ruth Bancroft gradually moved her clutch of potted succulents from windowsill, porch, and greenhouse to land no longer needed for the family farm. Collaborating with nursery-man and garden designer Lester Hawkins, Bancroft laid the foundations for a full-fledged landscape, devising a scheme of rounded, raised beds laced with meandering paths to allow each area to be examined and appreciated before the next was revealed. While the overall landscape was a joint effort, the beds' sensitive design is Bancroft's alone. The layout bears witness to her academic training in architecture, her uninhibited joy in experimentation, and her innate taste. For although succulents do bloom, this garden's beauty does not depend on flowers but rather on the near limitless diversity of shape, line, scale, texture, and structure of the sometimes surreal plants.

Visitors enter the garden through a lattice pavilion painted a soothing green.

The towering spires of the octopus agave can reach as high as 40 feet. Although the blo
add life to the Ruth Bancroft Garden, they signal the end of the plant's life cy

It is flanked by two shade houses where tender specimens find shelter from winter and relief from summer. The path continues on beneath a canopy of wispy desert willows, rare acacias, and bulbous bottletrees that pierce the sky and provide filtered shade. Beyond lie the islands of plants: self-contained compositions in contrast and complements. The spreading star of a giant agave explodes over dainty crown of thorns; a stiff fountain of yucca sprays beside the leathery catcher's mitt pads of opuntias. Hairy columns of Peruvian old man cactus sway above a fuzz of fluffy artemisia. Everywhere are barbs and thorns, razorlike leaf blades and prickly tips—the price these plants pay to collect and conserve water.

The tapestry of dusky blue- and gray-greens, this garden's predominant tones, is interrupted here and there by the brash lemon-lime of a kalanchoe or glossy purple-black of an aeonium. These produce blooms as striking as their foliage, such as the brilliant cerise daisies of the ice plant, the feathery ruby puffs of the Mexican flamebush, and fuzzy yellow flower stalks of the *Agave ferox*—wiry and wiggly and 30 feet long. There is also a real oasis here, a free-form pool edged with palms and puyas and stocked with yellow flag irises and six varieties of waterlilies. This was also the Garden Conservancy's first sponsored garden.

■ **RUTH BANCROFT GARDEN** (25 miles east of San Francisco) 1500 Bancroft Road, Walnut Creek, CA 94598 **TEL:** (510) 210-9663 **OPEN:** By appointment **TOTAL ACRES:** 4 **SPECIAL COLLECTIONS:** Desert plants, aloes, agaves, echeverias, piñon pines   **ZONE 9** C **F** **P** **T** **WS**

LUTHER BURBANK HOME AND GARDENS
SANTA ROSA

This 1.6-acre property in downtown Santa Rosa serves as a living museum and appropriate memorial to the foremost plant breeder in the United States, Luther Burbank. From 1884 to 1926, he conducted most of his hybridization experiments here in his four-acre garden, in hopes of improving plant performance. Burbank eventually introduced more than 800 varieties of fruits, vegetables, nuts, and flowers—including the 'July Elberta' peach, the 'Burbank' potato, and the Shasta daisy—many of which are still enjoyed today.

His former outdoor "laboratory" became a public garden in 1960 and features about 25 examples of his famous finds. In the rose garden, for instance, his pink *Rosa multiflora* 'Thornless' thrives alongside varieties developed by other California breeders. Spineless cactuses originally propagated as cattle forage pay tribute to Burbank's never-ending (although in this case fruitless) attempts to find new food sources. An orchard bears a number of his inventions, including the 'Santa Rosa' plum, 'Northblue' blueberry, and the "plumcot" (a cross between a plum and an apricot), although there remains only two specimens of his 'Paradox' walnut—a fast-growing, fine-grained hardwood suitable for cabinetry. Providing masses of color are 16 demonstration beds much like those Burbank used, filled with cannas, asters, gladioluses, and similar ornamentals, as well as a border of saucer magnolias, lilacs, amaranthus, and other flowering specimens. And perpetuating Burbank's spirit are beds with recent hybrids, such as mildew-resistant zinnias, which would have made the pioneering horticulturist proud.

■ **LUTHER BURBANK HOME AND GARDENS** (59 miles north of San Francisco) Santa Rosa Avenue at Sonoma Avenue, Santa Rosa, CA 95402 **TEL:** (707) 524-5445 **OPEN:** Daily 8-7, April through Oct.; daily 8-5, Nov. through March **TOTAL ACRES:** 1.6 **SPECIAL COLLECTIONS:** Roses, orchards, cactus, demonstration gardens   **ZONE 8** A C **F** **G** **H** **HO** **P** **PA** **T** **WS**

Mendocino Coast Botanical Gardens
Fort Bragg

A spectacular natural setting and a mild climate conducive to growing nearly everything form the foundation for the Mendocino Coast Botanical Gardens—a relative newcomer that has rapidly become one of the state's horticultural treasures.

Hovering on a rocky headland above the Pacific, the 47-acre property was first developed in 1961 by a retired nurseryman, but not opened to the public until 1992. The garden takes its role as a repository of indigenous and rare specimens seriously. About three-quarters of the site is cloaked in native flora: A forest of Bishop and shore pines buffers seaborne winds, western sword and deer ferns lushly line a creek racing through a canyon, and patches of California poppy, Indian paintbrush, and lupine carpet the coastal bluffs. The remainder is given over to more formal displays of 20 plant collections, including lilies, camellias, dwarf conifers, fuchsias, and Pacific irises. Outstanding among the collections are 300 heaths and heathers—tough moorland plants artfully arranged in a patchwork swatch according to foliage color. Here too thrive heritage roses, with more than 200 examples of varieties introduced no later than the mid-1900s. The garden's signature, however, is its rhododendrons. In addition to natives and hybrids propagated locally are exotic, sometimes intensely fragrant, and oft-temperamental specimens gathered from as far afield as New Guinea and the Himalayas.

Mendocino Coast Botanical Gardens (179 miles north of San Francisco) 18220 North Highway 1, Fort Bragg, CA 95437 **Tel:** (707) 964-4352 **Open:** Daily 9-5, March through Oct.; daily 9-4, Nov. through Feb., except Thanksgiving and Christmas **Total acres:** 47 **Special collections:** Native plants, heaths and heathers, lilies, irises, heritage roses ZONE 8 A G P PA R T

The waves of the Pacific lap at the edge of the Mendocino Coast Botanical Gardens, where cliffs are brightened by ice plants, marguerites, and poker plants.

Oregon

SHORE ACRES GARDENS
COOS BAY

Hidden among Sitka spruce, Monterey cypress, and shore pines on a secluded stretch of southern Oregon coastline lies Shore Acres Gardens. Originally the estate of lumberman and shipbuilder Louis J. Simpson, the house and grounds were developed in the early 1900s by young Simpson, who wanted his mansion built near the sea cliff. He also wanted a garden. Under his direction, workers cleared a large parcel of land just south of the house—an area, though level, thick with coast pine, downed timber, blackberries, salal, ferns, and wildflowers. Horse teams hoisted huge boulders from the rocky beach, which were then arranged to border the reflection pond.

Simpson also directed the captains and crews aboard his family's schooners and clipper ships to bring him varieties of rhododendrons and azaleas from around the world. Exotic tree species soon arrived as well. When finished, the estate was for a time one of the largest and finest showplaces in southern Oregon. In 1924, some 700 acres of the estate, along with its six-acre garden, were purchased by the state of Oregon. The mansion fell into disrepair and was razed in 1948. Although the garden also deteriorated, it was researched and restored in the early 1970s and is now maintained by state park workers along with a local group of garden lovers who comprise a foundation called Friends of Shore Acres. Although the garden looks much different from Simpson's original, it is definitely worth a visit. The first glimpse of the large formal garden section is via a wide-angle view that emerges from a covered wooden entry. First-time visitors will enjoy the enlargements of old photographs and the accompanying brief narrative history of the Simpson family displayed on the entry walls. The immediate impression of the garden is one of grand scale as your senses take in acres of sedate lawn bisected at regular intervals by straight paved walkways. These paths are bordered by low boxwood hedges and adjacent beds planted with seasonal annuals, hardy perennials, and ornamental shrubs.

The gardener's cottage, the only remaining and restored structure from the original estate, sits like a tidy dowager on the eastern border of the garden beneath towering Monterey cypress and Sitka spruce. Throughout the formal garden large circular and square island beds contain seasonal collections of annuals and perennials. In the rose garden, circular beds exhibit extensive collections of rose varieties including floribundas, teas, grandifloras, and some old scented varieties. The formal garden offers square beds filled with about 250 dahlias, some blooming well into September and October.

Formal walkways beckon visitors to the far south side of the garden, down a few stone steps, and into a secluded Oriental garden. Here a path encircles a large pond around which grow flowering trees and shrubs, irises, and dozens of azaleas and rhododendrons. A large Monterey pine towers at one corner. Giant rhubarb, delicate maple, bamboo, and ferns drape gracefully at pond's edge. In the center of the pond a pair of copper cranes reflect their graceful silhouettes on the water's surface, where waterlilies bloom pink, white, and pale yellow. A miniature Oriental-style bridge and small metal lanterns flank the pond's western edge, where Simpsons' bejeweled guests strolled during the lively Jazz Age of the early 1900s.

Spring arrives with a rush of blooms at Oregon's Shore Acres Gardens, made doubly colorful by the reflections in the Oriental Garden pond, where copper cranes pause to take in the view.

After leaving the garden, a stroll over to the sea cliff leads to the glass-walled gazebo, which contains more historic and photographic exhibits on the Simpson family. This is the site of the original mansion. A low rock wall offers sweeping views of the ocean and several uptilted outcroppings rising from the water, washed over and over by incoming waves. This garden is well worth visiting in winter as well as summer, with its stark tree and ornamental shrub silhouettes, and mild and misty coastal climate. But the winds can blow with gusto at times, and winter storm watchers like to come here in January and February for good reason. The autumn months are also a good time to visit, when vibrant red-hot pokers, African irises, kangaroo paws, penstemons, cosmos, snapdragons, dahlias, and, of course, colorful fall foliage on the deciduous trees, are in full force.

Shore Acres also offers a network of trails and paths in the park area. These meander high above the Pacific Ocean amid stands of the ever-present conifers. Along the way, visitors can find ground covers of dark green salal and, in early spring, spot wax myrtle blooming in pale pink and soft lavender. At this time of year, picnic tables nestled in secluded spots along the way prove particularly inviting. Travelers can also picnic and hike at rugged Cape Arago, a mile to the south of Shore Acres State Park.

SHORE ACRES GARDENS (117 miles southwest of Eugene) Shore Acres State Park, 13030 Cape Arago Highway, Coos Bay, OR 97420 **TEL:** (541) 888-3732 **OPEN:** Daily 8-dusk **TOTAL ACRES:** 6 **SPECIAL COLLECTIONS:** Estate garden, rhododendrons, azaleas, roses, dahlias   **ZONE 8** C F G H P T WS

HENDRICKS PARK RHODODENDRON GARDEN
EUGENE

Situated on a broad knoll within Hendricks Park on the east end of Eugene's forested southern ridge line, the Rhododendron Garden occupies a shady 20-acre garden glen. It dates from the early 1950s when members of the Eugene Men's Camellia and Rhododendron Society donated the earliest plantings of azaleas and rhododendrons from their own gardens and individual propagations. Because of their actions, rare species and hybrids are well represented in the more than 5,000 varieties that make up this impressive collection. In early spring 1954, the garden was dedicated by the newly formed Eugene chapter of the American Rhododendron Society.

Magnolias, dogwoods, viburnums, witch hazels, and hundreds of other ornamentals are also planted among the hardy azaleas and "rhodies." Towering over all, around the edges of the knoll, looms the much-loved Douglas fir along with stands of white oak. The garden's walkways twist and turn throughout the glen, offering visitors a close encounter with nature. Sunlight dapples paths and plantings. The flowers, ranging from delicate pastels to vibrant colors, are at their best from mid-May through June. One could easily bring a picnic and enjoy an entire afternoon in this lovely spot in the southern reaches of the Willamette Valley.

■ HENDRICKS PARK RHODODENDRON GARDEN (113 miles south of Portland) Summit and Skyline Drives, off Fairmont Boulevard, Eugene, OR 97401 TEL: (541) 682-4800 OPEN: Daily 6-11 TOTAL ACRES: 20 SPECIAL COLLECTIONS: Rhododendrons, azaleas, camellias, magnolias ZONE 8 H P PA T WS

Rhododendrons take center stage in the garden at Hendricks Park, which boasts 5,000 varieties that burst with color each spring.

Bush's Pasture Park
Salem

In 1877 newspaperman Asahel Bush II built his large Victorian house in Salem, soon adding lawns, a small greenhouse, a vegetable garden, and an orchard. Fine old vines of wisteria still drape the front porch of the house, offering a profusion of pale lavender blooms in early to mid-May. The sunny rose garden, just west of the residence, was planted in the mid-1950s and contains more than a hundred beds.

Today visitors can see and sniff more than 2,000 roses. Especially noteworthy is the Tartar Old Rose Collection, beds of some 300 old garden roses representing varieties and species that came across the prairies and around Cape Horn to the West Coast. The outstanding collection includes *Rosa mundi*, a striped ancient gallica, the oldest rose mentioned in literature; the 'Mission Rose', a wedding gift to early pioneer missionary Jason Lee and his bride, Annamarie Pittman; and, the lovely damask rose, 'Bella Donna'. Large perennial beds are located near the greenhouse and south of the barn. Many are being redesigned and replanted with huge peonies and gatherings of delphinium, astilbe, yarrow, and coreopsis, among other favorites. Also of note are espaliered apple trees and a fine collection of flowering trees and shrubs. Many of these varieties were planted in the early 1900s by landscape designers Elizabeth Lord and Edith Schryver.

The garden is family-friendly, offering large picnic and lawn areas and a small playground for children. The adjacent Bush Barn houses the 70-year-old Salem Art Association and a large art fair is held at the park each year in mid-July.

Bush's Pasture Park (51 miles south of Portland) 600 Mission Street S.E., Salem, OR 97302 **Tel:** (503) 588-2410 **Open:** Daily, dawn-dusk **Total acres:** 75 **Special collections:** Roses, peonies, perennials, flowering trees and shrubs   ZONE 8 A C G H HO P PA R T

Deepwood Estate
Salem

Salem is home to a period English garden designed in 1929 by northwest landscape designers Elizabeth Lord and Edith Schryver. The gardens were commissioned by Alice Brown, third owner of the estate's elegant Queen Anne Victorian residence. Together these talented women transformed sections of the grounds into various "garden rooms." The most formal area, the Boxwood Garden, is reached by stone steps from the upper lawn. Ornamental fencing borders its precisely clipped boxwood hedges. Back up the steps and through an intimate ivy archway unfolds the main lawn area, where visitors can pause in a white wrought-iron gazebo that dates to the 1905 Lewis & Clark Exposition in Portland. It was transported to Salem in the 1950s.

The Teahouse Garden, enclosed by an old-fashioned fence, is especially charming with a large collection of hardy perennials. Sheltered wood benches tucked here and there offer places to enjoy both colors and scents, especially when the lilac trees are in bloom. An old wisteria vine climbs a large tree near the wrought-iron entry to the estate. Along the eastern perimeter an elegant 250-foot-long bed of perennials marches in colorful profusion from early spring to late fall.

Deepwood Estate (51 miles south of Portland) 1116 Mission Street S.E., Salem, OR 97302 **Tel:** (503) 363-1825 **Open:** Daily dawn-dusk **Total acres:** 5.5 **Special collections:** English-style garden, boxwood, perennials, lilacs   ZONE 8 A C G H HO P T V WS

LEACH BOTANICAL GARDEN
PORTLAND

Located in southeast Portland, the Leach Botanical Garden, formerly known as Sleepy Hollow, was the home of plant-lover Lilla Leach and her husband, John. He said Lilla finally consented to marry him, in 1913, because he convinced her that he could handle a pack mule, throw a diamond hitch, talk mule talk, and go where the flowers were unusual and different. Lilla did in fact discover a rare rhododendronlike plant, with small deep rose blooms, on one of their pack trips into the Siskiyou Mountains of southern Oregon. Ultimately this plant was named for her—*Kalmiopsis Leachiana.* In all, she discovered four species and one variety new to science. One species she discovered, a wild yellow iris named *Iris innominata,* "iris the unknown," was introduced into domestic gardens and won various horticultural awards. Lilla Leach was the first person to receive the Eloise Payne Luquer medal for distinguished achievement in botany from the Garden Club of America.

At Sleepy Hollow, where they lived from the mid-1930s on, the couple developed a network of trails and added to their extensive plant collection. During the early years of marriage they had enjoyed these woodland acres along Johnson Creek as a weekend retreat. John Leach died in 1972 at the age of 90 and his wife passed away in 1980 at age 94. Their collection of over 2,000 species, hybrids, and cultivars can be enjoyed on a self-guided tour that winds around the manor house and down along the creek. The Oregon Fuchsia Society maintains a test garden for hardy fuchsias in the upper garden area that has been developed above the manor house. Cultivars such as 'Santa Claus', 'Jingle Bells', and 'Dark Eyes', are seen along with other old and new favorites that grow well in the Northwest. Close by is an impressive penstemon collection arranged in separate beds that represent varieties from the Northwest, Southwest, Baja, and Rocky Mountain regions.

Other beds planted with a variety of native bulbs are being developed in this upper terrace area. Garden lovers also can inspect the nearby home compost interpretive area with its labeled compost bins. This much-loved garden is now sponsored and maintained by Leach Garden Friends and the Portland's Bureau of Parks and Recreation.

LEACH BOTANICAL GARDEN 6704 S.E. 122nd Avenue, Portland, OR 97236 **TEL:** (503) 761-9503 **OPEN:** Tues.-Sat. 9-4, Sun. 1-4 **TOTAL ACRES:** 9 **SPECIAL COLLECTIONS:** Native northwestern plants, fuchsias

ZONE 7 G H HO L P T V

CRYSTAL SPRINGS RHODODENDRON GARDEN
PORTLAND

Founded in 1950, the Crystal Springs Rhododendron Garden contains some 2,500 rhododendrons and azaleas, representing over 600 species. After entering the garden, a path leads into the Jane Martin Entrance Garden, where many smaller hybrids are grouped. At the base of the path a natural waterfall tumbles down a small rocky section, creating a shallow stream that houses colonies of ferns and other water-loving plant varieties. Above, a graceful wooden bridge offers wide-angle views both north and south through lacy willows, Japanese maples, dogwoods, magnolias, and other deciduous varieties, as well as the region's majestic Douglas-firs.

Many pleasant hours may be spent walking the web of paths connecting the various wooded areas. Along the way, benches provide resting spots. One charming area is the wooden walkway that crosses the south portion of shallow Crystal Springs Lake, where ducks swim and splash in the water and songbirds twitter in low-hanging branches. Golfers may also be spotted on the far side of the lake, playing rounds at the Eastmoreland public golf course.

From mid-May to late June visitors are treated to rhododendron blooms ranging from the palest pinks, yellows, apricots, creams, and whites to deep pinks, reds, lavenders, and purples. Some of the older specimens reach heights of 25 feet or more, forming shady groves adjacent to paths and large lawn areas. The garden is cared for by staff from the Portland parks department and by a host of volunteers from the local chapter of the American Rhododendron Society.

■ CRYSTAL SPRINGS RHODODENDRON GARDEN S.E. 28th Avenue, Portland, OR 97286 TEL: (503) 771-8386
OPEN: Daily dawn-dusk TOTAL ACRES: 7 SPECIAL COLLECTIONS: Rhododendrons, azaleas

ZONE 7 A F G H P

A bench provides a nice place to rest and soak up the surroundings at the Crystal Springs Rhododendron Garden, which offers many species rarely seen in the Pacific Northwest.

ELK ROCK GARDEN AT BISHOP'S CLOSE
PORTLAND

Of the few Northwest estate gardens open to the public, Elk Rock Garden at Bishop's Close is also one of the best. Situated on an 11-acre stretch of volcanic basalt and native trees, it perches on a ledge high above the west bank of the Willamette River between Portland and the community of Lake Oswego. The estate was developed in the late 1800s by Scotsman Peter Kerr, who hired John Olmsted of the Olmsted Brothers firm to draw up a master plan for the estate garden. Kerr and Olmsted corresponded for more than ten years as the garden took shape.

Visitors today see an elegant historic estate, with its glimpse of life in another era, as well as Kerr's handiwork with his extensive collection of magnolias, one of

Portland's frequent rains nurture a variety of graceful trees and colorful shrubs at the Elk Rock Garden at Bishop's Close. This former estate was designed by John Olmsted.

his great loves. Elk Rock Garden has about 40 specimens, among them one of the first Campbell magnolias in the Northwest. Reportedly, Kerr planted this foot-tall seedling on his 90th birthday in 1942. His vast collection of mature rhododendrons, representing many species and hybrids, is also on view.

Paths lead from the ivy-draped manor house, now the Episcopal Diocese of Oregon, around a broad expanse of lawn, shrubs, and plantings that open to graceful vistas and mature trees around every turn. Light gravel crunches underfoot and waves of blue wood hyacinths and white trilliums bloom in shady places. A shallow stream bordered with delicate irises and dwarf Japanese maples comes into view and maidenhair ferns droop over moss-lined pools. A wood bridge affords a view back toward the manor house and to the tall sequoias lining sections of the path around the lawn. As the walkway ascends to the far southeast corner of the estate, it passes many native northwestern wildflower species and provides sweeping views of the wide Willamette River glistening below.

A small formal garden with precisely clipped yews and boxwood sits on a narrow ledge above the main lawn area. Just beyond, an enormous weathered wisteria drapes at the cliff's edge of the upper parking area. A stunning display of pale lavender blooms here in mid-May.

▮ **ELK ROCK GARDEN AT BISHOP'S CLOSE** 11800 S.W. Military Lane, Portland, OR 97219 **TEL:** (503) 636-5613 **OPEN:** Daily 8-5, Sept. through May; daily 8-6, June through Aug. **TOTAL ACRES:** 11 **SPECIAL COLLECTIONS:** Estate garden, rock garden, rhododendrons   **ZONE 7** **H** **P** **T** **V** **WS**

A field of early summer splendor at the Berry Botanic Garden features Shirley poppies, California poppies, and baby blue-eyes. Volunteers maintain seed collections of plants native to the Northwest.

BERRY BOTANIC GARDEN
PORTLAND

With a little advance planning, garden lovers can arrange a visit to the Berry Botanic Garden, a unique six-acre species garden located near the Willamette River and the community of Lake Oswego. It began as a home garden in 1938 when Rae Selling Berry, an avid plantswoman, subscribed to major plant hunting expeditions—first to southern and southeastern Asia (prior to World War II), then to South America and Europe. Her share of these seeds were nurtured into seedlings and mature plants—rhododendrons, magnolias, primroses, and alpines, the latter two being her special loves. After her death in 1976, Berry's friends helped to establish the Berry Botanic Garden in her honor. It has also been selected to represent the National Center for Plant Conservation. Volunteers maintain seeds and living collections of the rarest plants of the Northwest. The seed bank here contains some 250 species, subspecies, and varieties.

The lower herb lawn offers island beds of photinia, stewartia, and trees such as the primitive dawn redwood and an elegant Chinese magnolia, whose large blooms emit a poignant melon scent. A shady bog borders the upper lawn, supporting lush colonies of ferns, meconopsis, and dozens of wild primrose species. In addition, an alpine rock garden with more than 600 plant species spreads across the sloping, sunny area behind the main house. Just beyond the greenhouse is Berry's grove of some 150 grown-up rhododendrons, most now more than 50 years old. A self-guided native plant trail leads through a denser, wooded section of tall Douglas-fir and mature rhododendrons. Among the numerous native species are wild ginger, bleeding heart, and salal along with native berries and Oregon grape. Near a bubbling spring and footbridge, skunk cabbages and cobra lilies thrive.

BERRY BOTANIC GARDEN 11505 S.W. Summerville Avenue, Portland, OR 97219 **TEL:** (503) 636-4112
OPEN: By appointment **TOTAL ACRES:** 6 **SPECIAL COLLECTIONS:** Rock garden, alpine plants, rhododendrons, primroses, native plants

ZONE 7 F G HO L P T V WS

INTERNATIONAL ROSE TEST GARDEN AND JAPANESE GARDEN
PORTLAND

A visit to the gardens of Portland and the northernmost environs of the Willamette Valley naturally begins with the **International Rose Test Garden** in Washington Park. Situated on a wide bluff overlooking the city, the site offers one of the best views of Mount Hood, the 11,235-foot snowy peak rising in the Cascade Mountains to the east. On clear days you can also see Mount St. Helens to the northeast and the snowy top of Mount Adams farther to the east.

At Washington Park, visitors stroll among hundreds of beds of carefully tended roses of all varieties, including hybrid teas, floribundas, grandifloras, miniatures, and climbers. Dedicated volunteers from the Portland Rose Society, having weathered more than a century of aphids, donate hundreds of hours from June through September to help tend the beds and remove the spent blooms. The society began in 1888, when Georgiana Burton Pittock, wife of pioneer newspaper publisher Henry Pittock, invited her friends and neighbors to exhibit their roses in a tent set up in her garden. The society continues to sponsor a rose show during the city's annual Rose Festival, held during the first two weeks of June.

The rose test program started in 1917 and is open to commercial hybridizers around the world. Test roses are located in a separate section of beds, each rose labeled with an identifying code number. Over a two-year period the test roses are evaluated according to such criteria as shape and form, color, vigor, fragrance, and novelty. The formal evaluation is conducted by accredited members of the All-America Rose Selection (AARS); there are two such judges at the garden, including the curator.

The garden contains more than 10,000 roses representing some 520 varieties. Especially worth a visit is the Gold Medal Garden, located in the upper section. This provides a growing record of the roses that have won Portland's municipal gold medal since 1919. A stroll through the Shakespeare Garden, tucked behind a brick wall close to the southeast edge of the bluff,

Mount Hood offers a majestic backdrop to the International Rose Test Garden in Portland.

reveals a colorful assortment of the flowers and herbs mentioned in the Bard's works. In addition, the garden offers large plantings of azaleas, rhododendrons, and camellias. Douglas-firs, so characteristic of this mild, humid transition zone, tower in small groves around the garden's edges.

Above the rose garden and their neighboring tennis courts and parking areas, another botanical treasure awaits on the former site of Portland's old municipal zoo—the 5.5-acre **Japanese Garden.** A wooden entry gate, guarded by two rather fierce-looking stone dogs representing male and female energies, leads to paths accessing five traditional gardens. A curving path leads past an 18-foot-high stone lantern and down to *Chisen-Kaiyui-Shiki*, the Strolling Pond Garden. The garden's largest plantings of azaleas and rhododendrons are found here. Next comes *Rijiniwa*, the intimate Tea Garden, in which a small ceremonial teahouse is hidden among lush bamboo, ferns, and stones. Visitors then negotiate a wooden walkway along a bog area, where colorful koi swim and thick stands of iris bloom. The newly expanded recirculating Heavenly Falls cascade from rocky ledges at this garden's far side. The path gently climbs to *Shukeiyen,* the Natural Garden, where another series of recirculating ponds and waterfalls tumble down the hillside through northwestern native trees, shrubs, and ground covers. The path leads to the base of the Natural Garden, which provides sitting areas to enjoy the shady views. A short distance up the path lies the *Seki-Tei,* or Sand and Stone Garden, placed inside a traditional stucco and tiled wall. This area's main features, eight stones of various sizes, rise from carefully raked sand to provide a stark contrast to the Natural Garden. A short distance along the path lies *Hiraniwa,* or the Flat Garden. Here tidy ground covers, mostly thyme, grow around areas of sand and stone. Finally the walk reaches a large public pavilion that overlooks the Rose Garden, the city, and the distant Cascade Mountains.

This masterful garden was designed in 1962 by Professor P. Takuma Tono, a noted authority on Japanese landscaping. Water and the sounds of water are an integral part of the Japanese Garden, whether cascading over rocks and boulders, reflecting trees and plantings, or striking bamboo against moss-covered rocks hidden among colonies of ferns. In addition, several examples of authentic stone lanterns have been placed in special locations. In mid-May, wisteria cascades from a lovely arbor located near the center of the garden.

■ **INTERNATIONAL ROSE TEST GARDEN** Washington Park, 400 S.W. Kingston Avenue, Portland, OR 97201 **TEL:** (503) 823-3636 **OPEN:** Daily 7-dusk **TOTAL ACRES:** 4 **SPECIAL COLLECTIONS:** Roses, Shakespeare garden

■ **THE JAPANESE GARDEN** Washington Park, 611 S.W. Kingston Avenue, Portland, OR 97201 **TEL:** (503) 223-4070 **OPEN:** Daily 10-6, April through May and Sept.; daily 10-4, June through Aug. and Oct. through March **TOTAL ACRES:** 5.5 **SPECIAL COLLECTIONS:** Japanese garden   **ZONE 7 F G H P T WS**

Directly above the rose garden in Washington Park lie the Japanese Gardens, where visitors can enjoy year-round strolls through five tranquil areas that make up the remarkable gardens.

LAKEWOLD GARDENS
LAKEWOOD

One of the Northwest's last great turn-of-the-century estates, the ten-acre
Lakewold Gardens and Georgian-style manor house represent a prototypical
garden estate. Its late owner, Mrs. Eulalie Merrill Wagner, worked diligently for
many years to ensure that Lakewold possessed some of the most basic and
important northwestern species and varieties. Eulalie and her husband, Corydon,
purchased Lakewold in 1938. The two were avid collectors of trees, rhododendrons, roses, alpines, and rock plants. The results of their work over the years
are impressive. Large beds of azaleas and rhododendrons line both the curved
entry drive and the "garden room" around the swimming pool, in all with some
150 species and hybrids. Native deciduous trees and conifers grow tall and stately
throughout the estate grounds, offering myriad shades of green at every turn.
At times the vistas are wide and sweeping and, later, close and intimate.

One example is the tall dawn redwood visible from the terrace next to the
English-style knot garden. It was planted in the mid-1940s. A broad, sloping
lawn leads down toward Gravelly Lake. Beds along the lawn's edge contain a
much-loved collection of blue Tibetan poppies, black bamboo, hostas, conifers,
and magnolias. Below this area, a gravel path meanders next to the alpine and
native plant scree section, an area for species that love rocky homes, such as
bolax, saxifragas, miniature rhododendrons, dwarf evergreens, and gentians.

The rock and pool garden beyond offers a quiet, secluded area shaded by
maples, a dove tree, kalmia, and Chilean flame tree. Ample stands of ferns,
hostas, and water-loving plants crowd along the pond and stream area. This
section of the garden was under development for some 20 years. From here, the
path ascends for higher views of Gravelly Lake, glimpsed through the trees and
from weathered wooden benches and lawn chairs placed for rest and contemplation. Back on the main lawn level, the centerpiece of the shade garden is an
enormous, malformed Douglas-fir. Its large, rounded limbs curve into inviting
spaces in which to sit and climb. The Wagner grandchildren loved to play here,
calling it the wolf tree. Even on rainy days one can enjoy the varieties planted
in the shelter of this fir, including hellebore, orchids, ferns, trilliums, primroses,
and cyclamens. A brick walkway wanders among closely clipped, geometric-
shaped boxwood parterres, leading to the more formal sections of the garden.
These contain animal-shaped topiaries and seasonal plantings—pink tulips and
purple crocuses provide especially wonderful displays in early spring. The plump
swan topiary was a gift presented to Mrs. Wagner in the 1950s by San Francisco
landscape designer Thomas Church. He designed several garden areas at Lakewold,
including the curved entry drive, the herb knot garden located just outside the
kitchen door, and the elegant quatrefoil-shaped swimming pool and its attendant
garden sculptures.

At the far end of the brick walkway, just beyond the swimming pool, the
lattice-domed teahouse offers clay pots of colorful impatiens, cascades of fuchsias
in moss-covered hanging baskets, old climbing roses, and Roman-style garden
sculptures. Strolling back along the path toward the manor house, visitors find
thick, trailing vines of kiwi cascading over the sunroom wall; wisteria vines trail
over the open-air roof that protects the terrace to the left. To the right, toward the

The quatrefoil-shaped swimming pool at Lakewold Gardens was designed by Thomas Church, who was also responsible for the herb knot garden and the curved entry drive.

entry drive, is another view of the fine empress tree dominating the curved lawn area; a large copper beech grows behind this, at the edge of the drive. Garry oaks, Douglas-firs, dogwoods, and crabapples combine in pleasant groupings along with the ever-present azaleas and rhododendrons.

■ **LAKEWOLD GARDENS** (10 miles south of Tacoma) 12317 Gravelly Lake Drive, S.W., Lakewood, WA 98499 **TEL:** (253) 584-4106 **OPEN:** Mon., Thurs., Sat.-Sun. 10-4, Fri. 12-8, April through Sept.; Fri.-Sun. 10-3, Oct. through March **TOTAL ACRES:** 10 **SPECIAL COLLECTIONS:** Estate garden, rhododendrons, rock and pool garden, topiary, Thomas Church design   **ZONE 8** **F** **G** **H** **HO** **P** **T** **WS**

RHODODENDRON SPECIES BOTANICAL GARDEN
FEDERAL WAY

This 24-acre garden, adjacent to the corporate headquarters of the Weyerhaeuser Lumber Company, contains more than 2,000 different varieties of species rhododendrons and azaleas. It is one of the largest collections in the world. Visitors can get a helpful garden map to explore the Alpine, Pond, and Study Gardens accessed by a network of paths and trails.

Rhododendrons range in size from one-inch Chinese dwarfs to 100-foot giants from the Himalaya Mountains. The bloom colors are also wide-ranging, from soft white to clear yellow, and from brilliant red to deepest violet. Other plant collections include ferns, maples, heathers, and bamboo; a forest of conifers and deciduous varieties surrounds the garden. Visitors who climb to the gazebo near the garden's center are rewarded with a wide-angle look at the landscape. Just below the demonstration area is the fine Pacific Rim Bonsai Collection. Some 50 bonsai are featured in a natural outdoor setting, including such fine examples as trident maple, creeping juniper, ponderosa pine, and American (eastern) larch. In the nearby conservatory are more than 200 other intriguing bonsai, varieties that are tropical or that need winter warmth.

■ **RHODODENDRON SPECIES BOTANICAL GARDEN** (8 miles northeast of Tacoma) 2525 S. 336th Street, Federal Way, WA 98003 **TEL:** (253) 661-9377 **OPEN:** Sat.-Wed. 11-4, June through Feb.; Fri.-Wed. 10-4, March through May **TOTAL ACRES:** 24 **SPECIAL COLLECTIONS:** Rhododendrons, azaleas, bonsai

ZONE 8 C F G H P T WS

BLOEDEL RESERVE
BAINBRIDGE ISLAND

Before leaving the Seattle area, visitors would do well to plan a ferry excursion to nearby Bainbridge Island, driving out to its far northeastern tip. Here lies the Bloedel Reserve, the former estate of the Bloedels, a well-known northwestern family. Of the estate's total 150 acres, about 84 are comprised of second-growth forest. The remaining 66 acres were developed, over some 35 years, into a series of natural gardens, ponds, meadows, and wildlife habitats. Visitors are advised to call ahead to arrange a visit; reservations are required.

The gatehouse echoes the French heritage of the main residence. Illustrated maps are available here, detailing paths leading across the West Meadow and down to the bird refuge. In spring, red-wing blackbirds nest among the cattails, while ducks, geese, and swans make their homes amid native sedges and grasses. Great blue herons and kingfishers may fly in low, looking for the trout that are regularly stocked in the pond. The dense forest area known as the Woods is essentially undisturbed except for its access trails and wonderful footbridge. Evergreens dominate here, with towering Douglas-fir, western red cedar, and hemlock filtering sun and sky. The forest floor is thick with ferns, salal, and huckleberry. The loudest sounds may be breezes rustling and swishing through the tree branches. The tour continues over the boardwalk in the forested wetland, onto a driveway west of the Middle Pond, and on to the visitor center housed in the impressive French-style main residence. Here visitors can take a close look at the waterfall and the new Birch Grove Garden. The path then moves upwards through the Glen, where hundreds of rhododendrons thrive under the second-growth timber along with perennials, bulbs, and wildflowers, including thousands of cyclamens that bloom in the fall. The Orchid Trail (named for the coral-root orchids that grow here) leads to the Japanese Garden, a meditative space of simplicity, carefully placed rocks, and myriad shades of green. Crossing the drive one last time will take visitors to the Moss Garden and then the Reflection Garden. Here a rectangular pond, edged with narrow strips of clipped grass, reflects the surrounding tall western red cedar and deciduous trees. Wooden benches invite visitors to sit and contemplate, perhaps as waterfowl glide across the water's surface.

■ **BLOEDEL RESERVE** (9 miles northwest of Seattle) 7571 N.E. Dolphin Drive, Bainbridge Island, WA 98110 **TEL:** (206) 842-7631 **OPEN:** Wed.-Sun. 10-4, *by reservation only* **TOTAL ACRES:** Garden 66, grounds 150 **SPECIAL COLLECTIONS:** Estate garden, rhododendrons, cyclamens, wildflowers, Japanese garden, moss garden

ZONE 8 F H P T WS

Autumn brings spectacular foliage to the Bloedel Reserve, wh occupies 150 acres on Washington's Bainbridge Isla

WASHINGTON PARK ARBORETUM AND JAPANESE GARDEN
SEATTLE

Located on the University of Washington's Seattle campus, this 200-acre arboretum began in 1894 when a professor planted a small collection of trees. The wooded wonderland now contains more than 5,000 plants, shrubs, ornamentals, and trees. A good way to begin an exploration is by strolling down Azalea Way, the arboretum's main walkway, which is especially appealing in spring when the hundreds of azalea varieties and species are in full bloom. Large banked beds on both sides of the walkway overflow with luscious colors—pastel and deep pinks, pale apricots and yellows, whites and creams, and deep reds.

Park maps are available to help navigate the network of trails looping throughout the arboretum, passing by such unusual specimens as nootka false cypress and an elm hybrid 'Ice-cream Tree', along with the familiar Northwest varieties of conifers. Here too are such deciduous varieties as flowering cherries, crabapples, dogwoods, and magnolias. It is possible for the sharp-eyed visitor to identify hundreds of rhododendrons, camellias, lilacs, and hollies, as well as more than 25 different kinds of ornamental vines. Semi-aquatic plant species are also found along the waterfront trail bordering the Lake Washington shoreline in the park's northern section; the raised trail floats over peat bogs and water through a forest of cattails.

The arboretum plant life changes dramatically with each season. Autumn is a fine time to visit, with fall foliage colors of russet, brown, orange, and yellow showing mid-September through October and November. For the colder months, a visit to the Joseph A. Witt Winter Garden is rewarded by displays of witch hazels, sasanqua camellias, wintersweet, paperbark maples, and winter-flowering perennials. The arboretum also provides a year-round sanctuary for dozens of bird species and small animals as well as a retreat for city dwellers and travelers. Visitors can stop at the Donald Graham Visitors Center for information on seasonal activities and guided walks.

The arboretum's Japanese Garden's 3.5 acres surrounding a traditional reflecting pond was constructed in the early 1960s. An illustrated brochure and horticultural plant list are available at the entrance to facilitate a self-guided tour of this serene oasis. Large rocks brought from the nearby Cascade Mountains were carefully placed throughout the gently sloping terrain. Native and non-native plants and trees were then selected and planted to represent different natural landscapes found in Japan. The plant materials have matured and filled out over the years, resulting in a lush, green garden. An authentic teahouse, a delicate pagoda, and ten Oriental lanterns contribute to the sense of peace and tranquility in the garden. Entering through the south gate, next to the parking area, the visitor is enveloped by a dense, secluded forest of conifers, maples, ornamental trees, and ornamental shrubs that cover the twin mountains created here. Two streams flow from this location and join later to form the large central pond populated by brightly colored koi. Several alternative paths invite exploration of the entire garden and its secluded areas. Visitors also can take a trail beneath a waterfall. In the wooded area above the waterfall stands the 12-tier pagoda.

■ **WASHINGTON PARK ARBORETUM AND THE JAPANESE GARDEN** 2300 Arboretum Drive East, University of Washington, Seattle, WA 98112 **TEL:** (206) 543-8800 **OPEN:** Daily dawn-dusk **TOTAL ACRES:** 200 **SPECIAL COLLECTIONS:** Azaleas, rhododendrons, flowering trees, hollies, ornamental vines, winter garden, Japanese garden   **ZONE 8** A F G H HO P T V WS

Authentic stone lanterns grace the Japanese Garden in Washington Park Arboretum, b with the help of the Japanese government and Kobe, Seattle's sister city in Jap

Medicinal Herb Garden
Seattle

After years of neglect, the Medicinal Herb Garden began growing again in 1984, thanks to the efforts of a group of educators, students, pharmacists, herbalists, and garden enthusiasts. These volunteers help maintain the comprehensive collection of medicinal herb species, located on the campus of the University of Washington.

In May the raised beds bloom with old roses, European redbuds, and Johnny-jump-ups but color really arrives in June. By July and August fennel, thistle, Joe Pye weed, pokeweed, loosestrife, and goldenrod tower high over visitors' heads. Also visiting are those busy pollinators—leafcutter bees, honeybees, skippers, ants, butterflies, and moths. In September and October the palette softens and blurs with such fascinating seed pods as teasel, love-in-a-mist, cardoon, and shoo-fly plant. There are also scores of blooming autumn crocuses.

The garden friends weed and prune the beds, collect and clean seed for exchange with other botanical gardens around the world, and provide horticultural tours of the garden. Although ancient "physick" or medicinal gardens are somewhat rare on the West Coast, this internationally known garden offers a living library of over 600 species of medicinal and useful plants. The campus can be accessed from the Washington Park Arboretum via Montelake Bridge, or directions are available at campus gates.

Medicinal Herb Garden 15th Avenue N.E. and N.E. 40th Street, University of Washington, Seattle, WA 98195 **Tel:** (206) 543-1126 **Open:** Daily dawn-dusk **Total acres:** 2 **Special collections:** Medicinal herbs

ZONE 8 **H P T WS**

Tennant Lake and Hovander Homestead Park
Ferndale

Horticultural travelers seeking a unique experience in the Northwest should include on their itinerary this natural history area located near Ferndale, north of Seattle. First stop is the historic Nielsen House, which serves as an interpretive center for the complex. All summer and into fall an old-fashioned perennial garden blooms along the picket fence bordering the lawn. Such favorites as daisies, phlox, peonies, and delphinium combine nostalgically with basket-of-gold, cosmos, liatris, and hellebores.

A paved pathway loops through a fragrance garden created especially for the visually impaired. From aromatic angelica, herbal comfrey, licorice-flavored fennel, and scented lavender to peppery-tasting nasturtium, minty pennyroyal, lemon-scented southernwood, and sweetly scented woolly lamb's ear, the plantings are a cooperative project of the Chuckanut District Garden Clubs and the Whatcom County Parks. Next, a gravel path leads to the Tennant Lake boardwalk, just beyond a wooden observation tower (currently under reconstruction). The sturdy boardwalk zigzags in a half-mile loop out onto shallow Tennant Lake and along its marshy shore, offering prime spots to observe pond lilies, yellow irises, cattails, sedges, willows, and other water-loving varieties that thrive here in thick clusters. A pair of binoculars is handy for spotting some of the nearly 200 species of birds and waterfowl who rest here on their twice-yearly migration along the Pacific Flyway. Many stay at the lake year-round.

A short drive away is the historic Hovander Homestead Park. A bed of late summer dahlias often blooms near the entrance to this 60-acre farm, developed by Swedish emigrants Hakan and Louisa Hovander at the turn of the century. Visitors are invited to wander the grounds, see the horses, visit the barns, inspect the old farm equipment, and enjoy the old-fashioned flower garden on the south side of the well-preserved Victorian-style residence. Built by the Hovanders, the house is now on the National Register of Historic Places. In addition, master gardeners from nearby Ferndale cultivate and maintain a large vegetable garden here. Trails meander down to the Nooksack River where there are both sunny and shady places to picnic in this lovely setting.

TENNANT LAKE AND HOVANDER HOMESTEAD PARK (96 miles north of Seattle) 5299 Nielsen Road, Ferndale, WA 98248 TEL: (360) 384-3444 OPEN: Daily dawn-dusk TOTAL ACRES: 60 SPECIAL COLLECTIONS: Native plants, aquatic plants, perennials, fragrance garden   ZONE 7 A F H HO P PA T V WS

OHME GARDENS
WENATCHEE

The densely forested Cascade Mountains give way to the high desert of central Washington, revealing tan-colored hills clothed in sagebrush, bitterbrush, juniper, and other high desert plant varieties. One day in 1929, Herman and Ruth Ohme stood atop a rocky, sagebrush-covered hill near Wenatchee, with its superb view of the Columbia River, Wenatchee Valley, and Cascade Mountains, and decided this was where they wanted to build their home. But in those Depression days banks were not lending funds, so the couple decided to work first on their backyard next to the sky. Over the next ten years they worked weekends and after hours from their orchard business, digging out scores of sagebrush, hauling tons of rocks, fashioning pools and ponds, laying out paths and steps, and planting hundreds of trees, ferns, and alpine plant species.

By 1939 the Ohmes had two small sons, and had developed a two-acre alpine garden atop their rocky hill. This effort was a labor of love, done by hand with intuition rather than a grand design. Using mules to pull a wooden sled, the Ohmes transported enormous rocks, flagstone, and large jugs of water to the top of their bluff. Herman Ohme also built two log picnic shelters, a wishing well, and an outdoor fireplace. A stone and log lookout, called Vista House, was built on the highest point, 600 feet above the Columbia River.

They would spend many pleasant weekends here, picnicking and working on the paths and steps, the ponds and pools, and on planting and watering the seedlings gathered from the nearby mountains. Interested friends and community members urged the Ohmes to allow visits to their alpine wonderland and, later, the gardens were, somewhat reluctantly, opened to the public at 25 cents per car. After Herman Ohme's death in 1971, Ruth, along with son Gordon and his wife, Carol, continued the planting, and expanded Ohme Gardens another five acres. A carefully engineered automatic sprinkling system was installed to water the gardens at night. Without water, of course, the hilltop would eventually have been reclaimed by its native sagebrush, bitterbrush, and the aromatic juniper trees.

Travelers still flock to this alpine garden, attired in sturdy shoes to navigate the irregular stepping stones and narrow flagstone paths. These meander in and around shaded, fern-lined pools, next to large ponds reflecting sky and clouds, and around immense boulders that shelter low-growing alpine plantings and asymmetrical sweeps of lawn. In addition to more than 15 varieties of

Ferns and boulders play major roles in the Ohme Gardens, where the emphasis is on greenery and the spectacular views of the Cascade Mountains, Wenatchee Valley, and the Columbia River.

native evergreens gathered from the Cascade Mountains, the garden shelters many varieties of sedum—'Dragon's Blood' and yellow sedum predominate in the upper garden section—along with lavender creeping thyme, white and pink creeping phlox, alyssum, and dianthus. Numerous fern species grow in thick clusters near secluded pools shaded by tall trees such as western red cedar, mountain hemlock, grand fir, Douglas-fir, and alpine fir. Several quiet, contemplative places offer stone benches where one can sit and survey the Ohmes' hilltop domain and the high desert vistas to the east and south. This garden shows few flowers, depending rather on trees, stone, water, and low-growing alpine plant species to draw the visitor into its natural "garden rooms," terraced on several levels.

If time allows, it's worth the three-mile drive north to the Rocky Reach Dam Gardens. The Ohmes found many of their large rocks in this area. Today a sunny picnic spot overlooks sweeping lawns, a children's play area, and a fine perennial garden filled with many old-fashioned favorites, including several double holly-hocks. Baskets of colorful annuals hang from the eaves of the maintenance building. On Petunia Island, some 5,000 of the colorful annuals are planted each year in a sculptured design surrounding the fish ladders. More than 180 varieties thrive in the Dahlia Garden. And a floral display of the American flag, Old Glory Garden, unfurls in the lawn above the perennial garden, fashioned with red, white, and blue annuals. The 4,800-foot-long dam has a spillway of 750 feet; 11 generators produce over a million kilowatts of power for Wenatchee Valley residential and commercial consumers.

■ OHME GARDENS (155 miles southeast of Seattle) 3327 Ohme Road, Wenatchee, WA 98801 TEL: (509) 662-5785 OPEN: Daily 9-6, mid-April through Oct., until 7 during summer TOTAL ACRES: 9 SPECIAL COLLECTIONS: Alpine and rock garden   ZONE 5 F G P PA WS

Manito Park and Botanical Gardens
Spokane

Despite eastern Washington's higher altitude, which reaches above 3,500 feet in many areas, the region offers an elegant garden collection in Spokane's Manito Park. The tour begins at Rose Hill, situated on a four-acre slope overlooking the garden's other sections. Formal beds of some 1,500 roses represent more than 150 varieties, including borders of old-fashioned scented roses. These are cared for by Spokane's Parks Department staff.

A good place to begin is the Joel E. Ferris Perennial Garden, an oasis of lawns and large perennial beds. Visitors wander past borders of golden and coppery-orange blossoming heleniums, colorful hellebores, goldenrod, and cosmos. Here too bloom salvias, poppies, spiky liatris, and phlox. Large island beds contain plantings of yellow and white yarrow, creamy white and pink astilbes, towering Shasta daisies, and cheery yellow coreopsis. Other beds are bursting with long-stemmed red, orange, and yellow geums; spiky clumps of red and pink lythrum; and veronica in shades of pink, red, and bluish-purple.

Next on the tour are the Duncan Formal Gardens, just opposite Gaiser Conservatory. The stone steps next to the conservatory provide the best sweeping views of this three-acre garden. Rounded shrubs and conifers clipped into cone shapes march along the garden's borders, and large island beds are filled with seasonal plantings and flowering shrubs. Along the west perimeter, such plantings as tall stalks of deep purple, blue, and white delphinium or white cleome form a long border, contrasting with the dark green Douglas-firs beyond. The plantings are changed each year. The Gaiser Conservatory, a large glass conservatory located above the formal garden, contains splendid collections of hanging fuchsias and large pots of colorful begonias as well as cyclamen, poinsettias, chrysanthemums, and spring flowering bulb displays. Tropical plant, fern, and tree varieties grow in lush groupings in the large center glass dome area.

The visit ends at the secluded Nishinomiya Japanese Garden, located just beyond the Lilac Garden and accessed by a meandering path. A ceremony bridge, curved in Oriental tradition, extends over the reflecting pond. A small waterfall flows from the rising sun toward the setting sun and three vertical stones in the central pond suggest cranes or ships at sea. One large flat stone is reminiscent of a tortoise or island. Together the symbols represent long life and eternal youth. The Japanese garden is considered a creative art form and a reminder that nature can inspire peace and serenity in the viewer. Carefully placed stones, water, and plants as well as statues, lanterns, and sitting spaces are used to develop a tranquil feeling in this lovely, intimate space.

Also in the Spokane area is the **John A. Finch Arboretum,** a mile-long tract that stretches some 65 acres along the banks of Garden Springs Creek. In addition to the splendid collection of lilacs here, visitors can see a number of fine magnolias, dogwoods, and flowering crabapples. In the arboretum's Corey Rhododendron Glen, quiet paths take the visitor along the creek toward the hawthorn section, the conifer section, and the maple section. There is also a Touch-and-See Nature Trail designed for the visually impaired.

Manito Park and Botanical Gardens (284 miles east of Seattle) 4 W. 21st Avenue, Spokane, WA 99203 **Tel:** (509) 625-6622 **Open:** Daily dawn-dusk, except holidays **Total acres:** 90 **Special collections:** Roses, perennials, lilacs, rhododendrons, Japanese garden

ZONE 5 A C **H** P PA R T WS

Hawaii

LAWAI GARDEN
POIPU, KAUAI

On the south coast of Kauai, the gently contoured bottomland and steep sides of Lawai Valley cradle the Lawai Garden. Headquarters of the National Tropical Botanical Garden, a complex of five gardens and three natural preserves, the 252-acre Lawai Garden houses administrative, scientific, and research staff; as well as a library, lecture rooms, and a herbarium—all geared to provide education, instruction, and recreation.

The garden also holds the world's largest plantings of native Hawaiian species, more than half rare or endangered. Almost two dozen were considered extinct in the wild until rediscovered by the garden's intrepid field collection teams, who also discovered 28 new native species. A blend of research and aesthetics, Lawai is beautifully landscaped with green meadows showcasing rare trees and palms. Here shaded slopes and glens shelter extensive collections of colorful gingers, heliconias, and members of the coffee (or gardenia) family. Most plantings were grown from material collected in the wilds of Hawaii, the Pacific Islands, and both Old and New World tropics. Visitors enter the Lawai Garden through the lovely Allerton Garden, along a broad path bordering Lawai Stream.

LAWAI GARDEN (10 miles from Lihue) Access through Allerton Garden, 4425 Lawai Road, Poipu, Kauai, HI 96756 TEL: (808) 332-7324 OPEN: Tues.-Sat. 9-2, except Christmas and New Year's Day TOTAL ACRES: 252 SPECIAL COLLECTIONS: Native species, gingers, heliconias ZONE 11 F G L P T V WS

LIMAHULI GARDEN
KAUAI

On Kauai's north shore lies a significant archaeological site—agricultural terraces and house platforms built more than 700 years ago. The site is protected as part of the 17-acre Limahuli Garden, under the umbrella of the National Tropical Botanical Garden. At Limahuli, archaeological conservation is wedded to traditional agricultural practices. The garden, a living classroom and research center, attests to the resource management skills of early Hawaiians, who used terraces as ponded fields, called lo'i ai, to grow kalo (taro). The source of poi, a Hawaiian food made from taro root, kalo culture is an agricultural art that requires flowing water during the entire growing cycle. Ancient Hawaiians grew 300 different varieties of edible kalo, many with colorful ornamental foliage.

'Ulu, the beautiful breadfruit tree, shares the garden with wauke, or paper mulberry, from whose fibers the paper-like kapa (tapa) was made by beating

An estimated 5,000 different hybrids of the ever-blooming hibiscus may be seen in Hawaii, in a wide range of brilliant colors.

Limahuli Garden conserves 700-year-old agricultural terraces still used to grow kalo (taro) in the traditional manner. The 17-acre site adjoins a sprawling native plant preserve.

fine layers of crossing fibers into a flat sheet. Here too grow 'olena or turmeric, an ancient spice and dye, and mai'a, or banana. Hawaiians grew as many as 50 named varieties of banana.

Behind the garden a forested valley rises over 3,000 feet. The pristine Limahuli Stream, which provides water for the garden lo'i ai, begins here as a dramatic waterfall plunging a thousand feet to the valley floor. The valley forms the 989-acre Limahuli Preserve, encompassing two ecosystems that are theoretically capable of nurturing over 70 percent of Kauai's endangered species and 59 percent of those statewide. In 1997 the American Horticultural Society and the American Association of Botanical Gardens and Arboreta recognized Limahuli Garden and Preserve as one of the nation's top natural botanical gardens.

■ **LIMAHULI GARDEN** (42 miles from Lihue) Kuhio Highway 560, Kauai, HI 96766 **TEL:** (808) 826-1053 **OPEN:** Tues.-Fri., Sun. dawn-dusk, except Christmas and New Year's Day **TOTAL ACRES:** 17 **SPECIAL COLLECTIONS:** Native Hawaiian and ethnobotanical species ZONE 11 F G P T V WS

ALLERTON GARDEN
POIPU, KAUAI

As early as 1881 Kauai was lauded as "the garden island," a distinction based on its natural beauty and the quality of its man-made gardens. Today its premier landscaped area lies in the valley of Lawai-kai on Kauai's south shore: Allerton Garden. In 1938 new owners Robert and John Allerton envisioned an ambitious

The secluded bay at the mouth of Lawai Stream serves as an entryway to Allerton Garden, where the shore becomes a hallway connecting a series of expertly designed "garden rooms."

landscape development focused on the valley's stream. Art connoisseurs, world travelers, and avid plant lovers, they successfully executed a unique landscape combining formal European traditions with a flamboyant tropical setting. The genius of their design was in the alliance of impeccable taste and horticultural expertise. Today the Allerton Garden is managed by the National Tropical Botanical Garden for the Allerton Garden Trust.

Exciting vignettes, each an independent architectural space or "room," lead the visitor on a circuitous route flanking Lawai Stream. The ever-present murmur of water accompanies each turn of the broad walkway, where new vistas open to reveal a bamboo garden and the Mermaid Fountain, a 126-foot stepped water channel joining two bronze mermaids. Finally the path arrives at the Three Pools, a contemplative setting canopied by spreading trees and walled by luxuriant growth.

A highlight of the garden is the exquisite Diana Fountain. Here a statue of Diana, goddess of the moon, contemplates the reflection of a white latticed pavilion in the still surface of a long pool, forming a serene composition. Placing this formal piece amid an informal mass of dramatic tropical plants is a testament to the designers' skill. Rather than lacking harmony, the combination is visually logical, beautiful, and restful.

ALLERTON GARDEN (10 miles from Lihue) 4425 Lawai Road, Poipu, Kauai, HI 96756 TEL: (808) 742-2623 OPEN: Tues.-Sat. 9-2, except Christmas and New Year's Day TOTAL ACRES: 100 SPECIAL COLLECTIONS: Bamboo, landscaped tropical gardens   ZONE 11 F G P T V WS

Olu Pua Botanical Gardens and Plantation
Kalaheo, Kauai

On the lower slopes of 1,400-foot Pohakea, a visit to south Kauai's Olu Pua Gardens lives up to its name, which is translated as "at peace among the flowers." Once the private domain of pineapple barons, the gardens fringe a lush lawn crowned by a gracious residence. Within, rooms are furnished in elegant plantation style, featuring museum-quality Oriental antiques and commanding sweeping views of the distant ocean.

A bonus for the camera buff, Olu Pua Gardens provide color year-round in the moist, cool setting. The plant collections are typical of an old Hawaiian garden, without accent on special groups. Rather the selection provides a broad spectrum of carefully chosen ornamentals aimed at providing maximum flower and foliage interest. Flowering orchids, gingers, heliconias, bromeliads, and ornamental trees abound while calatheas and large crotons complement flowering displays. Here too are giant aroids, related to the garden's monsteras and philodendrons and prized by mainland houseplant growers. The winter flowering of the red New Guinea jade vine is particularly breathtaking. In addition, mature specimens of the strange Australian grass tree share attention with graceful palms and sturdy cycads.

Olu Pua Botanical Gardens and Plantation (11 miles from Lihue) Kalaheo, Kauai, HI 96741 **Tel:** (808) 332-8182 **Open:** Daily 9-4, except Thanksgiving, Christmas, and New Year's Day **Total acres:** 12.5 **Special collections:** General tropical ornamentals   ZONE 11 **F** G **H** HO P **T** V

Allerton Garden's impressive specimens of Moreton Bay fig trees anchor themselves to the earth with sturdy buttresses and sinuous networks of surface roots.

FOSTER BOTANICAL GARDEN
HONOLULU, OAHU

Located in four widely separated sites, the Honolulu Botanical Gardens complex of five gardens takes advantage of the dramatic climatic changes caused by elevation shifts and trade winds. Because of the range of climates, these five gardens constitute the largest tropical collection in the United States. Hawaiian plant terms can be confusing for those not familiar with the language of the islands. In Hawaiian, the name for a plant is the same for both genus and species, and most names were in use long before the adoption of Latin binomials. Most Hawaiian plants have only Hawaiian names and do not have a counterpart in horticultural nomenclature.

The oldest area of the Honolulu Botanical Gardens, the 14-acre Foster Botanical Garden serves as the complex's administrative headquarters. Here plantings reflect the horticultural history of the islands, representing 148 years of plant introduction. On display are a wide array and ever-changing pattern of eye-catching flowers, fruit, and foliage.

In the mid-1800s King Kamehameha III sent German-born physician and botanist Dr. William Hillebrand to the world's tropics to collect plants of economic promise for Hawaii. These strange and rare plants, mostly supportive of ship-building and repair, now include towering specimens of bunya-bunya, hoop pine, and kapok. There is also a huge earpod tree which, thanks to the shift from wood to steel in shipbuilding, never fell to the economic axe. Revealing an

Foster Botanical Garden is canopied by trees of cultural and historic significance, imported from the world's tropics. Orchids also compose a major collection here.

interest in more than just the practical, Hillebrand also imported the fragrant Mexican plumeria, or frangipani, for the Victorian gardens of Honolulu. It would later be grown in almost every Hawaiian garden, becoming the most popular lei flower, and every visitor to the islands today experiences its scent and color.

Mary Foster, a relative of the royal family, purchased the 4.5-acre garden in 1871. Following her conversion to Buddhism around the turn of the century, she obtained a small specimen of the bo, or sacred fig tree revered by both Buddhists and Hindus. Her planting, propagated from the tree in India under which the Buddha achieved enlightenment in approximately 500 B.C., remains an object of deep reverence. Mary Foster bequeathed her garden to the people of Honolulu in 1930. She is said to have

In a dormant caldera, Koko Crater Botanical Garden's notable hybrid plumerias display a range of colors prized for making leis.

witnessed her late husband, Thomas, riding his favorite horse through the garden by night. Perhaps she intended to preserve the area as a place where the two of them could always return.

■ **FOSTER BOTANICAL GARDEN** 180 N. Vineyard Boulevard, Honolulu, Oahu, HI 96817 **TEL:** (808) 522-7060 **OPEN:** Daily 9-4, except Christmas and New Year's Day **TOTAL ACRES:** 14 **SPECIAL COLLECTIONS:** Palms, cycads, orchids   **ZONE 11 F G H P PA T V WS**

KOKO CRATER BOTANICAL GARDEN
HONOLULU, OAHU

At 1,200 feet, the Koko Crater rim is the major east Oahu landmark. It is also the site of the 207-acre Koko Crater Botanical Garden—a tropical desert that is hot and dry, but not barren. Here, for example, a large grove of the summer-flowering endemic wili wili produces clouds of large burnt orange, chartreuse, or bicolor blooms. Other natives include the endangered nanu, a fragrant gardenia; several dryland loulu palms; 'alahe'e, a shrubby gardenia relative with dark green, shiny foliage and crowded clusters of highly fragrant white flowers; and kulu'i, a shrub with silver foliage. Growing wild throughout the crater are shrubby ground covers 'ilie'e, 'ilima, and 'ilima papa, the latter two exhibiting bright gold-orange flowers from which leis are made. Also present is the blue-flowered pa'u o hi'iaka. All of these extremely drought-tolerant plants have been incorporated into local xeriscapes.

With the exception of the centrally located palm section, exotic plantings are arranged geographically, showcasing approximately a thousand trees, shrubs, vines, and succulent species from the world's dry tropics. In early spring, the extensive hybrid plumeria, or frangipani, collection offers a rush of mass flowering in colors ranging from pure white through delicate pinks, rich gold, bright yellows and oranges, to deep, wine red—all perfuming the entire area. Flowering continues until mid-autumn.

■ **KOKO CRATER BOTANICAL GARDEN** c/o Foster Botanical Garden, 180 N. Vineyard Boulevard, Honolulu, Oahu, HI 96817 **TEL:** (808) 522-7060 **OPEN:** Daily 9-4 **TOTAL ACRES:** 207 **SPECIAL COLLECTIONS:** Palms, native species, xeriphytes   **ZONE 11 A P PA T WS**

Wahiawa Botanical Garden
Wahiawa, Oahu

Two mountain ranges form the island of Oahu, and in the cool, moist saddle that joins them sits the 27-acre Wahiawa Botanical Garden. Here tropicals from similar environments grow readily, including tree species of podocarps, figs, and gums, especially the Mindanao gum with its multicolored, green-beige bark. A rapid grower, reaching an excess of a hundred feet in height, it is now widely used for landscaping and considered a possible source of pulp to be grown on lands abandoned by Hawaii's nearly defunct sugar industry. Other notable plant exhibits include tree ferns, epiphytes, aroids, and heliconia and palm collections. Specimens of brownea display large orange flower clusters. Also highly photogenic are the pendant pale pink flowers of amherstia, "Queen of Flowering Trees." In addition, the garden offers an orange-flowered asoka tree of India, revered by Buddhists as the tree that sheltered Buddha's birthplace. The collection of native Hawaiian species features many mature loulu palms; a collection of hibiscus; several kinds of red, orange, or yellow flowering koki'o; and representatives of the white-flowering, fragrant tree hibiscus, koki'o ke'oke'o. Also of interest are the native 'Ohe'ohe and 'ohe makai, trees with highly ornamental foliage.

■ **Wahiawa Botanical Garden** (30 miles from Honolulu city center) 1396 California Avenue, Wahiawa, Oahu, HI 96786 **Tel:** (808) 621-7321 **Open:** Daily 9-4, except Christmas and New Year's Day **Total acres:** 27 **Special collections:** Palms, aroids, tropical conifers   ZONE 11 H P PA T V

Ho'omaluhia Botanical Garden
Kaneohe, Oahu

On the windward side of Oahu, at the base of the towering, verdant cliffs of the kane'ohe pali, lies the 400-acre Ho'omaluhia Botanical Garden. Featuring extensive collections from the world's wet tropics arranged in geographical sections, the plantings surround a 32-acre flood-control lake.

One area showcases an outstanding Philippines collection, the only one of its kind outside the Philippine archipelago. It offers visitors a range of unique trees, shrubs, vines, and palms. Other sections—Malaysian, American, Melanesian, Indian, and African—offer exotic flora, trees, vines, palms, and climbing aroids. Rattans, vining-climbing palms, torch gingers, and nearby flashy red, orange, yellow, and pink heliconias are favored subjects for the camera. In addition, nutmeg, clove, and cinnamon trees attract special attention. Ho'omaluhia offers two areas planted with Hawaiian species. One concentrates on the 'ohi'a lehua, the native tree most familiar to visitors from which brilliant, prized red or yellow leis are made. The second grouping features ethnobotanicals, those plants valued for food, shelter, clothing, dyes, and medicines. These include both heritage species, plants carried to the islands in great sailing canoes during the period of Polynesian migration over a thousand years ago, and useful native plants. Plantings throughout Ho'omaluhia evoke the spirit of the tropical rain forest. Visitors will relish views of the magnificent 2,000-foot sheer pali threaded with dozens of ephemeral waterfalls nourished by frequent rains.

■ **Ho'omaluhia Botanical Garden** (13 miles from Honolulu city center) 45-680 Luluku Road, Kaneohe, Oahu, HI 96744 **Tel:** (808) 233-7324 **Open:** Daily 9-4, except Christmas and New Year's Day **Total acres:** 400 **Special collections:** Palms, aroids, native species   ZONE 11 H L P PA T V

Aptly named, torch ginger sports brilliant red inflorescences on its tall ste
                                              It thrives in Ho'omaluhia Botanical Garden's rain forest conditi

LYON ARBORETUM
HONOLULU, OAHU

The 3,000-foot mountain Konahuanui dominates the head of Manoa Valley. Hugging its base, the Lyon Arboretum offers the ultimate tropical rain forest experience. At the turn of the century the 194-acre site was an eroded pasture, treeless and windswept. In 1918 the forestry division of the Hawaiian Sugar Planters Association began experimental plantings here to identify tree species capable of quickly covering similar sites throughout Hawaii. Their motivation was the protection of the water supply critical for sugar production. Eighty years later the arboretum, benefiting from a planting continuum and spurred by 160 inches of rainfall each year, is a luxuriant jungle of trees, vines, showy shrubs, and one of the world's top palm collections. The grounds now support some 7,500 different kinds of tropical plants.

Among Lyon's specialties are native Hawaiian plants and plants of cultural importance or used for food, pharmaceuticals, or fibers. It also holds a research collection of the maranta family, colorful foliage plants that include shrubby and ground cover species (many popular for indoor use and known as prayer plants). The arboretum's world-class collection of aroids, a large plant family that includes the ubiquitous philodendrons, is found throughout the arboretum—climbing trees, perched in trees epiphytically, or forming great shrubby masses of dark green foliage. A favorite, the double-flowered form of chaconia, a tall shrub from Trinidad, sprouts neon red sprays of flowers almost all year. A research institute of the University of Hawaii, the arboretum serves the international scientific community and visitors alike through programs ranging from its renowned micropropagation unit to Hawaiian ecosystem restoration. In addition, an extensive series of public education classes gives the arboretum high marks and a loyal volunteer following.

LYON ARBORETUM 3860 Manoa Road, Honolulu, Oahu, HI 96822 **TEL:** (808) 988-3177 **OPEN:** Mon.-Sat. 9-3, except holidays **TOTAL ACRES:** 194 **SPECIAL COLLECTIONS:** Palms, aroids, native plants, ti, chaconia
ZONE 11 G **H** P **T** V WS

Lyon Arboretum's luxuriant growth has been adroitly cleared to create jungle-lined walks through colorful collections of palms, marantas, bromeliads, and ornamental shrubs.

Waimea Arboretum and Botanical Garden
Haleiwa, Oahu

Once home to Hewahewa, High Priest to King Kamehameha I, Waimea Valley opens to Oahu's north shore. Today it shelters the Waimea Arboretum and Botanical Garden and a collection of rare and endangered plants from exotic places. In addition, the garden preserves a valuable cultural site comprising ancient agricultural terraces, house platforms, a burial site, and the restored Hale o Lono Heiau, a temple consecrated to Lono, Hawaiian god of agriculture. A significant collection of food and dye plants, medicinals, and other heirloom crops are grown where archaeologically appropriate. The priest's occupation of the valley began around A.D. 1090.

Chief among the garden's 36 special collections are its coral bean trees, the world's largest, with over 80 percent of known species. Their spring and summer flowering season provides a visual feast. (Coral beans are of modern pharmaceutical interest.) Also intriguing is the surprising array of material within the garden, both flowers and foliage, that

Waimea Falls, in Waimea Arboretum and Botanical Garden, has been the site of major archaeological finds. Here, garden displays focus on Hawaiian history and culture, such as the flowers and foliage used to make leis.

is used to make leis. In addition, the garden holds Hawaii's finest hibiscus collection, exhibiting hybrids from the turn of the century to modern times. Both collections display colorful blooms year-round. Other areas specialize in plants from threatened tropical island ecosystems, including some from the Ogasawara Islands, Fiji, Lord Howe Island, Guam, the Mascarenes, Bermuda, Madagascar, and Sri Lanka, plant combinations not found elsewhere.

Waimea's tree-canopied valley also shelters an array of colorful ornamentals, orchids, gingers and heliconias, spider lilies, impatiens, cannas, bauhinias, bromeliads, and numerous others. In addition, ground covers such as ferns, begonias, and many different kinds of peperomias, beloved of houseplant enthusiasts, also thrive here. Masses of the acanthus and spurge family's glowing shrubbery offer foliage color from mottled green-and-yellow, green-and-red, red-and-mahogany, to unlikely combinations of purples. Many sport leaves edged as though attacked by pinking shears. Botany and landscape design are happily joined in Waimea's beautiful grounds, which display more than five thousand different tropical species and provide a popular, cool retreat.

Waimea Arboretum and Botanical Garden (60 miles from Honolulu) 59-864 Kamehameha Highway, Haleiwa, Oahu, HI 96712 **Tel:** (808) 638-8655 **Open:** Daily 10-5 **Total acres:** 150 **Special collections:** Coral bean trees, plants from high tropical islands, orchids

ZONE 11 F G H P PA R T V WS

Kula Botanical Garden
Kula, Maui

On the island of Maui, a road gently climbs the flanks of the crater called Haleakala, eventually arriving at an oasis of abundant surprises: the 14-acre Kula Botanical Garden. Horticultural afficionados quickly discern that this place is from another world—part Australian, part South African, and part Andean—not tropical Hawaiian. The garden's 3,300-foot elevation, abetted by the cold night air flowing from the top of Haleakala's 10,000-foot crest, creates a temperate zone climate. Light frosts are rare.

Important in this hillside garden are the proteas, a vital cut-flower crop in this part of Maui. Here the amazing South African king protea displays its dinner-plate-size blooms, variously colored in pinks to white. From autumn to spring, the bird nest banksia of western Australia opens its large, fuzzy lime-green buds to expose a light yellow flower. The "old man" banksia of Australian fairy tales, native to coastal east Australia, here bears its silvery-gold cylindrical flower heads from midsummer to mid-winter, while its smaller relative, the rosemary grevillea, shows pink-and-white flowers all year.

Here too bloom the surprising Mexican tree dahlias, tall stems topped by clusters of large, single pink flowers. They vie for attention with multicolored fuchsias, snow-white or peach-colored pendant angels' trumpets, and the bold whitish-grey foliage of the plume poppy.

Even the garden's reptilian maintenance crew is international. Delighting the younger set is a monstrous Jackson's chameleon from Kenya, a large green frog from the Americas, and an assortment of other bug-eating helpers.

■ **Kula Botanical Garden** (20 miles from Kahului) Kula, Maui, HI 96790 **Tel:** (808) 878-1715 **Open:** Daily 9-4 **Total acres:** 14 **Special collections:** Proteas, tree dahlias   **ZONE 10 F G H P PA T V**

Kula Botanical Garden displays species from both Old and New World temperate zones. White herald's trumpets grow here as trees next to proteas, flowering eucalyptus, clivias, and fuchsias.

The ever-blooming orange-and-blue bird of paradise, a major cut flower found at the Maui Tropical Plantation, is prized for shipping as well as for home landscaping.

MAUI TROPICAL PLANTATION
WAILUKU, MAUI

Maui is composed of two great mountains—Haleakala, which rises to 10,000 feet to the east, and the west Maui mountain complex, which measures more than 6,000 feet in elevation. Dropping sharply, the two are connected by a broad, hot, dry isthmus, the site of intense agricultural activity where sugar is still king and pineapple abounds on upland slopes.

At the western edge of the isthmus, the Maui Tropical Plantation devotes its 112 acres to growing and displaying Hawaii's agricultural products. Here small working orchards supplemented by interpretive displays depict the roles of sugar, pineapple, coffee, macadamia nuts, and bananas in Hawaii's economic history. More recent exports—papayas, mangos, avocados, and guavas—are joined by colorful plantings of flower and foliage crops, red ginger, various heliconias, and both brash and subtly hued ti leaves. Visitors are encouraged to touch and smell.

An especially interesting display tells of supplying water to Hawaii's extensive agricultural fields in low rainfall areas, a triumph of hydraulic engineering. Well before the end of the 19th century, ditches and tunnels for carrying precious water from wet to arid lands were frequently dug through solid lava by hand labor. The plantation, itself receiving only 20 inches of rain per year, taps into the system created to carry water to the low-lying, parched isthmus from the west Maui mountains, which are deluged by 400 inches of annual rain.

The plantation's extensive entry grounds are generously landscaped with visually exciting, exotic tropical ornamentals representative of Hawaii's home gardens.

MAUI TROPICAL PLANTATION (3 miles from Wailuku) 1670 Honoapilani Highway, Wailuku, Maui, HI 96793 TEL: (808) 244-7643 OPEN: Daily 9-5 TOTAL ACRES: 112 SPECIAL COLLECTIONS: Tropical fruit trees

ZONE 11 G H P R T V

HAWAII TROPICAL BOTANICAL GARDEN
PAPAIKOU, HAWAII

The windward flank of snow-capped Mauna Kea meets the Pacific Ocean along the Hamakua Coast of the big island of Hawaii, an area of very high rainfall. Always green, the region is laced with deep, densely forested valleys, ravines, and countless white-water streams and waterfalls, many plunging over sheer cliffs directly into the sea. Onomea Valley, one of the coast's few readily ocean-accessible places, is also site of the beautiful Hawaii Tropical Botanical Garden. The garden is cut by two fast-moving streams—Boulder Creek, aptly named for its rock-strewn course, and Onomea Falls, a beautiful series of low falls and pools. The only other sounds breaking this peaceful environment are those of birds and the murmuring ocean. In the still, humid air, with the encouragement of 130 inches of annual rainfall, rampant growth works to replicate the environment of a lush, tropical rain forest. The almost continuous tree canopy is composed of mature mango trees, spreading monkeypod trees, breadfruit, brilliant orange-flowered African tulip trees, a grove of tall, slender hula palms, and a fine selection of other ornamental palms and tree ferns from the world's wet tropics.

The luxuriant understory has been developed with a sensitive and strong eye for color and texture. At any time of the year, masses of croton, hybrid ti, and a significant collection of calatheas and bromeliads provide brilliant foliage color while seasonal flowering plants furnish explosive accents. Notable among the flowering exhibits, the heliconia collection provides constantly changing hues in

Thoughtfully engineered trails lead visitors through the junglelike growth of the Hawaii Tropical Botanical Garden, a paradise of colorful foliage, exotic flowers, and rushing streams.

red, orange, and yellow. Included are spectacular specimens of *Heliconia rostrata* and *Heliconia mariae,* both bearing huge hanging inflorescences. More color is derived from the extensive orchid and anthurium collections, both species and hybrids exhibiting strange blooms in white, pink, orange, and red. A wide range of hibiscus, gingers, and other showy, tropical shrubby ornamentals add to the vivid palette. The startling pendant flowers of *Medinilla magnifica* from the Philippines appear here in both the glowing pink and red forms. A colorful, serene pond features such aquatics as tropical waterlilies with their many-hued, jewel-like blooms growing next to giant Amazon waterlilies and African papyrus, as well as a wide variety of floating and bog species.

A well-designed path system comfortably traverses the somewhat difficult topography, guiding visitors from one plant grouping to the next and providing rest stops. In addition, strategically placed viewing spots offer areas for contemplating waterfalls, the sweep of the surf, and the deep blue ocean. The garden, privately owned and operated through a nonprofit corporation, currently comprises 17 acres.

■ **HAWAII TROPICAL BOTANICAL GARDEN** (7 miles north of Hilo) RR 143-A, Papaikou, Hawaii, HI 96781 **TEL:** (808) 964-5233 **OPEN:** Daily 9-5, except Thanksgiving, Christmas, and New Year's Day **TOTAL ACRES:** 17 **SPECIAL COLLECTIONS:** Heliconias, palms, tree ferns, aquatic plants ZONE 11 F G H P T V WS

NANI MAU GARDENS
HILO, HAWAII
Nani mau translates to "always beautiful," a label aptly applied to this 20-acre gathering of tropical flower power on the island of Hawaii. Frequently refurbished beds of tropical annuals and perennials; dwarf ixoras with red, orange, and yellow flowers; salmon crossandras; pentas in red, pink, lavender, and white; and brilliant crotons accented by the rich blue of the Andean otocanthus and purple bougainvillea provide a kaleidoscope of color. Another ever-changing display features a mix of orchids in full flower. An anthurium collection grown "wild" on tree-fern trunks provides further photo opportunities. More color pulsates from the bromeliad display, where mature specimens of *Vriesia imperialis* offer impressive five-foot-long silver and purple leaves.

Yet color is not the only dimension explored at Nani Mau. Detectable throughout the garden are plants with especially fragrant blooms, delighting the senses with the perfume of pua keni keni, a popular lei flower; the Chinese kwai fah; and *Tabernaemontana crassa,* a rare flowering shrub from Africa with a potent, sweet fragrance. In addition, a large planting of tropical fruit trees display the tropical edibles found in island gardens. The very tall Caroline Island ivory nut palms add a visual treat, emerging well above the canopy on straight trunks bearing massive heads of leaves. Each leaf extends up to 20 feet in length, sheltering pendant clusters of fruit.

The carefully contoured grounds offer user-friendly grades and wide, paved paths along which the lush growth of well-groomed plantings is supported by an annual rainfall of 115 inches. Every turn of the path presents a new vista, and a visit to this garden lives up to its name: always beautiful.

■ **NANI MAU GARDENS** 421 Makalika Street, Hilo, Hawaii, HI 96720 **TEL:** (808) 959-3541 **OPEN:** Daily 8-5 **TOTAL ACRES:** 20 **SPECIAL COLLECTIONS:** Tropical bedding plants, tropical fruit trees, orchids
ZONE 11 F G H L P R T V WS

CHAPTER 7

CANADA

■

Nova Scotia

Quebec

Ontario

Manitoba

Alberta

British Columbia

Visitors enjoying the Sunken Garden at Butchart Gardens today find it hard to imagine that it was once a used-up quarry.

Halifax Public Gardens
Halifax, Nova Scotia

The Public Gardens in Halifax, the capital of Nova Scotia, have been a landmark in the city since they opened in 1867. The gardens are one of the best examples in North America of the ornate Victorian style. The landscape features a full

range of traditional Victoriana: elaborately designed carpet beds of scroll and serpentine shapes filled with annuals, perennials, roses, and show-type dahlias throughout an area that includes weeping beech and mulberry trees and impressive exotic and native specimen trees. The dove tree, catalpa tree, Japanese umbrella pine, ginkgo, American chestnut, copper beech, corkscrew birch, tulip trees, and both star and saucer magnolias are some of trees that can be seen here.

Rockeries display a mixture of chives, sedums, pinks, and speedwells. The greenhouse tropical collection is planted out each summer and includes palms, agaves, dracaenas, and bird of paradise. Impressive wrought iron gates from Scotland, classical-style stone bridges, statues of Roman goddesses, fountains, and a stone grotto all decorate the garden. A final touch in the center—a wonderful 1887

The bandstand at Halifax was built in 1887 in honor of Queen Victoria's Golden Jubilee.

bandstand capped in red and surrounded by 32 flower beds commemorating Queen Victoria's Golden Jubilee. Across from the gingerbread-style bandstand, ducks and swans swim in a scalloped-edged pond in this scene from a bygone era. Spring and summer are the best times to see the flowers in bloom in this 18-acre garden park.

■ **Halifax Public Gardens** (120 miles east of Portland, ME) Spring Garden Road and S. Park Street, Halifax, Nova Scotia, Canada B3J 3A5 **Tel:** 902-490-4894 **Open:** Daily dawn-dusk, May through Nov. **Total acres:** 18 **Special collections:** Formal Victorian-style gardens   **ZONE 6** C HO L P PA T

Jardin des Métis
Grand Métis, Quebec

On the northern coast of the Gaspé Peninsula, along a famous salmon run of the St. Lawrence River, a garden of English grandeur was created by Lady Elsie Redford. In 1919, she inherited a former fishing retreat from her uncle and within ten years, her passion for gardening and her worldwide pursuit of plants transformed her 45-acre estate into a horticultural showcase. She experimented with thousands of plants and introduced many never grown as far north before. Over 1,500 species, including some 500 different kinds of native and exotic perennials, grow in the garden. One of her finds, the intense Himalayan blue poppy is today the garden's symbol and can be seen in bloom during the month of July. The garden declined after Lady Redford's departure in 1954, but was acquired by the government of Quebec in 1961 and restored to its

Jardin des Métis in the province of Quebec had humble beginnings, when Lady Elsie Redford planted a small vegetable plot on her estate in 1919. The garden now encompasses 45 acres.

former splendor. Today, this garden is a major attraction for horticulturists and gardeners worldwide.

The proximity to the river and the indigenous white spruce trees that provide a shield from wind create an unusual microclimate, moist and warmer than the surrounding landscape. This tempered weather allows a profusion of beautiful blossoms from spring to autumn in six different ornamental gardens. Paths lined with wildflowers lead to a rock garden, a rhododendron garden, a crabapple garden, and a rose garden. The art of English landscaping is exemplified in the garden called Allée Royale, where exuberant borders of intense color are designed to bloom continuously throughout the season. Double perennial borders display blue delphinium, roses, lilies, lythrum, and, along the edge, cascades of dianthus and campanula. The primula garden features a variety of colors and species and two of the Métis Garden's most distinctive features: a Sawara false cypress, native to Japan, and a rare, indigenous silverberry bush. The newest area is a green garden with meadows and native plants. Surrounded by stately trees, this lush landscape is accented by rustic bridges across unexpected streams and an impressive overlook of the Métis River meeting the St. Lawrence. Villa Redford stands in the center of the garden and houses a museum and restaurant.

JARDIN DES MÉTIS (210 miles northeast of Quebec) Route 132, Grand Métis, Quebec, Canada G0J 1Z0 TEL: (418) 775-2221 OPEN: Daily 8:30-6:30, June to mid-Oct. TOTAL ACRES: 45 SPECIAL COLLECTIONS: Estate garden, native and exotic perennials, blue poppies   ZONE 4   A F G H HO P PA R T V

MONTREAL BOTANICAL GARDEN
MONTREAL, QUEBEC

In the half century since its founding, the internationally renowned Montreal Botanical Garden has grown to comprise 180 acres with 30 outdoor gardens, 10 exhibition greenhouses, and more than 30 behind-the-scenes service greenhouses. Although owned by the city of Montreal, the garden owes its existence to Frère Marie-Victorin, a brother in the Catholic Ecoles Chrétiennes community. An ardent propagandist for scientific cultivation and Quebeçois nationalism, Brother Marie-Victorin sought to promote the natural history as well as French-Canadian intellectual leadership. In 1931, as the city was just beginning to ponder how it might mark its tricentennial, Marie-Victorin presented his idea to honor Montreal's patroness, the Virgin Mary, by dedicating a "bouquet of flowers" to her in the form of a botanical garden. Brother Marie-Victorin's Jardin Botanique, as it is known, took several decades to achieve its current wide diversity of trees, shrubs, and herbaceous plants—an estimated 25,000 species from five continents.

The outdoor gardens, the first areas to be established, remain the main attraction. Near the entrance gate is the somewhat formal reception garden area dedicated to Marie-Victorin, whose statue stands at its center. From here a path leads north to small theme exhibition gardens, including a shrub garden, the Poisonous Plant Garden, the Monastery Garden, and the Medicinal Plant Garden. Many other specialty gardens of great charm lie tucked amid the garden's acreage.

The arboretum accounts for about half of the garden's total space, stretching north and containing nearly 3,000 species and horticultural varieties of woody

The Montreal Botanical Garden is composed of numerous theme gardens, including displays of annuals, perennials, vegetables, and poisonous plants.

plants. Many visitors see it for the first time via the garden's mini-train as it travels past specimens grouped according to their botanical families—maples in one gathering, dogwoods in another, and so on—thus showing the subtle differences of branching patterns, leaf shape, and color within each species. On the arboretum's eastern perimeter, a shade garden features Christmas and Lenten roses and masses of spring-flowering bulbs. To the west lies the Leslie Hancock Garden, dedicated to plants of the Ericaceae family—richly flowering broad-leaved evergreen shrubs such as rhododendrons, azaleas, laurels, andromedas, and heathers.

In winter, ten indoor exhibition buildings shelter more than 12,000 species and varieties of plants foreign to Montreal's temperate climate. Separate halls re-create such exotic environments as the tropical rain forests of South America and the arid deserts of Africa. Here, too, Henry Teuscher's personal collection of orchids, the nucleus of a collection of more than 700 species of orchids, is on permanent exhibition. Of special note is the garden's bonsai collection. Unusual by any measure, it is said to be one of the most complete and diversified collection outside of Asia, with nearly 500 specimens ranging from 10 to 350 years old.

Close by the bonsai/penjing pavilion are traditional outdoor Japanese and Chinese gardens. The Japanese garden is really three distinctly different gardens. The first, in the sansui style, combines typical Japanese plants and Japanese pines with classic water features and carefully placed viewing stones. The second, a tea garden, features a *tsukubai*, or low water basin, surrounded by fragrant plants. The third is the Zen garden, a plantless place of meditation set forth in classic severity with imported white ocean sand and eleven viewing stones.

At five acres, Montreal's Chinese Garden is the largest in the Western Hemisphere. Modeled after the classic *shan shui*, or mountains and water, tradition of southern China, it includes selected species of bamboo, Chinese peony, and lotus. There are also several architecturally authentic garden pavilions,

The Tower of Condensing Clouds is reflected in a lake dotted with waterlilies in the Chinese Garden.

bridges, and towers; a pond; and a symbolic "mountain" of stone. Many of the unusually contorted stones used here were handpicked from the sacred shores of China's Lake Tai-hu. The garden continues to grow in size and ambition, as do its nearby scientific and educational facilities. Recent additions include the Insectarium and the Biodome, the latter a living museum in which botanic materials and animal life are presented in four different ecosystems.

MONTREAL BOTANICAL GARDEN 4101 Sherbrooke East, Montreal, Quebec, Canada H1X 2B2 **TEL:** (514) 872-1400 **OPEN:** Daily 9-8, late June to early Sept.; daily 9-5, early Sept. to late June **TOTAL ACRES:** 180 **SPECIAL COLLECTIONS:** Orchids, bonsai, penjing, Chinese and Japanese gardens, arboretum

ZONE 5 A C **F** G **H** L P **PA** R T V **WS**

Laking Garden at the Royal Botanical Gardens showcases some 250,000 bearded irises, a highlight of the garden's Iris Festival each June.

ROYAL BOTANICAL GARDENS
BURLINGTON, ONTARIO

Spectacular gardens extend for 11 miles along the northwest shore of Lake Ontario across the townships of Hamilton, Burlington, Dundas, and Flamborough. Spread across a 2,700-acre complex, the Royal Botanical Gardens began in a quarry pit during the Depression in the 1930s and has become one of the great botanical gardens in the world. Renowned for its research and education programs, it also offers some of the most beautiful gardens anywhere. Thousands of magnificent displays, some intimate, some elaborate, fulfill the garden's motto: "where art and science meet." There are five major garden areas and some 30 miles of trails through the undeveloped forests, meadows, marshes, and a wildlife sanctuary. A car is essential and the tour should begin at the Visitor's Center where excellent maps and brochures are provided.

Beyond the Fountain Court across from the center await the formal gardens of Hendrie Park. The two-acre Centennial Rose Garden is the central feature with an abundant display of heritage and modern roses. Extensive trial gardens of summer annuals provide lavish spreads of color. Newer areas include a scented garden, a medicinal garden, and a comprehensive and glorious collection of clematis.

Laking Garden, about a half-mile west of the center, offers an enchanting series of old favorites. The entrance on the upper level is flanked by hundreds of modern and historic peonies. A pavilion overlooks herbaceous perennials in the style of the legendary designer, Gertrude Jekyll, with informal beds of pastel colors and luxuriant textures. Most stunning of all is the display in June of 250,000 irises, one of the largest iris collections in the Northern Hemisphere. Drifts of jeweled colors float in a panorama of exquisite blooms arranged by height and hue.

The boughs of a weeping willow reach down to greet beds of bright tulips in the Rock Garden, where more than 100,000 bulbs from Holland bloom each spring.

The most famous feature is the rock garden, considered the jewel of the garden. More than 46,000 plants are dramatically displayed on ledges, around boulders, throughout nooks and crannies, at the edges of ponds and among shrubs and trees. From mid-April until late May hundreds of varieties of tulips are ablaze everywhere, a warm up for begonias, impatiens, lilies, ornamental grasses, and myriad others in summer.

Here in a gracious parklike setting, the arboretum showcases copses of crab-apples, magnolias, dogwoods, and a varied collection of indigenous trees and shrubs, including a mazelike display of hedges. Twenty acres of the arboretum are devoted to the Lilac Dell, the world's largest collection of lilacs. In May more than 700 varieties offer a magnificent bouquet of blue, purple, magenta, and white within this natural landscape.

The most recent addition, in 1986, was the Mediterranean Greenhouse, an enormous garden under glass with collections from southern climates everywhere (despite its name). Special holiday floral exhibits are ongoing. A children's garden and teaching garden has been in existence since 1947 and provides individual plots for aesthetic and instructional purposes.

In keeping with its educational mandate, all plants at the Royal Botanical Gardens are carefully labeled. In addition, informative instructional brochures are provided on the care of many of the plantings. These gardens are wondrous in all seasons, and visitors are advised to set aside a period of days to see them, if at all possible.

ROYAL BOTANICAL GARDENS (36 miles southwest of Toronto) 80 Plains Road West, Burlington, Ontario, Canada L7T 4H4 **TEL:** (905) 527-1158 **OPEN:** Daily 9:30-dusk, except Christmas **TOTAL ACRES:** 2,700 **SPECIAL COLLECTIONS:** Irises, lilacs, roses, clematis, annuals, peonies, rock garden

ZONE 6 A C F G H L P PA R V WS

Niagara Parks Commission
Niagara Falls, Ontario

While horticulture is not the primary reason most travelers visit the Niagara Falls area, it is a rewarding and additional pleasure. This is primarily thanks to an extensive parks system that was organized in 1885 to curtail the commercialism around the majestic falls. A specially appointed commission developed a system of parks with recreational amenities and splendid gardens, stretching for nearly 35 miles from Lake Erie to Lake Ontario. The main garden within the Niagara Parks system is 200-acre **Queen Victoria Park,** with one of the largest exhibits of carpet bed planting anywhere. This popular Victorian style of planting is a floral extravaganza here, beginning in late April with more than a half-million daffodils in bloom, one of the most prolific displays in North America. Tulips, perennials, roses, and annuals follow in massive spreads of color.

Also of note is a densely planted rock garden and the Niagara Greenhouse, which provides the thousands of plants needed for the park's elaborate displays. From a series of small buildings built in 1894, the greenhouse has expanded into a complex of more than 6,000 square feet, with floral shows for the public. The entrance, a central glass dome with full-size palms and other tropical plants, leads to exhibition spaces filled with seasonal splendor. The commission has always encouraged the propagation of unusual species and varieties of flowers, including the popular butterfly flower, a delicate rose-colored bloom with an inner yellow butterfly pattern. In addition to traditional displays, the greenhouse offers impressive hanging plants and standards of fuchsias, hydrangeas, lantanas, and chrysanthemums.

Oakes Garden Theater, an outdoor Greco-Roman-style amphitheater poised against the stunning backdrop of Niagara Falls, is surrounded by elaborate geometric beds of Korean boxwood filled with begonias, conical yews, and standard lantanas. Potted urns and pleached linden trees along an ornamental garden wall add graceful touches.

Another popular attraction is the **Niagara Parks Commission Botanical Garden and School of Horticulture,** located six miles from Niagara Falls. Students have contributed to the design and collections of these interesting gardens for more than 60 years. Herb, vegetable, rock, and Victorian rose gardens are spread across some one hundred acres, along with an annual garden and a fine display of ornamental trees and shrubs. A new glass conservatory is devoted exclusively to the collection of more than 2,000 butterflies.

Less than a mile away, the **Floral Clock and Lilac Garden** boasts the world's largest functioning clock made of flowers. Inspired by a famous garden clock in Scotland, this area landmark of 25,000 plants spells out NIAGARA FALLS in hour positions. A ten-foot-wide water garden pool filled with lilies and stocked with goldfish curves along the front of the clock, while the second half of the circle is filled with multicolored flowers. The nearby Lilac Garden, commemorating Canada's centennial in 1966, was a gift from the U.S. branch of Rotary International. In late May and early June, its ten acres of fragrant lilacs bloom in a brilliant array of colors.

■ **Niagara Parks Commission** Niagara Falls, Ontario, Canada L2E 6T2 **Tel:** (905) 356-8554 **Open:** Daily dawn-dusk, except greenhouse and conservatory. Call for seasonal hours and directions. **Special Collections:** Victorian flower beds, rock garden, world's largest floral clock, lilacs, roses, butterflies

ZONE 6 A C F G H P PA R V WS

The winter sun brightens a snowy scene at Edwards Garden, which spans 35 acres. In spring, the ravine comes to life with thousands of bulbs and rhododendrons.

Edwards Garden
North York, Ontario

Situated in a ravine three miles north of Toronto, Edwards Garden is a picturesque combination of natural woodlands, steep hillsides of color, lavish floral displays, rustic bridges, and a beautiful rock garden. Once a private country estate, it rests on the banks of Wilket Creek. Masses of spring bulbs bloom throughout the 35 acres. A special feature is the outstanding collection of rhododendrons and azaleas in bloom along the banks of the stream from mid-April to late June. Lilacs, roses, annuals, and perennials brighten the summer months in this tranquil oasis. A Civic Garden Center is also located at the site, offering a library, workshops, lectures, and small floral exhibitions.

Edwards Garden is one of three garden parks that are part of the Metropolitan Toronto regional parkland system. Other interesting horticultural areas are **James Gardens** (Royal York Road), an intimate setting of terraced gardens, spring-fed pools, graceful bridges, and statuesque trees along the banks of the Humber River. The **Rosetta McClain Gardens** (Kingston Road), perched on Scarborough Bluffs, is the only garden park on Toronto's waterfront. There, small gardens of roses, raised flowerbeds around a pergola, mature specimen trees, and water views complete an attractive scene.

Edwards Garden (3 miles north of Toronto) 775 Lawrence Avenue East, North York, Ontario, Canada M3C-1P2 **Tel:** (416) 392-8186 **Open:** Daily 8-8 **Total acres:** 35 **Special collections:** Estate garden, rock garden, rhododendrons, azaleas   **ZONE 6** **G** **H** **L** **P** **R** **T** **V**

Assiniboine Park
Winnipeg, Manitoba

Sprawling over 280 riverside acres in Winnipeg, Assiniboine Park was founded in 1904. It encompasses several gardens established in the early 20th century, along with modern additions. Prominent among them is the English Garden, a three-acre landscape of meadows, wooded walking trails, and informal flower displays that opened to the public in 1929. Arranged around a central pool, this site incorporates a rock garden, a woodland garden, an ornamental grass garden, and borders abundant with delphinium, peonies, poppies, lilies, tulips, and other old-fashioned favorites—all interspersed among flowering crabapples, dogwoods, and lilacs.

In stark contrast is the Formal Garden, designed in 1907 with a precise geometric layout. The beds are aligned on two intersecting axes and filled with annual bedding plants. Around the perimeter is a U-shaped promenade lined with American elms whose canopies have joined to form an arcade over the roadway. The park's centerpiece is its conservatory, which was originally built in 1914. The entire structure was renovated in 1969, with a new conservatory being built over and around the old one. The new conservatory, at about 16,000 square feet, boasts a palm house and floral display areas and contains more than 8,000 specimens. The newest feature is the Leo Mol Sculpture Garden, established in 1992 to showcase the works of this Winnipeg resident. The naturalistic gardens, spread out around a heated pool of tropical waterlilies, include roses, irises, and impatiens.

Assiniboine Park (134 miles east of International Peace Garden in Brandon) 2355 Corydon Avenue, Winnipeg, Manitoba, Canada R3P 0R5 **Tel:** (204) 986-5537 **Open:** Daily 9-8, April through Sept.; daily 9-4:30, Oct. through March **Total acres:** 280 **Special collections:** English-style landscaping, perennial gardens, tropical plants   **ZONE 3 C H P R T WS**

Devonian Botanic Garden
Edmonton, Alberta

Opened in 1959 by the University of Alberta, the Devonian Botanic Garden features more than a dozen themed gardens spread over 80 acres of rolling landscape, pine forest, and wetland. The largest among them is the five-acre Kurimoto Japanese Garden, a sunny stroll garden where the geography of Alberta is interpreted in an authentic Japanese design. Plantings include both native and introduced species, ranging from spruce and tamarack to mock orange and daylilies. Traditional ornaments, such as lanterns, a pagoda, and a bell tower, punctuate this serene setting.

Indigenous flora are also prominent in the Plants of Alberta Garden, a collection of wildflowers, grasses, and shrubs, and in the two-acre Native People's Garden, where plants used by the aboriginal inhabitants of this region are displayed in a quiet grove of birch and pine trees. In the Alpine Garden, a thousand tons of rock were installed for a scree bed, a boulder bowl, and two ridges that are home to plants from the Himalayas, Alps, and Caucasus Mountains. Among the thousands of dwarf specimens are rhododendron, campanula, phlox, and narcissus. Other themed gardens include an iris dell, a peony collection, a lilac garden, an herb garden, and a primula dell. Most surprising is the Desert Plot, where cactus and yucca thrive on a natural sand dune and survive

Alberta's frigid winters. A special attraction at the Devonian is the Butterfly House, in which some 30 species of exotic butterflies flit among bananas, palms, lantana, and other tropical and subtropical plants.

DEVONIAN BOTANIC GARDEN Route 60, Edmonton, Alberta, Canada T6G 2E1 **TEL:** (403) 987-3054 **OPEN:** Daily 10-7, mid-May through first week of Sept.; daily 10-4, second week of Sept. to mid-Oct and first two weeks of May; Sat.-Sun. 11-4, mid-Oct. through April **TOTAL ACRES:** Gardens 80, natural areas 110 **SPECIAL COLLECTIONS:** Peonies, alpine garden, butterfly house, Japanese garden, native plants

ZONE 3 **F** G **P** PA WS

MUTTART CONSERVATORY
EDMONTON, ALBERTA

Looming above the North Saskatchewan River valley like the pyramids along the Nile, the Muttart Conservatory is both an architectural and botanical treasure. Four striking glass pavilions—ranging from 60 to 80 feet tall—rise from velvety lawns and protect a collection of some 8,500 species and hybrids from the bitter Edmonton winters. The conservatory is arranged around a central underground courtyard. The two largest pyramids, each measuring 7,100 square feet, are dedicated to tropical and temperate plants. In the former, which is a simulated rain forest, grow orchids, passionflowers, hibiscus, and birds of paradise beneath a leafy umbrella of palms and figs—all gathered around an 18-foot waterfall. In the latter, such giant canopy plants as sequoias and coast redwoods soar over an understory of magnolias, rhododendrons, and roses interspersed with irises, foxgloves, and other perennials. Although winter temperatures in this pyramid may dip to freezing, the Muttart successfully raises a number of tender specimens, including camellias and citrus trees.

Measuring 4,200 square feet each, the two remaining pyramids showcase arid plants and provide a

With the rectangular skyscrapers of Edmonton hovering in the distance, the pyramids at the Muttart Conservatory make their own geometric statement.

display area for thematic seasonal exhibitions that change ten times each year. The beds of the arid plant pyramid, as rocky and barren as the desert landscape, hold specimens from North and South America, the Mediterranean, and Africa. Along with the expected dryland natives, such as aloes, cactuses, and succulents, is a collection of economically useful plants, including olive, jojoba, and carob.

MUTTART CONSERVATORY 9626-96A Street, Edmonton, Alberta, Canada T6C 4L8 **TEL:** (403) 496-8755 **OPEN:** Sun.-Wed. 9-9, Thurs.-Sat. 9-6, except Christmas **TOTAL ACRES:** 9 **SPECIAL COLLECTIONS:** Orchids, pyramid design, desert plants, tropical plants

ZONE 3 C **F** G **R** WS

THE VANCOUVER PARK BOARD
VANCOUVER, BRITISH COLUMBIA

The coastal city of Vancouver hosts two magnificent parks and a world-class botanical garden, each with its own personality. **Stanley Park**, on the tip of a peninsula jutting into English Bay, is a thousand-acre nature preserve set aside in 1886 for public recreation. Largely undeveloped, the park is threaded with trails leading through mature forests of cedar, hemlock, and fir, which shelter drifts of ferns, foamflower, and other natives. The landscaped areas, primarily along the park's eastern edge, abound with such ornamental trees as stately London plane trees and dawn redwoods, while the main gardens feature outstanding collections of rhododendrons, magnolia, and perennials. The Rose Garden offers more than 3,500 plants, mostly modern varieties.

Queen Elizabeth Park, named for the consort of King George VI, covers 130 sylvan acres in downtown Vancouver on "Little Mountain"—a 500-foot-tall rock scarred by quarrying in the early 1900s. Opening in 1939, the park is home to two sunken quarry gardens—one with a 50-foot waterfall—and masses of conifers, azaleas, magnolias, and dogwoods interplanted with flowers. The park's main attraction, however, is the Bloedel Floral Conservatory, which opened in 1969. Rising from a terrace of pools, the 70-foot-high dome houses 15,000 square feet of tropical and desert plants, along with some one hundred free-flying exotic birds and a koi pool.

The Bloedel Floral Conservatory is the crown jewel in the spectacular Queen Elizabeth Park. The location offers sweeping views of Vancouver.

VanDusen Botanical Garden, just a few blocks from Queen Elizabeth Park, is a 55-acre collection of more than 7,500 different types of plants from six continents. Since its opening in 1975 on the site of a former golf course, the gardens have exquisitely combined the art of landscape with the science of horticulture. Set among picturesque rolling lawns, six tranquil ponds, and dramatic rockeries, the gardens are grouped either by geographic origin or botanical relationships of the plantings. Among the former type is the Sino-Himalayan Garden, where poppies, dove trees, and candelabra primula grow amid more than 200 species of rhododendrons.

The Mediterranean Garden features natives from that dry, sunny region, such as the cedar of Lebanon and lavender, while the Southern Hemisphere Garden contains such exotic oddities as the monkey puzzle tree and New Zealand flax. The gardens devoted to eastern and western North America include such familiar

The gardens in Queen Elizabeth Park lie in what was once the quarry that supplied much of the rock to build Vancouver's first roadways. Today the gardens overflow with flowers.

specimens as dogwoods, mountain laurel, madrona, maples, and pines. The related-plant collections range from dainty ground covers to soaring giant redwoods. Flowering cherries, magnolias, and narcissus are standouts in spring, while hydrangeas and lilies provide summer color. In fall, the maples and ginkgoes display their stunning foliage, and the garden glows in winter with spiky mounds of heath and heathers and with nearly 120 varieties of holly, many bearing bright berries.

VanDusen also offers a children's garden—with topiary figures, espaliered fruit trees, and such bizarrely shaped plants as Harry Lauder's walking stick. In the formal rose garden visitors will find hybrid teas, floribundas and shrub roses penned in symmetrical boxwood-lined beds. Another favorite attraction is an Elizabethan-style maze wrought from a thousand upright white cedars.

■ **STANLEY PARK** Georgia Street, Vancouver, British Columbia, Canada V6G 1Z4 **TEL:** (604) 257-8400
OPEN: Always open **TOTAL ACRES:** 1,000 **SPECIAL COLLECTIONS:** Rhododendrons, perennials, roses
ZONE 7 A **H** P PA R T WS

■ **QUEEN ELIZABETH PARK** 33rd and Cambrie Streets, Vancouver, British Columbia, Canada V6G 1Z4 **TEL:**
(604) 874-8336 **OPEN:** Daily 10-dusk, except Christmas **TOTAL ACRES:** 120 **SPECIAL COLLECTIONS:** Tropical
plants, spring bulbs, summer annuals
ZONE 7 C G **H** P PA R WS

■ **VANDUSEN BOTANICAL GARDEN** 5251 Oak Street, Vancouver, British Columbia, Canada V6M 4H1 **TEL:**
(604) 878-9274 **OPEN:** Daily from 10, closing times change seasonally **TOTAL ACRES:** 55 **SPECIAL COLLEC-**
TIONS: Holly, rhododendrons, rock gardens, maze
ZONE 7 **F** G **H** L P R T WS

UNIVERSITY OF BRITISH COLUMBIA BOTANICAL GARDEN
VANCOUVER, BRITISH COLUMBIA

Cloaked in dense coastal forest, the University of British Columbia Botanical Garden spreads over 70 acres of a promontory overlooking the Strait of Georgia. Its nine themed gardens hold more than 10,000 plants that thrive in this mild, protected microclimate. The largest area is the Asian Garden, 35 acres of plants indigenous to that continent, ringed by magnificent stands of Canada's native cedars, hemlocks, and firs. In addition to collections of Japanese maples, Yulan magnolias, and Korean stewartias, the garden holds what is considered the largest collection of rhododendrons in the country—from Tibet's diminutive *Rhododendron forrestii* to the 30-foot-tall *R. sinograde* from China.

As impressive in stature if not in size, the 2.5-acre Alpine Garden comprises an imposing rockery with dainty mountain specimens gathered from around the globe and grouped by geographic origin. The sun-drenched south-facing slope, constructed of some 2,000 tons of volcanic rock, dazzles with gentians, crocuses, sedums, trilliums, and tulips. Such ground-hugging rock plants are complemented by dwarf forms of trees and shrubs, including pine, spruce, and pieris.

Displaying local riches is the Native Garden, where ten acres of forest shelter a number of British Columbian botanical treasures. Ferns, wild ginger, and fawn lilies grow among the maples and buckthorns, while cranberry, Labrador tea, and bunchberry inhabit a bog. Demonstration beds are planted with natives suitable for home gardens—such as columbine and allium—and introductions derived from natives, including new varieties of blueberry and penstemon. The nearby Winter Garden comes into its own just when most others start to fade. In late fall, viburnums and winter jasmine begin a pageant of color and fragrance that heathers, witch hazels, hellebores, and daphnes carry through into spring.

A handsome garden pavilion anchors a number of smaller installations, including perennial borders abundant with yarrow, sage, black-eyed Susans, and ornamental grasses, and an arbor garden, where a cedar pergola is overrun with wisteria, clematis, trumpet vine, and bittersweet. The Physick Garden, patterned after a 16th-century engraving of a monastery garden, includes 12 geometric beds of medicinal plants arrayed around a bronze sundial. Enclosed within a boxwood hedge, the garden is home to such famed herbal healing agents as digitalis, chamomile, and poppy. The Food Garden features a range of edibles—from nut trees and raised beds full of vegetables to berry bushes and espaliered fruit trees.

Perhaps the most stunning display is the Nitobe Memorial Garden, a Japanese landscape designed by the prominent landscape architect Kannosuke Mori and dedicated to Dr. Inazo Nitobe, a respected diplomat. Located about a mile from the main garden, the Nitobe is an informal strolling garden where gravel paths wind through 2.5 acres of water features such as streams and waterfalls, as well as bridges, lanterns, and plants, many brought from Japan. Flowering cherries, azaleas, Japanese maples, and irises lend the few seasonal splashes of color amid this restrained, tranquil garden. Within the strolling garden is a traditional tea garden, with a stepping-stone path leading to a cypress teahouse.

UNIVERSITY OF BRITISH COLUMBIA BOTANICAL GARDEN 6804 S.W. Marine Drive, Vancouver, British Columbia, Canada V6T 1Z4 TEL: (604) 822-9666 OPEN: Botanical gardens: Daily 10-6; Nitobe Memorial Garden: Daily 10-6, mid-March to mid-Oct.; daily 10-2:30 mid-Oct. through Feb. TOTAL ACRES: 70 SPECIAL COLLECTIONS: Asian plants, particularly rhododendrons, Japanese garden, alpine garden, native plants

ZONE 8 F G P T WS

The Yukimi, a snow stone lantern, is sheltered by Japanese maples in the Nitobe Memorial Garden. Its beauty is thought to be best revealed in winter, when covered by a dusting of snow.

Sun Yat-Sen Classical Chinese Garden
Vancouver, British Columbia

The first full-scale classical Chinese garden ever built outside China, this serene, secluded site occupies one-third of an acre in Vancouver's Chinatown. It is dedicated to Dr. Sun Yat-Sen, an important political figure in early 20th-century China. Opened in 1968, the garden is modeled after a type used by scholars in the Ming Dynasty (1368–1644) as a retreat for contemplation and inspiration. It was built by some 50 Chinese craftsmen, who used traditional tools and materials shipped from China in more than 950 crates. The intricate roof tiles atop the garden pavilions were fired in Ming-era kilns, for instance, and many of the floors are paved in intricate patterns with pebbles collected from China's river beds, along with shards from Chinese porcelain bowls. Unlike western gardens, the Sun Yat-Sen is less a collection of specimens than of ideas, which are expressed symbolically through architecture, water, stone, and plants—it is an idealized version of the natural landscape. The main concept is that of contrast, reflecting the Taoist belief in yin and yang, whereby such opposing elements as a placid pool and craggy rocks are combined to create a harmonious whole.

The garden is enclosed behind thick stucco walls and entered through a series of passageways intended to create a tranquil, sheltered feeling. This entryway is planted sparsely, with golden bamboo, mondo grass, and azaleas. Beside it lies a small courtyard, one of whose walls is pierced with three "leak" windows that overlook bamboo, pine, and a camellia. There are 36 such windows throughout the buildings, each with a different lattice design and each framing a plant composition as a living painting. The garden is also designed to catch every possible breeze, with exterior walls pierced to allow in gently flowing air.

From here, a covered walkway leads to the main garden, and runs along one side of its large courtyard and allowing the entire setting to be viewed, including such plants as magnolia, camellia, witch hazel, banana, ginkgo, maple, and pine. Dominating the garden is a false "mountain" of fantastically contorted limestone that rises out of an opaque jade-green pool. The individual stones, which were taken from Lake Tai, near Suzhou, China, and fitted together to create the look of a natural rock outcropping, are planted with wintercreeper and winter jasmine. Atop the mountain is a t'ing, or garden pavilion, with extremely upturned eaves and low walls; beneath it is a waterfall grotto, from which the gentle streams of water that overrun the rock can be viewed. Water is an important element throughout the garden. Several areas have been designed so that rain dripping off the roof tiles creates soothing sounds while gently watering the plants below.

Along the pathway are two pavilions, the first featuring an intricate grillwork with an open center that frames the t'ing. The second pavilion provides an entry to the garden's collection of penjing, which, like bonsai, are trees whose growth has been stunted and which have been trained into artistic shapes. The walkway ends in the Scholar's Garden, a small courtyard intended for private contemplation and planted with magnolia and flowering plum. In the adjoining pavilion are three windows that look out onto the "three friends of winter"—a winter-flowering plum, a bamboo, and a pine, which represent rebirth, flexibility, and fortitude, respectively.

Sun Yat-Sen Classical Chinese Garden 578 Carrall Street, Vancouver, British Columbia, Canada V6B 5K2 Tel: (604) 662-3207 Open: Daily 10-4:30 or later, depending on season Total acres: Less than 1 Special collections: Symbolic plantings, precious Taihu rocks, winter-flowering plum trees

ZONE 7 F G H T WS

eak windows" in the main courtyard of the Sun Yat-Sen Garden, each with a
ferent lattice design, frame views of the plants beyond.

Minter Gardens
Rosedale, British Columbia

Geology and horticulture come together at Minter Gardens, where a valley landscape littered with rocks that tumbled centuries ago from nearby Mount Cheam provides the setting for 27 acres of exquisite gardens. Conceived by plant expert

A favorite for children of all ages, the evergreen maze at Minter Gardens is constructed in a circular design of some 1,000 pyramid cedars.

Brian Minter and opened in 1980, the garden was developed to take advantage of the stunning terrain and natural flora, including the 100-foot-tall cedars growing amid the shale boulders. Eleven themed display areas—from a manicured rose garden to a woodsy fern glade to an intoxicating fragrance garden—were added with an eye toward providing maximum seasonal color. They are augmented with a number of water features and miles of meandering pathways.

In spring, the Rhododendron Garden bursts into bloom, accompanied by daffodils blanketing the Meadow and Alpine Gardens. Some 100,000 tulips, along with hyacinths, lilies, and other bulbs, flower among stands of azalea, dogwood, magnolia, and cherry trees. Summer is the season for annuals at Minter, where countless thousands of alyssum, begonias, impatiens, and salvia, among others, fill beds, define geometric patterns, and spill from baskets. Annuals are also put to interesting use in the floral topiaries that have become the garden's trademark, such as a 12-foot-tall "peacock," whose 50-foot-long "tail" fans out with marigolds and ageratum. Come fall, the mountainside forests surrounding the gardens blaze with foliage, their color rivaled by Minter Garden's massive plantings of chrysanthemums, dahlias, and pansies. In addition, the Chinese garden features an important penjing collection.

▮ Minter Gardens (75 miles east of Vancouver) 52892 Bunker Road, Rosedale, British Columbia, Canada V2P 6H7 Tel: (604) 794-7191 Open: Daily 9-dusk, April through Oct. Total acres: 27 Special collections: Penjing, floral topiary, rhododendrons, roses   ZONE 6 F G H P PA R T WS

Butchart Gardens
Brentwood Bay, British Columbia

The craggy remains of a limestone quarry are now the site of a dramatic garden where sprigs of ivy creep over sheer stone cliffs and placid spring-fed pools lap against borders of colorful blossoms. Butchart Gardens sprawls across 50 acres of what was once the estate of the pioneering cement manufacturer Robert Butchart and his innovative, energetic wife, Jenny. Frustrated by the exhausted limepit that marred the grounds of their 1904 home on Tod Inlet, near Victoria, Jenny Butchart decided to turn the three-acre eyesore into a garden. She spent 40 years reclaiming the rest of the property as a horticultural showplace.

To create the Sunken Garden, Jenny had tons of topsoil carted down to the quarry floor and spread over mounds of rock rubble to form the foundations for planting beds. As in her day, the beds now bloom with a rainbow of annuals, which shimmer among subdued pockets of rhododendron, hydrangea, and pieris. The ivy, cotoneaster, and alpine plants that she laboriously tucked into cracks in the 50-foot-high garden walls, while dangling from a boatswain's chair, still cling to the stone face.

The deepest portion of the quarry was flooded to form a pond, where weeping willows, flowering cherries, and daffodils are mirrored in the deep-green water. An equally compelling feature is the Ross Fountain, a water jet that sprays some 70 feet in the air above a massive pond filling another abandoned quarry. Densely ringed with conifers and shrubs native to the Pacific Northwest, the raw rock walls have been intentionally left bare, as a contrast to the lushly planted Sunken Garden. A long, curving path—paved with cement, of course, and lined with masses of begonias, salvias, geraniums, and other flowers—bisects the garden, the remaining half of which is more formal. Closest to the house is an Italian garden, a former tennis court that Mrs. Butchart transformed into a raised lily pool with a series of symmetrical beds in classical designs. At its far end, through arches carved in a wall of Lawson cypress, is the Star Pond, a pool whose 12 "points" are trimmed with boxwood and surrounded by stately tulips in spring.

Flanked by emerald lawns is the Rose Garden, where arches of climbing and rambling roses lead the way to a sloping bowl of hundreds of hybrid teas and floribundas interplanted with delphinium, nicotiana, asters, and other flowers in box-lined beds. Reflecting the Butchart's interest in travel—they collected plants

Brightly filled urns perch atop ivy-covered walls in the Italian Garden, which includes a formal pond. This garden was once a tennis court at the Butchart estate.

The teahouse in the Japanese Garden at Hatley Park rests amid fiery autumnal foliage, highlighted by a Mount Fuji cherry tree and a Japanese maple. Some of the trees that may be found in the

yearly on their worldwide expeditions—is the Japanese Garden, whose entryway is marked with a towering red torii, the traditional Japanese gate. Sloping down to the waterside, the intimate garden teems with Japanese maples, azaleas, bamboo, and weeping hemlocks—all ornamented with bridges, lanterns, and sculptures.

As stunning as the Butchart Gardens are by day, they become even more spectacular after sundown when the entire property is illuminated, and countless lamps, artfully hidden, create soft plays of light and subtle shadow among the diverse plantings.

BUTCHART GARDENS (12.5 miles northwest of Victoria) 800 Benvenuto Avenue, Brentwood Bay, British Columbia, Canada V8M 1J8 **TEL:** (250) 652-4422 or (250) 652-5256 **OPEN:** Daily 9 AM, closing times change seasonally **TOTAL ACRES:** Gardens 50, estate 138 **SPECIAL COLLECTIONS:** Estate garden, sunken gardens, Japanese garden, roses, annuals, perennials ZONE 8 F G H P R V WS

HATLEY PARK
COLWOOD, BRITISH COLUMBIA

What was once the private estate of a coal and railroad baron now houses one of Canada's newest universities, which has preserved the grounds as an outstanding example of early 20th-century landscape design. Hatley Park is comprised of 140 acres of gardens at Royal Roads University, which opened in 1995 on the site of James Dunsmuir's palatial home. Dunsmuir, who was appointed lieutenant

second-growth forest surrounding the park are estimated to be 500 years old. This former private estate is now owned by Royal Roads University.

governor of British Columbia in 1906, began building Hatley Castle a year later on 650 acres adjoining a saltwater lagoon. The grounds were landscaped by Brett and Hall of Boston and are today maintained in the grand manner befitting Dunsmuir's original vision.

The gardens are framed by dense stands of old-growth forest, with cedars, firs, and hemlocks towering over patches of shooting stars, lady's-slippers, trilliums, and other woodland wildflowers. In contrast, the manicured grounds include three main garden areas, numerous water features, and a greenhouse. Spreading over four acres, the Japanese Garden includes three spring-fed lakes surrounded by original flowering cherries, Japanese maples, Japanese umbrella pines, copper beeches, and rhododendrons. Also remaining from Dunsmuir's time are a teahouse, lanterns, a waterwheel, and other garden ornaments.

The Italian Garden, whose entry pillars are clad in 80-year-old wisteria, is resplendent with delphiniums, clematis, chrysanthemums, and climbing roses. Climbers, trained on a post-and-rope fence, encircle the Rose Garden as well, whose center is filled exclusively with David Austen roses. Smaller garden areas include a scree bed with campanulas, veronica, and creeping phlox, and a bog garden of moisture-loving primulas, gunnera, flag, and lobelia.

HATLEY PARK (9 miles west of Victoria) Royal Roads University, 2005 Sooke Road, Colwood, British Columbia, Canada V9B 5Y2 **TEL:** (250) 391-2551 **OPEN:** Daily dawn-dusk **TOTAL ACRES:** 140 **SPECIAL COLLECTIONS:** Estate garden, Japanese garden, Italian garden, roses   **ZONE 8** C HO L P PA T WS

Index

Italic entries reference photographs.

Index

377

Index

Index

Index

Acknowledgements

All the gardens in this book represent the dedication and tireless efforts of those who created the gardens and to all of them I extend my gratitude. Many others associated with the gardens have provided detailed information, answered endless queries, and without their help we would not have been able to assemble this book.

Over the years my friends have been my cheerleaders to get this project done, and I thank all of them for their kind support.

The writers, photographers, and staff who have contributed to this guide all deserve accolades for their unstinting efforts on behalf of the project.

And, of course, my love and appreciation to my husband, Chris, for his patience, new-found culinary skills, and endless encouragement. *MZJ*

Composition for this book by Zaino Design/BNGO Books, New York, New York. Printed and bound by R.R. Donnelley & Sons, Willard, Ohio. Color Separations by Digital Color Image, Pensauken, New Jersey. Paper by Consolidated/Alling & Cory, Willow Grove, Pennsylvania. Cover printed by Miken Companies, Inc., Cheektowaga, New York.

Credits

Text copyright © 1998 Mary Zuazua Jenkins
Copyright © 1998 National Geographic Society

Published by THE NATIONAL GEOGRAPHIC SOCIETY

John M. Fahey, Jr.
President and Chief Executive Officer
Gilbert M. Grosvenor, *Chairman of the Board*
Nina D. Hoffman, *Senior Vice President*
William R. Gray,
Vice President and Director, Book Division
David Griffin, *Design Director*
Elizabeth L. Newhouse,
Director of Travel Publishing
Barbara A. Noe, *Assistant Editor*
Caroline Hickey, *Senior Researcher*
Carl Mehler, *Senior Map Editor*
Margaret Bowen, *Editorial Consultant*
Richard S. Wain, *Production Project Manager*

■

A Mary Zuazua Jenkins Book
Director
Mary Zuazua Jenkins
Art Director
Carmile S. Zaino
Designer
Kevin Callahan
Editor
Mary Luders
Copy Editor
Karen Ivory
Index
Jenifer Blakemore
Writers
Jane Mintzer Hoffman, Karen Ivory,
Mary Zuazua Jenkins, Laura Martin, Wendy
Murphy, Myrna Oakley, Rosemary Rennicke,
Michelle Strutin, Paul Weissich
Editorial Assistants
Maria Bradley-Moore, Laura Chappel,
Jean Cotterell, Anna Gallegos,
Carol O'Donnell, Mimi Wise

■

Library of Congress Cataloging-in-Publication Data
Jenkins, Mary Zuazua.
National geographic guide to America's public
gardens : 300 of the best gardens to visit in the U.S.
and Canada / by Mary Zuazua Jenkins.
p. cm.
Includes index.
ISBN 0-7922-7152-1
1. Gardens—United States—Guidebooks.
2. Gardens—Canada—Guidebooks. 3. United
States—Guidebooks. 4. Canada—Guidebooks.
I. National Geographic Society (U.S.) II. Title.
SB466.U6J45 1998
712'.097—dc21   98-4722
                                   CIP

Illustrations Credits
Murray Alcosser, 2-3, 269, 271, 335, 343, 344,
348, 350, 351; Ping Amranand, Cover, 5, 6, 65-
66, 104-106, 114-117, 123-149, 153-157, 160-
197, 200-201, 204-209, 213, back cover-top;
Timothy E. Barbano /Phipps Conservatory, 113;
James P. Blair, 258-259; T. Bonderud/First Light,
374-375; Botanica, 262; Rod Bradley, 255; Fran
Brennan, 274; Mark C. Brennan, 42; Richard W.
Brown, 60; Karen Bussolini, 63, 72-73; Tori
Butt/New York Botanical Garden, 67; Les
Campbell/ Positive Images, 88; Walter
Choroszewski, 101, 102; Jonn Coolidge/Courtesy
of Colonial Homes Magazine, 12, 297; Claire
Curran/Descanso Gardens, 301; John Elk, 264;
Richard P. Felber, 1, 19, 30-35, 45-57, 66, 68,
69, 74-83, 90-99, back cover #2, 4; Kevin
Fleming, 118; Michel Gagne/Montreal Botanical
Garden, 358; Mark Gibson, 254; Philip Gould,
211; Mick Hales, 71, 87, 317, back cover-3;
Tammy Hall, 279; Eric Hayes/ Fraser Photos,
356; Saxon Holt, 121, 322, 325, 327, 331, 354-
355, 370; Hal Horwitz/New England Wild
Flower Socie[ty]
22; Roy Inm[an]
Ivy/Fraser Ph[otos]
Monticello/Th[e]
Foundation, [
Johnson, 25, [
Ketchum, 30[6]
357, 365; Bal[
245; William [
Society, 41 (to[p]
366, 367; Mel[
314, 319 ; Me[
Long/New En[gland]
(top,left); John[
Flower Society[
Mann, 266-26[
Mastrovito/Mo[
McDonald/Phot[
Arts, Boston, 3[
John Nollendo[r]
333, 372; Jack [
Douglas Peeble[s]
Photo Resource[
304, 315; Allen[
228-239, 246-253, 257; Kevin Shields, 16-17,
20, 21, 40 (bot.,rt); Ted Spiegel/Kykuit, 84; Alan
Sirulnikoff/ First Light, 369; Steve Terrill, 10,
321, 328; Norman S. Track, 360-361; Jonathan
Wallen, 108; Tom Williams/Ohme Gardens,
294/295, 338; Don Wheeler/Philbrook Museum
of Art, 280; A. Wilson/Hearst Castle Gardens,
309; Michael S. Yamashita, 310-311

■

Visit the Society's Web site at http://
www.nationalgeographic.com

■

Cover: Rosedown Plantation, Louisiana